Native American Spirituality

A Critical Reader

EDITED BY LEE IRWIN

University of Nebraska Press
Lincoln and London

Library of Congress Cataloging-in-
Publication Data
Native American Spirituality: a
critical reader / edited by Lee
Irwin. p.   cm. Includes biblio-
graphical references and index.
ISBN 0-8032-8261-3 (pbk.: alk. pa-
per). 1. Indians of North America—
Religion. 2. Indians of North
America—Rites and ceremonies.
I. Irwin, Lee, 1944–
E98.R3 .N382 2000
299'.7—dc21   00-028664

Contents

Native American Spirituality

Native American Spirituality

An Introduction

LEE IRWIN

The themes in this volume are not necessarily new nor strictly an expression of developments within a particular field of academic study. They are, in many ways, as old as the earliest meetings, misunderstandings, and conflicts between Native and non-Native peoples that have led, more often than not, to confusion in trying to communicate the respective differences of their alternative worldviews. From the "other side of the frontier," these themes have long been woven around the problem of trying to communicate the value and importance of indigenous religious action, identity, and commonly shared lifeways that are not easily or accurately subsumed into standard "western" analytic categories. These themes involve something more than intellectual understanding, aesthetic appreciation, or a fascination for exotic cultural activities. From the beginning of cultural contact, Native religious practitioners have engaged in a struggle to sustain their authenticity in the face of sustained, oppressive cultural denials. This history of contestation requires contemporary non-Native persons to fully recognize the intrinsic worth and value of Native religious beliefs and practices that are, in fact, not simply accessible or publicly available for inspection or study. Any introduction to these traditions requires respect, patience, and commitment to understand even the most elementary aspects of Native beliefs as they relate to religious practices and values.

The disturbing history of religious persecution and denial of Native religious rights, coupled with an often irresponsible exposure of beliefs or practices regarded as deeply held facets of individual and communal identity, has led to a sheltering of Native spirituality from the public eye of non-Native spectators. The consequences of representation (and misrepresentation) by non-Native others has helped to create a climate of caution and mistrust that only additional generations of reciprocal care, listening, and responsiveness can fully heal. It is perhaps the theme of learning to hear and to respect the speaking of Native peoples that most powerfully motivates this collection. The key themes are ones of hearing, responding with respect, and letting the alternative view stand as that—alternative and fully authentic—without feeling the need to redress that view in alien clothes or new theoretical identities. These themes are "contemporary" insofar as they are cast into the language and interpretations of present concerns, as grounded in the integrity and commitments of each author. The theme of representation involves the double issue of representing the other in the context of self-representation as scholars (and the power they acquire in writing) fully open to critical view and evaluations, no longer protected by a one-sided valuation of majority social identity, academic standing, or majority privilege.

It would be simpler if all of us could learn to value the contributions of the other as that which enhances our own self-understanding. Native religious and spiritual traditions are no longer simply "objects of analysis" or mute data lacking either voice or rights in the process of becoming known. The context has changed, and the relationship among the various persons that constitute the contributors to this volume are interactive and complex, no longer credibly reducible to a theoretical stance that ignores or denies the central values of Native personhood and place. What is contemporary here is a developing self-reflection on the part of researchers and respondents that what we are all engaged in is not the reduplication of the cultural other but the negotiation of cultural understanding *among* responsible members of alternative communities whose concerns overlap to a degree that evokes insights and mutual learning in the process. This emergent understanding is primarily *dialogical* and part of a creative interplay among speakers; it is a matter of listening and speaking respectfully.

Where it was perhaps once thought possible for an outside observer to enter the world of the other and reproduce the nuances and complexity of that world "objectively," these articles show clearly that there is a tentativeness to such a process that requires much more of the observer than a theoretical language of analysis. The issue is not analysis but communication. One never becomes the other but only coexists through meaningful relationships that are more or less insightful and revealing, more or less central or marginal to the issues of the day, more or less in contact with the reality of the other. The complexity of this engagement requires a degree of honesty that allows for a transformation of perceptions, an awakening to the value of being other in a context of spiritual authenticity that often demands a recontextualizing of first impressions and then, more substantively, of later impressions. Such a process often reduces itself to discreet relationships with real people, sometimes just a few such persons in order to establish a vital communication. This takes commitment and a high degree of dedication and honesty in order to articulate what is valuable and meaningful in the relationship.

Clearly, the themes involve issues of negotiation and relatedness. In the relational context, what emerges is not disembodied speakers detached from the concerns that motivate the participants' communities nor an aggressive re-presentation in terms of the culture of the analyst but rather an increasingly engaged set of speakers, each trying to fathom the interests and needs of the other. Those needs are not merely intellectual but also emotional and existential; they involve struggle, the search for empowerment, social standing, degrees of expertise, political representation, sometimes confusion and contradiction, and often a battered response to a larger and more complex world found to be indecipherable when viewed from only one cultural perspective. The "information" is not so much information about things or actions or quantifiable beliefs as about the consequences of human decisions, the quality of life, the way things work, how life is valued and enhanced. At the heart of it is the community of relationships that sustain—in all its fractures, contradictions and non-agreements—a meaningful world of spiritual activities and deep-seated human engagements.

Perhaps the word "spiritual" needs clarification. My own understanding of spirituality in this context is something more than simply practicing a particular religion. This word "religion" doesn't sit well in such a context either, being as it is a postenlightenment concept often rooted in a polarity between ideas of the "sacred and profane." Such a distinction is an artificial and nonhelpful locus for understanding the primary foundations of Native spirituality. My perception of the interactive spheres of Native communal life is that they have a relatedness through personal relationships that finds common expression in mutual, everyday concerns. Ceremonial activity, prayer, or simply carrying out daily activities like driving a friend to work or struggling for political rights may engage individuals in aspects of "religious" concern. It is that connectedness to *core values and deep beliefs* that I mean by "spirituality"—a pervasive quality of life that develops out of an authentic participation in values and real-life practices meant to connect members of a community with the deepest foundations of personal affirmation and identity. In this sense, spirituality is inseparable from any sphere of activity as long as it really connects with deeply held affirmative values and sources of authentic commitment, empowerment, and genuineness of shared concern.

Insofar as these spiritual concerns or core values may motivate the actions and thoughts of an individual in a wide variety of circumstances, the contributors to this volume approach those concerns from a diverse number of perspectives. Native American studies are constituted by an intersection of many fields, all rich with diversity and multiple arenas of expression. Native American religion or spirituality is approached by those working in ethnohistory, anthropology, political science, linguistics, literature, women's studies, law, or the emergent field of Native American religious studies, to name only the more obvious disciplines. This volume represents a diversity of intellectual backgrounds, combining voices of both Natives and others in a montage of dialogues aimed at illuminating the rich thematic complexity of Native American spirituality. There is no authoritative view nor theory that shapes those dialogues other than a genuine concern to "get it right" in terms of the intersection of background training and authentic connections within a specific community of willing correspondents. It is not a one-way process but involves learning about the other on both sides and from many different perspectives.

THE PROBLEM OF REPRESENTATION

Perhaps the greatest frustration for persons first entering the field of Native American religious studies is the immense complexity of the subject. There is no easy summary and no immediately accessible texts that allow for a competent synthesis—a synthesis largely alien and of little interest to the members of many Native communities. Native religions are remarkably diverse and grounded in very specific languages, places, lifeway rites, and communal relationships embedded in a unique ethnic history often overshadowed by the more pervasive history of religious and political suppression. Untangling the knots of communication and misunderstanding among individual scholars, Native communities and the larger cultural context takes years of consistent, meaningful effort. Furthermore, the whole is in process—religious communities are not static but evolve and change continually in the pressure cooker of contemporary American society. This is certainly true of Native American communities, which are still being forcefully battered by numerous political, economic, and social upheavals and internal struggles.

In this process, when I think of the image of a Native person in the context of popular culture, it seems more like a Thanksgiving Day parade balloon-figure, blown up out of proportion and painted with totally artificial colors and designs. The non-Native people holding the ropes are marching in a display of cultural images far more reflective of themselves than of the peoples such images claim to represent. From "noble savages" to "shaman healers" and from "blood thirsty warriors" to "political radicals," these images seem to speak of something other than real people whose complexity and concerns cannot be reduced to such inflated, artificial images. Furthermore, such images deny the actual, deeply held communal aspects that inform the lives of many Native peoples, the family connections and the sense of obligation that unite the community in its struggles against internal and external tensions. The artificial images created by non-Natives seeking a simpler, unauthentic overview need to be thoroughly collapsed and deflated and replaced by a more complex, nuanced view of Native diversity and difference cocreated out of meaningful communal dialogues. The value of diversity and specific identity within a particular community is that it fosters a better understanding of the rich inheritance of the past and present that still needs to be understood.

Yet how do we best represent this diversity to others? One solution is the range of voices in this volume. Most of the contributors represent specific communities, usually in the context of living and meaningful relationships with members of those communities. And none of the authors speak for all Native communities or even other communities in adjacent areas. In the process of their representations, they bring themselves forward in relationship to community members as well as giving voice to community members through their own speaking and writing. In this sense, the thematic representation is dialogical and shared, moving between the sometimes coherent and, at other times, disjointed perceptions of various community members. The tensions among the experiences and bias of the author and those of the community members are not erased or denied or smoothed over with monological narratives. The representation is often a record of long-term negotiations or personal relationships that seem vital to an understanding of the community or to the appreciation of some facet of communal activities.

But what about self-representation, where Native peoples speak and write about their own traditions as seen and known by them and not by noncommunity members? Partially, the very writing of a narrative is a step into a negotiated realm between Native and non-Native worlds. Bookmaking, editing, marketing, printing, and construction are not part of the interactive, everyday world of most Native communities, though books are read and ideas transmitted in print. Yet there is a history of Native self-representation that stretches back over 150 years and provides resources for helping others to see from "the Native point of view." The list is long and complex, involving quite literally hundreds of sources and authors, many still in archives and unpublished manuscript holdings. On the other hand, today an increasing number of Native authors are writing on their own traditions. But this too can be problematic. Can all these Native authors claim to truly represent the communities of their birth or upbringing? Have they been empowered by their community to write these works or are they profiting from them to their own advantage without communal approval? Such writings seem to run the gamut from sincere articulations of Native tradition to completely unauthentic works spun for personal gain, popularity, or just plain cash. Thus the problem of representation has no easy answers. Much ethnography collected and written by non-Native authors is highly valued by Native peoples; others would deny the value of anything but Native self-representation. In this collection we have dual representation—almost all articles contain voices of Native people speaking in terms of their own causes and concerns.

The authors of the volume are Native, non-Native, and part-Native. All of them share the distinction of being members of academic programs or having appropriate academic degrees. Such positions and degrees are not superfluous, since they represent requirements for this kind of publication. The intimate connection among representation, non-Native norms of education, and the economic market as well as the struggle of academic presses in the face of mass-market publication is itself a context that powerfully affects narrative and contents. Representation does not occur in a "free space" uninfluenced by a host of motives, pressures, and needs, and these needs are not always coherent or aligned. The struggle for authenticity rides on a current of restless energy churned by complex social conditions demanding a constant effort on the part of writers to meet that energy and transform it into valuable social contributions. In this volume the authenticity of concern comes through, with all its turbulent asides, tensions, and contradictions, to celebrate the value of meaningful relationships among persons committed to moving beyond static views of ethnography or monological theory.

In that process historical research takes a somewhat secondary position to the reverberations and turbulence within the current academic context of Native studies. Part of the problem of representation is gaining a foothold that allows for the free expression of ideas and opinion. Such representation is slow in coming and long in process. Who has access to written productions and products of representation? Who can make it public? And whose expectations have to be met in order for that production to actually manifest? Normatively, this is not under the control or supervision of Native peoples. And the focus is not on the past but on the present, that is, the present struggle for representation in a context of either popular or scholarly publication. In the scholarly context, the pressing need is for greater self-representation by Native scholars on their own terms, in the present, in their own language, and from their own perspective. This does not always easily coalesce with a market view of "successful" publications, yet authentic self-representation requires more than a mere conformity to the means of production.

Part of the need in any form of representation is to hear the actual voice and grant it the freedom for self-expression. What is required is a willingness to hear others in their own voice, to recognize diversity and difference, and then to give the voice a place to manifest that allows others to value its content and concerns. It is exactly this concern that has motivated the present collection. To the best of my ability, I have invited individuals from both Native and non-Native communities to speak of their concerns and to present their insights as they see fit to express them. Subsequently, this has resulted in varying degrees of representation and a complex intersection of voices, all speaking with intensity about the worth and meaning of their own existential commitments in relationship to Native spirituality. The task of the reader should be not simply to side with one point of view or another but to take in all points of view and value each as part of an on going dialogue in which all speakers have a right to be heard respectfully. The challenge is to learn from every perspective and not just those with which we already agree.

In terms of theoretical perspectives, it is clear that representation involves many disciplinary views, ranging from anthropology through religious studies and into literature and history. There is no particular, shared theoretical perspective and no recourse to a monological theory or a single authoritative school of academic discourse invoked by the contributors to this volume. Each has drawn on complex, subtly articulated perspectives within and between disciplines more than they have drawn on the resources of a single theoretical school. These multivocal theories represent their concerns in the context of relationships to specific Native communities and what the authors regard as a meaningful readership. This perhaps reflects the very nature of religious studies as multidisciplinary and as nonreducible to either a single methodology or a single hermeneutics. As there is no authoritative perspective in the interpretation of specific religious worldviews and practices, the authors of these articles each work to assemble their writings in terms of methodologies that work best for them in the context of their own fieldwork and research rather than in terms of a strictly disciplinary approach. This, it seems to me, is clearly the direction of future thematic writings in Native American studies.

Furthermore, a Native voice is one that often emphasizes personalization and speaking from the perspective of an embodied, committed Native person rather than as a scholar whose identity is defined by membership in corporate (non-Native) institutional life or as one who is subsumed within disciplinary rhetoric. This sense of authenticity rings true in the writings of this volume, where Native authors write first and foremost as Native people. The sense of personalization is a refreshing early spring wind, a Chinook, melting some of the ice and snow of a long hard winter of overly rationalized theory-making that has largely depersonalized the community and spirituality of its participating members. The authors gathered together here are speaking about a deep-seated theme: the need to engage Native peoples in ways that fully recognize the value of the person (and personal experience) as central to the formulation of Native spirituality.

The social complexity of concern about native spirituality now involves, first and foremost, Native scholars whose voices and views have increasingly gained authority and place within the field of Native American studies; secondly, part-Native or non-Native scholars whose genuine concerns have involved them often in life-long commitments to native communities, peoples and religious activities; thirdly, both Native and non-Native individuals who are not scholars but who may have the highest degree of expertise in relationship to specific traditions in which they are trained, some through a life time of practice and instruction; and finally, Native and non-Native readers who, while having little background or familiarity with traditions other than their own, nevertheless have genuine interests in Native spirituality. These groups may be prioritized differently, but the intersection of their concerns is what is creating the complexity and diversity in the field of Native American studies today.

THEORETICAL CONCERNS

1

Mediations of the Spirit

Native American Religious Traditions and

the Ethics of Representation

INÉS HERNÁNDEZ-ÁVILA

I believe that autoethnographic expression is a very widespread phenomenon of the contact zone, and will become important in unraveling the histories of imperial subjugation and resistance as seen from the site of their occurence.

Mary Louise Pratt, *Imperial Eyes: Travel Writing and Transculturation*

First and foremost, a metaphysic of connection means discovering our own authentic voices. This happens in relation to the group in which I am historically and culturally rooted. . . . *Differentiation* not *assimilation* must ground right relation. What this connectedness may mean for a privileged group of women is that the only form of relation possible is to listen, to learn and to begin a journey of conversion as response to the lessons of history.

Mary Grey, "Claiming Power-In-Relation: Exploring the Ethics of Connection"

[I]n order to constitute ourselves as bicultural subjectivities, Indian identified writers must negotiate a politics of position and of representation. And in order to do so adequately, we must sharpen our awareness of the multiple relationships out of and into which we write.

Jana Sequoya, "How(!) Is an Indian?: A Contest of Stories"

SETTING THE SPACE OF MEDIATION

In this essay I would like to parallel Michael M. J. Fischer's threefold strategy in "Ethnicity and the Post-Modern Arts of Memory," by requesting the reader to engage in "ethnographic listening, attention to cultural criticism, and attention to experimental writing."[1] My own strategy stems from my intention to personalize my writing in order to represent a Native scholar, myself, who is at once cultural critic and informant. In thus validating the subjective experience, or as Mary Louise Pratt says, the experience "spoken from a moving position already within or down in the middle of things, looking and being looked at, talking and being talked at [and about],"[2] I am (re)inscribing what Pratt calls a " 'contact' perspective" that is multilayered, and though shifting, aligns me at once with segments of the Native community who are under study and with sectors of the academy who undertake that study. Jana Sequoya, in "How(!) Is an Indian?: A Contest of Stories," provides a useful and complementary discussion regarding the ethics of Native American representation (literary, scholarly, and otherwise) in the academy, particularly because her essay reveals the contestatory nature permeating discussions of identity, community, authenticity, representation, and culture (or "having stories") in and out of the university.

I also want to call on Betsy Erkkila's discussion of "the relation between minority discourses and post-structuralist theory in the study of American literature and culture" in "Ethnicity, Literary Theory, and the Grounds of Resistance" as a way to situate my own remarks in this essay.[3] I agree with Erkkila when she says, "[I]t matters very much who is speaking, about what, and from which particular social, historical, and political location."[4] I am keenly aware of my own location as I write. I am the daughter of a Nimipu mother and a Tejano father. On my mother's side I am a descendant of Hinmaton Yalatkit's (Chief Joseph's) band of the Nimipu (Nez Perce) from Nespelem, Washington (my mother's family and I are enrolled on the Colville reservation). On my father's side, I am of Mexican (and therefore, *mestiza*, and Mexican Indian) descent by way of the Texas-Mexican border town of Eagle Pass, then Galveston, Texas. I am a mother and a grandmother. I know my responsibility as a member of my various communities: as a Native American woman concerned with preserving the (intellectual) sovereignty of Native peoples (for my children and my grandchildren and our future generations); as a scholar and professor actively contributing to the evolution of Native American Studies as a discipline; as a Native Woman contributing to the articulation of Native American "feminisms"; as a creative writer intent on digging for the roots of originality of my own and other indigenous peoples; as the faculty member in our program who is entrusted to teach the "Native American Religion and Philosophy" course; and as a practicing member of certain Native American ceremonial traditions.

With these (and others) as my own "multiple mediations" (to borrow a term from Indian scholar Lata Mani[5]), my accountability in this essay is still to myself first, to my own Nimipu family, and then to the larger Native American community, diverse as it is, contestatory as it is, and to the women of that community. They are my first "implied audience." I am willing and prepared to say to them everything that I say here. I know this essay could, and indeed most likely will, come into the hands of some Native American people who will read what is here with interest, and hopefully with relief rather than indignation or disappointment.[6] The Native American community is not so fragmented as others might imagine; we tend to stay informed, sometimes seemingly in the most accidental ways, about what others of our community are doing and saying. My ethical responsibility as a recorder and "representer" of Native American traditions compels me to write with care and with utmost respect, and to not pretend to be what I am not. In the case of this essay, I want to use elements of my (life) story to foreground those issues which have emerged as critical ones for many Native people in this historical moment of our relationship with Western institutional(izing) politics. It is my hope that, as Fischer says, "What thus seem initially to be individualistic autobiographical searchings turn out to be revelations of traditions, re-collections of disseminated identities and of the divine sparks from the breaking of the vessels. . . . [T]he searches also turn out to be powerful critiques of several contemporary rhetorics of domination."[7]

AUTOETHNOGRAPHIC SKETCHINGS OR
PERSONAL / SOCIAL LOCATIONS

Even though, according to Pratt, "multiple pressures . . . militate against nar-
rative (mere anecdote) and devalue it as a vehicle of usable knowledge,"[8] it is my personal experience, informed, of course, by formal research, which has given me the authority to speak (and write), and for that matter, to teach what pertains to Native American religious traditions. Indeed, my own authority (including any decision to "talk about") emerges exactly from my understandings of the ethical frames, boundaries, and reciprocal protocols that attend to any discussion of Native belief systems. Also, because my own research project includes an articulation of Native American "feminisms,"[9] I often have been asked to participate in or contribute to feminist projects wherein I would have to reveal information about Native women's ceremonial matters. Several questions present themselves to me as I consider the task of describing a "woman-centered ritual" from a Native American perspective. As Sequoya has noted, "The problem, of course, is precisely one of context: what is misuse in relation to the sacred cultures of particular tribal communities evokes authentic atmosphere in relation to the secular humanist and popular cultures of the Euroamerican tradition."[10]

I am a sweat lodge person and a *danzante* (a traditional dancer within the Aztec Conchero tradition of Mexico City). I have participated in sweat lodge ceremonies since 1981, and in the Conchero tradition formally since 1979, not only as a dancer but as a *Malinche*. In the Conchero tradition, the woman who fills the role of the *Malinche* takes her name from the young Aztec girl who was given as a gift to Hernan Cortes by the Maya, to whom she had been enslaved. Because of her facility for languages, she became Cortes' interpreter (and his mistress) during the period of the "Conquest" (or "continuing invasion"). Because she was forced into the role of Cortes's "tongue," she is considered, in both popular and intellectual traditions in Mexico, the arch traitor and sell-out, who, in presumably opening her legs, gave over the people and the land to the invaders. But in the ceremonial tradition of the Conchero dance community, "*la Malinche*" is not seen negatively. She opens the paths, going ahead of the group, protecting them, holding the sacred fire, cleansing and blessing the way so that the others may follow. She is a dancer, too, but in her caring for the fire, she is caring for the community of dancers in her group.

As I think of writing about her,[11] I remember one year when a film crew set themselves up in Chalma (south of Mexico City), a major place of pilgrimage for the Concheros. It was impossible to ignore the cameras and the crew as they intruded into sacred space and began to set up their scenes. How could the filming not distract us, how could it not divert us from the (playful, in the sense of sacred recreation) prayerful intention that had brought us there? The main filmmaker of this crew had done a film about one Mexican pueblo's dance of the "*voladores*"; I had occasion, later, to watch the film, where I learned that after the filming, the dance died in that village—it was never performed again. How much might I write about "*la Malinche*" before someone decides to go down to the ceremonies to do their own investigation? At what price does the revealing of *danza*, or any ceremony, happen so that the world (and/or the academy) can "share" in the experience, given that the world tends to dismiss any ethical considerations in the fervor of "discovery." I agree with Sequoya when she suggests, "Perhaps one might consider such dismissive strategies as an institutional residue of the paradigm of the vanishing Indian[s]" who are objectified rather than recognized as subject and voice of their own stories.[12]

I have similar reservations about writing about the sweat lodge tradition. According to many people whom I consider teachers, the sweat lodge is female; she is referred to as the "grandmother sweat lodge"; when we enter the lodge, many say that we enter the womb of Mother Earth.[13] The sweat lodge tradition exists south as well as north of what is now known as the U.S.-Mexican border. In the Aztec tradition there is a song titled "Teteo Innan, Temazcalteci" ["Our Grandmother, the Grandmother Sweat Lodge"]. The song speaks to "Our Grandmother" as the "Heart of the Earth," and the "Tree of Life" whose flowers bloom in the four colors that represent the four directions of the universe. A "woman's sweat" is, in a pronounced way, a centering and gathering of female energy for the purposes of purification and healing.

I could describe how the lodge is built, and according to what tradition; how many rocks are used and what kind, and how they are heated; how the ceremony is structured; what kind of songs are sung, if any; how the prayers are said and in what language; what the order of speakers is and why; what each one of them says, and so on. But even if I were to write a disclaimer in such an essay, warning people not to imitate this Native American "woman-centered ritual," and even though in the world of academia I might feel I had not done anything improper in describing it, I know that in the Native American community, among the elders, I could not say the same thing because I am certain that just as there would be readers who would be truly respectful of the information, there are those who would feel that my description of details gave them permission to appropriate. Worse than that, I would have betrayed the confidence of the women in the sweat lodge circle that I described, because my intention within the circle of ceremony would have been not to pray, but to record and tell. In *Imagining Ourselves Richly: Mythic Narratives of North American Indians*, Christopher Vecsey does just this in his chapter, "The Genesis of Phillip Deere's Sweat Lodge," where he not only gives a brief summary of what Deere tells people within the lodge, he also states, "Like other '*New Age*' religious complexes, it [the sweat lodge ceremony] combined messages of spirituality, personal adjustment, and communal awareness with *cultic activity*" (emphases mine).[14]

In the sweat lodge ceremony people reveal themselves to the Supreme Being, who has many names, and in so doing, they reveal themselves to one another in an intimacy that must be respected. The circle within the lodge is the re-creation of the cosmos, so before the entire creation, you say what you have to say, do what you have to do, pray in the manner that you have to pray, cry if you have to, collapse if you have to. No one judges you or brings anything up to you afterward. It just happens that we might hear another's prayers in the lodge; it just happens that one person or another may be having a particularly hard time, for any number of reasons, and the rest of us support her (or him) with our prayers. Each of us knows that the next time it might be any one of us having the hard time. We know that we do not want the details of our life divulged in public; we are in the sweat lodge because that is our safe space; it is our place of trust. And so I choose not to write about the sweat lodge ceremony, except in a general manner.

I am clear that what I know about the sweat lodge tradition I have learned mostly from a pan-Indian perspective (at least on my part), all of which information I value and hold dear, and for which teachings I am deeply grateful. Teachers and elders of distinct traditions have been generous enough to share with me and with others like me their understandings and sometimes even their ceremonies. These particular people have had compassion for those of us who are Native American but who grew up away from the traditional teachings of our own people. Some of us grew up entirely in an urban area, away from our reservations or our land bases; our families ended up in the cities either by choice or because we were forcibly relocated. Some of us come from families who have converted almost entirely to (often fundamentalist) Christianity, or at least that generation of elders that still knows the traditional ways has converted, which amounts almost to the same thing. Many of us do not know how to speak our own languages. Perhaps we are trying to learn, perhaps we are waiting for the right moment to ask someone to teach us, but many of us learn how to sing beautiful songs from other traditions and in other languages. We also take part in the sweat lodge and other ceremonies, such as the different sacred dances, of traditions that are not our own, at the invitation and with the permission of those to whom these traditions belong. That does not necessarily make us become members of that tribe or that tradition.

I first took part in a sweat lodge ceremony on the late Muscogee elder Phillip Deere's land. I learned more and began to run (mostly women's) sweats at D-Q University during Sun Dance time in the early 1980s. My learning and understanding expanded as I began to take part in the encampments and ceremonies of the California Indian community, where I was for a time a "runner" for several of the elders.[15] That I only know bits and pieces of my own Nimipu sweat lodge tradition is due largely to the fact that my own family elders have been somewhat reluctant, for their own reasons, to impart these understandings to those of us who would like to know them. I remember my uncle, saying, years ago, that he knew all the family stories of the Nez Perce war with the United States during the Nez Perce attempted escape into Canada, but that he would die and take those stories to his grave unless he felt that someone deserved them. In recent years he has begun to share those stories with some of us, allowing us to record and transcribe them. Perhaps in time the other teachings will surface, and in the meantime, all I have learned from the generous people who have shared their wisdom with me in the Native American community will help me "to find my way home to what is mine," as the late Paiute elder Raymond Stone (known to many as "Grampa Raymond"), from Lone Pine, California, used to say. Meanwhile my responsibility is to honor and respect the way in which I was taught to "have" and to "know" the particular ceremonial ways that were shared with me.

Many Native American people who have been cut off from their traditions are hungry to recapture their ways or, at the very least, have a sense of what they have lost. Grampa Raymond always said, "The ceremonies, the language, the songs, the dances are not lost. We are lost; they are where they have always been, just waiting to be [re]called." I have found this to be true. I wanted to learn my Nez Perce people's old songs. I was sad that other people could sing their songs in ceremony, and I didn't know mine. I prayed for the songs to come back to me. With my mom's blessing, I asked my uncle, who my mom said would probably be the one to remember the songs, to please teach me. He said he would try to recall them, but I know that part of his hesitance is that he is a Pentecostal minister (albeit one who has been known to tell Coyote stories to his congregation). My aunties, who are Shaker Indian tradition, do not want me to learn those old songs; they want me to learn Shaker songs that, to them, are not only better but "safer" than "unChristian" songs.

I was beginning to despair when one day a former student of mine who was working in a store in Davis that sells Native products from the Americas called and told me excitedly that she had seen an ad for tapes of Nez Perce music and stories; she asked if I wanted her to order them; I said yes. The music tape turned out to be authentic Nez Perce songs sung by three elder men who, as it happens, were my relatives (they are no longer living). I took both tapes to the Colville reservation and showed them to another relative who is working on our tribal archives. He told me of a set of cassette tapes that had been recently prepared for distribution by Loran Olsen at Washington State University at Pullman. Thanks to Olsen's work, I now have a set of eighteen tapes, complete with an annotated catalogue, of Nez Perce music from archives throughout the United States. My retrieval process makes use of the advances of technology (not to underplay Loran Olsen's dedication to his project). Other Native American individuals and communities that I know of have had their songs come back during or through fasts or other ceremonies. They come back as they will. My prayers were for the way to be made possible for these songs to return to me and to those of my Nez Perce family and community who wanted them. I am certain that I was not the only one who offered those prayers, but I am thankful that several of the singers on these tapes are also my relatives.

My aunties and my uncle have begun to give me commentary on the music and the singers. These songs are my people's heritage; they belong to us and to our spirits as Nimipu people; still, many of the songs belong to individuals who must give someone permission to sing them, or they are associated only with particular ceremonies. It will take me some time to decipher these singular rules with respect to each of the songs. In the essay "How They Almost Killed Our Songs," Karuk writer and traditional singer Julian Lang writes about how the songs of his people have been sustained against great odds.[16] He, too, mentions the rules, the protocol, which go hand in hand with the songs, so that they will receive the respect they deserve and so they will continue.

POLITICAL, HISTORICAL LOCATIONS:
AMERICAN INDIAN RELIGIOUS FREEDOM IN THE UNITED STATES

That the American Indian Religious Freedom Act (AIRFA), P.L. 95–341, was passed so recently as 1978, and that it was even necessary is grievous given the first amendment to the Constitution that assures religious freedom to all citizens. Jack F. Trope echoed the assertion of the Native American community regarding AIRFA, when he called the act "a policy statement with 'no teeth.' "[17] The present struggle to "give it teeth" through legislation is a hard one, given what Russell Lawrence Barsh notes, commenting on *Employment Division vs. Smith*:

In its 1990 decision on the use of peyote by the Native American Church, the Supreme Court has lent support to those who argue that the United States is fundamentally a Christian nation rather than a nation based on religious freedom. . . . [In this decision the Court] adopt[ed] a rule of zero tolerance for the practices of *minority* religious groups wherever they conflict with laws made by the United States Christian majority.[18]

The decision allows the government to suppress a religious practice as long as it "suppresses it everywhere, for everyone, and claims that its goals are not religious."[19]

While Steven C. Moore, senior staff attorney for the Native American Rights Fund, says that the Native American Church "was not absolutely destroyed or driven underground by the Supreme Court's 1990 action on the use of peyote," he does say that the decision "invites the return to an era of religious persecution [that] one would hope a presumably enlightened and tolerant society such as ours had left behind."[20] Little has changed for indigenous peoples in more than five hundred years. The major area of conflict still arises out of Native peoples' relation to and reverence for their distinct land bases and all these land bases provide in terms of sustenance, healing, and the distinct cultural pedagogies that reveal and inform Native peoples' complex belief systems. As Trope has said, "When freedom of religion is discussed in the context of traditional Indian religion, it is the right of practitioners to maintain relationships with the natural world that is at issue."[21]

In fact, many Native communities are struggling to live with respect for the earth's rhythms. Today the Diné people of Big Mountain are being mandated by law into an urban way of life that threatens their continuance as a people. They resist the relocation (with the women elders like Roberta Blackgoat as the leaders) as they witness and struggle against the confiscation of their sheep, the uprooting of their medicinal plants, the denial of permits to repair their homes, and their actual physical removal from the land base that they know, where they were self-sustaining and lived creatively with their surroundings.[22] Whether it be Big Mountain or Guatemala, Hawaii or Brazil, the removal and attempted alienation of Native peoples from their ancestral land bases by government forces almost ensures cultural genocide. The land bases give form and sustenance to Native cultures; the ceremonial, spiritual life of any Native culture is guided intimately by the land base as teacher as well as provider.

The United States government finds it imperative that the claim to any kind of land base by indigenous peoples be continuously weakened, since this kind of claim of sovereignty would seriously impede both governmental and corporate projects. The protection of ancestral lands for ceremonial purposes was recently dealt a huge blow by the Supreme Court in a case involving the construction of a six-mile road (which would benefit the logging industry) through Yurok, Karuk, and Tolowa sacred land that lies in U.S. Forestry Service jurisdiction. In *Lyng v. Northwest Indian Cemetery Protection Association*, 485 U.S. 439 (1988), the Supreme Court reversed decisions by the federal district court and the Ninth Circuit Court of Appeals that "had ruled that the government's interest in building the road did not justify the destruction of the Indian religions that utilized the affected sites."[23] In its reversal, the majority opinion of the Supreme Court "held that the Constitution's free exercise clause [in the First Amendment] did not prevent governmental destruction of the most sacred sites of three small tribes in northern California."[24] The court determined that the establishment of the road would not intentionally prevent the practice of any Indian religion. While construction of the road was eventually abandoned, the precedent that private interests supercede Native religious rights remains the law of the land. Indeed, the prevailing message is that indigenous peoples are in the way of "progress" and development. As Trope states,

where western notions of resource development, i.e., logging, mining, tourism, conflict with the preservation of the integrity and sanctity of sacred sites, the inclination of most governmental (and private) authorities is to recognize and understand the goals and needs of those who want to develop, but not the deep-seated religious beliefs of Indians who might be affected by that development.[25]

Indigenous people are expendable precisely because our worldviews are in opposition to the policies of first-world societies and the needs of cultures of consumption.

FEMINIST (MISSED) CONNECTIONS

In her essay, "Claiming Power-In-Relation: Exploring the Ethics of Connection," Mary Grey writes of a feminist spiritual vision "rooted in respect for the context of a group's experience."[26] Grey delineates the obstacles that have impaired women from "bonding-in-solidarity" with each other; among the "key areas of difficulty" she lists class difference, the tenuous Jewish/Christian connection, black women's oppression, difference in sexual orientation, women's (internalized) negative self-image, damaged social structures, the exploitation of the planet, and the suffering of Third World women. Grey not only casts black women as the only women of color who are contrasted to white women, she seldom in her discussion mentions cultural differences with respect to any American women of color, except perhaps in her veiled (possible) reference to Native women when she addresses the "destroyed sense of community between

Western women and women living in communities still respecting nature's [or the earth's] rhythms."[27] Her mention of black women only calls attention to "the history of white women's collusion in [black women's] oppression."[28] Even her mention of Third World women does not consider issues of cultural and political sovereignty, but instead her focus is on Third World women's courage in the face of pain.

Yet Grey establishes the idea of "interconnectedness [as] both a new revelatory paradigm and a moral imperative" for women who seek to broaden the scope and vision of the feminist struggle.[29] This ethics of connection, which calls for a reclaiming of the "healing strength of nature,"[30] she says requires an understanding of the interdependence and interrelatedness of all life. Ironically, her "new" metaphysic of connection resonates (in broad sweeps) with long-held understandings regarding Native peoples' belief systems. As Peggy Beck, Anna Lee Walters, and Nia Francisco say, in *The Sacred: Ways of Knowledge, Paths of Life*, "The knowledge that is instilled in youngsters throughout their lives in Native American sacred tradition, is the knowledge of relationships and how these relationships are arranged and interact with each other."[31] What is more, "Through this interdependency and awareness of relationships, the universe is balanced."[32] Unfortunately, perhaps Grey has not been "situated" to realize that her "new" perspective is actually quite old.

Even though Grey calls for "privileged women" to "listen [and] to learn," from "other women" (women who are not privileged? By what? Class, race/ethnicity? How is privilege defined?), she also posits in the conclusion to her essay,

. . . [W]omen of privilege—for whom it has not been a great problem to discover a voice—have the responsibility to empower other groups of women, with whom we are as a political group *in relation*, to discover, own, celebrate and mourn a story in all its particularity.[33]

Besides the assumption Grey makes about the ease with which "privileged women" discover their own voices, she also presumes a responsibility, for herself and other "privileged women," that does not belong to them. Put specifically, Native women empower ourselves; other women have the option of standing in solidarity with us as we do so. We take back our power as we reclaim (and tell) our own and each other's stories and find in our stories the herstories and histories of our peoples. One of our tasks is to (re)view the work that has been done on Native healers, spiritual practicioners and leaders through the lens of ethical representation.

THE CASE OF MARIA SABINA

The story of Maria Sabina, the Mazatec elder from Huatla de Jimenez, Mexico who worked with the sacred mushrooms, is recorded in *Maria Sabina: Her Life and Chants*, written by Mazatec scholar Alvaro Estrada. The text demonstrates in a dramatic way the issues of exploitation, at several levels, of a Native woman and her spiritual foundations. Estrada, who speaks Mazatec, records Maria Sabina's autobiography, which is an account of how she came to be a "Wise One" who ingested the mushrooms (the "little saints," the "little children") and went into trances to cure people. R. Gordon Wasson, noted anthropologist, is credited with the "discovery" of Maria Sabina; Wasson facilitated a Folkways recording of her in ceremony, wrote about her in articles and books, documented her work on her patients, and had photographs taken of her in trance. Maria Sabina quite honestly admits in her narrative that once she began to divulge her ways to the investigators, she began to feel her powers weaken.[34] She says:

The day that I did a vigil for the first time in front of foreigners, I didn't think anything bad would happen. . . . But what was the result? Well, that many people have come in search of God, people of all colors and all ages. The young people are the ones who have been the most disrespectful. They take the children at any time and in any place. They don't do it during the night or under the direction of the Wise Ones, and they don't use them to cure any sickness either. . . .

[F]rom the moment the foreigners arrived to search for God, the saint children lost their purity. They lost their force; the foreigners spoiled them. From now on they won't be any good. There's no remedy for it. Before Wasson, I felt that the saint children elevated me. I don't feel like that anymore. The force has diminished. If Cayetano hadn't brought the foreigners . . . the saint children would have kept their power.[35]

Maria Sabina is consistently straightforward in this way throughout the text.

In his "Retrospective Essay," which is included in the book, Wasson replies that Maria Sabina's words "made [him] wince," and yet he insists that from the first time he attended one of her *veladas* (the all-night healing vigils), he knew he had to decide whether to guard the privacy of the tradition or to "present it worthily to the world."[36] He opted for the latter, actually determining that he and his wife "alone could do justice to [the presentation]."[37] He says,

The sacred mushrooms and the religious feeling concentrated in them through the Sierras of Southern Mexico had to be made known to the world, and worthily so, *at whatever cost to me personally*. If I did not do this, "consulting the mushroom" would go on for a few years longer, but its extinction *was and is inevitable*. [emphases mine][38]

Why is extinction inevitable? Is the parallel relationship between "discovery" and appropriation, desacralization and consumerism a guiding principle of the Western world regarding the treatment of Native peoples? Does "extinction" inevitably follow "discovery"? When is the cost too high? Maria Sabina tells us that as a result of the foreigners disrupting the places of the elves which are near her house, several children die.[39] Wasson's own wife died in late 1958, three years after they began writing up everything they saw ardently pursuing "his" discovery. In 1958, they taped a ceremony, which was finally released in 1974 as *Maria Sabina and the Mazatec Mushroom Velada*, a massive text which documents from moment to moment a healing vigil where, in this instance, Maria Sabina determines that the patient (a young man) cannot be cured.[40] She tells the young man of his impending death during the *velada*, and he dies shortly after the ceremony. While I cannot say that these deaths are all connected, I cannot help but wonder if they are. Paula Gunn Allen has said, "Preserving tradition with the sacrifice of its living bearers seems at best reasonless, at worst blasphemous. If people die as a result of preserving tradition in the white way of preservation, for whom will the tradition be preserved?"[41]

I read in the newspaper several years ago a notice of Maria Sabina's death on a December 22. Wasson says that everything he did was to preserve the tradition's "prestige" and Maria Sabina's "prestige." I think of how she was asked to ingest the sacred mushrooms so that she could be recorded in trance but not for any healing ceremony. In one of these transcriptions, from a recording in 1970 which is quite long, we read that she asks, "Do we still have a long ways to go?" and later, "Aside she asks [again], tired out, 'Is there much more to go?' singing until the tape runs out."[42] The chants themselves are tremendously powerful, but I am not at ease when I read them. Jerome Rothenberg, in his preface to her story, is concerned with how her language "as a great oral poet" fits into his notion of ethnopoetics. In a curious leap, he tells us that "in Mazatec, Maria Sabina's calling is, literally, that of 'wise woman' — a term that we may choose to translate as 'shaman' or, by a further twist, as 'poet.' "[43] As I notice how her story is framed, how it is cast, I am grateful to Alvaro Estrada for recording an interview he conducted with another Mazatec elder, Apolonio Teran, in 1969, which also appears in the book; Teran tells him that "not only was the divine spirit [of the mushroom] profaned, but that of ourselves (the Mazatecs) as well."[44]

Maria Sabina: Her Life and Chants presents us with her person as a teacher to all of us regarding the ethical representation of a particular spiritual tradition. The text mediates in a way that Rothenberg and Wasson probably did not envision. The same is true of the music from the Nez Perce archives. When my aunts heard a (now deceased) relative on one of the tapes singing "Seven Drum Religion" songs, they turned to me and said that these songs are usually not recorded. They were surprised to hear them and to know that he had recorded them. A little later in the conversation, not in any apparent relation to these previous comments, one aunt mentioned that this relative had to have both of his legs amputated late in life. She then went on to speak of other matters. I myself am grateful that these songs were recorded for the Nimipu people and subsequently collected into one set by Loran Olsen. Lang also expresses his appreciation that so many Karuk songs were collected and recorded by white ethnographer Helen Heffron Roberts. Lang writes, "When Helen was told that some of her recordings were being returned to the Indian people she collected them from, she was happy."[45] In the case of Roberts, however, Lang states that she was successful in her work partly because of "the understanding reached between the singers and herself: she was preserving the songs for them, [even though] in reality she felt it was very unlikely that the recordings would ever make it back to them in any form."[46] The questions remain: What to do considering that for every non-Indian who reads the book or hears the recording and who believes that the book or the tape place this information in the "public domain," there might be at least one Native person (from the community written about or recorded) who does read or hear the text and in whom something is (re)awakened? Is this the curse and the blessing?

Alvaro Estrada says that "investigators . . . added the adjective 'hallucino-genic' to the sacred mushroom, the ancient *teonanácatl*, the 'Flesh of the Gods.' "[47] He reminds us that the use of peyote (*teonanácatl*) was immediately repressed by the "Tribunal of the Holy Office" and has been condemned for centuries by the Catholic church, forcing "Native doctors to shift the rites and worship of the magical plants onto a private even secret plane."[48] Mexican scholar Gonzalo Aguirre Beltran, in his book *Medicine and Magic*, observes how the early chroniclers of Native cultures, for the most part, were "individuals whose religious principles prevent[ed] them from seeing anything but the work of the devil—the helpless and maligned devil—in Indian mysticism."[49] The demonization of Native belief-systems continues into the present and has implications for Native American religious freedom today. In some instances, this historical repression figures into the present reluctance of many Native peoples to share their belief systems with anyone. It also figures into the decision of some elders not to pass on their knowledge or even languages to their younger generations, in some ways to protect them.

SINCE 1992: STILL (RE-, UN-) DISCOVERING /INVENTING "AMERICA"

In *Inventing America: Spanish Historiography and the Formation of Eurocen-trism*, José Rabasa argues that "the invention of an unknown part of the world implied its inscription within a preexistent representation of the globe."[50] Sub-sequently, with the adjustments to global cartographies came a reassessment of the world as it had been known. "In the process, [Rabasa notes] European sub-jectivity [grounded in Western metaphysics and racist constructs] surfaced as a privileged perspective and definer of the totality."[51] The resulting "definitions" of "New World," enforced by the power of colonizing (ideological/institutional) forces, began to take on the veneer of "objective knowledge," from the sixteenth century on.

In the long run, the representations of "imaginary" constituents vanished from "realistic" accounts and maps, but . . . the passage that *naturalized* the West's history and picture of the world has never been complete and can always be redrawn. From this standpoint, the dismantling of how America was invented in the sixteenth century, and continues to be invented, is through and through a historical practice that seeks to open horizons for countering Eurocentrism.[52]

The constituent project of dismantling how "Indians" were invented necessitates a "rootdigging" from within Native communities to ascertain and correct the misrepresentations. Many Native Americans are working with a conscious and devoted love on the recovery and transformation of our histories, languages, and traditions, on the recovery and transformation of ourselves and our peoples.

After all, for more than five hundred years it has been beaten into Native peoples that it is absolutely the worst, ugliest, most loathsome thing in the world to be an indigenous person. The total dehumanization of indigenous peoples of the Americas was and is necessary in order to justify their continuing exploitation in the United States and throughout the hemisphere. Native peoples continue to be subjected (in varying degrees) to a regime of terror and punishment in order to strip them "clean" of their spiritual (cultural) foundations, with the intent of rendering them helpless. As a result of the many trails of tears, the dispossessions, the relocations, the boarding schools, the introduction of alcohol into our communities, and the other genocidal policies of the federal government, it is actually remarkable that Native peoples have held on at all to any of our spiritual foundations. It is my strong belief that the high rate of alcoholism and suicide among Native peoples is directly related to the immense despair and grief over our losses.

The missionization campaign among indigenous peoples has always been, and continues to be, intense. Many Native American communities have been very open to Jesus Christ, blending Christian beliefs easily with their original belief systems. Fundamentalist Christianity (and in some cases, as with the Navajo, Mormonism[53]) has made powerful inroads, however. The rigidity of fundamentalism has caused many Native people to be ashamed of or afraid to admit their "Indianness." In what George Tinker calls "the praxis of self-hatred,"[54] these Native people have become convinced that "Indian" truly is evil, savage, heathen, and that any "Indian" ways are the devil's work. Activist/poet/singer/actor Floyd "Red Crow" Westerman describes the process in his song called "Missionaries":

Go and tell the savage Native that he must be Christianized
Tell him end his heathen worship and you'll make him civilized
Shove your gospel-fostered values down his throat until it's raw
And after he is crippled, turn your back and lock the door.[55]

To complicate matters even more, the paradoxical historical moment we are in has "New Agers" anxiously seeking out Native traditions at the same time many Native people are disavowing their "Indianness."

NATIVE AMERICAN SPIRITUALITY AND THE "NEW AGE"

As many non-Indian people, including many feminists, search for "alterNative" ways of viewing the world and living in harmony with the universe, they are turning to Native American philosophies and peoples for guidance and inspiration, on issues such as holistic healing, ecology, respect for difference (as in sexual orientation), and respect for women, elders, and children.[56] While Indian people are still being denied their own full religious expression, many non-Indians are devouring Native American spiritual traditions in the same way they have consumed Native American art, jewelry, clothing, weavings, and crafts, once again with no thought to the real, present-day, political, social, economic, and cultural/religious struggles in which Native people are engaged. Where are these people when Native American sacred sites are at stake? Where are they when the religious rights of Native American women and men prisoners (and communities) are at stake? Where are they when the rights of Native Americans to use sacred medicines such as *hikuri* (peyote) are at stake? Where are they when Native American burial sites are being defended? Where are they when Native people are struggling for the repatriation of ancestral remains?[57] Where are they when Native American lives and continuance as distinct peoples are at stake? Does their respect and reverence for Native American spirituality increase or lessen in proportion to their ability or inability to participate in the ceremonies?

Many, if not most, non-Native Americans seem to feel an entitlement regarding Native American ceremonial and cultural traditions, artifacts, and gravesites, including ancestral bones, that can only be understood in the context of the original entitlement the first colonizers felt toward this land by "right of conquest" and soon after, "Manifest Destiny." This entitlement assumes the right to take what is indigenous, with complete disregard for Native peoples, in a manner in which the perpetrators would not think of doing so easily with other traditions. Oddly enough, this notion of taking what is indigenous is never characterized as "stealing," or as "theft," or even as disrespectful or outrageous. Imagine people wanting to find out what it "feels like" to take part in the Catholic ceremony of the Eucharist, or to wear a priest's garments, or the dress and hairstyle of Orthodox Jews, because it seems "cool."[58] Imagine going into any cemetery, and wandering around, picking up here and there different mementos that have been left at the distinct gravesites, to then display them as "treasures" in one's home. Imagine contributing to a museum your "private collection" of dead white people's clothes, jewelry, and other belongings taken from them at the moment of death, before they were dumped into a mass grave.

One spring, a nice enough white woman visited D-Q University,[59] where I was living and teaching at the time. She happened to participate in a sweat ceremony that I led, and she enjoyed the experience very much. Sometime later, I phoned her with a question about a journal she was editing because I was interested in contributing an essay to her. When she recognized my voice, she excitedly said, "Oh, is this my shaman?" I said no. "My medicine woman?" she went on. "No," I said. "But you led the sweat lodge ceremony!" she exclaimed, "What would you call that!?" I said, "I led the sweat lodge ceremony, that's all." Neither of us pursued any association after that conversation. She was not interested in me as an intellectual. She wanted me to play a role that suited and served her spiritual needs. One of the most popular Native American comedians, Charlie Hill, has a list of ten things white people always say to "Indians."[60] I'm not sure if "Won't you be my shaman?" is on the list, but it should be. The appropriation of Native American spirituality relies on the romanticization (and objectification) of indigenous peoples. Those who appropriate ignore the humanity, complexity and intellect of Native peoples, just as they ignore the history of oppression that has been the experience of Native peoples in relation to the United States government and "mainstream" society.

I have also been present at D-Q University when non-Native Americans (this time European women) have *insisted* on being allowed into a sweat. Would they themselves allow complete strangers to walk into their homes and demand entrance into a private family gathering, much less a religious ceremony? An example from my own family revolves around an article titled "Chief Joseph," complete with photos, which was produced by William Albert Allard and published in *National Geographic* in 1977.[61] I was astonished when I opened the magazine to find a double page photo of four women elders engaged in the ceremonial farewell to my grandmother at her funeral. The photo was taken with a long range lens; from the position in which they are standing (and because I know how their stance would correspond to a particular moment of the ceremony) I can surmise that these elders were literally on the precipice of the gravesite. Photos are not taken at these ceremonies, and this particular photojournalist did not have the permission of my grandmother's son or her daughters to document the funeral services in this way. Under the guidance of my mom, my aunts and my uncle, I corresponded with Allard and asked him to release to us whatever pictures he had taken. He was arrogant and rude in his refusal; as far as he is concerned, those photos (and the images) are his property, and he is entitled to them.[62] As the noted Lakota scholar Vine Deloria Jr. says, "The non-Indian appropriator conveys the message that Indians are indeed a conquered people and that there is nothing that Indians possess, *absolutely nothing*—pipes, dances, land, water, feathers, drums, and even prayers—that non-Indians cannot take whenever and wherever they wish."[63]

According to some New Agers, everyone was "Indian" in a past life, which then justifies the taking in this life of anything that is Native American. "Rainbow Tribe" (and lately I've heard "Eco-Tribe") encampments and gatherings abound in many places, even in Europe, especially, I understand, in Germany. There are non-Indians who think they are more Indian than the Indians, and there are Indians who have succumbed and catered to the demand for "Native ways." Deloria says:

Many Indians are irritated, and justly so, with the wholesale appropriation of American Indian rituals, symbols, and beliefs by the non-Indian public. Several national magazines and newspapers and a myriad of pamphlets, posters, and bumper stickers proclaim the wonders of studying with the likes of Wallace Black Elk, Richard Erdoes, [the late] Sun Bear, Lynn Andrews [the "Beverly Hills Shaman"], Edward McGaa, and a host of lesser luminaries in the New Age-Indian medicine man circuit.[64]

The International Circle of Elders, made up of Native American women and men elders from throughout this hemisphere, who have traveled around the world on behalf of indigenous people, have issued directives in the form of warnings against the selling of vision quests, sweat lodge ceremonies, "shamanic workshops," ceremonial objects, sacred medicines, and so on.[65]

Once money enters the conversation, the nature of the gatherings and ceremonies is altered. Money affirms entitlement on the one hand, since devotees of consumer culture believe that enough money can buy anything, and on the other hand, money encourages people to assume a false authority because it is profitable to do so. Throughout California, you can see flyers announcing all kinds of "experiences" modeled after some Native American tradition or another. The fee is always quite high, which to many consumers, of course, means that the product is "worth more." However, the warnings sent out by the Elders Circle speak of another cost that is more dangerous. The perversion of ceremonies and distortion of rituals can cause people to get hurt because they are "messing around" with spirituality, and they don't know what they're doing. Besides the fact that people could get hurt, physically, spiritually, emotionally, mentally, or in any combination thereof, what is costly for the

Native American community is the loss of potential and actual support for legitimate issues.

A few years ago I heard of an Indian "medicine man" running sweats in Northern California for (predominately) white women (usually women's sweats are run by women). He was known to drink large quantities of alcohol and make sexual advances toward the women, who permitted him to behave in this manner because he was ostensibly their spiritual leader. He was in fact abusing, debasing, and exploiting these women, at the very least, and harming them severely at the worst. Who is to blame here? Indian people are ruled often by economic deprivation. I am not excusing this fake medicine man; he was surely hurting himself as well, but what he did was to respond, perhaps at some subconscious, or even quite conscious, level, with cynicism to the expectation of non-Indians for a "sideshow." This time, though, he was "dancing for the white women" who wanted an Indian shaman, at whatever cost. Consumer culture is a culture that devours. With the indiscriminate "lifting" of certain aspects of particular Native American traditions by unconscionable people, both Indian and non-Indian, what results is the superficiality of a "quickie" spirituality.

There is debate within the Indian community itself, even among scholars and writers, about what is all right to "share" and what is not. As Sequoya elaborates in her own essay, well-known (mixed-blood) Laguna Pueblo writer Leslie Silko has been criticized severely by Paula Gunn Allen, who is part Laguna herself, for revealing too much of Laguna ways in her novel *Ceremony*. At the same time, Gunn Allen's *Grandmothers of the Light: A Medicine Woman's Sourcebook*, in its very title suggests that it was written with a New Age and (eco)feminist readership in mind.[66] What is so objectionable to Native people is the current phenomenon of the "instant" medicine women and medicine men and the ease with which they appropriate. Even more disheartening is when Native people themselves appear to invite the dissolution of distinct traditions by suggesting that it is fine to use whatever you want. Many Native people who work with New Agers insist that they have been "instructed" to share their learnings because the world as we know it is ending. To this, Deloria astutely comments,

If we accept these claims as true, we are basically saying that traditional Indian religions have become missionary minded and now seek converts in a larger intercultural context. This claim is contrary to every known tenet of any tribal tradition but it may be a new revelation given at the end of this world.[67]

Of these exchanges, George Tinker says, "In this 'meeting' of cultures, the communal culture value of Indian people is transformed by those who do not even begin to see the cultural imposition that has occurred, however unintended."[68]

In the non-Indian world there is a tendency to make certain people's ways the "most authentic" of Indian ways; in the United States, focus is often on the Lakota tradition, perhaps because it has been one of the most visible (it is certainly the one recognizable via Hollywood as well as through the work of anthropologists and ethnographers). New Agers are especially impressed if something or someone is Sioux. It is true that many of the Lakota traditions, such as the sweat lodge ceremony, the sacred pipe, and the Sun Dance, have been shared with many peoples, both Native American and non-Native American.[69] Deloria says, "For these losses we can thank the ever-present Sioux Indians and their intense desire to act as hosts for the wide variety of people who beat their way to the Pine Ridge and Rosebud reservations."[70] It is true, also, that the Sioux have a ceremony for "making relatives," so there are people who might be able to claim legitimately that they are members of the Sioux community even though they may not be by bloodline. The Sioux traditions have definitely penetrated into other indigenous communities, even to the point of Sioux Sun Dances being sponsored on other Indian nations' lands, including as far south as the outskirts of Mexico City. Deloria himself says, somewhat tongue-in-cheek, that perhaps "the Sioux have received some special revelation that demands they universalize their traditions . . . even to save the religious practices of other tribes."[71]

The Sioux and Aztec traditions partially filled a vacuum that was created by the intentional and systematic efforts of the United States government to bring about the disintegration and erasure of the cultures of distinct indigenous peoples and of the peoples themselves. There has been a mixing up of traditions—among the *mestizos* and *mestizas*, the mixed-bloods, the urban Indians, among even some of the reservation Indians. Sometimes Indians who come back in touch with a Native American spirituality manifest a "born-again" fervor—there are even T-shirts in the Indian community that say, "Born Again Indian," "Born Again Pagan," "Born Again Sioux," and so on. Sometimes these born-agains, and I include myself here, because I went through this phase, can themselves be extremely rigid and fundamentalist in their perspectives, insisting, for example, that there is only one way to conduct the sweat lodge ceremony, or only one way to pray, or sing, or fast, and so on. The Lakota and the Aztec traditions come to mind, because they are the ones, in the north and the south, respectively, that seem to attract ardent devotees. For those Chicanos and Chicanas who want to claim their indigenous heritage, the Aztec dance tradition has functioned in much the same way as the Sioux tradition has in the north. All people of Mexican descent, however, are no more Aztec than are all people of Indian descent in the north Lakota. And even though those traditions, for whatever reason, have opened themselves up to indigenous people from other traditions, and sometimes to non-Indians, the experience of participating in those traditions does not make someone Aztec or (necessarily) Lakota.

With what is known as Aztec dance, when it is brought up to the States, prayer becomes performance. Why? Who is to blame when poor workers come north to sell their labor and find that the "commodity" that many people want is their religion? The public manifestation that is an expression of religious devotion at sacred sites in Mexico City becomes, in cities like San Francisco, Chicago, or San Antonio, more a cultural exhibition, one that is often seen in the Native American community as a kind of "fancy dancing" and in the non-Indian community as a sort of folkloric dance. In such settings, the dance tends to become more outward, with attention on the exchange between those dancing and those watching. In many cases, the focus is on the execution of the steps for themselves; the steps are danced with a choreographed precision at a fast pace. The dance *vestuario*, or regalia, becomes an elaborate costume. There is an audience that must be impressed, and remuneration is often received for the "performance." In Mexico City, there are dancers who have similar inclinations. However, for the traditional, or "old style," dancers, the dance is more inward, with a conscious focus on the center of the circle and the circle as a whole; ideally, the steps are prayer and devotion manifesting the dance as life and life as dance. Within each dance group, old people and children are also given the opportunity to lead dances, at their own pace. The dance outfits are often quite humble, with mainly the elders wearing the more elaborate *vestuarios.* The "audience" is the Supreme Being and the whole of Creation. As elders have told me, each member of the circle of dancers is supposed to be striving to grow in *conciencia.*[72] The spirit is expected to triumph harmoniously over the ego and over matter within the circle, and, in the dance of life.

In contrast, the commodification and commercialization of Native American spirituality disturbs and disrupts the work of sustaining the spiritual traditions that belong to specific Native American communities, and the work of retrieving those traditions that, in many cases, have been almost forgotten. There is an integrity of form to each people's songs, to each people's ceremonies — what has been denied us through the process of colonization is being delicately and patiently rebuilt. Many Native American women and men, children and elders, are actively involved in the process of decolonizing our consciousnesses and reconstructing our belief-systems. At the same time, we are engaged in the overall struggle for the social, economic, and political betterment of our people. Since we are the most legislated of any peoples in the United States, the rebuilding and sustaining of our spiritual traditions is intertwined with our overall struggle.[73] It is insulting to hear non-Indians self-righteously proclaim their entitlement to our traditions—whether via New Ageism or because they have had the (class/economic) privilege of studying our languages, histories, and cultures in institutions of higher learning—while the young people in our communities still contend largely with a boarding school type of indoctrination and otherwise poor education that rarely allows them to finish high school. In academia, the "experts" assume the right to pass judgment on our authenticity by the rule of their supposed "civilized objectivity." These grievances are exacerbated by the fact that those who take from us do not care to know of our struggles in this life.

THE REPRESENTATION OF OUR SPIRITS

The issues that frame the question of Native American religious traditions within the Native American community are interwoven with questions of identity, community, and representation, from the personal to the hemispheric and global levels. There are as many Native American spiritual traditions as there are distinct "tribes" or nations in this hemisphere, even though, as Sequoyah says, "[I]t is one of the paradoxes of democratic government that without the appearance of a homogeneous political identity—an identity constituted in terms of the dominant system of representation—the issues crucial to Native American survival as regionally diverse peoples cannot be heard."[74] Still, many Native peoples are engaged in the struggle for sovereignty. Many Native American women and men, whether they are community activists, health workers, educators, cultural workers, visual and performing artists, curators, writers, filmmakers, scholars, elders, or students, to name a few, are contributing to the rethinking about issues of identity, community, spirituality, and "culture." Race, ethnicity, class, gender, sexual orientation, age, ability, in the context of the specific historical experiences of our peoples, factor into our reconfigurations, and into our representations. For many Native people, whether the issues revolve around our personal well-being or the well-being and continuance of our peoples, our distinct and evolving spiritual traditions remain the base of what we do as conscious human beings. Just as we show respect for the strength and beauty of each people's traditions and for the pain and joy of their histories, we must show respect to one another as women and men, acknowledging each other for our differences. As we honor each other's spirits, we honor women's and men's wisdom and women's and men's authority within the context of the communities we claim as our own.

NOTES

I dedicate this essay to the women and men elders who taught me strength and who stood by me as I learned to be myself.

1. Michael M. J. Fischer, "Ethnicity and the Post-Modern Arts of Memory," in *Writing Culture: The Poetics and Politics of Ethnography*, ed. James Clifford and George E. Marcus (Berkeley: University of California Press, 1986), 198.

2. Mary Louise Pratt, "Fieldwork in Common Places," in *Writing Culture*, 32.

3. Betsy Erkkila, "Ethnicity, Literary Theory, and the Grounds of Resistance," *American Quarterly* 47 (December 1995): 563.

4. Ibid., 572.

5. Lata Mani, "Multiple Mediations: Feminist Scholarship in an Age of Multinational Readership," in *Traveling Theories/Traveling Theorists*, ed. James Clifford and Vivel Dhareshwar (Santa Cruz: Group for the Critical Study of Colonial Discourse and the Center for Cultural Studies, University of California at Santa Cruz, 1989).

6. I have in fact presented the major points of this essay at a Native American Women's conference at Humboldt University in Arcata, California, and I have circulated it among several Native elders, mostly women, some men; in all, the essay has been well received.

7. Fischer, 198.

8. Pratt, 32.

9. I have qualified the term "feminisms" with quotation marks because Native women have not embraced it. At the same time, I am interested in re(or un)covering those aspects of distinct Native belief-systems that address the roles and power of women. I am also interested in the work of Native women in opposing and otherwise (re)negotiating a transformation of any such aspects which might repress and/or violate women's space and voice.

10. Jana Sequoya, "How(!) Is an Indian?: A Contest of Stories," in *New Voices in Native American Literary Criticism*, ed. Arnold Krupat (Washington DC: Smithsonian Institutional Press, 1993), 456.

11. I have written about *Malintzin*, or "*la Malinche*," in other essays, but I have not detailed exactly what the "*Malinche*" does, moment by moment, within the dance ceremony itself.

12. Sequoya, 456.

13. There are books that delineate the sweat lodge tradition within a range of specificity, such as *The Sacred Pipe: The Seven Rites of the Oglala Sioux* by Joseph Eppes Brown (New York: Penguin Books, 1953) and *Imagine Ourselves Richly: Mythic Narratives of North American Indians* by Christopher Vecsey (New York: HarperCollins, 1991).

14. Vecsey, 208.

15. A "runner" is a person who takes messages back and forth between elders and between distinct indigenous communities, often communicating the messages during ceremonial times. A runner might also simply give an elder an account of the proceedings of a particular event.

16. Julian Lang, "How They Almost Killed Our Songs," *News From Native California* 4 (winter 1990): 23.

17. Jack F. Trope, "Protecting Native American Sacred Sites and Religious Freedom," *Wicazo Sa Review* 7 (fall 1991): 53.

18. Russell Barsh, "The Supreme Court, Peyote, and Minority Religions: Zero Tolerance" *Wicazo Sa Review* 7 (fall 1991): 49.

19. Ibid.

20. Stephen C. Moore, "Reflections on the Elusive Promise of Religious Freedom for the Native American Church," *Wicazo Sa Review* 7 (spring 1991): 42.

21. Trope, 53.

22. I do not want to imply that life at Big Mountain is idyllic, but the land base is home.

23. Trope, 53.

24. David Wilkins, "Who's in Charge of U.S. Indian Policy? Congress and Supreme Court at Loggerheads over American Indian Religious Freedom," *Wicazo Sa Review* 8 (spring 1992): 40.

25. Trope, 53.

26. Mary Grey, "Claiming Power-In-Relation: Exploring the Ethics of Connection," *Journal of Feminist Studies in Religion* 7 (spring 1991): 17–18.

27. Ibid., 9.

28. Ibid., 8–9.

29. Ibid., 11.

30. Ibid., 17.

31. Peggy V. Beck, Anna Lee Walters, and Nia Francisco, *The Sacred: Ways of Knowledge, Sources of Life* (Tsaile AZ: Navajo Community College Press, 1992), 21.

32. Ibid., 13.

33. Grey, 17.

34. She performed the ceremony for the outsiders because the municipal authorities of the village, on the recommendation of her friend Cayetano Garcia, ordered her to do so.

35. She repeatedly comes back to this point because the tradition of the sacred mushrooms is a healing tradition. Once word spread about the "hallucinogenic" quality of the mushrooms, hippies and other people began to go down in huge numbers to "try them out" and, as they told her, "to know God." Alvaro Estrada, *Maria Sabina: Her Life and Chants*, trans. Henry Munn, ed. Jerome Rothenberg, New Wilderness Poetics, vol. 1 (Santa Barbara CA: Ross Erikson Press, 1981): 90–91.

36. Estrada, 20.

37. Ibid., 13.

38. Ibid., 20.

39. Ibid., 92.

40. R. Gordon Wasson et al. *Maria Sabina and the Mazatec Mushroom Velada* (New York: Harcourt Brace Jovanovich, 1974).

41. Paula Gunn Allen, "Some Problems in Teaching Leslie Silko's Ceremony," *American Indian Quarterly* 14 (fall 1990): 380.

42. Estrada, 147, 189. This recording session, we are told in the text, was arranged by Henry Munn, although "only Mazatecs were present" (p. 9), which I presume is an attempt to demonstrate that no foreigners intruded in any way. However, the session is called a "chanting session" as opposed to a "healing ceremony," and thus its nature is changed. (Munn, by the way, "married into the Estrada family," we are told, and is a "devoted student of Mazatec culture," p. 9).

43. Jerome Rothenberg, preface to Estrada, 7, 11. Rothenberg continues this association of "shaman" with "poet" in his more recent essay, " 'We Explain Nothing, We Believe Nothing': American Indian Poetry and the Problematics of Translation," in *On the Translation of Native American Cultures*, ed. Brian Swann (Washington DC: Smithsonian Institution Press), 65.

44. Estrada, 206.

45. Lang, 25.

46. Ibid.

47. Estrada, 23.

48. Ibid.

49. Quoted in Estrada, 24.

50. José Rabasa, *Inventing America: Spanish Historiography and the Formation of Eurocentrism* (Norman: University of Oklahoma Press, 1993), 213.

51. Ibid.

52. Ibid.

53. See Steve Pavlik, "Of Saints and Lamanites: An Analysis of Navajo Mormonism," *Wicazo Sa Review* 8 (spring 1992): 21–30.

54. George Tinker, *Missionary Conquest: The Gospel and Native American Cultural Genocide* (Minneapolis: Fortress Press, 1993), 3.

55. Floyd "Red Crow" Westerman, "Missionaries," from the cassette recording *Custer Died For Your Sins*, Red Crow Productions, 1982.

56. I am, of course, aware of the other side of this conversation, the position that Native people do not really have the belief systems that have been attributed to us, that instead, some well-meaning sympathizers to indigenous causes in their zeal to garner support for Native peoples have merely projected onto us, in a highly romanticized manner, this sophisticated consciousness of ecology, astronomy, holistic healing, etc. I would certainly agree that many Native people no longer have (access to) these belief-systems. However, I am also cognizant of the work of Native scholars, and groups like the Society for the Study of Native American Religious Traditions, who are developing the study (and recovery) of Native religious traditions as a disciplinary field of its own.

57. Trope, 54. In 1990, the Native American Grave Protection and Repatriation Act, P.L. 101–601, was passed which provides some protection to Native American grave

sites and requires the repatriation (by federally funded museums and federal agencies) of cultural affiliated human remains and associated funerary objects, as well as some unassociated funerary objects, sacred objects, and items of cultural patrimony.

58. I was startled several years ago upon seeing a fashion magazine (in the checkout lane at a grocery store) highlighting some famous designer's new styles patterned after religious habits from different denominations. One model wore a gown modeled after a monk's habit, another wore an outfit indeed copied in the style of Orthodox Jews, and so on. I have not seen those styles catch on in the general populace, though.

59. D-Q University is a private Native American college in Davis, California; its name combines the name of an Iroquois prophet known as "The Peacemaker" and the name of the Aztec god of wisdom, the Plumed Serpent, Quetzalcoatl.

The university was founded in 1971 as a "College of the Americas" where indigenous (and other) peoples could come to study from an hemispheric Native American perspective and where Native peoples could determine how their own histories and cultures would be studied. The school is referred to as "D-Q" because the Iroquois people requested that their prophet's name be shared only in trust.

60. While many Native people here in the United States have begun to call themselves "Native American," some still refer to themselves as "American Indian" or "Indian" (they are all generic terms). Everyone in the "Indian" community knows that the term is a misnomer, but it is a word we have made our own.

61. William Albert Allard, "Chief Joseph," *National Geographic* 151 (March 1977): 410–11. I was not able to attend the funeral. My mother was there and remembers seeing Allard on the periphery of the crowd and wondering what he was doing there.

62. My mother, without directly saying so, but I know out of respect for my grandmother's spirit, instructed me to "let it go."

63. Vine Deloria Jr. "Is Religion Possible? An Evaluation of Present Efforts to Revive Traditional Tribal Religions," *Wicazo Sa Review* 8 (spring 1992): 37.

64. Deloria, 35. Wendy Rose's essay, "The Great Pretenders: Further Reflections on Whiteshamanism," in *The State of Native America: Genocide, Colonization, and Resistance*, ed. M. Annette Jaimes (Boston: South End Press, 1992), is an important contribution to this discussion as is George Tinker's "New Age and the Continuing Colonial Invasion" in his book *Missionary Conquest*, 120–23.

65. See Lee Irwin's essay, "Freedom, Law, and Prophesy," this volume, appendix one, for an early statement of the Circle of Elders.

66. Paula Gunn Allen, *Grandmothers of the Light: A Medicine Woman's Sourcebook* (Boston: Beacon Press, 1991).

67. Deloria, 35.

68. Tinker, 122.

69. Other traditions, such as the Nez Perce, also had or have the sweat lodge, the Sun Dance, and the pipe traditions but in their own form.

70. Deloria, 36.

71. Ibid.

72. In Spanish, *conciencia* means both conscience and consciousness.

73. See Stephen L. Pevar's *The Rights of Indians and Tribes: An American Civil Liberties Handbook* (New York: Bantam Books, 1983).

74. Sequoyah, 455.

Cultural Identity, Authenticity, and Community Survival

The Politics of Recognition in
the Study of Native American Religions

JOHN A. GRIM

This article asks the question whether the current politics of recognition in American Indian studies provides new perspectives for the study of American Indian religions.[1] The politics of recognition is associated here with the public effort of many American Indian scholars and reservation community leaders to raise questions about the lack of sovereign voice among indigenous peoples and about the manner in which their cultural identity has been misrepresented. Closely related is Native American postcolonial theory which explores the structures of American imperialism and the ways in which structures of dominance have framed Native American ethnicity, race, gender, and religion.[2] This paper proposes that specific issues raised in the politics of recognition, namely, cultural identity, authenticity, and community survival, provide critical approaches to the study of American Indian religions. These approaches are not simply political perspectives but ways of illuminating social forces and ritual practices in Native American communities.[3]

Native American identity has rarely been understood in its cultural and social setting in mainstream America. Individualism and stereotypes of heroic warrior personalities have been emphasized in a way that distorts the actual Native stress on individual identity in the context of cultural community. The academic study of Native American healers, shamans, or medicine men has at times over emphasized the personal biographical and visionary formation of these healers with little or no attention to the community setting in which these religious healers practice. When Anglos, disaffected by their own religious traditions, turn to American Indian religions they often imagine themselves as autonomous, heroic visionaries. American Indian scholars sometimes speak of these practitioners as "whiteshamans." In drawing out the reactions of these Native scholars I am pointing toward the basis of their judgments regarding cultural identity as lying in the Native community. Moreover, the direction of their analysis constitutes a new dialogue between mainstream and dominant

America in which Native peoples are not simply spoken for but speak themselves about the study of their religions.

Authenticity is connected in this paper to the Native American regard for place. This approach does not collapse Native regard for land into a spiritual environmentalism but urges students of Native American religions to understand the fundamental link between Native community and place. Ward Churchill expressed this saying, "Recognition of the legal and moral rights by which a nation occupies its landbase is a fundamental issue of its existence."[4] For example, Native reservation spokespeople have struggled for decades to protect sacred sites as well as to restore the land base of their communities. Mainstream Americans wonder which is the "authentic" American Indian relationship with the land? Are Native peoples authentically religious in relation to sacred sites so that efforts to augment the community land base is understood as simply an expression and extension of the private property ethos protected by the United States Constitution for human members of the community? Using the concept of "wilderness," I take up a legal study as an inquiry into authenticity and place in the Native American politics of recognition. What does the Native struggle for sacred sites tell us about American Indian religions? Responding to this question constitutes an approach which also informs us about American Indian ethics and spiritual direction.

Many people in mainstream America were shocked during the Colombian Quincentennial in 1992 when they heard the term "genocide" used in describing the history of relations between the United States and the diverse American Indian peoples. Some Native American scholars have insisted that this term is descriptive of these relations into the present. Thus, they use the term not only for historical description but also for political purposes. The overtly political agenda of some Native scholars has dulled the sharper questioning of a mainstream American propensity to commodify everything. Objectifying and marketing Native cultures threatens the survival of viable American Indian communities according to this critique. One of the approaches suggested here, namely, community survival, explores the critique raised by the American Indian politics of recognition that a systemic global violence continues to subvert local, indigenous communities, their land, and their cultures. This approach to the study of American Indian religions urges students to develop "eyes" to see and "ears" to hear the new voice of Native peoples talking about the threats to their cultural ways. In responding to these challenges Native American religions have changed just as they have transformed themselves over centuries of encounters with other indigenous traditions. Understanding that change is not simply a historical insight, it has been an issue of community survival during the five hundred years of Native American encounters with Euroamerican colonization.

Students of Native American religions will see that in using these approaches —cultural identity, authenticity, and community survival—the interpretive act becomes less an application of the anthropological perspective and more of a dialogue. The anthropological perspective has emphasized the distinct worlds of diverse cultures. The dialogic perspective fostered in the politics of recognition is more interactive. Dialogic approaches presume that the different worlds of Native culture interact with one another and with mainstream American culture. Interaction is the key epistemological act in the approaches presented here. That is, understanding does not occur without reaching out to learn about other Native cultures. Understanding risks the possibility of change.

This dialogic perspective is not the same as the interreligious dialogue of institutional religions. There is more of a willingness to bracket the "truths" and structures within which most interreligious dialogues occur. A dialogic perspective requires that one learn in the exchange of ideas and practices about sharp differences and shared concerns. Ultimately, these dialogic approaches cause a student to ask questions about the study of religion itself.

The question continues to be raised: Does the current resurgence of critical voices in the Native American politics of recognition play a role in the academic study of American Indian religions? Native scholars have criticized the study of religion as having promoted demeaning images of American Indians. What critique can be brought to the work of Native scholars? Do the politically significant perspectives raised by Native scholars insinuate themselves as methods for the study of American Indian religions which may, in fact, have little to do with the traditional ways of the diverse indigenous communities of North America? Are Native scholars circumscribed by their political or personal agendas? Are Native scholars and the study of Native religions correctly described by Sam Gill when he wrote:

Native American members of the group [those involved in the academic study of religion] often talk about their experiences, both in terms of their own tribal cultures and as Native Americans (oppressed minorities in academia as well as American culture). . . . The publications, few as they are, by members of this field tend to be as much discussions about what should or should not go in the field, who should and should not contribute to the field, as they are productive studies of Native American religious topics. (Gill 1994: 972)

Gill's criticisms place academic study above discussions of the politics of recognition as approaches in the study of religion. Is it not also possible that the academic study of American Indian religions can be advanced by the politics of recognition?

Implied in Gill's critique is the "ethnic criteria" argument regarding the study of Native American religions. One standpoint says that only an American Indian can truly study and understand American Indian religions. Gill also describes a slightly different position based on languages and field studies:

The topics that have engendered lively discussion in recent years in the study of Native American religions are revealing. Discussion has frequently centered on whether or not active participation in the study of Native American religions should be restricted to those who speak Native American languages and have field experience. Another topic of recent interest is whether non-Native Americans should study and teach Native American religions. This discussion from start to finish has explored issues that divide along ethnic and racial lines (as even the question was formulated). (Gill 1994: 971)

Wendy Rose, a Hopi anthropologist, addressed this question when she wrote:

The fear exists among non-Native writers that we are somehow trying to bar them from writing about Indians at all, that Indian people might be "staking a claim" as the sole interpreters of Indian cultures, most especially of that which is sacred, and asserting that only Indians can make valid observations on themselves. Such fears are not based in fact; I know of no Indian who has ever said this. Nor do I know of any who secretly think it. We accept as given that whites have as much prerogative to write and speak about us and our cultures as we have to write and speak about them and theirs. The question is how this is done and, to some extent, why it is done. (Rose 1992: 415–16)

If ethnic and racial lines are not acceptable criteria for either Rose or Gill, what are the criteria that Native scholars propose regarding the study of American Indian religion? Would language study and field experience provide a response to Wendy Rose's question about "how" the study of American Indian traditions should be done? Do questions raised by the politics of recognition hold insights for thinking about "why" non-Native students study Native American religions?

Overstating the question, as I have done here, brackets efforts in the academic study of religion to reassess ritual studies and to rethink narrative traditions of myth-making.[5] Indeed, this caricature of the history of religions is as dubious as some of the ethnographies of Native peoples and many of the interpretations of American Indian religions. Drawing attention to interpretive constructs in the history of religions is part of the advance work that has already begun in the study of religion. Lawrence Sullivan undertook such a critique in his study of South American religious ideas in *Icanchu's Drum* where he wrote:

A number of obstructions block the clear view we desire of South American religions and values. Contrary to general impression, South Americans' ideas about themselves are not the biggest problem. Their imagery, unfamiliar to us, does not obscure South American religious life; it *constitutes* it and, therefore, remains the only true source of its clarification. Rather, our own interpretive constructs stand in the way of understanding.

To come into the light that South Americans themselves shed on their experience of humanity, we must first inspect our own way of thinking and the shadowy concepts that undergird it. For instance, no people refer to themselves as practitioners of South American religions in the way that others identify with Buddhism, Christianity, Sikhism, Islam, Judaism, or Hinduism. *South American religions* is a category constructed by outsiders who, in a way that calls for critical scrutiny, actually constitute the religious situation described by the term. (Sullivan 1988: 6–7)

Sullivan highlights self-scrutiny of the shadowy concepts often used to think about religion. The approaches presented here serve to emphasize investigative concepts that come from the communities being studied.

Misconceptions persist, especially in the teaching of American Indian religions by nonspecialists. Stereotypes often are used by students of religion to describe Native peoples as primal rather than contemporary; as categorized by theological questions rather than embodying local religious thought; as timeless (ahistorical) and caught in historical forces rather than as history-making; as incapable of the analytical distance of western Enlightenment rationalism rather than thought traditions which have subtle ritual and mythic modes of reflection. By deriving interpretive tools from the politics of recognition, this article seeks to provide perspectives for educators trying to teach American Indian religions. Such perspectives do not explain away but open possibilities for the academic study of American Indian religions.

In considering writings of the American Indian scholarly community I have selected statements by the Hopi-Miwok anthropologist, Wendy Rose, and the Lakota lawyer, Vine Deloria Jr., from the collection of articles titled *The State of Native America*.[6] In the discussion of cultural identity I also draw on the work, *Manifest Manners*, of Gerald Vizenor, a literary theorist of Anishinabe-Anglo heritage.[7] This is followed by a perspective from the study of the Osage theologian, George Tinker, in his work, *Missionary Conquest*.[8] While these scholars are American Indians, I do not intend in any way to present them as *the* Native position or to collapse their diverse standpoints into one Native view. Rather, I have gathered together isolated aspects of their work as articulating an American Indian politics of recognition to draw attention to a particular body of social criticism. This diverse "body" of writings has sharply criticized academic researchers as having fostered, knowingly or unknowingly, those unequal processes of representation by which indigenous peoples have been caricatured in the academy.

Following the sections on the three approaches to the study of American Indian religions, I will conclude with a brief case study, namely, a consideration of the *Ashkisshe*, the "Sun Dance" ceremonial of the Apsaalooke/Crow peoples of Montana.[9] My point is to consider the implications of cultural identity, authenticity, and community survival both for the Apsaalooke themselves as well as for myself as a student of the Ashkisshe ceremony. The example of the Ashkisshe/Sun Dance focuses on the reintroduction of this complex ceremony to the Apsaalooke from the Shoshoni of Wyoming and the first performance of a Shoshoni/Crow Sun Dance on the Crow Indian Reservation. This historic event, which occurred in 1941, has had political, social, and ideological implications for the Apsaalooke.

The Ashkisshe ceremonial also has been the focus of academic discussion by both Native and non-Native writers such as Thomas Yellowtail and Joseph Medicine Crow (Native), as well as Fred Voget and Ron Frey (non-Native). This article endeavors to bring some of the epistemological and methodological questions posed above to the study of the Shoshoni/Crow Sun Dance as a religious ritual. Moreover, the fiftieth anniversary Sun Dance performed in Pryor, Montana, in 1991, provides a significant example in which this particular Ashkisshe ritual was joined to its founding story, or myth. A brochure was prepared by the sponsor of the fiftieth anniversary Sun Dance, Heywood Big Day, and this particular ceremonial was the subject of a photographic essay by the sponsor with the assistance of Michael Crummett.[10] In this case study historical and religious dimensions of the Shoshoni/Crow Sun Dance were purposefully linked so as to bring the Crow into reflexive thought about this religious act.

What I hope to make clear at the conclusion is that many of the implications of the politics of recognition have already, to some extent, been implemented by traditional specialists who lead, as well as practice, the Ashkisshe ritual among the Apsaalooke people. Thus, Apsaalooke leaders of the Ashkisshe ceremonial, for example, have made connections between identity as interior attitudes to be cultivated during the ritual and the learning of Crow language and Sun Dance songs. Regarding authenticity, Crow elders speak of the interconnectedness of the dancers with sacred power, *maxpe*. The dance of the participants becomes the placement of authenticity and of spiritual blessings for all the community. Finally, the loss of their older traditional Sun Dance (*Baaiichkiisapiliolissua* "fringed ankle dance") in 1875 reminds the Crow of the fragile nature of ceremonial life especially in a pervasively hostile environment. For the Apsaalooke community survival flows from ritualization, the process of actualizing the imagined community, not in conceptualizations or interpretive schema alone.

IDENTITY AS DIFFERENCE

The lack of voice given to indigenous communities in history texts and the marketing of Indian consumer products illustrate nonrecognition by mainstream America of diverse American Indian cultural identities. Underlying dominant

American attitudes is the perspective that all Americans are located within the same economic and social milieu. The approaches offered here provide ways to think about issues, such as cultural identity, not as commodities or slogans with which to market a product but as integral voices which bring these different communities into being.

What has caused suffering and confusion of identity among Native peoples has now become a target for social criticism by Native scholars. Most problematic for many Native communities and scholars are those non-Native individuals who market American Indian religion and identity for self aggrandizement and profit. Can the academic study of American Indian religions be distinguished or separated from this exploitative activity? For example, what happens when non-Native individuals present themselves as pseudo Indians, fake shamans, or interpreters of Native perspectives? The anthropologist, Wendy Rose, considered some of these questions when she wrote:

The problem with whiteshamans is one of integrity and intent, not topic, style, interest, or experimentation. Many non-Indian people have—from the stated perspective of the non-Native viewing things Native—written honestly and eloquently about any number of Indian topics, including those we hold sacred. We readily acknowledge the beauty of some poetry by non-Natives dealing with Indian people, values, legends, or the relationship between human beings and the American environment. A non-Native poet cannot produce an Indian perspective on Coyote or Hawk, cannot see Coyote or Hawk in an Indian way, and cannot produce a poem expressing Indian spirituality. What can be produced is another perspective, another view, another spiritual expression. The issue, as I said, is one of integrity and intent. (Rose 1992: 416)

Let us take Wendy Rose's emphasis on "integrity and intent" as key terms for the self-scrutiny of the non-Native student using a cultural identity approach to study American Indian religions. No non-Native study of a Native religious practice can identify itself as an Indian explanation. Rather, all interpretations arise from worldviews and related perspectives whose values may have ideological force. Studying American Indian religions entails a reflexive step that activates self-scrutiny. That is, this approach encourages students to inquire into the images they have of Native Americans.

Examination of those images opens those dim and tentative beginnings of memories that have established directions for study in ways other than through critical analysis. From this self-scrutiny a student can research the historical journey of a people knowing that it is not his or her own journey. A student can develop an awareness of the limitations of a non-Native student with regard to the inner world, the "shadow-visions" of which Gerald Vizenor speaks when he writes:

The shadows of personal visions, for instance, were heard and seen alone, but not in cultural isolation or separation from tribal communities. Those who chose to hear visions, an extreme mediation, were aware that their creative encounters with nature were precarious and would be sanctioned by the tribe; personal visions could be of service to tribal families. Some personal visions and stories have the power to heal and liberate the spirit, and there are similar encounters with tribal shadows in the stories by contemporary tribal authors.

Nicknames, shadows, and shamanic visions are tribal stories that are heard and remembered as survivance. These personal identities and stories are not the same as those translated in the literature. (Vizenor 1994: 57–58)

Vizenor uses the neologism "survivance" to suggest the process of survival embedded in the daily narrative acts of personal identity. He reminds his reader that the inner world of visions is private and difficult of access but intimately related to the Native communities of a visionary. Because these visions are so inimical to translation some individuals yearn to take into themselves the personal direction and meaningful authority of these Native visions.

By "whiteshamans," Rose refers to non-Native individuals who, from a number of motivations venal or romantic, present themselves as actually Native or as authorized interpreters of indigenous thought and action. She does not seem to be pointing at non-Native academics in using this term. Indeed, her statement is written in an academic style, but her remarks raise questions about public statements regarding American Indian religions. Native individuals who publicly market American Indian thought for personal aggrandizement are not described in some critical settings as "whiteshamans" but as "plastic medicine men or women." Regardless of the terms, various communities of regard, of which the academic study of religion is one, feel compelled to examine the plausibility of disingenuous claims in light of knowledge and understanding of indigenous people.

In this sense, the Native critique and the academic analysis are quite close. Namely, in the indigenous community, questions might be, "What elders have authorized you to speak in this way? What are your kinship connections to Native peoples? What experiences empower you to speak publicly?" And in the academic context, the question often arises, "What is the critical and comparative relation of the whiteshamans' teachings to known religious teachings of this people?" They are different questions that arise from the conversations within these particular communities that study American Indian religions. Both communities distance themselves from those Native or non-Native individuals whose understanding of Native traditions is purely subjective, idiosyncratic, and profit-motivated. Yet, the crucial point in this identity approach is that the academic standpoint and the perspective of a Native community are necessarily different. Identity implies difference in American Indian studies.

Wendy Rose focuses on integrity and intent to provide criteria for evaluating poetic and artistic exchange in which Native themes are used by non-Natives. One striking difference embedded in Rose's emphasis on integrity and intent is the difference between these communities of communication. In the academy, the integrity of intellectual identity rests with the autonomous rational individual; whereas, in the indigenous community identity rests in the relationship between the individual and the collective. Collective cultural identities are primary in the religious lifeways of American Indian communities. This collective identity as relational knowledge set in Native worldview values is violated by the claims of non-members of indigenous communities who assert unsubstantiated prerogatives to speak for, or on behalf of, a Native community. Thus, it is not ethnicity alone or autonomous rational analysis but authenticity of intent and awareness of Native communitarian thought which are necessary evaluative criteria in the academic study of American Indian religions. Yet, who determines what is authentic intent and what constitutes communitarian thought remains to be developed more fully in dialogic studies.

AUTHENTICITY AND PLACE

The authenticity approach immediately raises questions about categories used to study a cultural community. If external distortions, such as bloodlines or literate documentation, are imposed on a people to determine inner authenticity, serious internal fault lines eventually may break a community apart. Several current legal battles on reservations regarding the authenticity of tribal governments revolve around this issue of recognition. Misrecognition occurs when a community is not allowed to speak for itself but finds itself the subject of interpretation and presentation by those who are not members. Distortions and misrecognitions become the standard of historical nonrecognition and legal manipulation. One major concern of Native scholars has been the ongoing misrecognition of American Indian sacred sites. The complicated issue of sacred sites has religious, historical, legal, and political dimensions for Native communities.

Ironically, the 1978 legislative effort to provide American Indians with religious freedom has failed in a sequence of legal tests most poignantly evident in the 1988 Supreme Court case, *Lyng v. Northwest Indian Cemetery Protective Association*. In this case, the court failed to uphold religious rights over a sacred burial and vision quest site of the Native peoples of northern California from intrusion by a National Forest Service road. A major argument in the legal process whereby this case came to be heard by the Supreme Court was built around a view that collapsed "wilderness" as a concept into "wilderness" as a worldview value.

The concept of wilderness, it was argued, corresponded to a perceived reality in dominant America in which humans could be separated out from the bioregion, or larger community of life in a geographical region. As a worldview value wilderness could be presented as a viable ethical goal with which to relate to land. This worldview value would be simultaneously projected onto American Indians and used to block their legal struggles to protect a sacred site. The projected worldview value presumes a dualism separating wilderness, as land undeveloped by humans, from developed land. This dualism directly relates to the types of dualism prominent in the Cartesian objectification of matter that also is embedded in the academic study of religion. Ideas of progress and metaphors for the study of cultures, derived from the theory of evolution, were used to discuss cultural and genetic differences between colonizers and colonized peoples. Early on, progress was the determinative concept for authenticity; of late, undeveloped "wilderness" has become another detachable label for authenticity. Neither "progress" nor "wilderness" are Native American concepts, but both have been used to interpret and evaluate American Indian thought.

Wilderness as a type is often laid as a template on American Indian sacred sites. In this sense, wilderness is a spiritualizing concept, or pattern, that is understood as corresponding to the view of American Indian communities. This is a fundamental misrepresentation that marks the inability of mainstream America to understand the sense of authentic relationships between diverse bioregions and the Native American peoples who inhabited them. Vine Deloria Jr., a Lakota lawyer and educator, observed that:

According to popular definitions of wilderness, its primary value is as an area in its pristine natural state, because this represents some intangible and difficult to define spiritual aspect of nature that has a superior value to commercial use of the area [the land contested in the *Lyng v. Northwest Indian Cemetery Protective Association*, 1988]. In a sense we have a generalized secular use, albeit one that represents a recognition of intangible values no matter how shallow they might be emotionally, now holding a greater value than a specific religious use of the same region. The question here is whether the Indian argument is to be considered inferior to the wilderness argument because of a racial distinction.

Unfortunately, at the circuit court level and later with the Supreme Court, the close parallel in motive and perspective was neither recognized nor understood. This neglect should be a warning to Indians and non-Indians alike that the popular belief prevailing that non-Indians can somehow absorb the philosophical worldview of American Indians and inculcate "reverence" for the land into their intellectual and emotional perspectives is blatantly false. Inherent in the very definition of "wilderness" is contained the gulf between the understandings of the two cultures. Indians do not see the natural world as a wilderness. In contrast, Europeans and Euroamericans see a big difference between lands they have "settled" and lands they have left alone. As long as this difference is believed to be real by non-Indians, it will be impossible to close the perceptual gap, and the substance of the two views will remain in conflict. (Deloria 1992: 280–81)

Directly related to Wendy Rose's questioning of the integrity and intent of non-Native perspectives is Deloria's insight into the perceptual gap between Indians and non-Indians regarding the concept of "wilderness." When Deloria critiques the court and the National Forest Management system for taking "wilderness" preservation as its motive and perspective, it is obvious how divergent non-Native and Native worldviews can be.

The Indian arguments in *Lyng v. Northwest Indian Cemetery Protective Association* were lost, according to Deloria, in a racial distinction. Indian arguments were: first, that the ancient forest has its own integrity; second, that three American Indian nations have long used this site as a burial ground and a vision quest location; and, third, that old growth forests are part of the national heritage, and the environmental impact of the logging road impoverished both Native and mainstream American communities. The Indian argument, which favored multiple use, was collapsed into one Indian religious position that the majority opinion of the Supreme Court could deny in the face of government usage of its national lands. Overtly, this case, and others in the ensuing years, have time and again decided for the American majority usage of such national lands over local American Indian claims of religious authenticity vested in those lands. Covertly these legal decisions have affirmed a dominant American view that the trust responsibility of the United States government does not extend to Indian spiritual relationships with the land.

In the quote above Deloria distinguishes these two points, namely, the negative racial character of the Supreme Court decision, and the incompatibility of Indian relationships with the land and the dominant American concept of "wilderness." Implied in his discussion is the challenge of differing worldviews in the study of American Indian religions. This challenge necessitates an authenticity approach to the study of American Indian religions in which motives and interpretive positions are subject to a critical regard. Often dominant American worldview values, associated with American inner authenticity, have disallowed us from seeing Native worldview values. The dominant America projection of "wilderness" and "first ecologist" images onto indigenous peoples has occurred with little or no awareness of the intimate communal conversations between Native Americans and the land that are an environmental ethics.

The question of the spiritual nature of "wilderness" as an American worldview value directly relates to the politics of recognition and the study of religion. That is, the insight of Native American scholars that such a fundamental view of the land embedded in the concept "wilderness," and in its opposite, namely, "developed," exemplifies a pervasive difference between indigenous and mainstream American worldviews. To study American Indian religions without some awareness of this difference is to project onto Native religion a spiritualizing dualism and to misrecognize what sacred sites actually make present to Native communities. Ironically, there are "conservative" groups apart from the academy who for purely political purposes appropriate and exploit the Native American critical mistrust of the "wilderness" concept. The conservative political agenda does not share the Native American regard for communities in relation to land, rather it seeks simply to subvert any and all environmental legislation as unnecessary opposition to the unbridled taking of profit.

SURVIVAL AND SYSTEMIC VIOLENCE

Community survival has made many Native individuals aware that their communities have the high moral ground in relation to dominant Anglo America. Many Native American communities have survived the genocidal assault of the past centuries. Native scholars have joined with others to communicate their awareness that the natural world, like Native peoples, has been objectified, emptied, and exploited in the name of western shadow visions of technological progress and national sovereignty. American Indian writers suggest that resistance to these mistaken ways is not simply a political act but a lifeway act in the sense that traditional religious acts are interrelated to a larger cosmology. Thus, the sacred does not manifest in fixed times or exclusive places but courses through the daily acts of life such as a legal-warrior's quest, a faster's mental journey, a mother's birthing, a dancer's presencing of power. Survival requires experience and evocation of sacred power in the daily round of activities. As an approach derived from the politics of recognition, community survival engenders an awareness that the assaults on global indigenous peoples and on the life of the earth are directly related to the historical genocide of American Indian peoples as well as to the international economy of corporate imperialism.

Community survival as an interpretive approach related to the politics of recognition derives from Native reflection on the history of relations between indigenous peoples and mainstream America. Survival resists imperialistic power that drains reservation communities, for example, of sovereign voice in their own financial expenditures. Survival resists a conceptual hegemony that inculcates systemic violence within a community so that Native Pentecostal Christians, for example, condemn their own traditional Native ways. Centuries of colonial subjugation may seem to be past, but conceptual hegemony lingers even in the academic study of religion according to the Osage theologian,

George Tinker. In his discussion of the linkages between Christian missionaries and larger civilizational drives in America, Tinker writes:

[T]he failure of the missionaries must be understood not just in individual terms but as systemic failure. The culpability of the individual missionaries for imposing their culture on Native Americans and perpetuating the lie of white superiority was in actuality prescribed from the outset by European and Euroamerican social structures. That is to say, it was impossible for any missionary to avoid complicity in the genocide of Native American peoples. Again in this case, recognizing the broader, structural impetus of Western social structures toward the assertion of white hegemony dare not become an excuse for exonerating the individual's participation in the dysfunctionality of the whole. Nevertheless, this recognition does push beyond the criticism of individual missionaries to an analysis of the systemic. This, in turn, raises two questions. First, what aspects of Western, Euroamerican culture have historically generated such myopic social and theological arrogance? Second, if the missionaries, with the best of intentions, perpetuated such havoc among Indian peoples, what does our own modern myopia conceal from us, whatever our intentions to the contrary. (Tinker 1993: 16)

The interconnectedness of social, economic, political, and cultural spheres in a systemic whole, according to Tinker, must be considered in every examination of interactions between Native and dominant America. Moreover, it can be said that the quest for harmonious sameness in mainstream America can bring the systemic whole into such massive human engineering movements as the westward expansion of the nineteenth century in America or research projects such as biogenetic engineering in the late twentieth century. Survival for Native peoples requires awareness of such shadow visions that generate "myopic social and theological arrogance." The politics of recognition decries the simultaneous masking of such visions in romantically constructed images of Native primitivity, militancy, and spirituality.

Reflecting on the academy, Tinker notes that exploitative agendas have penetrated into institutional policies, research agendas, and epistemological positions. He writes:

To begin to grasp the full spectrum of the systemic [modern world-system], one must plot everything from cultural patterns of social behavior to institutional development and economic interaction, political structures and processes, and especially to intellectual patterns of thought. As such, the social structures of cognition that are the basis for all academic disciplines and theoretical reflection participate in the systemic whole. (Tinker 1993: 116)

The survival approach in the study of religion derived from the politics of recognition calls for some understanding of the problems in claims of theoretical purity for academic study, of the limits in research, and of an awareness that all peoples are indigenous to the earth. Students are limited, as well as informed, by their social structures in their efforts to understand other cultures. Community survival as an approach in the study of American Indian religions promotes investigation of the social structures of cognition to understand what has been foisted upon the values and practices of indigenous peoples. This begins the possibility for reflexive understanding of one's own role in the systemic whole, for acknowledging the history of indigenous peoples in that whole, and for scrutiny of the role religion has played in the survival of Native communities. This communication challenges prior histories, initiates responsibilities to Native communities, and liberates a student to resist physical and conceptual violence as normative.

A CASE STUDY IN THE APSAALOOKE ASHKISSHE

The Apsaalooke/Crow are a Siouan-speaking people with a reservation in the Missouri River drift plains and Wolf, Pryor, and Big Horn Mountains of North America. Their current population of eight thousand is about that of prereservation days and their current reservation, of which Crow individuals and the tribe itself hold approximately 55 percent, is located within their traditional homeland described as "four-tipi poles."

The Apsaalooke/Crow ritual called *Ashkisshe*, or Sun Dance, is a major community event that has been discussed in academic literature during the twentieth century.[11] I have chosen it as a case study for a brief consideration of the three approaches derived from the politics of recognition because it has been the focus of my field studies on the Crow Reservation since 1983. From that first exchange I have developed, in concert with individuals and families among the Apsaalooke, an understanding that I would not publish written descriptions or reflections on ritual activity without consultation with the Crow. Toward that end this article has been deposited with the archivist, Magdalene Medicine Horse, at Little Big Horn College, the tribal college at Crow Agency.

Drawing on the issue of identity in the study of American Indian religions, questions can be raised about terminology used in this case study. That is, why would I use the terms "religion" and "ritual" when describing the *Ashkisshe*? Do these terms say more about my views than insight into this *Apsaalooke* activity? Having commented earlier in this paper on the use of "lifeway," I can readily acknowledge that the term is not Crow. "Lifeway," on the other hand, accentuates the interplay of social, economic, and cosmological forces in the sense of meaningful social and spiritual life.

The Crow term for "religion," *alachiwakiia/* "one's own way" is akin to the translated Crow expression, "It's up to you!" which suggests that experience and manifestation of the power that enables life is personal yet manifest in the communitarian setting which extends into the biological life of the region. Can the Crow term *maxpe* be translated as the sacred without immediately being suffused with Durkheimian epistemology? Is *maxpe* simply "supernatural" with all the transcendent theological implications of that term? The use of such Anglo-European terms not only manifests my preconceptions, which I use in an effort to gain some understanding of Crow cultural identity, but they may also mask creative tensions within Apsaalooke lifeway between the individual and the community.

It is important to note that the *Ashkisshe* ceremonial alone does not constitute Apsaalooke religion. It is possible to point to the endurance of ancient rituals among these northern plains peoples. Such rituals as the Tobacco [adoption] Society (*Baasshussheelaakbisuua*), sweat lodge (*auwusua*), "medicine bundles," (*xapaaliia*), also are practiced. In the nineteenth century not only other tribal dances and visions influenced the Crow but also Baptist and Catholic churches and schools were established. More recent twentieth-century religious arrivals among the Crow are the Peyote Way and Christian denominations such as the Holiness Pentecostal Churches. Tensions may exist between these sacred ways but among many Apsaalooke no one way is extolled to the exclusion of the others.

The identity approach also causes me to question my use of "ritual" as a bracketed or self-contained event. The *Ashkisshe* is a major ceremonial held in the spring but the ritual process of preparation may extend well over a year. One description of this ritual process can be found in the photographic essay, *Sun Dance: The 50th Anniversary Crow Indian Sun Dance*. It describes the sequence of actions which began before the actual Sun Dance on July 25–28, 1991. The text reads:

> The Sun Dance was but the culminating event in a long continuum of many events over an eight-month period. Starting on the winter solstice, 1990, there were four Medicine Bundle Ceremonies through the winter. Then, four Outdoor Prayer Services took place throughout the spring and early summer of 1991. Next was a magnificent trip to the top of the Big Horn Mountains to hunt two buffalo for the post-Sun Dance feast. Other journeys were made to the Pryor Mountains to harvest lodgepole pine, aspen, and fir trees for [the ceremonial] lodge construction. The actual Sun dance was merely the last in a long line of ceremonial activities. (Crummett 1993: xiii–xiv)

Using the identity approach I not only ask myself how I am using the term, ritual, but why. Obviously fixed notions of ritual as an event that happens at a set time and in a set place are inappropriate here. Perhaps, two terms are more helpful, namely, ritual process and ritualization. Ritual process emphasizes the span of time and the sequence of events that will occur before an *Ashkisshe*.

Ritualization can be used to focus on the stages of ritual enactment that occur during the specific four days of the ceremonial called *Ashkisshe.*

My role as an undergraduate teacher at Bucknell University is known among the Apsaalooke with whom I visit and have conversation. Using such a term as "ritual" signals both my limitations in understanding this Apsaalooke event as well as my efforts to be a cultural bridge so that Crow ways come into the classes I teach. Students reflect on these limitations, terms, and possible misrepresentations just as they consider the sequence of events before the *Ashkisshe,* the ceremonial itself, and the role of the dancers.

The authenticity approach derived from the politics of recognition builds on prior insights gained in the identity approach, regarding perspectives, terms, and agendas. However, the authenticity approach explores inner realms in which the "shadow-visions" play. This study of inner worldview values may lead to creative new perspectives for the study of American Indian religions, or it may generate distortions of Native American peoples and ceremonies. It may do both. The dialogue with the people whose ways are being studied is central for evaluating this authenticity approach.

During the Apsaalooke *Ashkisshe* the dancers are encouraged by family, friends, announcers, and one another to aspire to *diakaashe,* "he or she really did it."[12] *Diakaashe* points toward the sincerity of determination and effort to bring benefits to other individuals and to the community. *Diakaashe* also may bring about a unique encounter with sacred power. The spiritual powers, called "Without Fires" and "Other Side Camp," may adopt a fasting dancer and become his or her "Medicine Father," *Iilapxe. Diakaashe* as a Crow worldview value is at the heart of that mystery in which individuals acquire the privileges and responsibilities of personal spiritual power (*xapaaliia*).

No one explication of this exchange with cosmological power, *maxpe,* is accepted by the Apsaalooke as an explanation. *Maxpe* is itself the context of any understanding. It is at this point that the prospect for spiritualizing distortions can occur in the history of religions. Certain methods have developed in the academic field to correct diachronic distortions. Thus, historical changes in Apsaalooke understanding of *diakaashe* and *xapaaliia* are topics of research. But the authenticity approach emphasized here asks how both these Crow ideas interlock. Can they be understood and why?

My investigations make me aware of a single-minded and exclusive "spiritualizing" that can occur when *diakaashe* is conceptualized. Academic reflection and classroom teaching involve mental transmissions that can make this interior Crow worldview value something it is not. The experiences of the fasting dancers who undertake the *Ashkisshe* are personal, collective, and profoundly troubling. The pain and suffering of the exertion are understood by the Crow as acts which can benefit both humans and the community of beings in the bioregion. The determination of the dancer to reach *diakaashe* can be understood as ritualization in which social forces and spiritual forces meet. Paradoxically, the effort of the academic researcher to describe, discuss, and transmit this in a classroom results in the conceptualizations of events which are themselves physical, affective, and emotional. The imaginings of the academic community investigating a ceremonial are quite different from the imagined Apsaalooke community both inside and outside the ceremonial lodge of the *Ashkisshe*. Musings of the researcher, the teacher, and the class are not the *diakaashe* of the dancer, but they can meet in the authenticity approach that is a dialogue about the place of significant actions and orientation in meaningful life.

For the Crow, *diakaashe* has changed over time and is, no doubt, the focus for new Apsaalooke perspectives on their own tradition. Two observations regarding *diakaashe* come from the recently deceased Crow Sun Dance Chief, Thomas Yellowtail, who danced at the first Shoshoni-Crow Sun Dance, and from the work of the senior anthropologist, Fred Voget, who has studied the Sun Dance since its return to the Crow in 1941. First, as every Crow knows, *diakaashe*, which may lead to adoption by a spiritual power (*Iilapxe*), can result in personal revelations authorizing the gathering of physical materials in a "bundle." Assembling this spiritually nourishing matter is a ritual process and opening the bundle responsibly at appropriate times constitutes a ritualization which may bring blessings to individuals and communities. For the Apsaalooke the gathering of these materials, the process of opening bundles, and the responsibilities attached to "owning" them is spiritual.[13] Talking about them apart from that spiritual process is viewed negatively, that is, as useless or harmful. An authenticity approach raises questions about the sincerity of inquiry into medicine bundles or about the *diakaashe* of a dancer by a non-Native researcher. Thus, sincerity in appropriately different forms becomes an evaluative criterion for both the researcher and for the Native informant.

Fred Voget also has reflected on the importance of *diakaashe* as a core Crow worldview value in the current *Ashkisshe*/Sun Dance. He commented about changes from the old Sun Dance, lost in 1875, in which dancers expressed *diakaashe* by "skewering" themselves, or piercing their chest and pulling free after being tied by leather lines to the central tree. Voget compared this older practice to the current dance focused on fasting:

The present Sun Dance stresses physical suffering to gain some good . . . the medicine fathers informed the Crow in visions and in dreams that it was no longer necessary to skewer themselves. Now sincerity of purpose is expressed through abstention from food and water during the ceremony and the sending of prayers by steady dancing interspersed with cigarette smoke prayers. As of old, the preparatory sweat bath and prayers are vital to the sincerity with which a suppliant approaches the suffering in the Sun Dance. A steady and sincere dancer who "charges the buffalo" attached to the center pole at some time may be run over and in his [or her] unconscious mystic state may receive something good, perhaps a power to cure. (*Yellowtail* 1991: xxvi)

Fred Voget as a non-Native scholar notes the historical changes in the Crow Sun Dance especially regarding the revelation from the Medicine Fathers. A sequence of historical events gradually transformed the manner in which dancers strove for inner authenticity and sincerity. In that historical process, authenticity and community survival overlapped for the Crow who restored the Sun Dance. It is as if when one thing changed in the religious universe of the Crow, everything changed.

Thomas Yellowtail also understood these changes but, as a member of the Crow community itself, he addressed these changes from a different perspective. Using the authenticity approach we might say that Thomas Yellowtail was moved by an inherent politics of recognition to realize that *diakaashe* involved commitments to community survival. He narrated in his "autobiography":

There are other things that a member of the Sun Dance religion should try to learn. For example, it is important for a man who wants to participate in the Sun Dance to understand the Crow language; then he will understand more. He will also understand what I say in the prayers. This is very important for a sun dancer. It was wrong when our people were taught the English language and not their own tongue. . . .

It is the same with the Indian songs. The young people today should learn them. They should try to sing the songs; they must try to grasp them when they hear them. (*Yellowtail* 1991: 179–80)

Inner authenticity has always held responsibilities as well as privileges in Crow understanding and Thomas Yellowtail's reflections are connected to contemporary Native scholars concerned with the distorted presentations of Native American peoples and their religious ways. In this sense, Yellowtail's commitment to the authenticity of the contemporary Sun Dance made him aware of the danger to his culture from the dissimulations of global consumer culture. Yellowtail's concerns join with those of his fellow Crow, Heywood Big Day. Big Day undertook the sponsorship of the fiftieth anniversary Sun Dance in 1991. This major event was for Big Day an act of community survival which echoes the politics of recognition and provides insight into the history of the *Ashkisshe* and Crow religion.

When William Big Day arranged for John Treherjo, the Shoshoni-Crow medicine man and Sun Dance chief, to bring the *Ashkisshe* ceremony back to the Crow in 1941, his motivation was to heal his young son who had become ill. Holding that boy up to the sun he vowed to hold the Shoshoni Sun Dance, in which he had participated on the Wind River reservation in Wyoming, to his Crow reservation in Montana.[14] The boy he held that day and who was healed as the days passed was Heywood Big Day.

For Heywood Big Day and for the Crow people the celebration of this ceremonial was a complex religious, social, political, and historical event. Big Day prepared a brochure that gives some expression to his thoughts. This brochure not only gave some "rules and regulations" for those attending the ceremonial, it also had a textual statement on the "1991 Crow Sun dance" which, in effect, is a proclamation of survival. Of the six paragraphs let us consider two using the community survival approach derived from the politics of recognition. In his brochure Big Day wrote:

> In 1875 my tribe lost its Sun Dance ceremony under the federal government's policy to assimilate all Indian people. For sixty-six years we refrained from practicing this deeply religious ceremony, and though many of the Crows forgot the importance of the Sun Dance, many others kept it in their hearts. . . .
>
> The 1991 Sun Dance is particularly historical for us because it marks the fiftieth anniversary of the return of this sacred ceremony. Preparation ceremonies are already being held during the full moons of each month. My family is sponsoring this important Sun dance, and I am conducting it. To carry on the Sun Dance tradition is a special blessing for me, since I was the little son of William who's [sic] restored health made him determined to fulfill his promise.[15]

Big Day highlights the history of his people which resulted in the loss of their older traditional Sun Dance. He does not use conceptual language referring to a "systemic whole," but his use of "assimilate" signals the pervasive assault against his cultural identity as a Crow. What has survived, Heywood Big Day suggests is something "kept in their [Crow] hearts." The *diakaashe* sincerity in the heart is the value that the dancers will ritualize in the Sun Dance. Heywood Big Day evokes in his brochure a distinctly Crow reading of this ritual process. His English translation, namely, that the "Preparation ceremonies are being held," indicates what in English tense would express past events, but which the Crow understand as still occurring and as coming to fruition in the actual dance. The fiftieth anniversary *Ashkisshe* has become a realization of the shadow-vision that the people have survived in the face of this assimilation policy. The pain is all present, the liberating power of the ritual is also present.

Bringing together the myth/ritual, the telling of the story and the ritualization of power, marks a most significant theoretical change in the history of the *Ashkisshe* among the Crow.[16] While the ongoing importance of this joining of myth/ritual in the Crow *Ashkisshe* requires Native and non-Native investigation, its immediate effect can be seen using the survival approach as the internalization of *diakaashe* in a historical mode.

Such an internalization is much more than simply understanding the fiftieth anniversary Sun Dance as retributive justice through mere survival as a people. Heywood Big Day goes on to say that, "Our Crow belief is something we are proud of and wish to share with people of all backgrounds." Survivance shimmers here in the Crow style of openly inviting and adopting others into their ways.[17] Thus, the survival approach not only allows us to raise questions about the reflexive recognition of endurance among the Crow it also reverses our perspective so that we see our role in the history of the assault and the continuing power of the dance.

The photographic essay published after the fiftieth anniversary Sun Dance noted the wider sphere of support beyond the dance lodge. It reads:

. . . extended past the Sun Dance grounds . . . Roosting high on a foothill point over-looking Pryor Valley sat the minuscule figure of a white man, who had journeyed . . . to participate in this historical Sun Dance. As it was there were more dancing Indians than space, and the lodge had to be expanded by shrinking the entrance. The Anglo . . . joined in with his fasting, dancing, prayers and presence from a distance to the southwest, still close enough to hear the drumming, singing and whistling emanating from the lodge. (Crummett 1993: 60–61)

There are Native scholars who say that non-Native students should simply say "No" when invited into Native ceremonials. The invitation, it is presumed from this perspective, has been prompted from an epistemic violence in which the indigenous community invites into itself the very source of its cultural demise. In this sense, students of Native American religions should know that their presence in the Native setting may effect cultural change.

Crow sponsors of *Ashkisshe* have implemented this "No" of the Native American politics of recognition when they decide that some *Ashkisshe* are not open to non-Native, or even non-Crow, participants. Yet, the Apsaalooke welcome outsiders to view the dance and non-Natives have been known to participate in the *Ashkisshe*. Perhaps the white man roosting high on a foothill at the fiftieth anniversary Sun Dance is a dialogic figure in the politics of recognition. This person on the hill was allowed by the Crow to join by fasting at a distance in the effort at communitarian survival and renewal. Did the rigorous fast bring him to understand how nostalgic, alienated whites can exploit a Native ceremonial for personal purposes? Did he join in the collective experience? Did the Crow risk too much?

For a student to understand the *Ashkisshe* they must know the historical loss of the older ceremonial in 1875 as well as the transmission of the newer Crow/Shoshoni Sun Dance. Using the three approaches suggested here they can understand that recent changes in the *Ashkisshe* are themselves part of an ongoing process. Because the Crow have implemented these changes, study of the *Ashkisshe* reveals developing directions in Apsaalooke cultural identity and inner authenticity. Because some of these changes came about as a result of the ongoing exchange with Anglo America there are issues of community survival to be explored.

To critique changes in the *Ashkisshe* naively as negative influences from dominant America or as inappropriate adaptations is pointless for a non-Native student. Rather, these contemporary changes are part of the dialogic perspective in the study of American Indian religions. This paper examines some of the multiform dimensions, or approaches, that this dialogue is taking. That is, Native American scholars in the politics of recognition are exploring new rhetorical modes in their writings and public presentations which have impact both on their Native communities as well as on academic circles. Crow Sun Dance leaders, and by extension ritual specialists throughout American Indian communities, know that the spiritual, social, and political forces that meet in the ritualizations of ceremonial life are constantly changing. The convergence of these transforming forces create those shadow-visions that renew the community. Students of American Indian religions realize that the dialogic perspective, embedded in issues of cultural identity, authenticity, and community survival, calls for responsibility to the communities studied. Along with the insights into the ways that peoples have encountered and celebrated their place in the universe comes an awareness of limits and a recognition of reciprocal exchange.

NOTES

1. Particular names of indigenous nations and peoples, such as Apsaalooke, are preferable to English translations, e.g., Crow, or more general references such as American Indian, Native American, First Peoples, First Nations, and Indigenous Peoples. As no one English term is preferable, these terms are used here to refer broadly to the indigenous peoples of the Americas.

2. See Jaimes, *State of Native America*; Williams and Chrisman, *Colonial Discourse and Postcolonial Theory*; Duran, *Native American Postcolonial Psychology*; Churchill, *Struggle for the Land*; and Murray, *Forked Tongues*.

3. These terms, identity, authenticity and community survival, as terms in the politics of recognition are drawn from a response by K. Anthony Appiah, "Identity, Authenticity, Survival: Multicultural Societies and Social Reproduction," to an article by Charles Taylor, "The Politics of Recognition," in *Multiculturalism*, ed. Amy Gutman.

4. Churchill, *Struggle for the Land*, 33.

5. I have in mind the issues raised in the articles in Green, ed., "Settled Issues." One

need only look at a recent issue of the *Journal of Ritual Studies* such as the proceedings of the Santa Barbara Conference on Ritual and Power in vol. 4, no 2 (1990) to see the varieties of approaches in ritual studies.

6. Jaimes, *State of Native America.*

7. Vizenor, *Manifest Manners.*

8. Tinker, *Missionary Conquest.*

9. My use of scare quotes around Sun Dance is intended to alert the reader to the problematic usage of this term. See Schlesier, "Rethinking." Throughout this article I will follow conventional usage on the Crow Reservation and use both terms interchangeably.

10. Crummett, *Sun Dance.*

11. For example, Lowie, "Sun Dance"; Voget, *Shosoni-Crow Sun Dance*; and Yellowtail, *Yellowtail.*

12. See Frey, *World of the Crow Indians.*

13. See Yellowtail, *Yellowtail,* 69–76.

14. For a full discussion of these events see Voget, *Shoshoni-Crow Sun Dance.*

15. The brochure has a drawing of a dancer in Sun Dance attire with a name underneath, namely, "William Big Day"; the brochure is titled "CROW SUN DANCE Golden Anniversary July 25, 26, 27, 28, 1991, Itta'tbachisash Ceremonial, Pryor Montana, Sponsored by Heywood Big Day, Sr." The author received his brochure from Heywood the day before the dance began.

16. Smith explores this issue in *To Take Place,* 96–117.

17. An understanding of "adoption" in Crow religious life is explored in Peter Nabokov, "Cultivating Themselves: The Inter-play of Crow Indian Religion and History" (Ph.D. diss., University of California at Berkeley, 1988).

REFERENCES

Anderson, Benedict. 1983. *Imagined Communities: Reflections on the Origin and Rise of Nationalism.* London: Verso.

Bernardis, Timothy. 1986. *Baleeisbaalichiwee: Crow Social Studies Teacher's Guide.* Bilingual Materials Development Center, Crow Agency MT.

Berry, Thomas. 1976. Indian Future. *Cross Currents* 26: 133–42.

Churchill, Ward. 1993. *Struggle for the Land.* Monroe ME: Common Courage Press.

Crummett, Michael. 1993. *Sun Dance.* Billings MT: Falcon Press.

Deloria, Vine, Jr. 1992. "Trouble in High Places: Erosion of American Indian Rights to Religious Freedom in the United States." In Jaimes, *State of Native America,* 267–90.

Densmore, Frances. 1918. *Teton Sioux Music.* Bulletin 61, Bureau of American Ethnology. Washington DC: Government Printing Office.

Duran, Eduardo, and Bonnie. 1995. *Native American Postcolonial Psychology.* Albany: State University of New York Press.

Frey, Rodney. 1987. *The World of the Crow Indians: As Driftwood Lodges*. Norman: University of Oklahoma Press.

Gill, Sam. 1994. "The Academic Study of Religion." *Journal of the American Academy of Religion* 62, no 4: 965–75.

Green, William Scott, ed. 1994. "Settled Issues and Neglected Questions in the Study of Religion." *Journal of the American Academy of Religion* 62, no. 4.

Grim, John. 1994. "Native North American Worldviews and Ecology." In *Worldviews and Ecology: Religion, Philosophy, and the Environment,* ed. Mary Evelyn Tucker and John Grim. Maryknoll NY: Orbis Press, 44–51.

Grinde, Donald A., Jr. 1992. "Teaching American Indian History: A Native American Voice." In *Perspectives* American Historical Association Newsletter 32, no. 6: 10–16.

Gutman, Amy, ed. 1992. *Multiculturalism*. Princeton: Princeton University Press.

Jaimes, M. Annette, ed. 1992. *The State of Native America: Genocide, Colonization, and Resistance*. Boston: South End Press.

Krupat, Arnold. 1992. *Ethnocentrism: Ethnography, History, Literature*. Berkeley: University of California Press.

Lowie, Robert. 1915. "The Sun Dance of the Crow Indians." American Museum of Natural History *Anthropological Papers* 16: 1–50.

Mead, George Herbert. 1934. *Mind, Self, and Society*. Chicago: University of Chicago Press.

Medicine Crow, Joseph. 1992. *From the Heart of the Crow Country: The Crow Indians' Own Stories*. New York: Orion/Crown Publishers.

Murray, David. 1991. *Forked Tongues: Speech, Writing and Representation in Native North American Text*. Bloomington: Indiana University Press.

Peelman, Achiel. 1995. *Christ Is a Native American*. Maryknoll NY: Orbis.

Rose, Wendy. 1992. "The Great Pretenders, Further Reflections on Whiteshamanism." In Jaimes, *State of Native America*, 403–21.

Schlesier, Karl. 1990. "Rethinking the Midewiwin and the Plains Ceremonial Called the Sun Dance." *Plains Anthropologist* 35: 1–27.

Sharpe, Eric. 1986. *Comparative Religion: A History*, 2nd ed. LaSalle IL: Open Court.

Smith, Jonathan Z. 1987. *To Take Place: Toward Theory in Ritual*. Chicago: University of Chicago Press.

Sullivan, Lawrence E. 1988. *Icanchu's Drum: An Orientation to Meaning in South American Religions*. New York: Macmillan.

Swanson, Todd. 1994. "To Prepare a Place: Johannine Christianity and the Collapse of Ethnic Territory." *Journal of the American Academy of Religion* 62, no. 4: 241–63.

Tinker, George. 1993. *Missionary Conquest: The Gospel and Native American Cultural Genocide*. Minneapolis MN: Fortress Press.

Vizenor, Gerald. 1994. *Manifest Manners: Postindian Warriors of Survivance*. Hanover NH: Wesleyan University Press.

Voget, Fred W. 1984. *The Shoshoni-Crow Sun Dance*. Norman: University of Oklahoma Press.

Weaver, Jace, ed. 1996. *Defending Mother Earth: Native American Perspectives on Environmental Justice*. Maryknoll NY: Orbis Press.

Williams, Patrick and Laura Chrisman, eds. 1994. *Colonial Discourse and Postcolonial Theory: A Reader*. New York: Columbia University Press.

Yellowtail, Thomas. 1991. *Yellowtail Crow Medicine Man and Sun Dance Chief: An Autobiography*. As told to Michael Oren Fitzgerald. Norman: University of Oklahoma Press.

Spirituality for Sale

Sacred Knowledge in the Consumer Age

CHRISTOPHER RONWANIÈN:TE JOCKS

A friend of mine, a traditional Kanien'kehá:ka (Mohawk) woman, tells about being approached by members of a foundation dedicated to "New Age" spirituality. As she tells the story, they introduced themselves, described their various spiritual pursuits, and on the basis of these credentials requested to be allowed to participate in some kind of American Indian ceremony. "They were really insistent," she said. "They were convinced they were ready and deserving of this thing." She told them she would oblige them.

"This is what you do," my friend told them. "First, you prepare the feast. Cook up lots and lots of food. We Mohawks make corn soup, but you can substitute tofu stir-fry if you like. As you're cooking it, think about the people you'll be inviting, about their lives, and about your own. Think about the ingredients too, where they come from, and who helped bring them to you. Then invite everyone you know to come over. Make sure you have enough food. Everybody that comes, you feed them. And you listen to them, pay attention to their advice, their problems. Hold their hands, if that's what they need. If any of them needs to stay over, make a place for them. Then, next month, you do the same thing again. And again, four times, the same way. That's it! You've done an Indian ceremony!"

This friend of mine was not being facetious or making fun of these seekers. Her advice was completely earnest. Nor was she asserting that somehow hospitality is the essence of ceremony. Rather, as I understand it, her reply was based on a critical distinction between what might constitute a ceremony for members of the participating ceremonial community—in this case, an Iroquois Longhouse community—and those aspects of it that are considered useful or accessible or teachable to others. It had the further merit of politely but clearly unmasking the arrogant assumption that one can prepare to participate in ceremony, and in fact can earn the right to do so, in any way other than by *becoming a member* of the community enacting the ceremony.

I can discern at least two bases upon which an American Indian community might decide what is or is not to be shared with outsiders, in relation to traditional thought and practice. One is moral and political, and concerns the "unequal power relations," to put it politely, that continue to exist between American Indian peoples and Euroamericans. Here, the issue is this: sharing of spiritual practices and knowledge can only rightly take place among equals, in a discourse of mutual respect, with the permission of both parties. By contrast, today an entire industry has sprung up in which Indigenous spirituality is appropriated, distorted, used, and sold without respect or permission, *even while* physical assaults on Native people, lands, and ways of life, continue. The best intentions and most heartfelt rejection of injustice by Euroamerican *individuals* are simply not very relevant here as long as they remain mere sentiment; hard work and real change from within the larger society, not escapism, are requisite. In many variations, this is the most frequently heard critique by Native people of attempts to appropriate their spiritual lives.

The other distinction is perhaps less often articulated, and concerns not what *should* be taught, but what *can* be taught; or, what can be translated accurately out of a Native context into a non-Native one. The issues here are not only linguistic, but epistemological and ontological as well, coming together under the title of hermeneutics. They concern the very nature of knowledge, and of the reality enacted or enhanced by American Indian ceremonies. These are matters about which Native traditionalists cultivate and maintain vastly different perceptions from those familiar to Euroamerican intellectual and religious history.

For the remainder of this text I will do three things: First, I will briefly review and summarize the first of these two critiques, the moral-political. I say briefly because these matters have been amply addressed elsewhere. Second, I will extend my discussion of the second distinction, the hermeneutical, drawing on the remarks of Indian and non-Indian commentators, as well as events related to a tradition with which I am a little familiar. Last, I will engage in some reflection about the relationship between appropriations attempted by New Age enthusiasts and other "seekers," on the one hand, and the work of anthropologists and other seekers of comparative social and cultural "data," on the other. My thesis is that without firmly grounded and enacted knowledge about the internally prescribed limits of externally available knowledge, such "data" is liable to be not only ethically clouded, but logically and intellectually unreliable.

Before proceeding, however, I should clarify my own place in relation to this thesis: Although I am Kanien'kehá:ka as well as Euroamerican by birth and by law, and although I have participated in Longhouse ceremonies, my academic career and placement have prevented me from being a regular participant in any Longhouse community. Thus I write, compile, and arrange these comments not as a representative, official or otherwise, of any Native tradition. Rather, I write from an in-between perspective, as a member of the academic community who at the same time seeks to maintain and build relationships with my own and other Native communities. Based on these relationships, I am committed to clearing open ground for new kinds of discourse between this hemisphere's First Peoples and Euroamerican intellectual tradition, in which the former are active, critical participants rather than passive specimens or curiosities.

THE MORAL-POLITICAL ARGUMENT

Some of the most colorful and energetic attacks on the appropriation of American Indian identity and "wisdom" are those by Ward Churchill. Especially pronounced in them is the impression shared by many people involved with Indian communities, that most of these "adaptations" are patently ludicrous. Anger or outrage are later responses; the initial reaction is usually to laugh in disbelief at the depth of human gullibility. As, for instance, when Lynn Andrews claims that she was forced to strip naked and enter a luminous tipi in order to be initiated by "the grandmothers" into a planetary/cosmic "Sisterhood of the Shields" (Andrews 1981:49). Churchill describes the ridiculous nature of these revelations:

In her version of events, [these women] had apparently been waiting their entire lives for just such an opportunity to unburden themselves of every innermost secret of their people's spiritual knowledge. They immediately acquainted her with such previously unknown "facts" as the presence of kachinas in the Arctic Circle and the power of "Jaguar Women," charged her with serving as their "messenger," and sent her forth to write a series of books so outlandish in their pretensions as to make [Carlos] Castaneda seem a model of propriety by comparison (Churchill 1992a:189).[1]

There comes a point, however, when amusement gives way to indignation. Churchill's comic caricature of some forms of the "men's movement" inspired by the writings of Robert Bly is perhaps his least restrained satire (Churchill 1994:207–72), in which a sense of outrage renders all but transparent the veneer of amusement at such doings. The source of this anger, at least in part, is the astounding success of these and like enterprises, and the fact that this success often displaces, distorts, marginalizes, and belittles Native people's own cultural production. Churchill, as well as Wendy Rose (1992) and other commentators, have described this not only as cultural imperialism, but cultural genocide. Readers can easily consult these sources for more detailed discussion and examples of these critiques. I summarize them as follows:

1. Commercial adaptations and academic interpretations of American Indian knowledge and practice are often plainly inaccurate. Such inaccuracy can take several forms:

Outright falsification: In some cases events or people are described as representing or embodying authentic traditional practices and thinking, but are later shown to have been simply made up. The works of Carlos Castaneda and Lynn Andrews are most often mentioned under this category.[2]

Distortion: Descriptions of events and people considered authentic by the community to which they belong and by scholars as well can nonetheless distort through the use of inappropriate external categories or frames of interpretation. This is a particular problem in academic writing that has assumed congruity between American Indian religious understandings and European religious categories such as "the supernatural," "Supreme Being," "evil," and even such borrowings as the northern Eurasian "shamanism."[3]

Violation of context: There are numerous examples of descriptions that distort by selecting only the most pleasing (read, "marketable") elements of Native experience to "reveal." Typically, practices that seem to involve "mystical" individual experiences are promoted, while other elements considered equally or more important by Native participants are ignored: elements such as kinship obligations, hard work, suffering, and the sometimes crazy realities of everyday reservation life. Especially guilty in this regard are various how-to books that purport to teach individuals how to replicate Indian ceremonies on their own.[4]

2. Conversely, adaptations or interpretations can be *too* accurate, in the sense that they are too revealing. They can violate Native rules of privilege, designed to protect aspects of specialized knowledge and practice from dangerous exposure or misuse. This is rarely the case in popular writing, but has been an issue in anthropology at least since Frank Cushing threatened his way into the kivas at Zuni.[5]

3. In either case, such adaptations or interpretations can be severely unethical, in that perpetrators use knowledge without proper Native permission or attribution, and often do so as part of alien and deeply offensive commercial enterprises. To say that traditional ceremonies are not intended to be performed for cash or for profit is to miss the more fundamental point, which is that traditional American Indian ceremonial work is of a piece with traditional economic structures which, in turn, are based on reciprocal relationships within a community.

Thus a sacred practitioner is, by definition, a person integrated into the place and the community out of which she or he works. I have been fortunate enough to meet a handful of such people and to know a couple of them well, and in each case I have the feeling I am meeting not only a remarkable individual, but a kind of epitome of the community they serve. As I have witnessed, when traditional exchanges are offered in return for ceremonial work, within days this "payment" is usually spread in one way or another among relatives and friends, into and across an entire district.[6]

4. All such behavior demonstrates to the legitimate practitioners of these traditions that those who abuse ceremony in these ways do not actually believe in the power and efficacy involved. In a gesture of profound disrespect, powerful and potentially dangerous techniques whose use in the Indian context often requires years of study and training are treated as if they were merely edifying symbolic or meditative exercises. I can think of no clearer example than Thomas Mails' *Secret Native American Pathways: A Guide to Inner Peace* (1988), in which artificial versions of pieces of Hopi, Cherokee, Apache, and "Sioux" prayer forms are taught to unseen readers as "The native American way and your way to lasting inner peace" (226).[7]

Note that these critiques apply equally to those who write books about Native knowledge and practice—whether packaged as poetry, academic or popular non-fiction, or fiction based on privileged information—and those who profess to actually practice, teach, and perform such things in workshops and the like. Wendy Rose, for instance, treats both under the category of "whiteshamanism." Again, those unfamiliar with these arguments are referred to the sources mentioned. Note too that from an Indian perspective, while primary responsibility for such violations must be assigned to those who perpetrate them knowingly, once a follower is aware of the objections of Native communities, she or he is called upon to respond accordingly. However nobly an individual may understand her or his own motives, it is simply not up to anyone other than the members of the practicing community to decide what these limits should be.

THE HERMENEUTICAL ARGUMENT

It is my contention that each of the above abuses of American Indian religious integrity renders its product not only reprehensible but meaningless, to the extent that it poses an interpreted part for the original whole. This assertion follows logically from what I proposed originally as an Iroquois Longhouse epistemological framework, extended here as a general theory:

In American Indian contexts, the only knowledge that is meaningful is that which is enacted ("walk your talk"). It is enacted by individuals, but individuals act, whether they are aware of it or not, only as part of a community, and thus, a participant in that community's history.[8]

To the extent that this is true, the history and intentions of a speaker, or by extension a writer, are an integral and inescapable component of the message she or he expresses.[9] Thus, knowledge as a timeless, pre-existing abstraction, or data that can be transmitted independent of the "accidents" of its encodation, is simply undefined, unverifiable, unapproachable. From this perspective knowledge cannot be traded in some imagined neutral "marketplace of ideas," as if it were itself a neutral, disembodied object. A falsified claim of identity or authority, then, can render the message moot just as in many traditions a mistake either of execution or of attitude can render a ceremony ineffective.

Responding to a paper at a recent academic conference, I found myself searching for an image with which to convey a sense of this intimate approach to knowledge. I ended up speaking about skin. "For Indians," I said, "these ceremonies and the knowledge they express are like our skin. That's how close to us they are. When people we don't know, or people we do, pretend to use these ceremonies away from their proper setting, it really is like stealing the 'skin off our backs.'" The Center for the Support and Protection of Indian Religions and Indigenous Traditions (CSPIRIT) put it this way in 1993:

Traditional ceremonies and spiritual practices . . . are precious gifts given to Indian people by our Creator. These sacred ways have enabled us as Indian people to survive— miraculously—the onslaught of five centuries of continuous effort by non-Indians and their government to exterminate us by extinguishing all traces of our traditional ways of life. Today, these precious sacred traditions continue to afford American Indian people of all [nations] the strength and vitality we need in the struggle we face every day; they also offer us our best hope for a stable and vibrant future. These sacred traditions are an enduring and indispensable "life raft" without which we would be quickly overwhelmed by the adversities that still threaten our survival. Because our sacred traditions are so precious to us, we cannot allow them to be desecrated and abused. (CSPIRIT 1993)

Such language further supports Churchill's own remarks criticizing the casual approach of many New Age enthusiasts who dabble in multiple "spiritualities":

I thought about protesting that spiritual traditions cannot be used as some sort of Whitman's Sampler of ceremonial form, mixed and matched—here a little Druid, there a touch of Nordic mythology followed by a regimen of Hindu vegetarianism, a mishmash of American Indian rituals somewhere else—at the whim of people who are part of none of them. I knew I should say that to play at ritual potluck is to debase all spiritual traditions, voiding their internal coherence and leaving nothing usably sacrosanct as a cultural anchor for the peoples who conceived and developed them, and who have consequently organized their societies around them. (Churchill 1994:213)

At the very least, then, this places a necessity on anyone writing about such matters to state clearly and accurately the kinds of experience, collaboration, and authorization upon which statements are based. Interpretations of, say, Iroquois spirituality, produced by other than duly recognized representatives of Iroquois communities, need to be identified as such, and the relationship between such interpreters and those communities specified. It is even more important for publishers, both academic and popular, to adhere to standards along these lines in evaluating submissions, and to refuse to publish work that violates them.[10]

None of this should be construed as if to suggest a "party line" of Indian political (or spiritual) correctness, however, in which only those with the most complete or pedigreed knowledge have any right to speak. Such authoritarianism is completely antithetical to all the North American traditions I know of. Sit around Indian campfires or kitchen stoves very long and one is bound to hear differences of opinion, of interpretation, even on spiritual matters, enjoyed and passed around, chewed over and disputed, once the anthropologists have gone home and the tape recorders are turned off—at least among those interested in such things. In fact it would be yet another mark of racism, smacking of nineteenth-century stereotypes of communal "primitive mentality" to expect drab uniformity or inarticulateness of belief around these fires.

We simply need to demand that those who put forth their interpretive opinions in public fora, printed and otherwise, stand up and tell their stories fully—"put their belly out before us," in Frank Waters' memorable phrase—and not hide behind cloaks of holier-than-thou, or more-learned-than-thou, arrogance. Once they have stood up, they must expect the same kind of sharp, even combative, scrutiny that visitors sometimes experience when visiting Indian communities. In my experience, bearing such attacks, showing what one is made of, can be the best way to make friends.

This is the case whether the "authority" in question is of Indian descent or not.[11] A number of the most sharply attacked "plastic medicine men" are of Native blood, and some of them can recount deep connections to their Indian contexts earlier in their lives. Once they have started on the road of selling their Native spirituality to paying customers elsewhere, however, relations back home invariably go bad. Some, like Ed McGaa (also known as "Eagle Man"; 1990 and 1992), assert nonetheless that their "mission" to the wider world was the result of visionary experience, a claim that leaves nonparticipant readers as well as many Indian people in something of a quandary. The line between authenticity and quackery is not always easy to draw, and in fact many of the most traditional-minded will simply refrain from doing so as a matter of policy.

As a teacher, I am not interested in silencing anyone, not even a Lynn Andrews. Yet when I am faced with strong evidence that an author's claims are deceptive, or if their interpretation of a community's religious life is far askew of what is known from those people's own perspectives, I will work to call such an author to account. If the accusing evidence is clear I will urge others not to buy the book, not to pay for the workshop—not only for ethical reasons, but because what is being sold is probably not "the real thing" anyway; won't do what it is claimed to do, and might just do harm instead. Then there is one other judgment I am forced to make: Which books or articles will I have my students read, and how will I present them? In these decisions I will always prefer works that show strong evidence of real, ongoing connections within a community. An author may dispute predominant interpretations or attitudes in a community; I will only insist that she or he do so from a basis of demonstrated understanding of and familiarity with the life of that community.

THE PRIVILEGES OF SCHOLARSHIP?

The same Kanien'kehá:ka woman whose story begins this essay was preparing to begin her graduate work in religious studies when she was contacted by the professor she would mainly be working with and asked to bring with her whatever information she could gather from Longhouse elders on the so-called "False Face" society—in Mohawk, *ato'wíhtshera*—who play an important but highly privileged and protected role in Longhouse spiritual work. This "data" the professor hoped to include in a comparative study of "masking." My friend protested that as a traditional person, she could not do this. As far as she was concerned, the work of this society was real; the power its members associate with, potentially dangerous. As someone not initiated into the society, for her even to inquire about it would be to invite harm. This much she said to her professor; but I think she would agree with me that even if she had been a member, the same harm would result from giving out elements of that understanding—in effect, selling it—to outsiders who are, by definition, unprepared to understand and respect it. Thus, the accuracy of the information she might or might not have been able to obtain, from the narrow standpoint of academic/scientific "data," was never the issue. The whole network of context and intention, was.

Unfortunately, at least as this graduate student recounted the story to me, her reply initiated an increasingly hostile exchange with her professor that ended in the termination of their working relationship.[12] According to her under-standing, this representative of the academic establishment refused ultimately to credit or respect her conviction that academic inquiry be limited by, and thus in some sense subject to, the demands of Iroquois traditionalists, the "subjects" of this proposed study. The question then becomes, does this kind of external limitation damage the integrity of such a study? Can an academic discipline privilege the authority of religious stricture in the formulation of its own research, as indeed has been demanded recently by the Hopi Tribal Council?[13]

In a recent assessment of the academic study of religion, Sam Gill, once recognized as an authority on Native American religion in particular, strongly criticizes what he sees as the emphasis of the entire discipline on "discourse conducted on the authority of vision, insight, or experience," rather than on "rational discourse, hypothetical inference, and the application of scientific method"; claims that the discipline has thus abandoned its academic foundations to become "the religious study of religion"; in other words, that "the academic study of religion has often failed to acknowledge what it is. It is academic; it is *Western*; it is intellectual" (Gill 1994:967–68; emphasis mine).[14]

The same conflict my graduate student friend encountered, over academic self-limitation in the face of Native community demands and concerns, is implied in this critique. As a scholar I have no interest in promoting *irrational* discourse; but as an Indian I would counter that the religious discourse of any Native People responds to its own rationality. Yet if we ask to whose rationality academic work ought to respond, Gill's answer is clear: *Western* rationality must continue to be the norm.

I respond that cross-cultural study can never break out of its "ghetto" in this way. Under this regime, rather than contributing to and broadening theory, method, or epistemology, *they*—meaning the "other" culture—become merely another "subject," another kind of specimen, for Euroamerican intellectual frames, categories, or tools. The stipulation of Iroquois elders that *ato'wíhtshera* is out of bounds for academic research thus becomes merely an impediment without intrinsic merit, to be overcome if possible. This too is appropriation, dressed up a bit but just as offensive to Native thought and practice as the ludicrous concoctions of commercial would-be shamans.

Dealing with these real and substantive issues involves the very theoretical basis—the *what* and *how*—of cross-cultural academic work. Professor Gill, by contrast, shifts the focus to questions of *who*. He asserts that the field at present is hopelessly sidetracked by issues of academic qualification; more specifically, whether work in the field should be restricted to those with fieldwork and linguistic competency in the community under study, or even more narrowly, to those who are ethnically Native American. Thus, he asserts that participation in the field is being dictated by Indian people (scholars?) along ethnic and racial lines, so that graduate programs "encourage primarily those who are ethnically Native American," producing scholars who "engage only cultural materials absent of conversation with any academic community whatsoever" (Gill 1994:971–73).

As an Indian scholar of religion who has been active in the field for five years, I must report I have never encountered a single incident in which such an exclusionary strategy has been promoted. Furthermore, any survey of the small body of literature on American Indian traditions in religious studies journals will find that Native scholars are in fact *underrepresented*. The issue is not and has never been whether non-Natives should "be allowed" to work in this field, and no Native scholar I know has ever insisted that one must be Indian in order to understand or study Indian communities. To do so would embrace notions of "wisdom in the blood" that carry cultural and philosophical relativism to its untenable extreme.

Rather, the issue is how the work is to be done. Again, the crux of the matter is both hermeneutical and political. It is hermeneutical in that one simply cannot gain an accurate understanding of what goes on in Indian Country without living in and around an Indian community for a long time. American Indian life does not work by the same rules or categories as life in the "mainstream," and it usually takes years to become aware of the subtleties of perception, history, and communication that inform it. In fact, one really needs not just to reside, but to reside *as a relative*, since there are vast dimensions of meaning that are only acted out in this way. Even this is not a matter of blood, however. There are full-blood Indians who have lost this ability to participate in kinship, and yet in every Indian community I have ever visited there have been one or two whites who have gained it.

And the issue is political in that power, status, money, and sometimes passionate mainstream public emotions continue to surround Indian issues, and hinge on their resolution. In the current American climate of racial and economic tension, these supposedly intellectual arguments quickly reveal their provocative political undersides. This is no news to Indian people, who have been eyewitnesses from the beginning to the confluence of Western intellectual history and the inescapable reality of the genocidal invasion of the Americas. It is news to many scholars, however, and not very welcome news at that. For example, Sam Gill laments that "the matter [of academic qualification in the study of American Indian religions] has become almost purely political and has failed to raise any substantive academic issues" (Gill 1994:971). In fact, by disdainfully ignoring the presence of political history at the academic table, Gill is led to an odd but telling non-sequitur. He writes:

The question of whether or not one ought to know one's subject in terms of the language and cultural setting seems to be the question of whether or not the area of study is an academic one. For there to be any discussion is evidence that it is not (Gill 1994:971).

In other words, the discipline itself—which, again, Gill understands as dominated by ethnic American Indians—is to be discredited as non-academic and thus blamed for even raising the issue of research competence. No mention is made of the fact that it is the incompetence and inaccuracy of generations of mostly non-Native "authorities" on Indian religion, as perceived by Native people, that has necessitated the focus on this issue.

In a larger sense, however, the hermeneutical and the political domains of this response merge. Traditional American Indian communities do not conceive of "religious knowledge" apart from its complex relations with other domains, including economics and politics. There is no knowledge other than what is lived out, and there is no living out that is not political and historical. In other words if, as a colleague has written, "being born Indian is being born into politics" (Alfred 1995:1), then how can any attempt to study Indian life avoid the political? How can any study of adaptations to "modernity" in Native religious life ignore the direct and indirect attacks that modern Euroamerican institutions have made and continue to make on Indian ways of life? To put it bluntly, while academicians may pretend to cloak themselves in a pure mantle of scientific detachment, virtually all the institutions we work for, in one way or another are connected to and supported by—in fact were built on—enterprises involving the exploitation of American Indian land and lives.

Of course historical study is the only way to achieve depth in the analysis of religious, political, or other developments and questions. I often tell people that I have never encountered a people more attuned to and interested in historical questions than those in my ancestral Mohawk community of Kahnawà:ke. My inquiries there were not even taken seriously until I was able to demonstrate knowledge of, and opinions about, Kahnawà:ke's history. Thus I would find highly suspect a synchronic community study that lacked historical depth. Conversely, historical studies that exhibit no relationship with the present, no input from today's descendants of that history, strike me as pallid and decapitated.

In fact, strong political disputes are often sparked and churned up around historical questions. A particularly difficult pass is reached when historical documents dispute an Indian community's own perception, in oral tradition, of its history. This is tricky ground for any scholar who cares about her or his standing in the community. But again, I would argue against choices that smother disagreement and enforce conformity to a party line. Rather, the best answer might be to focus on presentation. Such contradictions need not be reported simply because they have been found, first of all—this calls up the question of motivation; the purpose of the study in the first place. But even when the choice is to present the contradiction, I have found that it can be done in such a way as to *explain* it; to suggest reasons for the discrepancy; to see it in larger frames, and thus usually to some degree to turn it into an occasion for thoughtful exchange rather than polemics.

At the very least, therefore, those involved in academic inquiry ought to reexamine both the means and the ends of research involving Native Peoples. How did the academic tradition of prying and cajoling and tricking "information" out of Native "informants"—then expertly demonstrating the real, hidden reasons and motivations for such outlandish behavior and beliefs—arise? What has motivated it, and how much of that motivation remains? Rather than scientist interpreting specimen, can we imagine a model in which Indigenous and Euroamerican intellectual histories meet and conduct authentic exchanges in a context of real respect?

If scholars of religion continue to insist that such a model surrenders too much control to believers, tainting scientific method with theology—becoming "the religious study of religion"—then scholars and traditional practitioners will continue to inhabit largely unrelated worlds. Such scholars will find themselves increasingly placed by angry Indians on the same platform with a whole crowd of commercial neo-Native "hucksters" whom the scholars themselves once dismissed and scorned. As an alternative, I list a few bare suggestions toward building the kind of model I am hoping for:

1. If an academic career built on the study of an American Indian community provides a living for a scholar and the scholar's family, she or he should feel obliged to reciprocate in some substantial way toward that community. This is especially true if that community faces imminent threats to its survival, which few Indian communities today do not.

2. As stated above, scholars need to provide clear and comprehensive accounts of their relationships with the Indian communities they study. Moreover, the issue of motivation—*why* they are involved in this work—ought to be considered an integral part of its justification. Mere curiosity or filling in lacunae in "the research record" should not be thought of as adequate reasons to probe into peoples' lives.

3. Scholarship ought to look on American Indian systems of knowledge and practice not as new, untried fields of data with which to test existing Amer-European essentialist theories; but as sources for new theories, new categories—even new frameworks with which to study and evaluate aspects of non-Indian life.

4. Indigenous sacred work and Native interpretations of such work ought to be considered as intellectual property, subject to all the appropriate permissions and credits.[15]

5. Given the profound linguistic, philosophical, historical, and political chasms between modern, literate, Amer-European civilization and the oral world of traditional American Indian communities, no written source, whether the author is Indian or not, should be exempted from the closest critical evaluation.

In this essay I have tried to demonstrate two things: first, how the appropriation of American Indian religious or spiritual systems involves not only ethical but political and hermeneutical failures; and second, how these same issues, which can appear in such exaggerated, obvious, cartoon form in some manifestations of popular enthusiasm, lie also more subtlely beneath the rarefied realm of academic inquiry. But in my estimation, if we are to speak in general of "contemporary issues in Native American spirituality," as this collection of essays attempts to do, this issue of appropriation and intrusion by academics and "New Age" enthusiasts is but one of perhaps three areas of deepest concern to Native traditionalists these days. The other two are (1) continuing threats to Indian landholdings and land use, especially in relation to sacred places—although all Indian land is understood as sacred in a basic sense; and (2) continuing economic and cultural invasion of Native communities, causing erosion of self-sufficiency and the decay of *integrity* in ceremonial work.

Current land issues include the conflict over the University of Arizona's Mount Graham observatory complex, as well as such long-standing issues as the Big Mountain relocation; the Lakota, Dakota, and Nakota claim to the Black Hills; and a long list of other Native land claims, large and small.[16] Examples of economic and cultural invasion issues include the forced imposition of educational methods and programs antithetical to traditional values, language, and ways of life; the invasion of consumer culture via television, alcohol, and most brands of Christian missionization; ongoing lobbying by powerful private and government entities to locate radioactive waste dumps, and other toxic byproducts of technological excess on Indian land; and of course, the long history of the reservation system, the removal of Native children to boarding schools, and other forms of economic and cultural exploitation that make these new get-rich-quick schemes so attractive to many Indian communities. How can ceremonial life fail to suffer degradation when the natural environment is degraded, when economic demands upon time spiral out of control, when Native languages rapidly erode, and when a whole gamut of market-driven alien substitutes crowd around every Indian home?

Of these areas of concern, the focus of this essay is probably the most abstract in terms of its actual threat to Indian ways of life, yet its importance to Indian communities is apparent from the sustained intensity of their response. Even so, because of its secular and scientific foundations, the non-Indian Euroamerican world continues to respond cynically to all protests based on traditional indigenous values, characterizing such activism as merely political—as public relations strategy—rather than religious or spiritual.[17]

All these matters particularly implicate scholarly research and publication, which is why I thought it important to include at least a brief treatment of them in this collection. The point is that if academic research on "contemporary issues in Native American spirituality," in whatever specific context, is to be of any use or relevance to Indian people, and if it is to move beyond the kinds of controversies and friction that have characterized it recently, it cannot but concern itself with these issues, as well as with internal issues involving cross-cultural methods, theory, and motivation. Rather than impeding, compromising, or polluting pure academic inquiry, however, these matters ought to be embraced as enlivening it. This is the fertile theoretical ground to which Sam Gill points when he remarks that "nearly everything about [small-scale exclusively-oral] cultures and their religions questions the assumptions and approaches of the academic study of religion" (Gill 1994:970). In a sense, I am only advocating additions, primarily political, to his understanding of this challenge, and pointing out that it is a challenge to expand and deepen the "assumptions and approaches" not only of one relatively small sub-discipline, but of all cross-cultural academic work.

NOTES

1. I am aware of the questions raised in the last few years about Churchill's own claim to "Creek/Cherokee Métis" identity. I am not in a position to evaluate either the questions or his response, but quote his writing because I find it useful. Certainly the irony of these accusations in light of his stance on the issue is lost on few who are aware of it. The issue of politics, scholarship, and Indian identity are addressed further along in this essay.

2. Castaneda's series of immensely successful popular books began with his *The Teachings of Don Juan: A Yaqui Way of Knowledge* (1968), a revised version of his dissertation in anthropology from UCLA. The evidence against its authenticity is presented in de Mille 1976 and 1980. I am aware of no such exposé regarding the equally popular Andrews titles, beginning with her *Medicine Woman* in 1976, although Wendy Rose dismisses a few of Andrews' baldest assertions in her critique mentioned above (1992). Pointedly, despite their transparent falsity, both these series of works continue to be listed in libraries and bookstore shelves as works of anthropology, ethnography, or religious studies, rather than as fiction.

3. Sometimes the scholar writes as if proving the existence of the phenomenon named by the category, such as Åke Hultkrantz's work on "the High God" in American Indian traditions (1971; 1979: ch. 2). The alternative is always the absence of the phenomenon; the very applicability of the category is not seriously questioned. Thus, in a real sense what was to be proven is assumed.

4. Two excellent examples are Michael Harner's trademark "Harner® Method" of do-it-yourself "core shamanism," described in his *Way of the Shaman* (1982), and the instructions included in Thomas Mails' *Secret Native American Pathways* (1988).

5. For a recent review of Cushing's odd career, see Green 1990. See also Don Talayesva's passionate Hopi attack on the depredations of the missionary, photographer, and "ethnological collector" Henry R. Voth (Talayesva 1942:6, 41, and 252). Talayesva is less diplomatic than scholars have been, describing Voth as a brutish, acquisitive thief. He writes, for instance: "The land was very dry, the crops suffered, and even the Snake Dance failed to bring much rain. We tried to discover the reason for our plight, and

remembered the Rev. Voth who had stolen so many of our ceremonial secrets and had even carried off sacred images and altars to equip a museum and become a rich man." (Talayesva 1942:252)

6. In a humorous but entirely typical case, I remember an occasion when a friend of mine gave a respected Singer a fine new western shirt in appreciation for the knowledge he had shared with her over the years. Minutes later he was trying it on when a relative appeared, a middle-aged man somewhat the worse for wear. Sure enough, a few minutes later this "uncle" left, the proud owner of the same flashy new shirt, leaving my friend temporarily nonplused.

7. In an almost unbelievable display of either ignorance or arrogance, Mails continues, "Remember that different approaches will suit different people. In this respect, we are more fortunate than the native Americans were, for while they had only their own pathways to follow, we can choose from those of four different tribes. . . . Test the ways and make your own choices" (Mails 1988:228–29).

8. This theory is stated more elaborately in Chapter 1 of my dissertation, "Relationship Structures in Longhouse Tradition at Kahnawà:ke" (1994). As I note therein, "knowledge about traditional procedures is but a pale shadow of the active ability to perform them—to rekindle them, in the Longhouse idiom" (Jocks 1994:5). Gary Witherspoon makes a similar observation in a different context: "Navajos taught me that anything you cannot remember without writing down is something you do not know or understand well enough to *use* effectively" (Witherspoon 1977:7; emphasis mine).

9. Something very similar in a much wider context seems to be articulated in philosopher Donald Davidson's work on "propositional attitudes," as summarized by Hans Penner in his presentation of "holistic analysis" (Penner 1994). Penner writes, for instance, that "what a person says or does is not just dependent upon what she believes, but also on what she desires, and hopes for" (980).

10. Unfortunately, given the power of market incentives, this is unlikely in the absence of any significant legal means for Native communities to protect the intellectual, emotional, and spiritual rights inherent in their traditional knowledge and practices.

11. The other side of this coin—the question of legitimate participation in American Indian religious life by non-Natives—is taken up in the next section of this essay.

12. Out of courtesy and because I have never taken the opportunity to speak with this professor about the matter, I refrain from naming either of these two parties. My purpose in mentioning it at all is not to accuse an individual, after all, but to illustrate an attitude that seems to me obviously characteristic of much academic inquiry.

13. As I understand it, the Hopi Tribal Council has announced that it must approve and review all future academic research involving Hopi people, land, or culture.

14. Portions of the remainder of this section have been submitted in somewhat different form to the *Journal of the American Academy of Religion*, as a response to Gill's article. Professor Gill announced several years ago that he would no longer teach or publish in the study of American Indian religions, as I understand it for many of the

same reasons mentioned in his critique. I regret his departure, having admired much of his work in the field, especially that done before 1987.

15. In a curious twist, I recently encountered a situation in which academic appropriation involved giving more credit than was due to a Native contributor. The latter was listed as co-author of an article, but in fact his contribution was the telling of a traditional narrative whose interpretation was left almost entirely to the other, non-Indian, co-author. In today's market, having a Native co-author listed on the cover will sell more books; yet the product may not be substantively Native at all.

16. An overview of many of these issues can be found in Jaimes 1992. I recently encountered a worthwhile overview of the Mount Graham issue in *High Country News* 27 (13), dated July 24, 1995; its address is: P.O. Box 1090, Paonia CO 81428.

17. For example, see the collection of mainstream critiques Clifton 1990. See also Ward Churchill's evaluation of the book (1992b).

REFERENCES

Alfred, Gerald R. 1995. *Heeding the Voices of our Ancestors: Kahnawake Mohawk Politics and the Rise of Native Nationalism.* New York: Oxford University Press.

Andrews, Lynn. 1981. *Medicine Woman.* San Francisco: Harper and Row.

Castaneda, Carlos. 1968. *The Teachings of Don Juan: A Yaqui Way of Knowledge.* Berkeley: University of California Press.

Churchill, Ward. 1992a. *Fantasies of the Master Race: Literature, Cinema and the Colonization of American Indians.* Ed. M. Annette Jaimes. Monroe ME: Common Courage Press.

———. 1992b. "The New Racism: A Critique of James A. Clifton's The Invented Indian." In Churchill 1992a: 163–84.

———. 1994. *Indians Are Us?: Culture and Genocide in Native North America.* Monroe ME: Common Courage Press.

Clifton, James, ed. 1990. *The Invented Indian: Cultural Fictions and Government Policies.* New Brunswick NJ: Transaction Books.

CSPIRIT (Center for the Support and Protection of Indian Religions and Indigenous Traditions). 1993. "Alert Concerning the Abuse and Exploitation of American Indian Sacred Traditions." Press Release (?), quoted in Churchill 1994: 279–80.

de Mille, Richard. 1976. *Castaneda's Journey: The Power and the Allegory.* Santa Barbara CA: Capra Press.

———. 1980. *The Don Juan Papers: Further Castaneda Controversies.* Santa Barbara CA: Ross-Erikson.

Gill, Sam. 1994. "The Academic Study of Religion." *Journal of the American Academy of Religion* 62: 965–75.

Green, Jesse, ed. 1990. *Cushing at Zuni: The Correspondence and Journals of Frank Hamilton Cushing, 1879–84.* Albuquerque: University of New Mexico Press.

Harner, Michael. 1982. *Way of the Shaman*. New York: Bantam.

Hultkrantz, Åke. 1971. "The Structure of Theistic Beliefs among North American Plains Indians." *Temenos* 7: 66–74.

———. 1979. *The Religions of the American Indians*. Trans. Monica Setterwall. Hermeneutics: Studies in the History of Religions, no. 7. Berkeley: University of California Press.

Jaimes, M. Annette, ed. 1992. *The State of Native America: Genocide, Colonization and Resistance*. Race and Resistance Series. Boston: South End Press.

Jocks, Christopher Ronwanièn:te. 1994. "Relationship Structures in Longhouse Tradition at Kahnawà:ke." (Ph.D. diss., University of California, Santa Barbara.)

Mails, Thomas E. 1988. *Secret Native American Pathways: A Guide to Inner Peace*. Tulsa: Council Oak Books.

McGaa, Ed (Eagle Man). 1990. *Mother Earth Spirituality: Native American Paths to Healing Ourselves and Our World*. San Francisco: Harper & Row.

———. 1992. *Rainbow Tribe: Ordinary People Journeying on the Red Road*. San Francisco: Harper San Francisco.

Penner, Hans H. 1994. "Holistic Analysis: Conjectures and Refutations." *Journal of the American Academy of Religion* 62: 977–96.

Rose, Wendy. 1992. "The Great Pretenders: Further Reflections on Whiteshamanism." In Jaimes 1992: 403–21.

Talayesva, Don C. 1942. *Sun Chief: The Autobiography of a Hopi Indian*. Ed. Leo W. Simmons. New Haven: Yale University Press.

Witherspoon, Gary. 1977. *Language and Art in the Navajo Universe*. Ann Arbor: University of Michigan Press.

This May Be a Feud, but It Is Not a War

An Electronic, Interdisciplinary Dialogue on Teaching Native Religions

RONALD L. GRIMES

After a lecture in Montreal by a non-Native professor, a First Nations woman from Manitoba rose and spoke with considerable passion: *Much of what you say,* she declared, *is probably true, but suppose you were a Jew and you had just heard your spirituality or your history presented to you by the grandchild of a Nazi. How would you feel?*[1]

Because of critiques like these, academic institutions where indigenous religions are taught are undergoing a crisis of conscience and of methodology. The majority of faculty teaching such courses are non-Natives; like me, they are North Americans of European extraction, heirs of colonialist forebears. To be sure, the majority of those teaching Buddhism and Hinduism are not Buddhists or Hindus either, but the historical relationship of Native people to Euroamerican institutions and their representatives is not that of Buddhists or Hindus. However much we like to think we are living in a postcolonial era, we are not—not yet. The conquest continues, and some say that its most dangerous contemporary battlefield is that of the classroom (or of the weekend workshop). The bone of contention is no longer gold; it is spirituality.

Natives and non-Natives alike have their reasons for not wanting to engage this issue head-on. It is easier not to—sacred matters being what they are. Churches and sweat lodges are not places for argument, and classrooms are too often turf dominated by the party in power. These days, a space that more regularly tolerates ongoing debate of issues like the ones raised here—is cyberspace. Although access to it is not perfectly democratic—depending as it does on having sufficient equipment, time, know-how, and money—there is nevertheless a strong and articulate Native presence on electronic discussion lists. The constituency of Natchat, for instance, is extraordinarily active; as is Native-L, its more news-oriented counterpart. Natives and non-Natives regularly engage one another in virtual "places" like as these. However disembodied the medium of internet discourse, and whatever the peculiarities of arguing without benefit of face, gesture, or tone of voice, cyberspace is a locus of cross-cultural encounter, a frontier. Engagement is possible, perhaps, because cyberspace engagement is distanced even when it is passionate.

Not long ago, driven by a moral and pedagogical quandary and realizing there was something seriously wrong with carrying on a debate only with one's own conscience, I initiated an interdisciplinary discussion on academic teaching about Native spirituality. It transpired simultaneously on three electronic discussion lists.[2] Since the members of any one list would not have known what was being said on the other two lists, I collected the replies and reposted them to the three groups. The statement that initiated the discussion was as follows:

I am submitting this query to invite reflection on three questions:

1. Should or should not European Americans be teaching courses on Native religions of North America?[3]

2. If we should not, why not, and what would be the results of our deferral?

3. If we should, how best can we proceed?

I am giving much thought these days to the question of cultural imperialism, especially its religious and academic forms. While on leave from my home university, I have been asked by the Department of Religious Studies at the University of Colorado, Boulder, to teach a large, publicly visible introductory course on the religions of Native North America.

Vine Deloria teaches here. So does Sam Gill. And so do Ward Churchill and Deward Walker. This is an sizeable concentration of authorities on indigenous cultures, politics, law, and religion. Ordinarily, I teach courses on indigenous religions at Wilfrid Laurier, a small Canadian university with few Native students, at considerable remove from indigenous populations of the American Southwest (where I do most of my fieldwork), and out of sight of high-profile scholars whose names are regularly associated with Native studies.

Currently, the Boulder campus is the locus of a highly charged stand-off that no one talks much about. In part, the issue has to do with academic, religious, and cultural turf. Sometimes it does not have to do with who is right or wrong on a given issue, but with who ought to be speaking about such issues. Anyone who has read Ward Churchill's (1992) critique of Sam Gill's *Mother Earth* (1990) or heard Vine Deloria's public but unpublished reflections on that book knows there are good reasons for Euroamerican scholars not to rush in, fools, where angels fear to tread.

In fact, some are rushing in the other direction: out. I know of several instances in which white male colleagues are giving up longstanding research and teaching commitments to Native, Black or feminist spirituality. For a few, their exiting is an ethical matter: make room for the oppressed; don't speak about what you are not, and so on. For most, it is a matter of feeling embattled or unappreciated. Exiting white scholars feel they will never get respect or credit for attending to such matters; they complain about political correctness. Some may find this minor exodus an occasion for joy. I do not.

A colleague asked me after seeing the video "Gathering Up Again: Fiesta in Santa Fe," "Shouldn't we just abandon such topics [the conflicts among Native American, Hispanic American, and Anglo American religious traditions]? Isn't scholarship, like art and ethnography," he asked, "just another way of appropriation, just another form of cultural imperialism? Why do you keep teaching on the topic of indigenous religion?" This was the question of a non-Native colleague; Native ones are raising the question as well. The notion of abandoning academic turf (as if it were bad land) and giving it back to "the Natives" (as if it were a gift that "we" previously owned) seems to me a piece of bad choreography to which we have danced several times before.

The question of cultural imperialism is especially acute when the subject matter is religion rather than, say, law, economics, or politics. Religion is, after all, supposed to be a protected domain. We religion scholars ought not be desecrating what we study. In *Ritual Criticism* (1990) I wrote about the problem of desecration, especially as it occurs when indigenous cemeteries are excavated or sacred objects displayed in museums. But the questions I must ask myself are not much different from those I have put to archaeologists and curators: Does teaching about religions indigenous to the Americas desecrate them?

In religious studies we like to feel we honor a religious tradition by taking it seriously enough to teach it. The act of paying attention is, or ought to be, a way of valuing. What are we to make of the accusation that our teaching of religions—forced by historical necessity into linking sanctity with secrecy—is really a way of appropriating or desecrating? Our first line of defense is that we teach about religion; we do not teach religion. Unlike "those" New-Ager wannabes in California, "we" responsible scholars do not put on Plains garb or do the Santo Domingo Corn Dance. But we do read the ethnographies (some of them distorted, some of them in violation of confidences) and contemplate the museum objects (some of them stolen, some of them falsely named and ritually underfed). We may not be responsible for the sins of our forebears, but we certainly make intellectual capital on the basis of their colonial activities.

An anthropologist friend said to me, "Grimes, if we took all the stuff you say seriously, we'd be paralyzed—like the proverbial centipede suddenly made aware of its own legs and completely immobilized by that fact. You would paralyze us with self-consciousness or guilt." I said I thought that was probably right but that being stilled and silenced for a while might not be a bad thing. He accused me of being a Buddhist.

But what form, I had to ask myself later, should this immobility and silence take? Should we white folks give up teaching about Native religions, leaving it to those who can teach it from their own hearts and traditions? (In many cases given-up courses would not be taught, because there are not yet many Native Ph.D.s in religious studies.)

I can hear other religiologists object, "Surely you don't think that only Hindus can teach Hinduism, only Muslims, Islam," and so on. One unspoken subtext of this response is the worry that thinking such a thought would surely put us out of business. If this were the only motive for the objection, I'd say, "Let's go out of business." But another subtext—one with which I am in more sympathy—is the belief that all kinds of academic study require the sympathetic exercise of imagination. If we taught only that which we embodied by virtue of our upbringing, gender, class, or ethnicity, we would all be reduced to autobiographical confession or mere reiteration of our traditions. I'd be teaching Grandma's peculiar brand of frontier Methodism, which would certainly insist on the obvious superiority of "my kind" over other folks.

So I have not chosen to exit. I continue to write and teach about religious practices of groups in which I do not hold membership. Some of them do not object to such study, but others do. Scholarship, I have come to believe, necessarily incurs guilt. We should not pretend otherwise. Scholarship, though it can be a kind of honoring, is also a kind of hunting. So we should do it with great care—identifying our fates with the fate of what we hunt, taking only what we really need for survival, and hedging our activities with considerable prayer. I dislike the hunting analogy. I am, of course, borrowing it, because in the hunting tradition I grew up with we did it for sport. I invoke the hunting analogy as a way of reminding our (white)selves of the violence of our actions even when we intend to be nonviolent. Though we may not experience scholarship as violence, thus not a form of hunting, we are certainly being told that others experience our study as violation. We need to pause to consider this charge, because some of our colleagues, students, and friends are making it. So for me the question is not, "What is a nonviolent way to study religion?" but "What is the least violent way to do it?"

Once in a brief public discussion with Vine Deloria at the American Academy of Religion I tried to press him to say forthrightly that he thought white scholars should not study or teach Native religions. He pulled up short of taking such a position. Instead, he said that European American scholarship should content itself with description but forego interpretation. I objected that description was already interpretation. Even if it weren't, I said, insofar as descriptions become the basis of interpretation, a white person's description was still just that, a point of view. Did he really think a Native interpretation based on a non-Native description would be of any value?

We didn't finish the discussion. We became circumspect, wry, and humorous with one another, because it was an emotionally loaded topic. But the bigger question, which this little scene illustrated, continues: What are the limits and ethics that bear on the teaching of indigenous religions by non-Natives in public institutions? We all know that anyone who teaches anything should be qualified, but what constitutes qualification? And what constitutes disqualification? Is ethnicity itself one of the qualifications? I am not asking a legal question so much as an ethical and a methodological question.

I suspect that we white male scholars will never get it quite right when we either describe or interpret things Black, things female, things Native. If true, this observation can lead to several possible conclusions: we should stop trying; we should try harder and harder (with effort we will get it right); we should do what we do with humility and open ears.

I could not pursue the first option without abandoning Indian friends, students, and colleagues. I am still too much a Protestant to believe that effort alone achieves much. So I prefer the last conclusion. And I have to ask what it might mean to teach a course on indigenous religions on this premise.

It might mean that we ought not try to teach courses directly on Native North American religions as such but rather on the encounter between religio-cultural traditions. When I first went to Santa Fe to do fieldwork, an anthropologist asked me why I wasn't going to study the Pueblos. I quipped, "Because the Pueblos are studying the Pueblos." I decided to work on the Santa Fe fiesta because that was where "my kind" was encountering "other kinds." I had both a responsibility and a right to study it because my ethnic group was partly responsible for making it the Gordian knot that it is. The problem with this approach is that it forces Native traditions to share the stage without being a subject matter in its own right. So it is a less than perfect solution.

Second, it might mean that we require readings that emphasize indigenous voices. One way to do this would be to incorporate indigenous autobiographical material and then deal with all the theoretical issues that surround the model (that is, indigenous informant/white editor) that produced most of these works. A problem with this model is that Anglo-American scholars write most of the theories that would frame the discussion.

Third, it might mean focusing on the conflicts that mark the study of indigenous religions (for instance, the *Black Elk Speaks* controversy, the *Mother Earth* controversy, the Carlos-Castaneda-Lynn-Andrews-Jamake-Highwater phenomenon or the Frank-Waters-and-the-Hopi controversy). The obvious problem with this model is focusing on aberrations and missing what is central to indigenous traditions. Another difficulty would be finding sufficient material written by Indians to balance the debates.

A fourth possibility is a course, one-quarter of which would introduce the general issues and three-quarters of which would concentrate on a specific indigenous people and then perhaps even on a specific individual (as represented by an autobiography). I have taken this approach, typically focusing on the Southwestern United States. One can easily be torn between the dated ethnographies that directly describe rites and retell sacred stories and the contemporary fictional works (by Leslie Silko, Scott Momaday, Paula Gunn Allen, and others) which are more circumspect. What are the respective virtues and liabilities of these two kinds of literature as windows on the sacred—the one supposedly factual but which, for lack of understanding and meaningful context, necessarily falsifies; the other fictional and therefore not necessarily bound to reflect actual practice?

I am not entirely happy with any of these ways, but I have given up teaching the kind of survey that uses works by Åke Hultkrantz (1981) and Joseph Epes Brown (1988). I find these works largely naïve about issues of appropriation and cultural imperialism. In addition, no matter how often you say to students, "It's Native religions, not Native religion," the degree of abstraction and generalization in surveys is so high that the force of the course's structure presses students in the direction of overgeneralization and stereotype. (The structure of a course always teaches more profoundly than its content does.)

On the Religion List there were fifty-four responses; on the Native List, forty-three; and on the Anthropology List, sixteen. Because of the length of the electronic discussion and lack of space, my aim is less to represent individual points of view than to articulate a position in the context of a summary of responses. Although one is even less sure about identity in cyberspace than in geographical space, my impression was that few First Nations people and few scholarly teachers of Native spirituality participated in the interchange. Indian participants, a few of them self-identified, appeared almost exclusively on Native-L. The most prominent of the scholar-teachers of Native religions were not members of the electronic lists but colleagues whose responses I solicited and then funneled to the lists. In short, most participants, I believe, were scholars interested in the topic or its implications for teaching in general. A discussion confined to either Native people or professors who teach on the topic of Native religions might have taken quite a different turn.

The responses of many non-Native discussants seemed to assume that an unqualified prohibition against teaching indigenous religions was the normative Indian stance. However, not one respondent argued that Euroamericans should be prohibited from teaching Native religions. The nearest anyone came to such a position was in a letter sent to me from a director of the Western Shoshone Historic Preservation Society. Its author, who had heard about but not read the e-mail discussion, claimed that "true traditional Natives" would never agree to such teaching. Since there were so few negative responses, it might be tempting to dismiss the issue I raised as specious. One respondent said she imagined that the discussion was exaggerated until she read the posting by Sam Gill, which I will consider shortly.

To avert further speculation that the issue is either trumped up or merely local, I will begin with the responses of Vine Deloria and Sam Gill, both of whom *seem* to offer negative replies to my first question.[4] I represent these participants by name for two reasons: their visibility (largely through their public writing and lecturing) and the reflective and sustained nature of their responses in the e-mail discussion. They offered longer, more considered, one-time statements rather than brief, daily interchanges.

Vine Deloria took the most sustained negative stance, but it was far from unqualified. "I see nothing wrong with [European Americans teaching courses on Native religions]," he writes, "but I personally wish they would not do so." In summarizing his position, he refines it: "I don't see why non-Indians cannot teach courses on Native religions, as long as they understand and accept the fact of modern American political life, [and act] with the knowledge that they are intruding on the emotional commitments and experiences of a specific group of people who may not appreciate their efforts, and are willing to take the consequences." The facts of American political life to which he refers are those that politicize teaching in a society whose history is fundamentally conditioned by colonialism.

Deloria suggests conditions under which teaching would be less of a problem: "The reason [for his personal preference] is that unless and until religious studies, as well as every other social science, adopts new language and a new orientation—unless Euroamericans grow up about what it is they think they know—they will simply continue to perpetuate misconceptions and misperceptions." Among the misconceptions mentioned in his communication are: the assumption that Native teachers are political and that Euroamerican ones are not; the distortions that necessarily arise from studying and teaching religion with no personal interest in it; and the application of non-Indian theories derived from Near Eastern, monotheistic religions; and the "incredible smugness" with which non-Native scholars talk about "the little they do know" about things Native.

Although Deloria does not sound optimistic about the possibility of over-coming the biases that make the non-Native teaching of indigenous religions so troublesome, he actually issues a call for the continuation of teaching: "It is essential that teaching Native religions in some form, and in spite of criticism, be continued . . . provided new ways of arranging and articulating the religion are found." The motive for this turn in Deloria's argument seems to be that of countering New Age appropriation of indigenous ways. A refusal to teach would risk making New Age appropriation easier.

The other position that warrants being identified by name is that of Sam Gill. In an "open letter" Gill narrates his decision, announced on Columbus Day 1992, to make what he called "a rubric shift." After decades of thinking of himself as a student of Native American religions dedicated to dispelling "romantic images" and resisting "a discourse of domination," Gill decides "to shift from this area," that is, to turn "a significant amount of [his] attention from the study of Native American religions." He describes his motives variously: He finds the area "too politicized," and he feels that what he or any other white male might write or say is "regarded [by Native American scholars, I assume] as irrelevant." He writes, "So my decision to switch rubrics came when I found myself angered by some of my Native American colleagues, disappointed in some of my Native American students, dismayed by the flood of action motivated by superficial political correctness, and distracted from the study of Native American religions by the impossible attempt to justify what I was doing."[5]

Sam Gill's response is in many ways the opposite of Vine Deloria's. Deloria is an Indian unhappy with the way whites teach indigenous traditions; Gill is a white male unhappy about criticism that he regards as racist. Like most opposites, they can appear to coincide. On the surface both are negative responses to the question of the appropriateness of non-Natives teaching Native religions in academic classrooms. Deloria wishes white people would *not* teach Indian religions, and Gill is *no longer* going to teach under the rubric "Native American religions." On the surface it appears that Gill has conceded to Deloria's wish.

However, in the final analysis, something else transpires: Deloria calls for teaching to continue (albeit, on different premises) because of the dangers of not doing so, and Gill still believes in "the whole humanistic enterprise," (including, one assumes, the academic study of Native American religions). Gill does not really concede to Deloria in principle but rather exercises a strategy, namely, waiting. "The political agenda and climate will change as time passes," he reflects. Although Gill "has other [academic] loves" and is turning his attention elsewhere (for instance, to Australian Aboriginal religions), he does not so much give up territory as make a strategic retreat in order to search for a better vantage point. Nowhere does he concede that white research and teaching are invalid. His rubric change is predicated on what he calls the "impossibility" of research and teaching in the current climate, not on an admission of its lack of validity.

Both Gill and Deloria imply that their disagreement is not merely a local political battle over turf. Rather it is replicated elsewhere, in the American Academy of Religion, for instance. The University of Colorado is not unique in having trouble over the teaching of Native American religions. It is only unique in the degree of visibility that this trouble has assumed, and this visibility is largely the function of its having prolific, widely read, generally respected scholars in the field.

There were few other negative responses. One was more confessional than prescriptive. A doctoral student, for instance, admitted that in the current contentious atmosphere she found herself paralyzed by self-consciousness and wondered whether she would ever teach on such a troubled topic again. Another respondent was prescriptive rather than confessional. He argued that "there are topics which we should not write about and which our predecessors probably should have avoided (for instance, religious secrets, sacred ceremonies kept hidden from outsiders, myths owned by individual clans)." An Indian student asked his non-Indian readers, "How would you like it if Indians were the authorities teaching you your own history?"

The electronic discussion did not articulate the full range of reasons that have been advanced against the non-Native teaching of Native religions, so for the sake of further discussion, I will try summarizing the negative arguments, drawing on oral discussions and debates, as well as on the e-mail interchange. There seem to be three fundamental but related issues. One is the issue of the sacrality of the subject matter. The argument is that sacred things are necessarily objectified and thus profaned by:

- being taught about in the academy;
- being taught solely or largely by outsiders, that is, people with no social or emotional commitment to the traditions;
- being construed as religion rather than as spirituality (or vice-versa).

One Native participant objected to having her practices and traditions referred to as "religion." Although she did not specify what made this usage offensive, two common reasons are that the notion of religion confines spirituality to an institution, and that it treats spirituality as a sector of life alongside other sectors rather than as something permeating all life. However, a Mohawk respondent objected to the term "spirituality," understanding it to connote a New Age mishmash of borrowed ideas and practices. Obviously, much depends on how each term is defined.

A second reason for objecting to the teaching of Native religions by non-Natives has to do with control and rights. The argument is that sacred lore (like land before the arrival of Europeans) belongs to First Nations people. Thus, non-Natives have no inherent right to it—no matter how much they may desire or need such knowledge. To assume such rights in an argument or to imply them by one's actions, amounts to a continuation of colonialism. One anthropologist was critical of the fact that debates, including this one, too often are centered in the academic rather than the tribal world. The implication is that such displacement amounts to colonialism no matter how sincere or humane the intentions of participants. Indians sometimes argue that scholarly works are used in political ways (for instance, in courts of law) no matter what scholars intend. Therefore, research and teaching on things indigenous is necessarily political (which does not make them any less religious).

A third issue is that of qualifications. The argument is that teachers of indigenous religions are typically unqualified to teach those religions. If, on the one hand, one assumes that religious instruction occurs in the classroom, no elders or tribal bodies have trained or authorized most teachers. If, on the other, one assumes that teachers are teaching about religion, they are not typically well-qualified. They have likely had no graduate training from a legitimate program in the field, and they regularly fail to consult, cooperate with, and render services to, Native communities. Even in cases where instructors are themselves Native, they may know one indigenous tradition well but have little knowledge of others.

Positive answers to the question of teaching Native religions were of two sorts: the "yes, of course" variety and the "yes but" sort. The former took it as obvious that Euroamericans should be able to teach Native religions. The resulting position often was relatively unqualified in its assertions and usually appealed to some single, sacredly held postulate. There were only a few such responses. The "yes if" or "yes, provided that" response was the majority one. Those who espoused it were more likely to argue than to assert, and to posit qualifications or conditions under which teaching should occur. Since both attitudes sometimes appeared in a single communication, there was no hard line between them.

A significant division among the "yes" replies was between those that actually addressed the issue with arguments and those that took the form of ad hominems, red herrings, collegial advice, one-liner throw-aways, or wound-licking. These are worth listing because of their recurrence both in the e-mail discussion and in classrooms. In the decontextualized form below they are not really arguments. Some of them could be reframed as arguments, in which case they would require serious debate. I am not claiming that there is no truth in some of these statements, only that they easily function as shields for staving off debate. All are quoted or tightly paraphrased. I have played philosopher and interpolated [in square brackets] what I imagine to be some of the unspoken implications.

• All this criticism is just white-academic bashing. [Therefore, since it is so indiscriminate, one should not take it seriously.]
• Whites who argue for restraints on teaching Native religions are just being politically correct. [Therefore, their positions are not seriously held; they are mere fads.]
• Indians who argue against the teaching of indigenous religions by non-Native academics typically lack strong tribal roots. [Therefore, take their opinions with a grain of salt.]
• Belonging to some group (e.g., being an Indian) is no guarantee of superior knowledge. [Therefore, Whites can teach as well as Indians.]
• There is no ethnic purity anyway — only the blurring of cultural identities — so an "ethnic cleansing" of the teaching profession by Indians is impossible. [Since there are no pure Indians, there is no one to legislate against or otherwise constrain non-Indian scholars.]
• The split between non-Indians who study and Indians who are studied is a "false binary," since many Indians have mixed identities anyway. [The distinction between Indian and non-Indian is therefore specious.]

• Indians don't understand their forebears any better than white people understand their seventeenth-century ancestors, so they have no privileged point of view.

• Native intellectuals need to understand how complicated the issue of who studies whom really is. [If they did, they would be less likely to criticize white intellectuals who, we all know, understand such complexities.]

• Who can say what lands are sacred and what texts are forbidden to the white man? [Who can say what means of retaliation are forbidden to the red man? Or, if no one can say, then Indians have no right to legislate what White scholars can study.]

• White angst is paralyzing: "If you didn't do the deed, don't take the blame." [If you don't let yourself feel guilty, you will not have to assume any responsibility for the way things are.]

• Indians sometimes depend on ethnographic literature collected by whites in order to know more about their heritage. [So Indians have no right to complain about scholarship done by non-Natives.]

• Indians don't all agree on whether non-Indians should teach Native religions. [Therefore non-Indians are free to make up their own minds about whether they will or won't teach.]

• If Indians are free to become Christian priests, then Whites should feel free to become shamans. [There are no important differences between the status of priest in Christianity and that of shaman in Native religions.]

• The real issue [for Indians] is control. The debate is really about politics, not about religion. [Therefore, Whites need not worry about the possibility of desecration.]

• "Stand your ground." "Fight back and damn the torpedoes." [This is a war, not a debate.]

Now to the substantive arguments. They proceeded on the basis of three premises that amount to primary European American cultural values: the premise of a common humanity, the premise of objective knowledge, and the premise of individual freedom. On these grounds, arguments were advanced in favor of the teaching of Native religions by non-Natives.

The premise of a common humanity posited a universal or common human nature on the basis of which any human being can, at least in principle, understand any other human being or group. Its motto could be something like Freud's "Nothing human is foreign to me." The fact of a common humanity implies that, yes, Native religions can be taught by non-Natives, just as Hinduism or ancient Egyptian religion can be taught by non-practitioners. "Am I to be forbidden to do anything with ancient Israelite religion because I am Catholic?" asked one teacher. "One would never dream of saying that physics should only be done by Englishmen," wrote another.

Many participants assumed rather than stated this premise, or else they implied it in their contention that restricting the teaching of Native religions to First Nations people amounts to racism. Several participants held that prohibiting or circumscribing teaching on the basis of ethnic identity constitutes racism. Some implied—but no one actually said—that this conclusion obtains regardless of historical circumstances. One participant, appealing to Ernest Gellner, rejected the position of "embodied authenticity," that is, the claim that one can only speak about the culture that she or he embodies.

One person argued that studying or teaching only about oneself or one's own people would unduly narrow a scholar's worldview. The result of European American scholars following such advice would be to make dominant ethnic groups even more oppressive, the person contended. The ignorance that would result from not studying Native religions, said another participant, would be more dangerous than making the inevitable, ignorant mistakes that one commits in studying them. Maintaining a common humanity requires that groups study one another. Since we are all human beings, argued one, we are naturally curious about each other.

A second premise was that of objective, which is to say, non-political, or disinterested, knowledge. Not only is such knowledge a value but the pursuit of it is inevitable, implied one discussant. People, white and Indian alike, are always making observations about each other, he said, so the question is not whether but how knowledge is obtained. Most discussants assumed the inherent value of disinterested knowledge. Several defended a specific subtype of it, namely, the knowledge provided by outside observers. For instance, one said, "Outsider points of view can often be valuable, especially if the insiders are factionalized." Some of the participants asserted that such knowledge is valuable not just to non-Natives but to Native people as well. One claimed that scholarship itself has sometimes empowered indigenous peoples. It has had, he argued, the effect of validating aspects of indigenous cultures that were about to be lost by members of those cultures or that were not appreciated by the non-scholarly members of non-Native cultures.

Some discussants defended not only the value of disinterested knowledge but the institution that claims to be its custodian, namely, the university with its various departments. One person argued that if teaching Native religions is wrong, then so is the whole enterprise of anthropology, since it consists largely of description and interpretation garnered by outsiders. One scholar argued that the very questions that framed the e-mail debate threatened higher education, the values of which, he seemed to assume, were shared by most of his audience. The argument in defense of disinterested knowledge (that is, "teaching about") occasionally appealed to precedent: We are already teaching about other religious traditions, so there is no good reason to make an exception in the case of Native religions. Some participants in the discussion worried that making an exception for Native religions would bring the whole academic house down: "To assume that the only people who should study a group are members of the group is to totally invalidate anthropology, sociology, linguistics and so on."

The third premise was that of academic freedom, specifically, a subgenre of it: individual academic freedom. In its bald form the premise is that anyone has a right to study and teach about anything without restraint, in other words, all things may become subject matter for all people. In principle there are no limits to this freedom, even though there may be limits in fact. The argument asserts that even though a scholar may be limited by ability and resources, he or she should not be constricted by design or principle. Many discussants felt they had to resist pressure. One argued that if established non-Indian academics yielded to the pressures of Indians, then who would scholars be subjected to next—Muslims? Christian fundamentalists? Republicans? Correspondents cited examples of suppressed data and oppressed scholars—the Qumran scrolls held hostage, Gershom Scholem anathematized for teaching that the Zohar was a thirteenth-century rather than a first-century text, and so on. Some participants seemed worried that Native people could or would exercise censorship. One person, who conceded that Indians had a right to control the teaching of religion, denied that they had a right to control teaching about religion. The premise of personal academic freedom occasionally inspired a turn from resisting censorship to asserting rights. "I should not be prohibited from learning their ways. How else am I to enrich my life?" complained one respondent.

Most of the arguments in favor of teaching were not absolute but predicated on desiderata. These were the "yes, if" responses, and I believe they constitute the most constructive aspect of the e-mail discussion. Typically, respondents enumerated only one or two conditions under which they considered teaching Native religions appropriate. Assembled into a list and treated as conditions, they become formidable. It seems to me that a fruitful debate might arise around a proposition that runs something like this: Teaching Native religions by non-Natives is desirable and/or permissible provided (again, most of these are quoted or paraphrased from e-mail postings)

• the sanctity, privacy, feelings, and clan rights of the various religions are respected;
• the topic is taught critically and contextually, that is, in view of the history of oppression and in dialogue with those whom such teaching might offend;
• teachers work outside of class to rectify imbalances, for instance, by lobbying to hire indigenous faculty, helping protect Native land, or defending Native rights;

- the larger economy and prevailing politics are made less oppressive to Native people;
- there is a multiplicity of interacting voices, for instance, Native voices are heard in class by reading Native authors, inviting Native speakers, collaborating with Native colleagues, and attending to Native students' concerns;
- learning is from and with, not just about, Indians;
- attention is repeatedly called to the limits of one voice;
- Native views are allowed to challenge the dominant worldview and question European American values, resulting in "indigenous critiques of world religions."
- the products of research are valued by Indians and are not for the benefit of scholars alone, that is, research results are made useful to Native people;
- the object of study (for example, a myth, symbol, or rite) is not currently in local use;
- the presentation is comparative and/or cross-cultural;
- European-American teachers admit their mistakes publicly and continue to learn from them;
- the aim and effect is tolerance and/or appreciation;
- the aim goes beyond mere appreciation [this one contradicts the caveat immediately above];
- knowledge of Native religions is not held separate from oneself;
- knowledge is for the sake of decision and action;
- the teacher is respectful; and, finally, provided
- the teacher doesn't try to be Indian.

Only a few participants explicitly stated their willingness to treat desiderata as criteria binding on those who teach Native religions. So a debate over this list would have two tasks. One would be to consider each of the constituent items, struggling with definitions and implications: What constitutes being respectful? Is toleration a worthy goal, or should it be subordinate to some larger one? Is being out of current use a valid criterion? To which specific Native groups should research be useful? And so on.

The other task would be that of deciding what force this, or some modified, list might have: Is it merely of things desired but up to individual faculty to implement? Should it have binding force, but only if individuals choose to enforce the conditions? Should they become the basis of a formal guideline or the purview of a committee formed on the analogy of university ethics committees? Do items on the list have moral or only pedagogical weight?

Lest I be accused of trying to keep my hands clean by merely managing this discussion, I conclude by saying briefly what my own position is. I continue to teach courses on indigenous religions, because the alternatives seem to me worse. Not to teach could easily be construed as, if not actually be the result of, regarding such religions as inferior. So for me the question remains how, when, why, and where to teach. I adhere to some of the conditions on this list above, but the selection varies from year to year, teaching situation to teaching situation.

In my view a primary qualification for teaching Native religions is attitude, and it is always easier to recommend one than to embody it. In my view the requisite attitude is a combination of humility, collegiality, and sensitivity. Evidence of such would likely manifest itself in some of the conditions listed above: Does said scholar actually collaborate? Do Indians find that he or she actually listens? And so on. I agree with the Native accusation that arrogance is a fundamental premise (attitudinal, not logical) of Euroamerican scholarship. It may be easy to identify personal arrogance, but it is much harder to identify and change institutional or collective arrogance.

I continue to advocate self-imposed, locally informed, and interethnically negotiated limits. In teaching I set aside certain materials as inappropriate for classroom use now or in this situation. I regularly make compromises. Some colleagues view this position as trading off academic freedom for a mess of pottage. I do not. Some of my colleagues experience it as an insult if they are expected to question, much less negotiate, the terms of their teaching of Native religions, arguing that we should not have to consult Indians. I believe we must. But I also believe that such negotiating is no different from the constant negotiation that we are always in the midst of when we teach other traditions. Every course I teach, every book I write, is some sort of compromise with the market, the expectations of readers, and with the time and energy I am willing to spend. So it does not seem to me anything unusual to have to negotiate, thus exist in a politicized atmosphere, in order to study indigenous religions.

In the library of the Anthropology Laboratory in Santa Fe there was a locked glass case containing, among other things, a volume on Pueblo religion. It was there because it kept getting stolen, according to the librarian, by Pueblos for whom making such knowledge public was a sacrilege or by white folks burning with desire to know sacred secrets. The result was that only we scholars with letters of recommendation in our pockets could get at that volume. My question was whether we should read, discuss, assign, and analyze such a work? We who do fieldwork work do so under both ethical and legal constraints regarding our consultants. Stealing sacred secrets would not pass the ethics committee at my university. Is such knowledge, obtained under colonial conditions, legitimate for us to use? Much (not all) of what we know about indigenous religions was obtained under shady circumstances. Methodologically speaking, how do we proceed—if our data is shady, our qualifications questionable, and Indian students and colleagues feel ripped off by acts of cultural imperialism?

I believe the study of any religion requires that those who teach it take seriously the history of their relationship to those who practice it. I resist, then, the attempt to circumvent the issue of teaching Native religions by merely assimilating it to the study of religion in general, thus implying that teaching about, say, Pueblo religion is the same as teaching about Tibetan Buddhism is the same as teaching about Sunni Islam. Most of us who teach indigenous religions are descendants of colonialists, and we continue to reap benefits from that colonialism. In such circumstances, appealing to objectivist epistemologies (functioning as ideologies) is not only ethically naive, it is immoral. In my view, then, sustained self-criticism is a prerequisite for being able to speak on the topic with credibility.

I advocate preferential hiring. That indigenous students would want to study with Native scholars makes sense to me. In their position, I am sure I would argue as they do for role models and for teachers who share their traditions and values. Sure, I would feel bad if, as a result of my advocacy, Indian students no longer took my courses and doubted my authority, but in the long run doubting professional authority is probably a good thing.

I reject the metaphor of embattlement and worry about the role it played in the e-mail discussion. I was counseled more than once to hold down the fort, damn the torpedoes, and not give up the fight. If we are not careful, we whites will trap ourselves with such metaphors. We will begin to feel as if we are hiding, rifle in hand, under a Conestoga wagon, with Guess Who pointing arrows in our direction. I have had enough of embattlement. I refuse to treat this issue as if we are defending some academic Alamo. I take metaphors far too seriously to be very tolerant of the martial ones.

Does my position threaten the university and its humanistic goals? Some have said so. Even though I share most of those goals, I still view them as culture-specific. They represent an institutionalizing of "our" worldviews. I doubt that humankind really depends on the future of the university any more than it does on the future of churches or nonprofit organizations. I am committed to humanistic scholarship, but I think its future depends on the capacity of intellectuals to listen and act with a deeply grounded sense of respect. The listening is sometimes hard. There is shouting and anger, then sulking and backbiting. So if we are to suffer through all this, we will need something better than martial metaphors: family metaphors maybe. We white scholars shouldn't walk away from angry or critical Indians, whether colleagues or students. They are family, and this may be a feud, but it is not a war.

NOTES

1. Part of this article was published in Grimes 1995; it is reprinted with the permission of Westview Press.

2. The three lists were as follows: Religion (listserv@harvarda.harvard.edu); Anthro-L (listserv@ubvm.cc.buffalo.edu); and Natchat and Native-L (both at listserv@tamvm1.tamu.edu).

3. I use the term "religion" rather than "spirituality" simply because I teach in a department of religious studies. Here, I refrain from entering the debate about how to define and apply each term to the ways of First Nations people.

4. Neither Deloria nor Gill was subscribed to the three lists. I called their attention to the debate and asked if, because of their reputation in the field and high public profiles, they would like to make a response to it. Both wrote statements that, with their permission, I posted to all three lists. Subsequently, both scholars approved of my representation of their positions before this article was submitted for publication.

5. Whether Gill still holds this position is not clear to me.

REFERENCES

Brown, Joseph Epes. 1988. *The Spiritual Legacy of the American Indian.* New York: Crossroad.

Churchill, Ward. 1992. *Fantasies of the Master Race.* Monroe ME: Common Courage Press.

Gill, Sam. 1990. *Mother Earth.* Chicago: University of Chicago Press.

Hultkrantz, Åke. 1981. *Belief and Worship in Native North America.* Ed. Christopher Vecsey. Syracuse: Syracuse University Press.

Grimes, Ronald L. 1990. *Ritual Criticism: Case Studies in Its Practice, Essays in Its Theory.* Columbia: University of South Carolina Press.

———. 1995. *Marrying & Burying.* Boulder CO: Westview Press.

DIALOGICAL RELATIONS 2

Voice, Representation, and Dialogue

The Poetics of Native American
Spiritual Traditions

ROBIN RIDINGTON

Monologue is finalized and deaf to the other's response, does not expect it and does not acknowledge in it any decisive force. Monologue manages without the other, and therefore to some degree materializes all reality . . . Life by its very nature is dialogic. To live means to participate in dialogue.

Mikhail Bakhtin, *Problems of Dostoevsky's Poetics*

During the past five hundred years a substantial literature representing Native American spirituality has come into being as outsiders and Native Americans themselves sought to explain, objectify, and analyze what participants have known through direct experience. The best of these representations are the product of dialogue. They are reports of the conversations through which Native Americans communicated an understanding of their spirituality to one another or to an interested outsider. Like the conversations that constitute Native American spirituality itself, successful representations speak to the reader as a sentient and intelligent person. They speak from a position of respectful mediation between the Native voice and that of the reader. Writing in this Americanist tradition is of necessity multivocal, reportorial, and reflexive. Its authors are most successful when they have documented and interpreted Native American spiritual traditions in conversation with them.

Concerns about voice, representation, and ethnographic authority are prominent today in both academic and Native American communities. A volume on contemporary issues in Native American spirituality should articulate the purposes of its own enterprise in relation to what has gone before. As a contribution to that end, this paper reviews some of the writing strategies that Native and non-Native authors have used to represent Native American spiritual traditions. It concludes with a discussion of voice, representation, and authority in contemporary writing about Native spirituality.

Spirituality is both intensely personal and distinctively cultural. As an experience, it needs no representation and carries the authority of its own voice. As a cultural phenomenon it has become the subject of scholarly cross-cultural comparison. For Native Americans, spirituality is at the core of an identity that is deeper than ethnicity. Native American spiritual traditions are as indigenous to this land as are the First Peoples themselves. Native spiritual traditions live in song, story, and ceremony. They live in the experiences of those who bring them into being. They live in the dream-space intensity of personal vision and in the shared cosmic ordering of words and actions that people of knowledge perform in ceremony. Songs, stories, and ceremonies have an internal consistency. They represent the way things are. They constitute a language of performance, participation, and experience. They represent the cosmic order within which the world realizes its meaning.

Native Americans did not have to address the issue of representation as we now think of it until they were confronted by people whose traditions were radically different from their own and often radically opposed to them. Indian Nations have both honored differences and celebrated similarities as they met and communicated with one another. As Tagish Athapaskan elder Angela Sidney told Julie Cruikshank, "Well, I've tried to live my life right, just like a story" (Cruikshank 1990:1). Native Americans have always shared stories of spiritual experience between individuals and between nations. They have lived in a world of storied experience. They have lived in conversation with the spiritual. They have brought a world into being through discourse. Movements such as twentieth-century pan-Indianism, the Native American Church, and the nineteenth-century Ghost Dance undoubtedly have analogs in earlier sharings of spiritual and cultural traditions. The Southeastern Ceremonial complex of Mississippian times, for instance, probably reflects a set of social and spiritual symbols that spread throughout the southeast and midwest at the end of the first millennium A.D. (Galloway 1989; Hall 1997).

Traditions flow from aboriginal Nation to Nation through conversation, not through proselytization. As Dennis Tedlock (1999) has pointed out, while Native creation stories bring the world into being through dialogue, dialogues between worlds can lead to destruction when colonizers impose their monologue on indigenous people. In an article on "Creation and the Popol Vuh," he writes, "the continuing growth of creation requires not a series of commands from a single source but an ever-widening discussion" (Tedlock 1983:270). Similarly, he says, ethnographic reporting is often monologic. The ethnographer typically retains strict control over the reader's access to the Native voice and masks the ever-widening discussion that is the ethnographic experience. It is common to hear only what the ethnographer has heard or what he or she wants you to hear, rather than the conversation out of which an understanding emerges.

Ethnographic writing about spirituality inevitably reflects the author's bias as much as it does the aboriginal experience on which it is based. Much of it is uncritical of its own purposes and underlying assumptions. It is framed, consciously or unconsciously, in the discourses of Western religion, science, or spiritual curiosity. As Joel Sherzer points out, Franz Boas, Edward Sapir, and their students insisted on the collection and publication of texts about Native American spirituality but "they were not analyzed as discourse per se" (Sherzer 1987:296). More recently, he says, researchers such as Dell Hymes, Tedlock and Paul Friedrich are recognizing that discourse is "an embodiment of the essence of culture" (Sherzer 1987:297).

NATIVE AMERICAN DISCOURSE

The conversations that create and sustain the world of Native American spirituality "embody the essence" of a different discourse than that of the people who came here from elsewhere. Hymes writes that Native American texts "display ways of speaking, of narrating, that are themselves simultaneously linguistic and cultural" (Hymes 1981:8). "In vain," he reports, Native Americans have "tried to tell" about themselves to outsiders who fail to understand their ways of speaking. He writes: "If we refuse to consider and interpret the surprising facts of device, design, and performance inherent in the words of the texts, the Indians who made the texts, and those who preserved what they said, will have worked in vain" (Hymes 1981:5).

Ronald and Suzanne B. K. Scollon (1979:186) point out that fieldworkers in the subarctic often "find it virtually impossible to follow a discussion or argument" because they lack a shared context of knowledge and experience within which conversation becomes meaningful. In particular, outsiders are unprepared to understand the spirituality of conversations that create a world that is alive with storied voices. Conversation is possible only when storyteller and listener respect and understand one another through shared knowledge and experience. It is possible only when every person can realize a place in every other person's story. It is possible only when the circle of stories includes all the relations of a world that is alive with meaning.

On the other side of the cultural divide, Native Americans often experience the discourse of non-Indians as insistently pushing toward monologue. They resent being interrupted by people who do not recognize the moments of silence that punctuate a speaker's narrative. They are surprised at what appears to be a lack of respect for the sharing that brings a story into being. They are shocked at having their spirituality regarded as primitive. In schools, Native American children are often uncomfortable with the assertive style of discourse their teachers identify as the mark of a "good student." Their skills as respectful listeners go unacknowledged. Sto:lo First Nation scholar and educator Jo-ann Archibald writes about the empowering circle of conversation that characterizes Native American spiritual knowledge:

The movement of power is not hierarchical, as from the teacher (the top) down to the student (the bottom). I picture the movement of power as flowing between concentric circles. The inner circle may represent the words, knowledge itself that expands and moves as it is taught to and shared with others. The other circles may represent the individuals, family, community, nature, nation, and spiritual realm that are influenced and in turn influence this power. I call this knowledge-as-power movement cultural reciprocity grounded in respect and responsibility. Respect is essential. Everyone has a place within the circle. Their place, their role is honored and respected. All also have a particular cultural responsibility to their place, their role: the storyteller-teachers to share their knowledge with others; the listener-learners to make meaning from the storyteller's words and to put this meaning into everyday practice, thereby continuing the action of reciprocity. (White and Archibald 1992:161–62)

The circle of discourse Archibald refers to is at the core of Native American spirituality. Respect operates at every level of conversation. Listening and speaking are of equal importance. What might appear to be a storyteller's monologue is in fact a contribution to the conversation; what Richard Preston has called, "soliloquies [that are] often eloquent and personally expressive as well as culturally meaningful" (Preston 1975:18).

The reciprocity, as Archibald writes, is "to make meaning from the story-teller's words." Listening and speaking are equally authorial activities. Respect for the authority of a speaker prevails across a wide range of First Nations cultures. Words have a physical quality that bridges the space between communicants. First Nations such as the Sto:lo have well-crafted conventions about the circle's formal properties. A speaker's place in relation to others is determined by his or her spiritual authority.[1] In Native American cultures generally, conversational communicants include all sentient beings: animal persons, the voices of natural places and forces, and the voices of those who have gone before. Coyote may be there, too, making fun of it all.

STORIES OF THE VISION QUEST

I can think of no better place to begin a survey of texts representing Native American spirituality than with stories of the vision quest. As Ruth Benedict observed in her 1923 monograph on "The Concept of the Guardian Spirit in North America," the quest for empowerment through visionary transformation is at the heart of spirituality in many Native American societies. What Benedict did not address was the meaning of visionary experience. Her interest was in the distribution of a cultural pattern, not in its reality as an experience. That reality may best be approached through an understanding of Native American oral tradition.

The experience of visionary transformation is fundamental to Native American spirituality. Although it is ultimately personal and begun in isolation, the quest for it is fundamentally conversational and social. Power comes from a person's conversation with the supernatural. It comes from an encounter with sentient beings with whom humans share the breath of life. It appears when a human makes contact with the nonhuman persons of the cosmos. It comes to a person when he or she is humble and pitiable. It comes to children and it comes to adults who make themselves like children. Power comes to people who listen carefully to the storied world around them. It comes when the story of a person's life joins the circle of conversation. Power comes when a person realizes a story that already exists. Power comes when he or she adds a new episode to that story. It comes when the story of a person's life becomes that of life as a whole.

DUNNE-ZA TEXTS

Although I had read about the vision quest and guardian spirit complex as a graduate student in anthropology, my first personal knowledge of this tradition began during the first month of anthropological fieldwork with the Dunne-za of northeastern British Columbia. I was privileged to witness an elder named Japasa tell the story of his childhood vision quest a week before he died. I learned later that, in Dunne-za tradition, a person normally communicates information about his or her spirit friends through symbolically coded action rather than through direct narrative. This story was special because the old man was letting go of the helpers he had known most of his life. His son translated the narrative for me, and I wrote it down in the form of fieldnotes. Later, in a narrative ethnography (Ridington 1988), I described the experience of hearing the old man's story as a pivotal moment in my evolving understanding of Native American spirituality. When I wrote about Japasa's story, I chose to present the text in poetic line-for-line transcription. Johnny Chipesia, the old man's son, narrated the story for me in the third person. The story begins as follows:

My dad said that when he was a boy, about nine years old,
he went into the bush alone.
He was lost from his people. In the night it rained.
He was cold and wet from the rain,
but in the morning he found himself warm and dry.
A pair of silver foxes had come and protected him.
After that, the foxes kept him and looked after him.

He stayed with them and they protected him.
Those foxes had three pups.
The male and female foxes brought food for the pups.
They brought food for my dad too.
They looked after him as if they were all the same.
Those foxes wore clothes like people.
My dad said he could understand their language.
He said they taught him a song. (Ridington 1988:57)

Japasa's story went on to describe how the wind came to him as a person.

That person said,
"See, you're dry now. I'm your friend."
The wind has been his friend ever since.
He can call the wind. He can call the rain.
He can also make them go away.

In Japasa's story, power comes through conversation with natural and spiritual beings who appear as persons. It is negotiated as a social relationship. The spirit helper is a friend, not a superior.

Among the many other stories relating to vision quest experiences that Dunne-za people told me, I recorded one from Mrs. Mary Pouce-Coupe. Her story touches on themes that are similar to Japasa's, but Mrs. Pouce-Coupe's is more generic and archetypal than the one I heard from him. It describes a man's initiation into the powers of a "medicine man."

One time there was a boy who married young.
Maybe he was ten or twelve.
Then his wife and children all died and he was very lonely.
"I will go in the bush," he decided.
"Maybe some monster will kill me there."
He went out.
Every night he would sleep on some animal's trail
without fire.
He wanted to get killed.
"If I had been a medicine man
my wife and children wouldn't have died," he said.
For ten years he stayed out in the bush.
The people all thought he was dead
so they didn't look for him.
But no animals would kill him
so he decided to try to be a medicine man after all.
But no animals would talk to him.

One night he went to sleep in a moose lick.
While he was asleep something woke him up.
He looked up and there was a big fat man.
"What are you doing here," he asked.
"My wife died. My children all died.
For ten years I have been in the bush
hoping some animal would kill me.
For ten years I haven't seen people."
The big fat man leaned down
and put his lips to the man's forehead.
He sucked and drew out blood.
He did the same thing on the back of his head—
and again he drew out blood.
"That's why no animals like you," he said.
"Now you can make friends."
The big fat man took him with him
and he opened a doorway in the lick and they went inside.
The next day he told the man to hunt
and he went out hunting.

Mrs. Pouce-Coupe's story takes the form of conversation reported by a narrator. This genre of narrative with embedded dialogue is typical of Native American oral literature. The form itself is emblematic of the experience of empowerment. Native American oral tradition truly tells of life "lived like a story."

GEORGE NELSON'S NARRATIVE

Because vision quest stories are at the core of Native American spirituality, they occur in narratives by non-Native writers as well as within Native tradition. In 1823, Northwest Company trader George Nelson wrote a journal letter to his father in Montreal describing the spiritual traditions of the Cree-Ojibwa people with whom he lived and worked. He assumed the voice of a third person narrator, describing the Cree in terms of their difference from his own culture.

They make themselves a bed of Grass, or hay as we term it, and have besides enough to make them a covering. When all this is done—and they do it entirely alone, they strip stark naked and put all their things a good way off and then return, ly [sic] on this bed and then cover themselves with the rest of the Grass. Here they remain and endeavor to sleep, which from their nature is no very difficult task. But during whatever time they may remain, they must neither eat or drink. If they want to Dream they may remain, then must neither eat or drink. If they want to Dream of the Spirits above, their bed must be made at some distance from the Ground — if of Spirits inhabiting our Earth, or those residing in the waters, on the Ground. Here they ly [*sic*] for a longer or shorter time, according to their success, or the orders of the Dreamed. (Brown and Brightman 1988:34)

George Nelson touches here on the simultaneously solitary and conversational nature of visionary empowerment. In order to come close to the spirit world, a person must be alone and removed from ordinary events. The spirits that come to a person in dream, he says, deliver messages such as "You will see many winters! Your head will grow quite white" (Brown and Brightman 1988:34). In an editorial aside, Nelson ventures the opinion that, "the language is not very dissimilar to that of our version of the Bible. But the stile [*sic*] seems to me to be the language of Nature." In that language, Nelson observes, "Every thing in nature appears unto them, but in the Shape of a human-being" (35). He goes on to describe a typical conversational encounter:

They dream they meet a man who asks them (after some preliminary conversation, of course), "Dost thou know me? (who or what I am)?"
"No."
"Follow me then," replies this stranger. The indian follows — the other leads him to his abode and again makes the inquiry — the answer is perhaps as before. Then the Stranger assumes his proper form, which is perhaps that of a Tree, a Stone, a fish &c, &c. and after rechanging several times in this manner, till such times as the 2nd becomes perfectly to know him, then this stranger gives him to smoke, learns him his Song, &c, thus addressing him: "Now don't you remember my Song? . . . Whenever you will wish to call upon me, Sing this Song, and I shall not be far — I will come and do for you what you require" (Brown and Brightman 1988:35).

Nelson writes about spiritual empowerment using what appear to be novelistic genre conventions. Against the background of his own voice as omniscient narrator, he inserts a dialogic representation of the conversations that constitute spiritual encounters. Nelson's writing strategy, however, probably reflects the style of Cree narrative as much as it does that of the eighteenth-century novel. Nelson adapted the letter writing of his own culture to the task of representing Cree and Ojibwa narratives. His work is best when it is free of his own interpretive voice.

Nelson's editors, Jennifer S. H. Brown and Robert Brightman, include a commentary on "The Ethics of Publishing Historical Documents" by First Nations scholar Emma LaRocque in their publication of his journal. LaRocque takes Nelson and Western authors generally to task for writing within a framework she calls "the dichotomy of civilization versus savagery" which, she says, "is pervasive in scholarly and popular literature on native peoples." While praising Nelson for the accuracy of his ethnographic detail, she faults him and scholars at large for failing "to accept native thought and organization as of equal worth to European thought while acknowledging the differences" (LaRocque 1988:201). Cree writer Stan Cuthand takes a more charitable view in an essay also included in the volume. It is possible, he says, that Nelson "did not understand the background of these stories in the context of the Atayohkanak [mythical beings called to the shaking tent] because it is almost another language which is used to describe the spirit world." Still, he says, "the events and stories he relates are compelling. . . . George Nelson's text is like a voice out of the past reminding us of our spiritual history" (Cuthand 1988:197–98).

HARRY ROBINSON'S STORIES ABOUT NATURE POWER

Nelson wrote in 1823. He identified the style of Cree stories as "the language of Nature." More than a century and a half later, anthropologist Wendy Wickwire used the term "Nature Power" to title the second volume of stories by Okanagan elder, Harry Robinson. Nature power, she says, is "the life-sustaining spirituality that guided Harry throughout his life" (Robinson 1992:10). According to Wickwire, "the very concept of fiction was foreign to him" (Robinson 1992). Robinson's stories, like all stories of spiritual encounters, are true. Robinson describes these encounters as follows: "You got to have power. You got to, the kids, you know. They got to meet the animal, you know, when they was little. Can be anytime till it's five years old to ten years old. He's supposed to meet animal or bird, or anything, you know. And this animal, whoever they meet, got to talk to 'em and tell 'em what they should do. Later on, not right away. And that is his power" (Robinson 1992:10).

Robinson's work is remarkable because he told the stories in English, using the Okanagan narrative style with which he was familiar. His work is also remarkable simply for his mastery of the genre. Native author Thomas King says of Robinson: "I couldn't believe the power and the skill with which Robinson could work up a story, in English, (they weren't translated, they were just simply transcribed) and how well he understood the power of the oral voice in a written piece" (Interview with Peter Gzowski, CBC Radio, April 5, 1993).

Robinson's stories embed direct discourse dialogue within the text of an omniscient third person narrator. As in the story told by Mrs. Pouce-Coupe, Robinson uses his own voice to carry the narrative line and cites the voices of characters in the story as directly quoted dialogue. The result is vivid and compelling. "I can go for twenty-one hours or more when I get started," Harry told Wendy, "because this is my job. I'm a storyteller" (Robinson 1992:7).

One of the stories in *Nature Power* tells about a boy who was taken out to gain power from a stump that had survived for centuries in an avalanche-strewn gully. The hunters he was traveling with told the boy:

You stay here.
You wait here.
It's too far for you to walk.
You stay 'round here.
We can hunt that way, make a turn
and a circle
and then we come back.
Towards evening we come by
and then you can go back with us to the camp.

Harry's story is vivid with the authority of narrated first person discourse.
The boy stays until he sees a chipmunk who appears to him as another boy.
The boy/animal speaks to him as a friend and guardian spirit.

You my friend.
You boy, and I'm a boy.
We both boy.
So, it's better to be friends instead of making fun out of me.
Now, I'm going to tell you something.
This stump—you think it's a stump—
but that's my grandfather.
He's very, very old man.
Old, old man.
He can talk to you.
He can tell you what you going to be.

In Harry's story the boy gains power and identity from an animal, from a
boy like himself, and from a grandfather. Because the stump has survived for
a long time, it has the authority of an elder. Because it is home to a chipmunk,
it shares in that animal's life. Because the boy is open to its conversations, the
stump is also a boy like himself. The empowering conversation is multivocal.
From the old man, the boy learns of the stump's power to ward off bullets:

You see me.
You see my body.
It was hit by the bullet for many, many years.
Hit by the bullet.
That's why you could see, all smooth.
That's the bullet marks.
And the bullet, when they hit me—the bullet—
they never go through my skin.
They never go through my body.
For a long, long time.

You know how old I was.
I been hit with a bullet for many years.
I never get killed. (Robinson 1992:27–29)

In Harry's narrative, spirit helpers appear as voices in conversation. As in the other vision quest stories, power comes through a person's storied conversation with the spiritual powers surrounding him. All of Harry's stories are true. As Wickwire explains, "the truth and accuracy of Harry's words in Nature Power have made me think anew about what is 'real' and what we 'know' . . . The people in Harry's stories experienced nature deeply and directly in a way that I cannot know, but that Harry wanted me, and others, to appreciate" (Robinson 1992:20).

STORIES TOLD BY ETHNOGRAPHERS

Ethnographers are professional narrators. Their job is to find a language in which to explain the life of another culture. More often than not, as Tedlock and others have observed, that language has tended to be a monologue that masks the dialogue from which it derives its information. Mikhail Bakhtin writes that "monologism, at its extreme, denies the existence outside itself of another consciousness with equal rights and equal responsibilities." While he is writing about novelistic literary strategies rather than those used by ethnographers, his observations provide a critical perspective on conventional ethnographic writing. Monologue, he says, "pretends to be the ultimate word. It closes down the represented world and represented persons" (Bakhtin 1984:292–93). Ethnographic monologue is almost a contradiction in terms. Unlike fiction, ethnography is by definition a communication between cultures. Like Harry Robinson's stories, ethnographic narratives must be true stories. To illustrate this point, I will cite only a few examples of monologic ethnographic writing about Native American spirituality. I chose them largely because I think they were original and important at the time they were written. I will also cite some examples of ethnographic writing that is the product of shared ethnographic authority and a freer use of the dialogic imagination.

TALES FROM ZUNI

One of the first professional ethnographic studies of a Native American spiritual tradition was Frank Hamilton Cushing's "Zuni Fetiches," published in 1883 in the *Second Annual Report of the Bureau of [American] Ethnology*. Cushing began his study with an attempt to explain what he called "Zuni Philosophy." He was unusual for his time in recognizing that Native American spiritual traditions can be understood as a systematic philosophy, but his opening words are a dense authorial monologue compressed into a single sentence. "The Ashiwi, or Zunis, suppose the sun, moon and stars, the sky, earth, and sea, in all their phenomena and elements; and all inanimate objects, as well as plants, animals, and men, to belong to one great system of all-conscious and interrelated life, in which the degrees of relationship seem to be determined largely, if not wholly, by the degrees of resemblance" (Cushing 1883:9).

This kind of writing requires careful study, in the way that a complex Latin passage is worthy of study. This is a written text, not a spoken one, although Cushing's mentor, Spencer F. Baird, reports that he may have dictated it to a stenographer (Green 1990:222). His study of Zuni Fetiches is important, for it is the first attempt by an anthropologist to represent a Native American philosophical system in terms of its own conceptual categories. What it lacks, however, is the Zuni poetics through which these categories become real to "the represented world and represented persons."

More than a century later, Dennis Tedlock published a volume of Zuni narrative poetry, *Finding the Center* (1972). In contrast to Cushing's self-centered monologue, Tedlock's work is the product of an ethnographic authority he shares with storytellers Andrew Peynetsa and Walter Sanchez. Tedlock conveys a sense of orality and actuality in his written presentation of translated Zuni oral texts. He invites the reader to lend his or her own voice to a reading of them. In Tedlock's rendition, you hear the verbal styling of Andrew Peynetsa. You experience him as "another consciousness with equal rights and equal responsibilities," not simply an ethnographic other. A scene from the story of "The Boy and The Deer" describes the spiritual encounter of a deer mother entering a Kachina village:

> And their mother went to Kachina Village, she went o— —n until she reached Kachina village.
> It was filled with dancing kachinas "My fathers, my children, how have you been passing the days?" "Happily, our child, so you've come, sit down," they said.
> "Wait, stop your dancing, our child has come and must have something to say," then the kachinas stopped.
> The deer sat down
> > the old lady deer sat down.
> A kachina priest spoke to her:
> "Now speak. You must've come because you have something to say."
> > "YES, in TRUTH
> I have come because I have something to SAY." (Tedlock 1972:7–8)

Tedlock's *Finding the Center* presents Deer woman as a person with "something to say." Almost twenty years later, his essay, "The Speaker of Tales Has More than One String to Play On," (Tedlock 1991) playfully and respectfully presents both scholars and Native American storytellers as people in conversation who have something to say together. As a way of critiquing Albert Lord's thesis that Homeric narrative is the archetypal form of oral discourse, Tedlock braids his own voice with a canonical Zuni text, about "a time so remote that newness was being made."

> "The Word of Kyaklo"
> which is recited every four years or so
> is the official, canonical version of the story of newness
> not produced by oral formulaic composition
> but repeated verbatim
> by a masked performer who studies for the part for a year.
> The other is a hearthside interpretation of the story of newness
> and partly redrawn, or resounded, edited and elaborated
> by a particular narrator
> Andrew Peynetsa
> on a particular occasion.

He concludes:

> Tales have no canonical versions
> no Kyaklo who recites them verbatim.
> They exist only
> in the form of interpretations
> and it takes a multiplicity of voices to tell them.
> Andrew Peynetsa was skilled at telling tales, and that's why he was able to
>   change the monotonous chant of Kyaklo into a decent story. (Tedlock
>   1991:338)

THE OMAHA TRIBE

The Omaha Tribe by Alice C. Fletcher and Francis La Flesche (1911) is another important classic ethnography. It is a comprehensive documentation of a Plains tribe's ceremonial life during the nineteenth century. It is also important because it is jointly authored by an Omaha anthropologist and an outsider. Passages written by Fletcher assume the voice of a third-person narrator, while La Flesche gives a first-person autobiographical narrative. Fletcher wrote, like Cushing, in an attempt to explain Native American philosophy. Her prose is powerfully evocative when she writes about a universal life force the Omahas know as *wakon'da*. In a particularly beautiful passage, Fletcher describes her understanding of this central concept of Omaha spirituality. I have chosen to render it poetically, line for line, because it deserves to be read as Fletcher's engagement with Omaha spiritual principles. While monologic in form, it clearly reflects a respectful dialogue with Omaha spirituality, mediated by her coauthor and adopted son, Francis La Flesche.

> An invisible and continuous life
> permeates all things, seen and unseen.
> This life manifests itself in two ways:
> first, by causing to move;
> all motion, all actions of mind or body,
> are because of this invisible life;
> second, by causing permanency
> of structure and form,
> as in the rock, the physical features
> of the landscape, mountains, plains, streams,
> rivers, lakes, the animals and man.
> This invisible life
> is similar to the will power
> of which man is conscious
> within himself,
> a power by which things are brought to pass.
> Through this mysterious life and power
> all things are related to one another
> and to man;
> the seen to the unseen,
> the dead to the living,
> a fragment of anything
> to its entirety.
> This invisible life and power
> is called wakon'da.
> (adapted from Fletcher and La Flesche 1911:134)

In contrast to Fletcher's statement of abstract principles, La Flesche's contribution to the coauthored ethnography is a narrative from his memory of ceremonies he participated in as a boy. In his wistful first-person "boy memory of these ancient ceremonies of the Sacred Pole, now forever gone," La Flesche identifies himself as "the only living witness who is able to picture in English these far-away scenes" (Fletcher and La Flesche 1911:245). He leaves generalization to his reader:

When every family in the tribe excepting those of the hon'ga gens had thus been called upon to make an offering, the priests began to sing the songs pertaining to this peculiar ceremony. I was now very much interested and watched every movement of the men who officiated. Four of the fattest pieces of meat were selected and placed just at the foot of the Sacred Pole. A song was sung and a man stood ready with a knife near the meat; when the last note died out the man made a feint at cutting and then resumed his position. Three times the song was repeated with its accompanying act, when on the fourth time the man in great haste carved out all of the fat from the four pieces of choice meat and put it in a wooden bowl. After the fat had been mixed with burnt clay and kneaded into a paste, another song was sung, and the same priest stood ready with bowl and brush in hand beside the Pole. At the close of the song he made a feint at the Pole with the brush and resumed his former position. Four times this song was sung, each time followed by a feint. Then a new stanza was sung, at the end of which the priest touched the Pole lightly with his brush the entire length. This song and act were repeated four times. Then a different song was sung, the words of which I can remember even to this day: "I make him beautiful! I make him beautiful!" Then the priest with great haste dipped his brush into the bowl and daubed the Pole with the paste while the singing was going on. Four times the song was sung, the anointing was finished, and the Pole stood shining in fresh paint. Then many of the people cried: "Oh! how beautiful he is!" and then laughed, but the priests never for an instant changed the expression of their faces. I did not know whether to join in the merriment or to imitate the priests and maintain a serious countenance; but while I stood thus puzzled the ceremony went on.

A SACRED OBJECT AS TEXT: BLESSING FOR A LONG TIME

Ceremonies honoring the Pole re-create a spiritual language that may well go back millennia (Hall 1997:102–7). They provide readings of this sacred object as a cultural and historical text. The Pole is both a storied person and the center of a circle of stories. Each reading of the Pole in ceremony evokes conversations that create and sustain Omaha spiritual life. The son of an Omaha chief long ago read what was to become the Sacred Pole as "a wonderful tree." His father read the same object as "a tree that stands burning." The older man understood it as a sacred place where "the Thunder birds come and go . . . making a trail of fire that leaves four paths on the burnt grass that stretch toward the Four Winds." The Pole is now a person who stands for all the people. He spoke directly to a generation undergoing change and dislocation in early historic times. He continues to speak to contemporary Omahas, who call him Umon'hon'ti, "The Real Omaha." He is a metonym, a person who stands for all Omahas. The Sacred Pole has been a voice of shared authority within the Omaha tribe since a chief's son first encountered "a wonderful tree." The chiefs recognized him as center toward which all members of the tribe could turn: "You now see before you a mystery. Whenever we meet with troubles we shall bring all our troubles to Him (The Pole). We shall make offerings and requests. All our prayers must be accompanied by gifts. This (The Pole) belongs to all the people, but it shall be in the keeping of one family in the Honga clan" (Fletcher and La Flesche 1911:219). Umon'hon'ti represents the idea of a tribal center toward whom each family and clan may turn for direction. When the Peabody Museum returned him to the tribe in 1989, elder Lawrence Gilpin spoke to the people assembled in the tribal arena. He reminded Omahas that: "It belongs to you, each one, each Omaha that is here. You have an undivided interest in this Sacred Pole." Following his talk in English, he began a prayer to Wakon'da by speaking directly to *Umon'hon'ti* in the Omaha language. His sister, Elsie Morris, translated his words as follows:

> Aho! Umon'hon'ti!
> Umon'hon'ti!
> We're humble people in the Omaha village
> That you have come home to.
> Today you have come home.
> There's a few words I want to say to Wakon'da.
> Umon'hon'ti.
> You have come home to the Omaha camp.
> I am very happy that you have come home.
> Umon'hon'ti,
> I am very happy that you have come home today
> To our poor, humble reservation.
> And towards Wakon'da, I'm going to say a few words.
> (Ridington and Hastings 1998:174–75)

Fletcher and La Flesche shared authority with Omaha elders and with one another in writing their classic 1911 ethnography. Dennis Hastings and I collaborated with tribal members and academics to tell the story of the Sacred Pole's return. The story we told in our 1997 book is our reading of written texts, recorded speech events and the Sacred Pole himself. Like Umon'hon'ti, each story in a circle of stories is both a fragment and entirety. In our introduction we wrote:

Indian stories do not begin and end like the lines of words that make up a book. Rather, they start and stop at meaningful points within a circle. Stories, songs and ceremonies constitute a body of tribal literature, passed down from generation to generation. Omaha tribal historian Dennis Hastings and I are writing a book, but we are also telling a story that connects to the tribe's body of knowledge. We will try to stop at meaningful points in the story and start again as one story suggests another. Each story suggests every story. Each story contains an essence shared by all. Each story is both a fragment and an entirety. (Ridington and Hastings 1997:xvii)

Beginning with the pioneering novels of D'Arcy McNickle, Native American novelists and biographers have told true stories about how the lives of individuals continue to exist in conversation with spiritual traditions. Those well-known today include N. Scott Momaday, Leslie Marmon Silko, James Welch, Louise Erdrich, Gerald Vizenor, Louis Owens, Thomas King, Tomson Highway, Jeannette Armstrong, and Greg Sarris. I will focus on three members of this group, Silko, Sarris, and King.

Leslie Marmon Silko
Leslie Marmon Silko's novel, *Ceremony*, begins with the lines:

> Ts'its'tsi'nako, Thought-Woman
> is sitting in her room
> and whatever she thinks about
> appears.
>
> . . . . . .
>
> She is sitting in her room
> thinking of a story now
> I'm telling you the story
> she is thinking.
> (Silko 1977:1)

The idea that thought and substance combine in the creation of storied lives is central to Native American spirituality. Interspersed between episodes describing the life of Tayo, a young Laguna man who has been damaged by World War II, Silko inserts episodes of Laguna narrative, many of which may also be found in Boas's 1928 *Keresan Texts*. Unlike Boas, who collected the stories but did not contextualize them, Silko weaves them into Thought-Woman's narrative creation of the world. Like Harry Robinson's stories of nature power, those of Thought-Woman must be taken as true stories rather than fiction. Silko's novel takes the reader through stories of creation and destruction. She blends episodes from stories of Fly and Hummingbird with those of Tayo's quest to restore the rains. This quest leads to a visionary encounter with Yellow Woman, a spiritual being who dwells on the sacred mountain that centers the Laguna universe. Mythical and personal stories become one when Tayo speaks to elders in the Kiva at the time of winter solstice. Once again, narrative recreates the world: "It took a long time to tell them the story; they stopped him frequently with questions about the location and the time of day; they asked about the direction she had come from and the color of her eyes. It was while he was sitting there, facing southeast, that he noticed how the four windows along the south wall of the kiva had a particular relationship to this late autumn position of the sun" (Silko 1977:257).

Greg Sarris

On the dust jacket of *Mabel McKay* (1994), by mixed-blood author Greg Sarris, Leslie Marmon Silko writes: "Greg Sarris's biography of Mabel McKay is wonderful, and is urgently needed in these days of confusion of Native American identity and Native American spirituality. As charlatan "medicine people" proliferate, and make huge profits from their chicanery, Mabel's story shows us the truth about the ways in which the spirit voices manifest themselves."

Sarris entitles section 3 of this four-part weaving of biography and autobiography, "Medicine Woman," thus reclaiming the fraudulent and appropriative use of the phrase by Lynn Andrews (see below). Like the other stories of spirituality cited above, Sarris writes about Mabel McKay's empowerment as an authorial narrative embedded with direct discourse dialogue. The following passage illustrates Sarris's style and the conversation through which Mabel McKay gained her power.

Mabel slept for days. Sarah couldn't wake her. It was hot, summertime in the valley, and Mabel was feverish. Sarah prayed. "Oh, if my father was living you wouldn't be like this," she kept saying.

Then, in the middle of a hot afternoon, Mabel heard the screen door slam. She opened her eyes and saw a hummingbird fly in. It hovered over her. She saw that it had the face of a man. "Hello, Mabel," he said. He introduced himself, telling her his name. "You've seen me before. I've been following you, hiding here and there. Spirit told me to watch until you were ready."

"Where did I see you before?" Mabel asked, uttering her first words in days. She squinted her eyes and studied the man's dark wrinkled face. She was certain she didn't know him.

"When you were little I came and took you to a cave where an old woman ground poison on a red rock . . ."

Mabel nodded, remembering the small colorful bird that appeared before her on a willow branch while she sat by the creek waiting for Sarah. A hummingbird, she thought, looking up at the scarlet throat and metallic green body of the bird flying in place above her.

" . . . Yes, and you refused me . . . You need to know about the poison and lots of other things. You're ready now to become a doctor. So now it's time. You need someone to help you with things on earth. So here I am. Will you accept my help now?" (Sarris 1994:69–70)

Sarris's work is both biographical and novelistic. It engages outsiders in the discourse of Native American spirituality in a way that ethnographic monologue seldom achieves. Silko is correct in calling for writing that "shows us the truth about the ways in which the spirit voices manifest themselves."

Thomas King

Green Grass, Running Water is King's reading of North American literature, literary theory, Native American history, and popular culture through the images and genre conventions of American Indian oral tradition. No single reader will understand all the references, since the communities with which he shares experience include Indians and academics, Americans and Canadians, mythic characters and friends. King contextualizes his story within a multitude of biographies and experiences. By crossing borders, King also expands them. Just as Herman Melville read the Bible, Shakespeare, and classical mythology into an American whaling saga, King reads all of the above as well as Melville, Northrop Frye, James Fenimore Cooper, John Wayne, and a host of other literary and cultural icons into a quartet of American Indian creation cycles as seen through the juggled eyes of Coyote.

What would happen, King asks, if Coyote rather than Jehovah created the world? What would happen if Jehovah turned out to be Joseph Hovaugh, the head doctor in a mental institution for old Indians? What would happen if an Indian author read the canon of white history through the narrative conventions of Indian history? The first thing that would happen, in King's version of the story, is that Coyote would be asleep and fall into conversation with his own dream. Creation, as Tedlock points out, has to begin with dialogue.

King acknowledges that Harry Robinson influenced the narrative voice he used in the novel. Both storytellers delight in making conversation with Coyote. In "Write It on Your Heart," Robinson tells a coyote creation story about names and identities. King's Coyote enters a similar creative dialogue with himself:

> Who are you? says that Dream. Are you someone important?
> "I'm Coyote," says Coyote. "And I am very smart."
> I am very smart too, says that Dream. I must be Coyote.
> "No," says Coyote. "You can't be Coyote. But you can be a dog."
> Are dogs smart? says that Dream.
> "You bet," says Coyote. "Dogs are good. They are almost as good as Coyote."
> Okay, says that Dream. I can do that.
> But when that Coyote Dream thinks about being a dog, it gets everything mixed up. It gets everything backward. (King 1993:1–2)

Following Coyote's opening dialogue with his dog dream, the rest of the book carries on a series of conversations that attempt to make the world right again. These conversations appear as the stories of First Woman, Changing Woman,

Thought Woman, and Old Woman, four mythic persons from Native American tradition. In the novel, these goddess figures first appear disguised as four old Indians named The Lone Ranger, Ishmael, Robinson Crusoe, and Hawkeye, who have escaped from a mental institution run by Dr. Hovaugh. Like Coyote in Harry Robinson's story, these creators play with names and the stories they invoke. Also like Coyote, Thomas King plays with a multitude of mutually intersecting stories. Some of the stories he cites are classic Native American myths. Some of them are from the canon of Western literary tradition. Some are from the lives of fictional characters who live only within the world of King's writing.

Green Grass, Running Water is set in the town of Blossom, Alberta. A central figure in the book is Blackfoot English professor Alberta Frank. The book ends as Alberta becomes pregnant at the sundance. Beyond King's coyote tricks, the spiritual message of *Green Grass, Running Water* is that of a sundance renewal. Blossom Alberta. As both coyotes and English professors know, the placement of a coma can change the meaning of words and the world.

FRAUDS AND DECEPTIONS

Not all of the books purporting to represent Native American spirituality are true stories. Indeed, some of the most popular "new age" books about Indian spiritual tradition are patently fraudulent and shamelessly appropriative. *Medicine Woman* by Lynn Andrews (1981) is a case in point. In a typical passage, she claims to represent her own empowerment by the "medicine woman," Agnes Whistling Elk.

Agnes smiled at me. "You are a black wolf."

She watched my reaction and then put out a hand and touched my forehead. "Waken within yourself." She took her finger away. The touch gave me a peculiar sensation throughout my body. (Andrews 1981:106)

Both internal and external evidence suggest that Andrews and her then partner, David Carson, set out to create "the next, female, Castaneda," perhaps even consciously loading the narrative with anachronism and cliche (Adolph and Smoley 1989:26). Native American activist Russell Means has reacted to such commercialization of Native American spirituality by saying: "When they wanted our land, they just announced that they had a right to it and therefore owned it. Now, being spiritually bankrupt themselves, they want our spirituality as well" (quoted in Adolph and Smoley 1989:97).

More subtle examples of the genre are *Lame Deer, Seeker of Visions* (1972) and *Lakota Woman* (1991) by Richard Erdoes and Native coauthors James Fire Lame Deer and Mary Crow Dog respectively. As Julian Rice points out in an article called "A Ventriloquy of Anthros: Densmore, Dorsey, Lame Deer, and Erdoes," ghost writer Erdoes "speaks less to enlighten than to preserve the illusion of a heroic presence with whom everyone will identify and whose wisdom everyone will buy." He uses "a Euroamerican journalistic tradition with an antithetical agenda—to create characters and events that will sell as many books as possible" (Rice 1994:169–70). What is particularly interesting, according to Rice, is that "the real authors of much of the culturally authentic material in Lame Deer" are ethnographers James Owen Dorsey, Francis Densmore, and Eugene Buechel, all of whom collected compelling first person accounts of Lakota ceremonial life and spirituality. Rice observes, "whereas an oral narrator uses story elements from the past to enlighten the present, Erdoes uses the written record to preserve an image and to fulfill the yearnings of the disaffected youth he projects" (Rice 1994:170).

Even a Native American author can appropriate and misrepresent Native American spirituality, as Hyemeyohsts Storm's recent *Lightningbolt* (1994) amply demonstrates. In an act of astonishing appropriation, Storm reworks virtually every Native American tradition to his fancifully autobiographical monologue. At one point in the narrative he claims that "the early settlements and Kivas found throughout Utah, Arizona, Colorado, and New Mexico are the work of the intermarried peoples of the Temple Doors [people he claims brought "the Great Circle of Law and all the Medicine Wheels to the North"] and Sweet Medicine ["blue-eyed fair-haired" Vikings whom the Cree and Northern Cheyenne referred to as "White Water Spider"] (Storm 1994:314–23). The synthesis is brilliant, creating as it does the opportunity for "new-age" white people to claim authorship of even the most venerable of Native American spiritual traditions. Storm puts it all up for sale but pays the heavy price of losing touch with the real story of his own life.

A REPRISE OF REAL VOICES

The sun, moon and stars, the sky, earth, and sea, in all their phenomena and elements; and all inanimate objects, as well as plants, animals, and men, to belong to one great system of all-conscious and interrelated life. (Cushing 1883:9)

An invisible and continuous life
permeates all things, seen and unseen.
(Fletcher and La Flesche 1911:134)

"Now speak.
You must've come because you have something to say."
"YES, in TRUTH
I have come because I have something to SAY. (Tedlock 1972:7–8)

Ts'its'tsi'nako, Thought-Woman
  is sitting in her room
and whatever she thinks about
  appears.
  (Silko 1977:1)

Respect is essential. Everyone has a place within the circle. Their place, their role is honored and respected. All also have a particular cultural responsibility to their place, their role: the storyteller-teachers to share their knowledge with others; the listener-learners to make meaning from the storyteller's words and to put this meaning into everyday practice, thereby continuing the action of reciprocity. (White and Archibald 1992:161–62)

As Bakhtin observed, "Life by its very nature is dialogic. To live means to participate in dialogue." Native American spirituality manifests itself as an ordered, sometimes ecstatic, always respectful conversation with the myriad persons of a sentient universe. It comes into being when an individual's experience becomes part of that storied life. Respect is essential to the act of creation. The boy in Harry Robinson's story respects the chipmunk who tells him that a weathered stump is his grandfather. The spirit helper is a respected friend, not a superior. The wind came to Japasa as a person. It has been his friend ever since they first met. Silko's Thought Woman creates a story that a troubled young man can realize in the ceremonial directions of his own storied life. Mabel McKay remembers "the small colorful bird that appeared before her on a willow branch while she sat by the creek." Much later, she knew that it was time to resume the conversation and accept "someone to help you with things on earth" (Sarris 1994:69–70). The dialogue of Native American spirituality takes place through respectful listening and learning. As Jo-ann Archibald observed, listener-learners "make meaning from the storyteller's words and . . . put this meaning into everyday practice" (1992:161–62).

Writing about Native American spirituality is successful to the extent that it is both intelligent and respectful. It fails when it appropriates spiritual dialogue to an alien monologue. It does worse than fail when it fraudulently misrepresents Native American experience to satisfy the romantic fantasies of people who lack the knowledge and understanding required to be good listeners. Whether reported by anthropologists or set out by Native American writers themselves, the best representations have been those that give voice to people who try to live their lives right, "just like a story." The stories that have come down to us tell about a circle of relations. They tell about a respectful circle of dialogue. In Indian Country today, events are often punctuated with the words: All My Relations.

NOTE

1. Some of the ideas in this section came from a conversation with Ed Labenski regarding his documentation of the stories of Sto:lo war veterans.

REFERENCES

Adolph, Jonathan and Richard Smoley. 1989. Beverly Hills Shaman. *New Age* (March/ April).

Andrews, Lynn. 1981. *Medicine Woman.* New York: Harper and Row.

Bakhtin, Mikhail. 1984. *Problems of Dostoevsky's Poetics.* Ed. and trans. Caryl Emerson. Minneapolis: University of Minnesota Press.

Boas, Franz. 1928. Keresan Texts. *Publications of the American Ethnological Society* 8(1). New York: American Ethnological Society.

Benedict, Ruth. 1923. The Concept of the Guardian Spirit in North America. *Memoirs of the American Anthropological Association,* 29.

Brown, Jennifer S. H., and Robert Brightman. 1988. *"The Orders of the Dreamed": George Nelson on Cree and Northern Ojibwa Religion and Myth, 1823.* Winnipeg: University of Manitoba Press.

Crow Dog, Mary, and Richard Erdoes. 1991. *Lakota Woman.* New York: Harper Perennial.

Cruikshank, Julie, in collaboration with Angela Sidney, Kitty Smith and Annie Ned. 1990. *Life Lived Like a Story: Life Stories of Three Yukon Elders.* Lincoln: University of Nebraska Press.

Cushing, Frank Hamilton. 1883. Zuni Fetiches. *Second Annual Report of the Bureau of Ethnology, 1880–1881,* 9–45.

Cuthand, Stan. 1988. On Nelson's Text. In Brown and Brightman.

Fletcher, Alice C. and Francis La Flesche. 1911. The Omaha Tribe. *Twenty-seventh Annual Report of the Bureau of American Ethnology, 1905–1906.*

Galloway, Patricia. 1989. *The Southeastern Ceremonial Complex: Artifacts and Analysis.* Lincoln: University of Nebraska Press.

Green, Jesse. 1990. *Cushing at Zuni: The Correspondence and Journals of Frank Hamilton Cushing.* Albuquerque: University of New Mexico Press.

Hall, Robert L. 1997. *An Archaeology of the Soul: North American Indian Belief and Ritual.* Urbana: University of Illinois Press.

Hymes, Dell. 1981. *In Vain I Tried to Tell You: Essays in Native American Ethnopoetics.* Philadelphia: University of Pennsylvania Press.

King, Thomas. 1993. *Green Grass, Running Water.* Toronto: Harper Collins.

Lame Deer, John Fire and Richard Erdoes. 1972. *Lame Deer Seeker of Visions: The Life of a Sioux Medicine Man.* New York: Simon and Schuster Touchstone.

LaRocque, Emma. 1988. The Ethics of Publishing Historical Documents. In Brown and Brightman.

Preston, Richard. 1975. *Cree Narrative: Expressing the Personal Meanings of Events.* Mercury Series Paper No. 30. Ottawa: National Museum of Man.

Rice, Julian. 1994. A Ventriloquy of Anthros: Densmore, Dorsey, Lame Deer, and Erdoes. *American Indian Quarterly* 18(2):169–96.

Ridington, Robin. 1988. *Trail to Heaven: Knowledge and Narrative in a Northern Native Community.* Iowa City: University of Iowa Press.

———. 1993. A Sacred Object as Text: Reclaiming the Omaha Tribe. *American Indian Quarterly* 17(1):83–99.

Ridington, Robin, and Dennis Hastings. 1997. *Blessing for a Long Time: The Sacred Pole of the Omaha Tribe.* Lincoln: University of Nebraska Press.

Robinson, Harry. 1992. *Nature Power: In the Spirit of an Okanagan Storyteller.* Comp. and ed. Wendy Wickwire. Vancouver: Douglas and McIntyre.

Sarris, Greg. 1994. *Mabel McKay: Weaving the Dream.* Berkeley: University of California Press.

Scollon, Ronald, and Suzanne B. K. Scollon. 1976. *Linguistic Convergence: An Ethnography of Speaking at Fort Chipewyan, Alberta.* London: Academic Press.

Sherzer, Joel. 1987. A Discourse-Centered Approach to Language and Culture. *American Anthropologist* 89(2):295–309.

Silko, Leslie Marmon. 1977. *Ceremony.* New York: Viking Penguin.

Storm, Hyemeyohsts. 1994. *Lightningbolt.* New York: Ballantine.

Tedlock, Dennis. 1972. *Finding the Center: Narrative Poetry of the Zuni Indians.* New York: The Dial Press.

———. 1983. *The Spoken Word and the Work of Interpretation.* Philadelphia: University of Pennsylvania Press.

———. 1991. The Speaker of Tales Has More Than One String to Play On. In *Anthropological Poetics*, ed. Ivan Brady. Savage MD: Rowman & Littlefield. 309–40.

———. 1999. Dialogues between Worlds: Mesoamerica After and Before the European Invasion. In *Theorizing the Americanist Tradition*, ed. Regna Darnell and Lisa Valentine. Toronto: University of Toronto Press.

White, Ellen, and Jo-ann Archibald. 1992. Kwulasulwut S yuth [Ellen White's Teachings]: Collaboration between Ellen White and Jo-ann Archibald. *Canadian Journal of Native Education* 19(2).

Pimadaziwin

Contemporary Rituals in Odawa Community

MELISSA A. PFLÜG

From ongoing fieldwork, I have learned that some Algonkian-speaking Odawa Indians in the Great Lakes region support actions aimed at reclaiming sovereign identity by engaging in traditional behaviors and values. Currently, people who call themselves Odawa "traditionalists" are acting to overcome a long-term process of socioreligious marginalization. This marginal social identity has been imposed on them by Euroamericans and largely derives from loss of land and language. To counter these severe threats to a unique Odawa identity, traditionalists look to a *corpus* of rituals as a powerful means to uphold the integrity of their community. We will see that rituals locate the attributes of religious actions and values in the practice of ethical cooperation among caring and sensitive people. This article articulates the theme that one way Odawa traditionalists enhance and reinforce social relations and sociocultural status is by enacting the value of empowerment contained in collective moral behavior and carefully considered acts of giving.

Traditionalists like Great Elk aim for *pimadaziwin*, which A. Irving Hallowell identifies as the central value that organizes all Algonkians' lives and the core of their worldview.[1] Hallowell defines *pimadaziwin* as The Good Life, "a long life and a life free from illness and other misfortune," a life of longevity and well-being (1955:104). *Pimadaziwin* counters such socially disapproved and collectively disruptive acts as inhospitality, stinginess, greediness, and, especially, ridicule. He tells us that achieving this goal requires constructive interaction on the part of each person with "dream visitors" who confer power on the individual to overcome personal adversity (1955: 121). Hallowell also relates that:

pimadaziwin [can] only be achieved by individuals who [seek] and obtain . . . the help of superhuman entities and who conduct . . . themselves in a socially approved manner . . . it is important to note that superhuman help [is] sought in solitude, that the "blessing" or "gift" [can] not be compelled, but [is] bestowed because the superhuman entities [take] "pity" upon the suppliant who, in effect, ask[s] for Life (i.e., pimadaziwin) (1955: 360).

Important as this insight is, Hallowell does not address the significance of "superhuman" and human agents mutually interacting to uphold The Good Life. As a behavioralist, Hallowell locates the goal of *pimadaziwin*, and its harmonious state-of-being, within the self and as an individually driven motivation (1955: 174). By doing so, however, he overlooks, or at least underplays, how the value of *pimadaziwin* informs the interrelational nature of the Algonkian socio-cosmos.

Lone Wolf is informative about this interrelational nature of the socio-cosmos and the value *pimadaziwin*. When I asked him about how he approaches the world and identifies his place in it, Lone Wolf replied while sketching on the ground a kind of interpersonalistic cosmographic map:

I see myself standing here in the center, and immediately encircling me is my family. Surrounding them are all our family members. Out from them are those who share my clan dodem. In a wider circle are all Odawa.

Encircling them are all Indian peoples, then all people. Around them are all the ancestors. Out from them are the animals and plants. Then come A-ki [Earth], Mishomis [Sun] and Nokomis [Moon]. The next largest circle are the great powers, or *manidos*. It's everyone's job to keep these relationships held together, across all the circles, and from their own place as center.

When all are connected, that's what we mean when we say, *Mino gwayako pima'adizi*, "he lives a good and honest life."

As Lone Wolf's cosmography suggests, ethical beings who make up the world—what Hallowell calls both human-persons and other-than-human persons, including the ancestors—give to the human-person and community, and the ethical person and community give back to them. This exchange maintains a continual connection among all ethical persons, human and otherwise.

We can see from Lone Wolf's description that the spectrum of relationships is ever-expanding. Thus, I suggest that for Algonkians, like the Odawa, the central purpose of each person is to behave morally in order to uphold *pimadaziwin* on a collective level of positive interpersonal relations. For Odawa traditionalists, *pimadaziwin* has much more to do with collective social identity and moral integrity than Hallowell seems to realize from his Ojibwe study. From Lone Wolf's statement, we can begin to see that Odawa traditionalists understand *pimadaziwin* as a state of being that every person, human and otherwise, ethically is charged with upholding. Each person doing so contributes to the goal of attaining a good, healthy and interactive moral life for the collective and, therefore, a unique and empowered sense of community.

Traditionalists underscore the relational nature of socio-cosmic life. Black Bear explained:

The gift has spiritual power, *gi-be manidoowaadese*. Power is in everything through Ki-je Manido, Grandfather, the Great Power-Person. It is in the burning of tobacco that we offer Ki-je Manido and the many *manidos*, or little grandfathers. It's in the prayers for me and the food eaten for me while I'm up on the hill [vision quest]. There's power in returning food to A-ki [earth]. It's in my use of *mashkiki* ["medicine," or more accurately, "power of the earth"] in the pipe ceremony to heal. It's in the *wiikonges* [feasts] that we have for our families and for members of other clans. It's also in the councils we have between our many Anishinabeg groups [the Odawa, Ojibwe and Potawatomi, plus the ancestors].

This statement suggests that showing Odawa ethical behavior through compassionate acts of giving empowers ethical people. Where unethical people withhold, ethical people become exemplary models for others, especially by their demonstrating the obligation (the "ought" of ethics) to give gifts, particularly the powerful gift of knowledge. Such displays of generosity diminish differences. Through the action of exchanging powerful knowledge between other-than [or more-than] human persons, such as the *manidos* and some human persons, the power of life is shared with humanity and, furthermore, ethical people giving back ensures the benefits of harmonious life: *pimadaziwin* in its most comprehensive and connotative sense. So, the Odawa ethical system can be understood as action-based instead of belief-oriented. It is not just an ideal, where a separation exists between ethos and worldview (as in some aspects of Christian belief). Rather, because of the immediacy of the interrelational nature of the Odawa's socio-cosmic life, ethos and worldview are fused. This perpetual union of ethos and worldview forms a system of ethical action wherein people are identified as ethical by their actions that benefit, invigorate and renew the community, and are not simply focused on the reward of the individual in the next life.

Renewed identity through expanded ethical relationships is possible for Odawa traditionalists because, as Brown Otter said:

All life is circular and continually changes. It has many phases. But everything, in all their different phases, is related and we must honor that relationship by giving to each other.

He went on to say that individuals acting together create a "circle" — which he used in the fullest connotative sense of the word — so that the connection between all ethical people is continually regenerated. Traditionalists contend that because life is in a constant state of motion, it is essential for the person, the community, even the world, to ritually transform the present moment and emerge with a renewed identity; social solidarity that is accomplished through compassionate acts of giving.

Odawa traditionalists stress ritual acts, especially of gift exchange, as the primary medium to create relationships, establish social solidarity and carve a collectively determined identity. For them, one must enact the value of gift to maintain proper ethical relations. Individuals have been, and are, respected for their knowledge and achievements that reflect and create their ethical being. Gift-giving, or what the Odawa refer to as "gifting," is the primary social act that lends respect and prestige; it also reflects power.

As a continuum of sharing and reciprocity, gifting follows rules for bonding the giver and receiver. On one end of the continuum, personal survival often depends on sharing between kin. On the other end of the continuum, reciprocity is one form of gifting that can dramatically enlarge family units to include clans, other tribes and "foreign" others such as Euroamericans. As a continuum of sharing and reciprocity, gifting extends to include exchange within the family group, between groups, among the ancestors and, ultimately, to relations with all ethical people.

In their rituals, Odawa traditionalists enact the ethical value of gifting to unite groups through the socio-religious duty of exchange. What is exchanged does not have to be goods and wealth, real and personal property, or things of economic value, such as lands and rights through treaties (see Mauss 1967). Because traditionalists establish intragroup and intergroup bonds, as well as bonds with the *manidos*, or power-persons, through acts of exchange (associated with the value of gift), such institutions as marriage, initiations and the *dodem* system unite, cement, and expand interpersonal alliances. For these Odawa, all such activities include ritual gifting, so that gift exchange becomes the main social means to create solidarity. Traditionalists clearly understand that failing to engage in socially building reciprocal exchanges results in the individual's loss of status and dignity and, on a larger scale, deteriorates alliances as well as communities, social organization and collective identity.

For Odawa traditionalists, to establish proper interpersonal relationships, contracts and alliances, receiving is as important as giving. They regard a person's or a group's refusing to either receive or give as slamming the door on friendship, which annihilates social relationships and, therefore, introduces danger. For traditionalists, gifting enacts proper ethical and social justice in a most immediate manner. They see it as their most significant way to create bonds between human persons as social groups, and between human persons and other-than human persons, such as the *manidos* and the ancestors. Gifting is the source to powerfully reduce the distance between ethical people and others who are unethical—we versus they—and to mediate the potential hazards of social distance, such as competition and hostility.

Examples of powerful actions associated with the value of gift are the traditionalists' healing rituals. Elders explain that curing is a process of gifting: The person to be healed gives the religious expert a gift, such as tobacco or silk, to honor the religious expert's position as initiating donor. The religious expert acts as the mediator between the person and the *manidos* in times of personal crisis. The gift exchange between the person seeking guidance in healing himself or herself and the religious expert differs only slightly from the religious expert's ceremonial gifts of prayers and tobacco to the *manidos*. Using the healing event as an example, the function of gifting can be illuminated by applying Marshal Sahlins's (1976) theoretical model as a heuristic device to show how social distance conditions the way persons interact and how the range of interactions drives aspects of the traditionalists' lives.

"A" (the person in need of spiritual or physical guidance for renewed health and empowerment) gives to "B" (the religious expert), who acts as the mediator to transform the gift into something else (knowledge, revelation and guidance transformed into profoundly realized power) in exchange with "C" (the *manidos*). The power given by "C" through "B" stems from "A's" initial gift, so that it acts as something of a catalyst. The benefit of this power, therefore, is transferred to "A." This process of exchange creates a closed loop (A <—> B <—> C). The presence of an intermediary party, "B," or the religious expert, is necessary to maintain interpersonal equity and ensure that the gift is used for powerfully benevolent acts. "The use of power can become harmful," warned Black Bear, if this closed and circular relationship is not reciprocal in its purpose. He continued:

A person's gift cannot be allowed to become another's power to do bad things. Life has to have balance—male/female, human/*manido*, person/person and among our many groups. When things get out of balance is when we're in trouble. This is why I honor you for your gift, I honor Ki-je Manido—Grandfather, the Great Power-Person—with my gift, and we're both honored by Ki-je Manido's gift of power [to us].

It is also why we seek the Red Road: the right way of living that Ki-je Manido set out in the First World. The Red Road keeps things in balance if one accepts the calling and uses well the power of what Ki-je Manido has given. This is the path toward a good life [i.e., *pimadaziwin*].

Conceptualizing the exchange process in the healing ceremony through the above model suggests that degrees of empowerment and solidarity result from different types of exchange. In this type of exchange, gift-giving itself provides an initial act of social organization. For traditionalists, gift exchange structures relationships between human persons and more-than human persons ("A" to "C" through "B"). Sharing and reciprocity are the ethical acts of interpersonal exchange that concretely organize the traditionalists' internal community and external relationships.

Sharing proper, or pooling, are purely intragroup activities associated with kinship solidarity (Sahlins 1976: 188). Pooling is when clan segments come together and amass needed resources within the kin group without the expectation of return. Family members simply gather and share resources for the common good and survival of the group. An unspoken understanding exists among traditionalists that the current "have not's" eventually may become the "have's," so not having is never held against anyone. Having something and withholding it is regarded as the most abhorrent behavior. The ethical duty of kin is to take care of each other with equality and altruism.

Reciprocity expands the personal level of exchange (sharing) beyond family relations to the broad collective level. While sharing solidifies and reaffirms kin relations, reciprocity extends these in-group associations to include non-kin members. Reciprocity has the power to mediate differences between disagreeing people—for example, between traditionalists and others who oppose them—because it reduces hostility and averts dissension. Through gifting, giving with the expectation of a return, traditionalists use reciprocal actions in ritual to mediate conflict. But, enacting the value of gift through reciprocity introduces tension into the system, for always the question exists, "What if the recipients withhold the expected return?" Because withholding undermines the ability to expand the social sphere and maintain solidarity, traditionalists expect positive or balanced reciprocity (Sahlins 1976) to alleviate, at least temporarily, tensions between groups, individuals, bands, clans, tribes, or Euroamerican "foreigners." Positive or balanced reciprocity mediates greater social distance between groups than sharing or pooling resources. Reciprocity creates alliances through a contractual agreement and addresses the structural tension felt between non-kin groups. Both sharing and reciprocity are equated with the value of gift and define ethical personhood.

For these Odawa traditionalists, giving creates proper relations between ethical people and ultimately is empowering by identifying "friend" versus "foe." Ritual acts of giving, with more-than human persons and between human persons, powerfully mediate the differences between ethical people and others who threaten social solidarity. The danger that others present is a problem primarily because it results from distance between people. As a central theme of the Odawa traditionalists' ritual activity, the problem of social distance and relation is mitigated through acts of gifting. Individuals and social groups invoke the value of gift to mediate the many and often chaotic forms of "otherness," and to transform its potential danger by abolishing distance. Gift exchange automatically creates a bond between people because doing so is to give part of oneself, as the gift is part of one's personal identity; to receive is to take part of another's being (Mauss 1967). Thus, gift-giving is a perpetual exchange of power in the form of social solidarity. Odawa traditionalists insist that a person does not "own" things like eagle feathers; they are a gift. By giving them to someone else, the person shows compassion and generosity, which is interpersonally empowering.

For Odawa traditionalists, the value of gift is the umbrella under which all acts of exchange on a continuum of giving and withholding derive. Ritual acts of sharing and reciprocity define, maintain and reinforce the traditionalists' social and cultural orientation. A model for ethical exchange behavior is revealed, for example, in such ritual acts as greeting each other with "*Bozho!*": that is, in an abbreviated form of the name of the Odawa culture hero, culture bringer and Great Transformer, Nanabozho.

For the Odawa, gift exchange always has been the central means to practice the model for ethical behavior associated with the organizing principle of gift. For traditionalists, gift is not impersonal: It is *very* personal. To enact the value of gift through exchange behavior heals and empowers because it mediates the sense of danger created by others' interpersonal distance. Exchange shows that compassion, an enactment of gift, is a responsibility that perpetuates interpersonal solidarity and, therefore, generates an empowered sense of community identity.

RITUALS OF COMMUNITY AND EMPOWERED IDENTITY

We can begin to explore how two types of rituals create a community with empowered identity; personal prayer and communal ceremonies. In these performances, traditionalists diminish, or annihilate, differences between individuals and groups. For them, ritually interacting with the *manidos*, or power-persons, produces a profound metamorphosis: They regard the presence of the *manidos* and their powerfully acting on these encounters as the source of dramatic transformation. Such religious attitudes and values give the traditionalists' social action its real salience and power. Lone Wolf affirmed this:

Personal prayers and ceremonies are very important to us. They show commitment to our ways of being Odawa. I wake up every morning and go outdoors to a little place in the yard and, facing east, give thanks and offer tobacco to the *manidos* for the good morning. People forget to give back. It's just like cooking and eating. I only prepare what I can eat, and should there be anything left, I bury it with tobacco. I do this because it's proper. Everything we eat has been sacrificed for us and has sacrificed itself for our gain. It's only right that thanks be given for that sacrifice and that the remains be treated respectfully. I return it to A-ki with thanks and make a sacrifice of my own of tobacco to Ki-je Manido and all the powers to show my appreciation.

This statement suggests that Odawa traditionalists look to the *manidos* as a source to create powerful interpersonal relationships. The *manidos* supply ways to establish ethical relations through ritual: Their purpose, according to Odawa religious experts, is to show how ritual actions restore right relationships. The goal of ritual to establish right relationships raises questions of how traditionalists do this and, perhaps more importantly, why. For these Odawa, interactions with the *manidos*, coupled with their own ingenuity, powerfully reconstitute and reaffirm tradition, which allows these ritual encounters to be personally and collectively transformative and (re)vitalizing.

Ritual empowerment through encounters with the *manidos* demonstrates the individual's commitment to community solidarity. Through ritual ceremonies, encounters with the *manidos* establish a bond between the person and others so a community emerges. The community in turn demonstrates responsibility to its members. Traditionalists approach rituals as the most significant way to mediate interpersonal distance that threatens collective identity with social division. They regard ritual — personal and collective action directed toward communication with the *manidos* — both as an ahistorical act tied to the classic practices of religious experts, and as a contemporary practice with vital social, economic, and political effects.

Ritually seeking the guidance and constructive intervention of the *manidos* reflects the older, historical Odawa social pattern. In winter, the larger group splintered to pursue subsistence, separating the individual and leaving him/her with a "me-and-the-world-at-large" orientation. In summer with the reuniting of clan networks, this individual orientation shifted to we-and-the-world-at-large. With these shifts in personal orientation and social organization, ritual established proper relationships between human persons, and between human persons and more-than human persons, such as the ancestors and especially the *manidos*.

Ritually enacting the value of gift is a medium of empowerment between persons, human and otherwise. It allows participants to transform ordinary time and space, and to mediate disagreements and misunderstandings stemming from interpersonal distance. Interaction with the *manidos* through ritual is a traditional way to affect proper relationships between all ethical people and to transform others who are unethical to being more benign. Interactions with the *manidos* are sources to re-create right relationships because they mediate the relations between human persons and more-than human persons, and between human persons and other people who are hostile. An essential means to counter threats of social disruption, ritual encounters with *manidos* perpetually work to restore the unity of all persons, human and otherwise.

Traditionalists use ritual as a channel to direct the power gained from encounters with the *manidos* for benevolent acts to achieve *pimadaziwin* — and so create an identity that is collectively determined. For these Odawa, rituals are events that address a reality that is ontologically and phenomenologically organized as I/You and We/They, where actions confirm who I am to You and who We are to Them. A world structured by a duality between ethical people and unethical others calls for a system to guide proper behavior and mediate conflicting disagreements. The problem of "otherness" dictates a rationale for traditionalists to use ritual action to mediate personal forces of good or ill. Traditionalists comprehend the nature and challenge of "otherness" through ritual encounters with others and the *manidos*—a repeated announcement of one's moral responsibility to others.

CONTEMPORARY PERSONAL RITUALS

Odawa religious experts understand their special skills as powerful gifts gained from communicating with a *manido*. Fulfilling his or her responsibilities to exchange the powerful knowledge gained from these encounters, the acts of pipe-carriers and "medicine-people" benefit the group. Above all, religious experts are the master interpreters, the allegorists. Charged with this responsibility, they are the ones who identify spiritual and physical empowerment and healing as the prime source of *pimadaziwin*. Thus, these religious experts invigorate Odawa identity.

Those Odawa who call themselves, or whom others call, elders complement the religious expert's physical and spiritual healing. Elders are identified as having the primary responsibility to work to unify the community through their assigned significance as the keepers of traditions, especially oral history. Like religious experts, elders are empowered by special and astute knowledge gained from direct encounters with the *manidos*. Lone Wolf, a pipe-carrier and elder, remarked that: "The elders teach things. I'm Anishinabe, even though I grew up believing that Indians were 'dirty, drunk, and worthless.'" When I asked if he was an elder, Brown Otter said: "I've been called that. I just keep learning and sharing this with others." Grey Squirrel said: "The elders are the keepers of traditional knowledge and the teachers of how to use that power. Their life experience, not their talk, and their willingness to share with others make them elders." Instead of writing down their knowledge, religious experts and elders pass it on orally because as Lone Wolf said: "I like to see what people are hearing from me. If it's important, they'll remember."

The community acknowledges religious experts, especially "medicine-people" of the Bear clan and other elders, generally, as having a profound relationship with and understanding of the *manidos*. These religious experts and elders are the spiritual leaders of the community who retain essential shamanic features and, therefore, are regarded as "vision people" with special power. The pipe-carrier, particularly, has had a revelatory message from the *manidos* of the nature, substance and destiny of the world, and of the individual's and community's *place* in the world. Elders, together with pipe-carriers and people of the Bear clan (who specialize in knowledge of herbal healing), teach how to keep the community intact and comprise the social category of "medicine-people" or religious experts.

As a specialist in healing, the pipe-carrier's responsibility is to protect the sacred pipe, a religious symbol that empowers persons, human and otherwise. During communal gifting ceremonies led by the pipe-carrier, the power that results from "knowing" the *manidos* is transferred to the community. Through the vision, the pipe-carrier facilitates religious expression to address community problems, and to adapt to a world in constant motion.

Elders believe the ability—or honor—to teach results from knowledge, or the power to heal and renew identity, solidarity, and empowerment. Elders retain traditions through ritual endeavors when knowledge and, therefore, power is given by the *manidos* to them and religious experts, and through them to the community. These agents-in-society are vital critics of social relations who find their strength and inspiration from the entire Odawa religious sphere, a framework they use to challenge people to renew socio-cosmic harmony. Traditionalists contend that renewal may be personal spiritual and physical healing, or it may be community regeneration.

Prayer for Odawa traditionalists includes dreams and visions. From an early age, they learn to remember dreams, which are interpreted by religious experts. The *manidos* revealed in dreams guide the dreamer to wisdom, which is a means for personal empowerment. Dreams are freely discussed among traditionalists, and often people faced with an important decision will say, "I'll have to dream on it." Ritual dreams are understood as a direct interpersonal link with the *manidos.*

Vision quests or fasts, what the Odawa call "going up on the hill," also create a link to the *manidos* and with one's personal *dodem.* Today, individuals of all ages and both genders "go up on the hill," often repeatedly, and they emphasize the need to be trained in this rite by a religious expert. This teacher prepares the person to communicate directly with the *manidos* and to find more succinctly one's own source of power so as to attain *pimadaziwin*—the good, healthy, and moral collective life. Before going up on the hill, a person must uphold the "Seven Ways of Being Odawa," so enhancing his or her power that will contribute to collective *pimadaziwin.* The "Seven Ways" are: to be pure in heart, in body and in soul; humble; honest; loving; and, respectful—a state-of-being that may take months, even years to achieve. As reassurance, the teacher may accompany the person on the hill, which is always held at a power place dreamed of by the questor. "Many things can happen," said Lone Wolf, who was preparing for his own vision.

You have to have seven things purified and in balance: mind, heart, and body, plus be humble, honest, loving and respectful. If one's out of balance, Ki-je Manido will know. Grandfather will show me something, even if it's that my life isn't together yet. I may have some subconscious stuff still there that I haven't reconciled yet. And if so, Grandfather will show me that I've got more work to do. I may have to meditate some more on the proper ways to be Odawa and live a good life [i.e., *pimadaziwin*]. This is what we think about when we go up on the hill.

Lone Wolf explained that the person on the quest abstains from all food and often even water for several days (usually four), although the teacher may bring along "medicine-water" in case of emergency. He also emphasized that one cannot anticipate or direct the result of the fast: if an attempt at impure manipulation happens "the *manidos* will not speak through the dreams."

The form a *manido* may take when encountered during a vision quest is uncertain and often surprising. While preparing for his quest, Lone Wolf told about a friend who went up on the hill because he was unsure of the direction his life should take.

This man was sitting quietly when suddenly a little yellow finch flew into the branch of a tree in front of him. The two began to talk and they understood each other perfectly. It wasn't as if the bird spoke English, or Odawa, or the man spoke the bird's language, or anything like that. They suddenly just had absolute knowledge of each other. And, the little bird told my friend that he must prepare himself to be a great leader and go back to his people and guide them. And, you know, he did. He's now a very important elder and pipe-carrier. But it was funny to think about a little bird talking to this guy. He's a big, huge fellow. Bear I might have expected, or Elk. But, not a little bird.

This description underscores that the contact with the *manidos* during vision quests and the message gained are powerful sources of transmutation and empowerment—two paths toward *pimadaziwin*.

Vision fasts essentially are purification rituals that re-create a connection with all-powerful dimensions of life through the religious experience of suffering, "death," and renewal. The *manidos* encountered in a vision produce a powerful transformation through this ritual. Traditionalists see that a person has been "ill," because he or she is impure of heart, mind, soul, and not humble, honest, loving and respectful. Therefore, each person must be trained to purify himself or herself, a state-of-being crucial to successful communion with the *manidos*. Paraphrasing Lone Wolf, traditionalists also understand that before direct communication can happen, the individual must "suffer" (fasting for many days is a form of self-sacrifice); through the dream, the person "knows" (knowledge = power) and "sees" the *manidos* so that this power is transferred as a gift; and, the person is renewed in the sense that the individual's identity is transformed.

Thus, when traditionalists say the person "died up on the hill and a new person came down," they mean that the individual re-emerges with new strength and wisdom gained from the *manidos*. He or she, then, is spiritually charged with taking this power back to morally benefit the community. Traditionalists regard the knowledge and power gotten from vision fasts as one's ethical duty to apply for the benefit of society. For example, knowledge of the power of herbal medicine to cure, *midéwiwin*, originally descended through the *manido*, Medicine Bear, (Midewiwi Makwa, a more-than human person who is one of the Great Persons of Odawa mythology). One who has had a powerful vision is charged with ethically applying it for beneficial purposes.

Unlike religious experts who ethically act with powerful benevolence for the sake of community welfare, especially through contacts with the *manidos* in dreams and vision quests, pipe-carriers and elders indicate that some unethical people use knowledge for harm, which disrupts socio-cosmic harmony. The most widely known example of people who act with powerfully intentional malevolence are bear-walkers (*me'coubmoosa*). They constitute one sort of socially internal "otherness." Most people know who bear-walkers are and try to avoid crossing them. They often express real fear of the bear-walker's power to harm, and their ability to change from human form into a malevolent bear. Great Elk insisted that I not study bear-walking too intensely, as he feared for my safety. Lone Wolf described having been bear-walked when he was a teenager, "way before I began to follow the traditional ways."

One day, I became seriously ill and spent several weeks in the hospital only to have the doctors scratch their heads with confusion about what was wrong with me. I couldn't move my whole right side, and I had trouble breathing. So, one of the elders in the community, after hearing I was sick, visited me in the hospital and reported that my problem was that I'd been bear-walked.

He went on to say that a pipe-carrier, responding to his need, went to the hospital and conducted a series of self-empowering rituals. Lone Wolf said of the experience: "I've never been the same. I really changed. It was then I stopped drinking and started to think about people other than myself. I started to respect the traditional ways again. I discovered my own center of power." Although he did not die physically, he died metaphorically and was reborn.

When bear-walked, one is guided to self-curing by a religious expert. This agent-in-society consults with the "patient," meditates on the source of the problem, and conducts a pipe-ceremony to communicate with the *manidos* and ask for guidance in addressing the problem. The process enables the individual to heal himself or herself through a series of powerful actions. Smudging is the first step: opening two windows and smoking out the house, especially the corners, beginning at the lowest level in the southeast and proceeding clockwise. Smudging is the key: burning certain substances in a bowl and letting the smoke emanate. Smudging with sage drives out malevolent spirits; smudging with tobacco invites in benevolent beings. The second step is to hang a piece of red willow tied with red yarn over an entry way. Third, one puts salt around all windowsills and doors leading outside; another effort to keep malevolent spirits out. The fourth step is to place four branches of cedar tied together on each of the four sides of the house. If the bear-walker's malevolent purpose is particularly powerful, an individual may require stronger measures and "medicines," including "shooting" the bear-walker and then reviving him or her in a purified state. The bear-walker epitomizes powerful malevolent acts: the religious expert, or pipe-carrier, "medicine-person" and elder, exemplifies the ethical obverse.

CONTEMPORARY COLLECTIVE RITUALS

As presently practiced, the central aim of collective rituals is twofold. First, they preserve healing traditions, especially as they perpetuate collective *pimadaziwin*—the good, healthy, and moral collective life. Second, they are used to transmit knowledge and the initiation into a powerfully renewed identity. "Medicine-people" retain their responsibility as master interpreters of this sacred knowledge, and they heal by keeping and using sacred water-drums and medicine-bags to re-create the connection of the person and the community with the *manidos*.

The pipe, one of the contents of the *pinjigosaum*, or medicine bag, is a central component in most Odawa communal rituals.[2] Laying down or burning tobacco or sweet grass extends the pipe ceremony. The ritual participants smoke the pipe while all are joined in a circle. The pipe-carrier chants a prayer and holds the pipe up to the *manidos*. As the pipe passes to each person, he or she absorbs the many powers called on by the pipe-carrier: combined powers from collective social identity, the ancestors, the environment, the earth and the plethora of *manidos*. The pipe passes around the circle in "the direction of the sun" (to the left). After each person has smoked and silently prayed, he or she swings the pipe in "the direction of the sun" and passes it to the next person. Pipe-carriers are special people with enhanced power but the power of the ceremony does not directly derive from them; its source is the *manidos*. The pipe-carrier simply is charged with keeping and protecting the pipe. "Ki-je Manido, the Great Power-Person, and the other grandfathers speak through the pipe," explained Soaring Eagle. Pipes usually are made of cedar and have stone bowls with decorations that, according to Soaring Eagle, "represent the four vertical and horizontal directions of space" and eagle feathers representing "*manidos* associated with the sky and earth like Mishomis [Sun], Nokomis [Moon] and Animiki [one of the Thunders].[3] Soaring Eagle continued:

The pipe represents the unity of heart, mind, and body that is possible within each person. The bowl is Grandmother's, Nokomis', heart—just like the drum-beat. It creates a center, the bond between A-ki [Earth], and Nokomis [Moon] and Mishomis [Sun]. Each section of the pipe points to each section of the person, and smoking it guides them in purifying themself; unifying their body, mind, and heart. Each grain of tobacco put in the bowl represents all forms of life. Add fire so a person smokes the sacred tobacco and, while praying, the breath of Ki-je Manido enters them.

Here, we can see clearly that in effect, A-ki is equated with the body, Nokomis with the heart and Mishomis with the mind, and that the "breath of Ki-je Manido" is power: powerful knowledge gained through ritual interactions.

Like the pipe-ceremony's purifying purpose, sweat-lodge rituals are for collective purification and empowerment. During the ritual, the participants chant: "Bathe in the breath of Ki-je Manido [the steam] and be reborn." Brown Otter said:

Sweats are held for spiritual purification. The problem in this community today is two things. People have strayed from the Right Path, they aren't living a good life. They've been indoctrinated into Catholicism, and they think that we who practice the Old Ways are practicing magic—voodoo or something. Also, it's hard to have a sweat, or any other ceremonies, without having land to build the lodges on and conduct the ceremonies.

Despite these worries, religious experts and pipe-carriers lead two types of "sweats." A person may take part in a sweat-lodge for either spiritual or physical healing; officiants specialize in one type or the other. Also sweats are for an individual's or a group's empowerment.

In group sweat-lodges, men and women generally participate separately. Laughing Gull said: "Many people think women don't need to take sweats at all because they're purified every month." For a sweat-lodge ceremony, the religious expert builds a round lodge covered with cedar with a central fire. People enter the lodge through an east door and sit in a circle around the fire, with four people named as the "Keepers of the East, South, West, and North Doors." Tobacco passes to each participant. Lone Wolf described his first sweat-lodge ritual.

When I entered the lodge, I could feel incredible power coming both from all the people there and from somewhere else. When the pipe passed to me, however, I couldn't see anyone else in the circle except for the Keepers of the Doors. Suddenly, there was a green light that radiated from the ceiling over the hearth. When the ceremony was through and I came out of the lodge, it was very dark, but I looked up into the trees and could see every branch, every leaf. I suddenly looked down at my side and saw a bright concentrated light right along side my leg. I thought I was hallucinating, maybe from the heat and being dehydrated. I said to the guy standing by me, "Hey, you see this?" He said, "What?" I said, "Up there; the lights in the trees. This, by my side." He said he didn't see it, but it must be very powerful and I should go and talk to the healer about it. So, I did. He said this kind of thing didn't happen very often, and it may never happen to me again. But, this is exactly what the sweat ceremony is all about. He told me, "You have been shown that you can harness great power. The light by your side is your spirit-helper."

This powerfully describes how sweat-lodges lead to the religious experience of transmutation and, ultimately, empowerment.

Through the sweat-lodge, the elders and religious experts simultaneously guide the person and group to encounter the benevolent *manidos*, or power-persons. "Bathing in the breath of Ki-je Manido" is an empowering ritual that effects a rite-of-passage: a transition from one moment to another, as well as a change in being. Sweat-lodge rituals cleanse a person's impure state. Personal power is enhanced through group solidarity. Each person emerges from the lodge with a changed state-of-being and identity. For those who receive a vision during the ceremony, solidarity is established with the group and directly with the *manidos*, sometimes in the form of light as we saw in Lone Wolf's description. The group comes together and establishes a proper relationship; not only is the individual empowered by other individuals, but more importantly by the *manidos* to the person through the community. The ritual concretizes power as a gift that transpires between a community of ethically empowered persons. The community of participants itself, therefore, becomes an organizing center, a virtual lightening rod for empowerment.

Other contemporary communal rituals are more visible than pipe-ceremonies or sweat-lodges. Probably the most widely held community ceremonies are dances, intratribal or intertribal, called powwows.[4] They are get-togethers in which both dancers and traders interact to uphold the value of gift exchange to generate positive ethical relationships. Powwows are events that renew old friendships and invite new ones. Black Bear said: "The sound of the drum is the heartbeat of our Grandmother, and when you're dancing you try to get into the rhythm—get in harmony with Aki." Grey Squirrel said: "Powwows are a strong spiritual event where you can show Grandfather and all your ancestors that you're doing what you can to keep traditions going." The arbor, an open-framed circular lodge made of cedar posts and covered with cedar boughs is in the center of the dance circle, where the drumming occurs.

Powwows that are open to both Indians and non-Indians, generally, include dances called "intertribals" in which everyone is invited to participate (except menstruating women, who "on the honor system" stay outside the dance circle because of their enhanced power). These rituals also include other dances in which only Indians may participate, such as honor-songs. Today, powwows play a key role in the maintenance of Indian traditions.[5] Despite the fact that Odawa traditionalists seem open to the participation in powwows of non-Indians, they are, however, still guests: these Odawa understand the ritual as essentially Odawa and use it to assert a unique identity and create solidarity.

Although male "fancy dancers" and grass dancers, and female shawl dancers and "jingle-jangle" dancers, have become quite popular, these performances are not indigenous to the Great Lakes but to the Plains tribes. "Part of their popularity is the young people's attraction to the associated dress," explained Great Elk. Only what are called "traditional dancers and dance dress" are indigenous to the area.[6] Those who are called, or who call themselves, "traditional dancers" are the pipe-carriers, elders, and "medicine-people." Their talent and skill are crucial to the success of the event. Each dancer's regalia is unique and usually stems from the person's dream and *dodem*, which one's movements also express.

By consecrating the land, building the arbor, and lighting and tending the central fire, the powwow ritual begins well before the actual dancing: dancing starts with a Grand Entry early in the afternoon, with a second in the evening. Dancers line up and enter the dance circle through an eastern-facing opening, which reaffirms the east as the direction where life starts. They then dance "in the direction of the sun." The first dancers to enter the circle are the head dancers, whose positions are by invitation and are a gift from the group that acknowledges an individual's importance to the community. Head dancers always are traditional dancers who are charged with being responsible for ensuring protocol, solving problems, and resolving conflicts. They need extensive knowledge of specific dances and styles, dress and protocol, such as the proper action to take when an eagle feather is dropped. For example, when an eagle feather is dropped, all dancing stops and the dancers leave the circle, except for a few male head dancers who perform a dance to ritually neutralize the feather's power. It is then picked up and given to the host dancer, who decides to whom it should be passed. The feather is never returned to the person who dropped it.

Invitation as a head dancer, who enters the arbor first, is both an honor and financial responsibility, as it calls for extensive gift-giving in exchange for prestige. After the head dancers come the veteran dancers, who represent all Odawa people who have died in battle, including veterans of U.S. wars. Then come the flag bearers, who carry the Canadian and U.S. flags (the U.S. flag sometimes upside down to honor the American Indian Movement), a veterans' flag and a tribal flag with eagle feathers honoring the *manidos* who guide Odawa life. Then come the male traditional dancers. Behind them come the male "fancy dancers" and grass dancers. The women follow and the children come last. The entire group makes a loose circle to honor the *manidos*, after which they stop to sing the flag song. After the flag song, an elder gives an invocation, then the dances begin.

The drum controls the dances themselves. A group of musicians and singers called "the drum" generally play one large drum in the center of the dance circle under the arbor. The songs and dances are structured, the order determined by the head singer. Drums must have an extensive repertoire. Not knowing a song, a prayer, called for by the head dancers causes an embarrassing loss of prestige and requires passing the right to another drum.

Different chants combine with the rhythm of the drum to determine the dancers' patterns of movement. While the women tend to be sedate and the men flamboyant, a visible transformation occurs in both. As Laughing Gull explained, power is transferred "through the energy of one person to another," which results in group enhancement, and it moves "directly from the *manidos* to the person through the energy of the dance itself."

As one type of collective ritual, powwows traditionally ensured successful hunting or victory. Today, Odawa traditionalists use powwows to express unity, solidarity, and social identity. Like all rituals, they happen in a concentrated and consecrated time and space, which creates a bond between human persons and other-than human persons, especially the ancestors and the *manidos*. Powwows establish proper relationships between all people. Being a place to both trade and dance, they enact and reinforce the value of gifting—sharing and reciprocity—to mediate social distance and disagreements between people. At powwows, ritual dances establish and maintain the life perpetuating connection with the *manidos*, which sustains collective *pimadaziwin*. The power of dance, the drums—"the heartbeat of the earth"—and the central arbor make real the concentrated creative power within each person and through which communal solidarity is voiced. The unity within each person extends out to the group, and it remains an active source of solidarity throughout the year. Through dance, the person purifies himself or herself, changes his or her state-of-being, and unites with other people and the world at large. Power is amplified by encounters with other-than human persons, including the ancestors and the *manidos*, and between human persons. Through the power of the dance, the person, in harmony with "the circle of life," momentarily separates from his or her everyday identity and becomes part of the identity of a unified and harmonious world, both social and cosmic. Differences are annihilated. The dancer "becomes" the "eagle" or some other powerful life-form. Each dancer creates a different image and identity through a different visual channel. Powwows teach the proper expression for a specific person and reaffirm group membership and kinship relations. This experience is crucial for young children whose attention spans may be too short to take part in other communal rituals and, therefore, the elders teach "the Old Ways" through dance with special enthusiasm.

Giveaways, as part of complex ceremonies such as powwows, are another type of community ritual. For example, at an annual powwow the group recognized a young woman who lost a child the previous winter. To honor the child and acknowledge the support of the group, this woman led a ceremony in which she gave gifts first to the host couple, then to a veteran dancer, next to all the dancers, then to the children. Before she distributed her gifts, however, she offered a prayer, a gift, to the *manidos*. She held tobacco out before her to the north, behind her to the south, to her right (east), and finally she swung her arm over her head to the west (reenacting the power of the pipe-ceremony). This action reaffirmed "the connection of the Four Worlds and Four Doors [cardinal directions]," as she explained, and both her own and the group's central position in this cosmographic architecture.

Another example of a giveaway, one of the first ceremonies in traditional weddings is for the "warriors to capture a tree to give to the wedding couple as a gift from the earth (A-ki)," explained the mother of a bride. The men find a young tree, dig it up, and give it to the wedding couple as a sign of their union with each other and with the earth. An eagle feather (a power sign associated with the *manidos*) is placed at the top of the tree, and the women cover the roots with earth before a pipe-ceremony begins.

An extremely popular form of communal rite is the naming ceremony. Most traditionalists desire an Odawa name. Like giveaways, naming ceremonies occur in many circumstances, and a person may receive several names throughout his or her life. The community gives an Odawa name to honor special deeds. Most often the name results from dreams. In a community naming ceremony, the individual calls on a "vision person" to fast and confirm the appropriateness of the name, and to conduct the ceremony. People also may have secret names used in prayer to generate a direct connection with the *manidos*. Lone Wolf said he received his Odawa name, *Nazhikewizi Ma'iingan*, after his teacher dreamed it was his "proper identity." This is a particularly noteworthy name, he explained, as it refers "to the separation of animals and humans, but also to their continuing bond." Lone Wolf said that, besides this name, he has a

Christian name, a family name and "two other names that I can't say but that I use in the mornings when I go out to pray with Grandfather." Today, there is particular importance put on naming ceremonies, which usually take place in the spring. Most people have Christian names on their birth certificates and driver's licenses. The gift of an Odawa name is a means of cementing one's position in, and identity with, the community. Accumulating names expands one's personal definition and social identity.

By far the most visible communal rituals are feasts. Various seasonal feasts stress the ethical importance of giving. For example, fall feasts commemorate the tradition of groups coalescing for the summer months and then sharing a harvest before separating for the winter. Similarly, summer berry feasts commemorate the tradition of groups rejoining and reconfirming kinship ties after separating for the long winter.

The contemporary *Gi-be Wiikonge*, or "Ghost Supper," a descendant form of the earlier Feast of the Dead (Pflüg 1992a), happens primarily on the night of October 31/November 1 but also throughout November. The ritual begins before the actual feast with members of the community decorating the graves of relatives and friends. People go about to various cemeteries and burial sites, tidy up the general area, and place ribbons and boughs of cedar on the markers. Often, bits of food and tobacco also are left. Then, someone who has lost a relative, or simply wishes to honor the dead, announces that he or she is hosting a *Gi-be Wiikonge*, saying "I'm cooking . . . ," and prepares food in enormous quantities. Word spreads rapidly through the community. In the evening, people from near and far attend. Everyone, including dead relatives and dead friends, "eats." "It's real important to have lots of people come," Soaring Eagle said, "because the more who come and eat, the more spirits are fed." "You feed the guests in honor of the dead," said Lone Wolf. "Each person represents someone who has died. So, it's real important to attend as many as your stomach can handle. Last year, I went to eight in one night."

Although the menu, which depends on one's financial means, differs slightly from house to house, typically the meal has various combinations of corn soup, wild game and fowl, potatoes, wild rice and squash. One feature appears on all menus: fry-bread. Laughing Gull explained that to share fry-bread is particularly important, "as it's something people can always give, despite how poor they are."

At the ritual feast, usually one large table is set where a group is seated and served by the host(s). There is no particular order to who eats when; that is, in terms of some rank by elders, gender, adults/children. Those people for whom there is no room at the table simply wait their turn, chatting, gossiping, telling family stories and milling about. When the first group finishes, another group is seated and served. This rotation continues until the food is gone, which ends the ceremony. Considerable gaiety and few overt ritual components are present besides the consumption of food itself, except that the host quietly observes two additional ritual acts. First, feeding of the *Gi-be*, the host picks someone nearest the age of the deceased being honored and serves this person either tobacco or special foods the deceased particularly liked, thereby "feeding" the dead. Second, the host burns a plate of food and tobacco or places a plate of food out on a table all night. As hostess of a *Gi-be Wiikonge*, Laughing Gull said the plate is burned or set out for the ancestor who most recently died, and "if it's gone in the morning, the spirit of the dead person has received it. The power of the food is transformed and passed to the dead person, making their spirit strong." Lone Wolf explained his understanding of the *Gi-be Wiikonge*:

It's not only a time set aside to honor our dead, but the dead, the *Gi-be*, are here. Gaiety and eating are important. If the occasion isn't fun, it'd be solemn, and we want to give thanks for all we have by showing our relatives, and friends from other groups—both living and dead—that we're happy and prosperous, and we want to share that with them.

Grey Squirrel offered how she approaches these feasts:

The *Gi-be Wiikonge* is an Odawa get-together when we can all break bread together. Sharing our food, and exchanging our legends and oral traditions, lets us remember our dead, keeping them alive. Sharing our customs brings us closer to our ancestors and to each other. It's a very important dinner because it helps get us back on the Red Path, the way to live a good life.

Clearly, these Odawa traditionalists understand that their identity depends on an ongoing interdependence with the dead. Identity is religiously bestowed, culturally maintained and socially transformed. In this way, the living may substitute for the dead within the ritual context.[7]

The *Gi-be* feast establishes proper relationships between various subgroups: between the individual (human person) and the world at large; between the individual and other individuals (both human persons, other-than human persons, and the dead); and between the individual and other individuals as a group, thereby perpetuating *pimadaziwin*. The feast also cements human relations because it supplies personal and collective orientation and empowerment, and it establishes alliances through gift exchange, especially the exchange of food.

Today, among these other socially constructive and healing actions engaged in by Odawa traditionalists are Elders Councils and Spiritual Get-togethers. These collective activities affirm and strengthen traditional values and ethics, especially *pimadaziwin*. They reserve time to recount oral tradition and provide a place for participants to remove themselves from their everyday lives and live the traditional ways. They generate a non-secular space-time for people to reassess their current lives, to become empowered through the guidance of the elders, and to return to their everyday lives with a (re)new(ed) collective identity. In other words, they consciously aim to restore right relationships, which makes them a powerful ritual event. During these gatherings, the elders speak, but they also demonstrate ethical behavior to create proper relationships through their ritual actions, and the setting allows all participants active involvement. Everyone receives attention, but the main focus is on young people and those struggling with substance abuse.

Elders Councils and Spiritual Get-togethers that generally take place in the summer months follow a common pattern. Various numbers of elders, pipe-carriers and people from throughout the community gather for four days, preferably in a secluded, wooded area. Resources such as food and firewood are pooled, tents are set up, and a cedar-covered arbor is built. One person is charged with building a fire in the center of the arbor and tending it for the four days and nights. Each morning begins with a sunrise pipe-ceremony, followed by breakfast. The day is spent on recreational activities, such as walking and canoeing, unstructured storytelling, one-to-one chats with elders and pipe-carriers, recounts of oral tradition, demonstrations of traditional crafts, and instruction in the Odawa language. Gossip is passed about what is regarded as the unethical behavior of other people, especially those Odawa who direct their efforts toward non-Indian "wannabes" and people who claim to be keepers of Odawa traditions who are not Indian at all. After dinner, everyone gathers under the arbor.

Each person enters the arbor through an eastern door, walks around the fire clockwise three times, places tobacco in the fire with a silent prayer, then sits down. The organizers of the Council pass a bowl of burning tobacco and sweetgrass to each person, who bathes in the smoke and is thus purified. Each person then receives a gift of tobacco, often in the form of cigarettes. Next, the elders pass an eagle feather, the powerful medium for both purifying the individual's thoughts and empowering him or her to speak honestly. Everyone present knows that the source of the person's voice is a *manido*; this power-person's knowledge being transferred through the feather to the speaker. No social pressure exists for any individual to speak, but those who desire to do so, get up one by one, go to the central fire, and while holding the eagle feather, present their concerns to the group. Most revelations are personal admonitions about transgressions from traditional ways of behaving. For example, at one Elders Council a woman told how she lost three children due to alcohol abuse. At another, a man just out of jail discussed how he beat his wife while under the influence of drugs. At a third, a person revealed that he had gotten drunk the previous night. Following these confessions are formal discourses by the elders and pipe-carriers that address the people's problems and concerns. Afterward, the group disperses and smaller groups gather around campfires, talking informally, sometimes the entire night.

It seems appropriate to regard Spiritual Get-togethers and Elders Councils as ritual events that reaffirm a unique Odawa identity and sense of community. Like all rituals, they happen in a concentrated and consecrated time and space, when transformation of both the person and the community happens through insight. As a healing event—a call for *pimadaziwin*—they are a medium for restoring right relationships. "They're a time of intense training," said Grey Squirrel. "Many ideas are offered and the Old Ways illustrated." The motive for holding these meetings stems from the deep concern that "traditions are being lost, and the loss of traditions means the loss of power and, therefore, our spiritual wellness and identity," as Lone Wolf put it. Spiritual Get-togethers and Elders Councils are directed to young people, particularly, because they are "our community's most valuable resource."

In all these ritual contexts, one can witness how elders, pipe-carriers, and "medicine-people," by showing more than telling, use special techniques of communicating with the *manidos* to guide people to proper relationships, which makes these gatherings of traditionalists a ritual, or religious, event. By sharing their knowledge of these powerful communications, in which the wisdom received is power, persons are giving gifts to each other. Thus, the setting is empowering for the entire collective. Such activities as Elders Councils and Spiritual Get-Togethers allow the group to discuss problems, issues and difficulties, and to use them as a means of both personal renewal and collective solidarity. The elders and spiritual leaders do not merely ask people to rid themselves of their problems and show them how through their own behavioral example, they also use the problems constructively as a means of total socio-cosmic renewal. They integrate the problem of alcoholism and social marginalization, for example, into the action of completely renewing their sense of community and empowered identity.

Odawa rituals suggest transformation and empowerment as important ritual events. Traditionalists use these experiences because they generate a collectively determined identity. This can be conceptualized as follows: Having overcome his or her "illness" through "death" and "rebirth," the ritual participant transforms his or her human condition by "knowing" the concentrated power of the *manidos* through visions or dreams. Traditionalists regard personalistic dream-knowledge as a powerful "medicine" that it is one's duty to take back to the community to help it "heal" and empower itself. Traditionalists understand that this exchange contributes to *pimadaziwin*—the collectively good, healthy and moral life.

For many Odawa, dreams are the ultimate personal ritual, the principle means for human persons to directly elicit their own power. One's power is the basic source to communicate with, share the attributes of, and transmit power among all ethical persons, human and otherwise. Traditionalists stress that this communication between people keeps traditions alive because it illuminates or directs one to the "Right Path," *pimadaziwin*. Since dreams are the essential guide for personal life, they ultimately function to maintain a healthy community life that results from ethical tradition and action.

Elders stress that collective rituals such as powwows, the "capturing of a tree" at traditional weddings, pipe-ceremonies, naming ceremonies, giveaways, feasts, Spiritual Get-togethers and Elders Councils all "unite the vertical Four Worlds and the horizontal Four Doors," as Laughing Gull put it, placing the ritual participants squarely in the center of this cosmographic map. Although people hold giveaways on many occasions, the purpose is to enact the value of gift by showing generosity and compassion, to thank the human community for being part of it, and to thank the *manidos* for being a part of the larger community of ethical persons. Proper relationships are either reaffirmed or established through giveaways. As we have seen, the head dancers at powwows hold a giveaway in which they give all participants, whether actual dancers or supporters, token gifts: an act of exchange or thanks for participating. They give back something in exchange for the prestige they receive. The giveaway, therefore, is a process of mediation and social reciprocity. Receiving an Odawa name is like a giveaway. It collectively acknowledges a person as part of a traditional Odawa community: as with all of their contemporary rituals, the recipient's self-esteem is enhanced, personal power is increased and identity confirmed—*pimadaziwin* in its fullest connotative sense.

NOTES

1. Because of the sensitive nature of their current social activism—especially in the eyes of non-Indians—to protect their individual identities, all names of consultants are pseudonyms; traditional Odawan translated into English. For extensive discussion of various aspects of the nature and sensitivity of some Odawa's social activism, see Melissa A. Pflüg 1992b, 1996a and 1996b.

2. For a discussion of American Indian pipe-ceremonies, generally, see Jordan Paper 1988.

3. After seeing many pipes for sale at powwows, I asked several people, including a pipe-maker, what they thought about just anyone—especially non-Indians—buying them. They assured me that the sacred and powerful pipes were never bought or sold. But, I also was told that people who buy the pipes at powwows do not understand their

meaning: "Folks who buy pipes usually just hang 'em on the wall or want them as a show piece on their mantles."

4. See David Whitehorse 1988 for a concise general description of the pan-cultural role of these events. "Powwow" is an Algonkian word that early Euro-American explorers associated with the healing rituals of shamans.

5. Benjamin R. Kracht (1993), focusing on the Kiowa, has begun to explore this application.

6. The Odawa do not use the term "costume."

7. Fred Ettawageshik (1943) and Wesley Andrews (1984) offer further insight into the function of the "Ghost Supper."

REFERENCES

Andrews, Wesley. 1984. *Ottawa Mortuary Ritual, Belief and Practice*. Master's thesis, University of Chicago.
Ettawagishik, Fred. 1943. "Ghost Suppers." *American Anthropologist* 45: 491–93.
Hallowell, A. Irving. 1955. *Culture and Experience*. Philadelphia: University of Pennsylvania Press.
Kracht, Benjamin R. 1993. "The Kiowa Ghost Dance, 1894–1916: An Unheralded Revitalization Movement." *Ethnohistory* 39 (4): 452–77.
Mauss, Marcel. 1967. *The Gift: Forms and Functions of Exchange in Archaic Societies*. New York: W. W. Norton and Company.
Paper, Jordan. 1988. *Offering Smoke: The Sacred Pipe and Native American Religion*. Moscow: University of Idaho Press.
Pflüg, Melissa A. 1992a. " 'Breaking Bread': Ritual and Metaphor in Odawa Religious Practice." *Religion* 22 (3): 247–58.
———. 1992b. "Politics of Great Lakes Indian Religion." *Michigan Historical Review* 18 (3): 15–34.
———. 1996a. "Indian Tribal Justice Systems and Tribal Courts in Indian Country." In *Rural Criminal Justice: Conditions, Constraints and Challenges*, ed. Thomas MacDonald, Robert Wood and Melissa Pflüg. Salem WI: Sheffield Publishing Company.
———. 1996b. " 'The Last Stand?': Odawa Revitalizationists v. U.S. Law." *Questioning the Secular State*, ed. David Westerlund. London: Hurst Publishing Company, Ltd. and New York: Saint Martin's Press.
———. 1998. *Myth and Ritual in Odawa Revitalization: Reclaiming a Sovereign Place*. Norman: University of Oklahoma Press.
Sahlins, Marshal. 1976. *Culture and Practical Reason*. Chicago: University of Chicago Press.
Whitehorse, David. 1988. "Pow-Wow: The Contemporary Pan-Indian Celebration." *San Diego State University Publications in North American Indians*, No. 5.

The Church of the Immaculate Conception

Inculturation and Identity among the
Anishnaabeg of Manitoulin Island

THERESA S. SMITH

Christian mission work among the Anishnaabeg (Odawa, Ojibwe and Pot-towatomi) of Manitoulin Island, Ontario, began when the Jesuit priest Joseph Poncet arrived to spend the winter of 1648 with the Odawa. Incursions by the Iroquois quickly forced the Jesuits from the island, and it was not until 1844 that a permanent mission was established at Wikwemikong. Within fifteen years, the mission work had reached West Bay where a church was built in 1910.[1] Missionary activities have since been continuous and here, as elsewhere, have served not only to promote Christianity but frequently to deny the sacrality and legitimacy of Anishnaabe tradition. As was the case with the religion of earliest missionized Algonquians—the Montagnais—Anishnaabe beliefs, practices and symbols were not only replaced by Christian ones but were denounced as demonic in origin.[2] Sixteen years before Poncet set foot on Manitoulin, Paul Le Jeune had set the tone for centuries of Roman Catholic interaction with Native lifeways, declaring that "fear is the forerunner of faith"[3] and rejoicing that "The dread of punishment is beginning to gain such an ascendancy over their minds that, although they do not soon amend, yet they are little by little giving up their evil customs."[4]

This is not to say that evangelizing through fear mongering is or was exclusive to the Jesuits or even to the Roman Catholics. Nor was it, as Kenneth Morrison has pointed out, entirely or consistently successful despite the cleared ground of cultural anomie available for these seeds in seventeenth-century North America.[5] As Le Jeune himself was to note, "The savages agree very readily with what you say but they do not, for all that, cease to act upon their own ideas."[6] In other words, the practical political and economic necessity for nominal conversion did not always entail the transformation of consciousness for which the Jesuits had hoped. The life-worlds of many Algonquians, while deeply scarred and changed by political and religious invasion, still provided islands of continuity with tradition. These islands, like the one founded by Nanabush after the primordial flood, may have rested upon chaos and yet they, too, were constructed from bits of the old order. Taken together, these remainders of tradition have been used to create—on Manitoulin at least—a resurgence of traditional lifeways. And the Catholic Church has been forced to recognize that Anishnaabe spirituality never disappeared despite threats of eternal damnation. As Kitty Bell, a member of the *midewewin* (medicine society), told me, "It was always there. Now the people are admitting 'yes, we gave up a lot.' And it was always taught from the pulpit. 'Don't go that way, that fire will surely lead you to hell.' They used these scare tactics. But it was always there, people always used these medicines."[7]

In the face of Native revitalization and post-Vatican II reformation, the Roman Catholic Churches on the island have recanted the old messages and have entered into a dialogue with Anishnaabe elders. The Church's preaching and ritual celebrations have begun to reflect the insights and the demands of Anishnaabe as well as Christian teachings. As Raymond Armstrong, an elder from West Bay and former usher at the Roman Catholic Church put it:

You know, I was at a workshop last fall where there were about 8 or 9 priests present who were apologizing to us Native people because of what had been done in the past, calling us pagans for doing our traditional things. . . . The missionaries were sent to the reserve to change our lives. We were worshipping the devil, they said. Today whenever we do a sweet grass ceremony they want to be present too and they are apologizing. Why did they change? Because they didn't know what they were talking about.[8]

Many Roman Catholics, including Pope John Paul II, have indicated their agreement with Armstrong's assessment. Speaking to a Native American audience at Phoenix, Arizona, in 1987, the Pope said:

The early encounter between your traditional cultures and the European way of life . . . was a harsh and painful reality for your peoples. The cultural oppression, the injustices, the disruption of your life and your traditional societies must be acknowledged. . . . From the very beginning, the Creator bestowed his gifts on each people. . . . I encourage you, as Native people, belonging to different tribes and nations in the East, South, West and North, to preserve and keep alive your cultures, your languages, the values and customs which have served you well in the past and which provide a solid foundation for the future. . . . these things benefit not only yourselves but the entire human family. This sharing of cultural riches must also include the Church native cultures are called to participate in and enhance.[9]

Clearly we hear a new evangelism coming from out of the Roman Catholic Church and from Christianity in general. It is an evangelism that is no longer so concerned with the Christianization of Indians as with the Indianization of Christianity. This new Roman Catholic evangelism reflects the general shift in Christian missionizing that David and Boonstra have termed "mission as solidarity,"[10] an approach that argues for inculturation, and apparently the introduction of syncretic forms, under the leadership of Christian Natives.[11] This move toward inculturation is necessarily fraught with problems including, and for some beginning, with matters of definition. Peter Schineller, while affirming the imperative of inculturation, urges the rejection of the term "syncretism" as historically and irredeemably pejorative and equating the word with what he calls "invalid or inadequate" inculturation.[12] Schineller quotes a number of African and Asian theologians, including the following: "A theologian from India speaks of the 'fusion of incompatible elements' and the 'mingling of authentic notions and realities of the revealed faith with realities of other spiritual worlds.' The concern is that one may borrow elements of another religion without critically passing them through the screen of Christianity, with Christianity being watered down or destroyed in the process."[13]

Of course Native people who stand on the other side of the altar rail necessarily raise complementary objections to the idea of syncretism and to the complicated character of an inculturated, "Indianized" Christianity. They would object strongly to Schineller's "top-down" approach in which Church officials, "with the help of anthropologists and social scientists, stand in judgment over the merits of particular aspects of culture.[14] Native theologians are more likely to "pass Christianity through the screen of Native lifeways," fearing not for the destruction of the essence of Christianity but for the "watering down" of their own cultural integrity. This appears to be George Tinker's view when he says, "Today there can be no genuine American Indian theology that does not take our indigenous traditions seriously. This means, of course, that our reading of the gospel and our understanding of faithfulness will represent a radical disjuncture from the theologies and histories of the Western churches of Europe and America as we pay attention to our stories and memories instead of to theirs."[15]

And then there is yet another voice, different from Natives and non-Natives who argue enthusiastically for inculturation and even syncretism, different from those who place strict limits on the amount and character of aboriginal contributions to belief and practice, different because these people don't stand on either side of the altar rail. The "Traditionalists" stand outside the church altogether and don't worry about whose religion is being diluted, rather they are concerned that traditional Native ways are being stolen or perverted in the name of inculturation. It is with these people that I have had many of my dialogues in the course of my field studies with the Anishnaabeg and, in many ways, it is their words that reverberate most resoundingly in my ears as they speak of their rejection of syncretism, not as an historically pejorative term but as a problematic reality.

On Manitoulin Island, the site of most of my field studies, the apparently syncretic movement that embraces belief, practice and symbol is most radically represented by the Church of the Immaculate Conception at West Bay First Nation. In its architecture, artwork and in the inclusion of traditional Anishnaabe ceremonies, the church appears to seek a fusion of spirituality that has proven to be both enlightening and sometimes confusing to Natives and non-Natives alike. It is my thesis that the Church of the Immaculate Conception constitutes the instantiation of a large and complex discussion that may be summarized in the question: Is the move to syncretic structures and worship in this context a responsible and appropriate response to the past and promise for the future ("mission as solidarity"), or are we merely witnessing the appropriation of one symbol system in the service of another? In order to understand the message that this church communicates and the problems and possibilities inherent in that message, I turn to several sources: 1) the structure itself 2) interviews with parishioners and with Fr. Michael Murray, the Jesuit priest who was instrumental in the design and construction of the church 3) interviews with Leland Bell, an Anishnaabe artist who produced the Stations of the Cross for the church 4) interviews with non-Christian Anishnaabe people who see their symbols taken up within the framework of a traditionally antagonistic religious institution and 5) background consultations and research I've been conducting on Anishnaabe religion on Manitoulin since 1988. I do not assume that this church holds the key to understanding the success, failure and motivation of Indianized Christianity—merely that it presents, quite literally, a structure around which discussion of past repression and current reconciliation may occur.

In 1971 a propane explosion leveled the church and its immediate surroundings, leaving only a damaged statue and bell and a few gravestones. Fr. Michael Murray, six months into the priesthood and newly posted to the parish, remembers the long and difficult discussions that preceded the new design:

I had no experience or preconceived thoughts or notions about Church. When it burned down, all of a sudden we were faced with a community and no building—what do we do? It was a learning process as much for me as for the people. Some people said let's rebuild it exactly the way it was. We were used to it, people were married, buried, baptized there and we know the feel of what that place had been in the past.[16]

Fr. Murray added that the group engaged an architect who drew up plans for a "Native" church in the form of a tepee—not a traditional Anishnaabe structure. The parishioners felt that the design looked disturbingly like the conical buildings built by the highway department to store gravel and salt for winter road maintenance. Understandably, the community dismissed these plans and turned to books on church architecture and to their own traditional structures—especially the wigwam, sweat lodge, *midewewin* lodge, shaking tent and powwow arbor. Here, as elsewhere in Native North America, the circle is omnipresent in "architecture" as it is in the rituals that are enacted in sacred space. Drawing upon memory and gesturing toward a resurgence in traditional teachings and practices, the community combined what Murray saw as three ideas: that the church should be a place in which the circle of healing could be remade, a place in which shelter could be sought and a place of prospect.[17]

The church does, indeed, appear to take up the symbolism Murray describes. Its circular white frame form is sunk into the earth and the cross on the roof points toward the top of the building where the traditional Christian steeple is replaced by a kind of raised "smokehole." It is through this hole that the church is opened to the sky with the only window in the entire building—save those in the vestibule. Double doors open outward to admit one into the vestibule. Created by Mervin Debassige, the doors invite entry into the syncretic symbolism that characterizes the church. Here we see a red sun on a blue background emitting four large rays and twelve smaller ones. The center of the sun is decorated with traditional Anishnaabe floral motifs and the smaller yellow rays contain black crosses. The brochure produced by Immaculate Conception parish tells us that this sun should be read as a "symbol of Christ, the Light of the World, with the four rays outlining the cross. The twelve minor rays represent the twelve Apostles taking Christ's message to the four corners of the earth."[18]

Yet there is a traditional Anishnaabe reading as well: the sun is a common symbol of Kitche Manitou, the Great Manitou, the Creator. All Christian Anishnaabeg with whom I have spoken indicate an identity between the Christian God and Kitche Manitou, though this identification appears to exist between the first person of the Trinity—the Father, rather than the son—and Kitche Manitou. In the language of Anishnaabe iconography, the large rays do speak of the four directions but the smaller ones would indicate the twelve moons. The blue background signifies spiritual power—especially within the midewewin or medicine society and the yellow, black and red are directional colors on the medicine wheel: yellow is East/knowledge, red is South/new life and black is West/cleansing. The church is white, the fourth color, the North, the direction of healing. On the interior of these doors, Debassige has carved clan totems as an expression of the community that the church serves.

From the vestibule one enters the church proper. Here the most striking features are the circular construction, the central sunken altar area and the stepped seating area which, like the lower area and the walls of the church, is covered in blue carpeting. The altar area is beneath ground level and the seating arrangement recalls traditional teaching circles. While blue symbolizes spiritual power for the Anishnaabeg it is also the color associated with the Virgin Mary. There is, indeed, an effective syncretism exhibited in the use of blue and in the mirroring of the number four: above the tabernacle set against the rear wall, a painting of a circle with four feathers; supporting the altar that rests in the center of the church, carved wooden posts of the four evangelists; and, on the lectern, a refrain of the circle of Kitche Manitou, the Creator, the sun, the Christian god, with the four feathers—the directions, the gospels.

When the church was first opened, it contained little else. Fr. Murray recalls the gradual process through which images entered the church—a process and resultant collection that he calls "eclectic" rather than truly syncretic. Statues of Mary and Joseph were placed on either side of the altar, only to be joined by two totem carvings. No one associated with the church had any idea what, precisely, was represented by these carvings, especially in light of the fact that the carving of totems is an import—largely for sale to tourists—from the Northwest. A colleague of mine noted that they communicated a weird disjunctive symbolism to her, not unlike the impression made by kitschy renderings of Santa Claus kneeling at the manger. But as the carvings were the gift of a parishioner, they were accepted and placed at their posts and their presence may indeed be merely decorative.

The baptismal font was also the gift of a parishioner who carved it from a large pine knot. The basin is supported by a pine pedestal that rests on the back of a carved wooden turtle, signifying the island of North America. Like the totem pole, this turtle image represents an import—this time from Huron and Iroquois mythology. But unlike the totem this symbolic influence is fairly old—at least among the Southern Ojibwe—and has been included as an element in earth diver narratives for two generations. It has resonance and meaning to people who always have understood the earth as an island resting on the waters of a primordial flood, and the turtle has been fully adopted as a religious symbol by the Anishnaabe on Manitoulin.

And then there is the tabernacle in the shape of a tipi—a design for the church itself that was, as we recall, rejected. This would appear to be a non-Native's idea of generic Indian symbolism, not Anishnaabe in origin or usage. Yet it is worth noting that the tipi has, in the spirit of the pan-Indian movement, lately come into use on the island, especially at intertribal powwows. This pan-Indianism—which tends to confound scholars who wish to maintain their own definitions of tribal traditionalism—has been both a source of strength and unity for Native North Americans and a point of controversy. On Manitoulin, for instance, the recent import of the Sun Dance has been met with a good deal of enthusiasm and some measure of criticism. The Sun Dances are held in isolated locations in part to protect participants from the picture-taking tourists who are welcomed at pow wows. But when the dances were initially begun a few years ago, they were also "hidden" from members of the Anishnaabe community who disapproved of the adoption of this "foreign" dance. The disapproval seems to have largely abated but is still voiced by some who feel that Anishnaabe ways need to be totally reclaimed before the community can understand or embrace the rituals of their neighbors. This insistence on the particularity, even exclusivity, of Anishnaabe spirituality plays a large part—as we will see—in the judgments that both Christian and non-Christian Natives make regarding the Church.

To return to the structure of the Church of the Immaculate Conception, as we look around its walls we see what is perhaps its most well-known feature—the Stations of the Cross painted by Anishnaabe artist, Leland Bell. There are fifteen in this series as Bell included the Resurrection, on the assumption that the suffering depicted in the Stations is rendered meaningless without this final act in the Passion drama, saying, "We can't celebrate death. What we celebrate is life." Bell is not a Christian but a committed traditionalist and member of the midewewin society. In creating this series he struggled with two challenges: first, the depiction of violence—a subject he has intentionally avoided in his art—and second, the need to create Christian iconography while using an artistic style that, in its use of color and form, is founded on mide teachings. Bell has said: "I wanted to try to say something from my point of view, but I also wanted to respect the other tradition. . . . I found the balance in Love. With the Stations it was a great time of healing, a great time of purification. That's my cultural perspective."

In Bell's description of the fifth station we see an example of his translation from one symbol system to another:

The three circles are the Trinity. I use a path. Jesus has taken this path. He accepts his situation and walks the path, the way of the cross. Simon is dressed in a yellow frock because in my tradition yellow is the color of the east and symbolizes knowledge. He must possess knowledge and wisdom if he helps another man who is suffering.

The same symbolic gestures appear frequently in Bell's non-Christian paintings, but with different connotations. In his own work the colors carry the familiar midewewin meanings (as above) but the path is the path of life or of the midewewin, and the circles may represent spirit helpers or, when they are seven in number, the seven teachings, the seven fires. We should note that Bell is not merely inserting midewewin vocabulary into a Christian context, but translating a story, not so much communicating the Stations to Anishnaabe people as handing Anishnaabe teachings to Christians. For Bell, this is an important difference:

I guess to me it's partly a job. If someone from a Jewish community asked me to do paintings, I would do them. I would study [Judaism] first, which is what I did with the stations. . . . It was Native people that asked me to do the thing, and I'm not saying that I'm trying to convert them back to Indian things, and I'm not saying they converted me to Christianity, because I'm not up for conversion—I never was.

Bell's paintings of the Stations are the focus of a book produced by the Jesuit Anishnaabe Spiritual Center, *Beedahbun: First Light of Dawn*. In this text the paintings are heralded as an example of the inculturation of Anishnaabe spirituality in the "new" Native Roman Catholic Church. Bell takes exception to the claim of the book, contending that it does not tell the whole truth about him or his paintings. As we were looking at the book, he pointed, for instance, to a photograph of Elder Ernest Benedict presenting Pope John Paul II with an eagle feather on the occasion of the pontiff's visit to Midland, Ontario in September, 1984. "I'm not into that at all," he said, "that melding of traditions." For Bell, we each have our own paths:

This is just my opinion, but I think if those people want to go toward the church, then let them go toward the church, and I'll go this way . . . but I'm not going to go around saying this is the right way and you are the wrong way . . . I don't think anyone in the world has the Truth. I think what people have is partial truth. Each spiritual tradition has truth according to its environment, its institutions . . . and what I believe is that now and again you can maybe touch base with some people. . . . I don't want to belittle the way of the cross—whatever it is—but the thing is, when they see the paintings, they also see somebody who is not a Christian person. Although in the interviews [for *Beedahbun*] they might have twisted—not twisted—but changed, some words that I used in the actual explanation of things.

Leland's wife, Kitty Bell, also a member of the midewewin, participated in some of our conversations. She became angry on the subject of the Jesuits' "creative editing" of her husband's words, accusing them of intentionally Christianizing midewewin teachings. Her reaction to the Church and to attempts to Indianize Christianity is unequivocal.

"They're whoring," she said, adding that the practice of Anishnaabe rituals and inclusion of ritual objects in and around the church is both inappropriate and foolish:

I've never seen any priest come into the [mide] lodge and sit with us and partake in these ceremonies and see how they are supposed to be done [Here Mrs. Bell was referring specifically to the ignoring of ritual proscriptions against women's participation in the sweet grass and pipe ceremonies during their menstrual periods]. It's a mind game. I think they are playing, fooling around with what they know nothing about. . . . And I see it like it's going to make our people sicker instead of healing them.

In other words, the priests and congregation—like the new age practitioners whom Blake Debassige has called "shake and bake shamans"—are making use of rituals without paying heed to the impelling sacrificial demands that go hand in hand with the life-affirming practices. When I asked Mrs. Bell why she thought that the Church was including Anishnaabe ways, she indicated that she perceived a cynical motive at work, a simple change in method on the part of a missionary religion that has lost its hold on Anishnaabe consciousness: "I think they are just redoubling their efforts to dispirit us."

None of my other consultants expressed such a strong rejection of the Church but all—including former and current parishioners—indicated varying levels of confusion and/or discomfort with some aspects of the building, its contents, and the inclusion of Anishnaabe rituals. A case in point is the use of sweetgrass, braids of which are frequently placed in front of the tabernacle at the Church of the Immaculate Conception. Frs. Leach and Humbert have said, "The sweetgrass ceremony readily emphasizes and portrays the mood of the liturgy at the beginning of the Eucharist as well as reinforcing the cultural spiritual consciousness of the Anishnabek. On occasion this ceremony has been inserted into the Roman Catholic liturgy as a means of blessing the assembly. It can substitute for, or enhance, the Penitential rite." This was one of the ceremonies that Kitty Bell objected to and her words are echoed by Anishnaabeg on the other side of the theological debate. Raymond Armstrong told me, "I've seen people going out [leaving the Mass] and because I was an usher I would sometimes ask what their trouble was and they'd say, "well, I can't smell that sweetgrass." There are, indeed, a number of people—especially older parishioners who have, according to Armstrong, "been driven away on account of what they have in the church now." For Christian Anishnaabeg who were told to hand over their medicine bundles to the priests and to reject the old ways as demonic, inculturation must appear as a remarkable and troubling contradiction—and one that is not easily articulated.

Another consultant, a former parishioner who wishes to remain anonymous, addressed this issue:

When it [the new church] first started, I was very excited about it and thinking that it was about time Native spirituality was taken seriously and that it may have a part in the church. But as time has gone by, I have thought about it again and I don't think it can be done. I talked to my father and asked how he felt about it and he didn't think it was right—that it was either one way or the other. And he also told me to have a look at what I'm doing and make my choices. . . . He's very loyal to the Church and he intends to stay that way. At one time we had the teachings in the church—the drum was taken in there and I told my dad about it and he said it's not right, it's two different things. And so I thought about it all the more and I listened to those [traditional] teachings and [I thought] maybe we are overstepping—stepping on each other's rights and I felt very, very awkward about the drum being in the church. I couldn't tell at the time why it was bothering me so much.

This consultant, who has chosen the traditional path, added that she felt the church was a sacred place but was most comfortable going there alone and praying to the Creator in private.

Raymond Armstrong who had trained to be a deacon at one time, is an elder who sponsors sweat lodges and performs a number of traditional rituals. He still considers himself a Christian even though he has drawn away from the church lately due to some political disagreements with church members. His thoughts on the church and its integration of Anishnaabe spirituality were at once clear and complex. As we sat in his kitchen surrounded by paintings of Jesus and inhaling the scent of the sage he had just used in an Anishnaabe purification ritual, he remembered his wife, Delores's, brief experience with the church. She had tried going to services but had stopped because it seemed to interfere with her ability to find traditional healing herbs: "She couldn't find the medicine she was looking for, she couldn't see it, yet it was right at her feet."[19] Delores Armstrong felt forced to make a choice and chose the traditional ways.

For Raymond, however, there did not appear to be a problem in integrating spiritualities, that is, until we began discussing the Eucharist. Armstrong said that he did take communion but that he would *never* dispense the host. When I asked him why not, he said, "It's like they say, you can't serve two masters."[20] While I was initially confused by his stance I later realized that Armstrong had made a clear choice: he had drawn a line between the two traditions that he could not cross, and this line was not one given to him by the priests or the traditionalists. It was purely individual and, in his own apprehension of Christianity and tradition, absolutely consistent. For Raymond and Delores Armstrong the line was drawn at different points but in the same manner and between the same categories of experience. Neither was tripping up on a point of doctrine or belief, instead both stopped at an intersection of power and practice and chose to go no farther on the Christian path.

To Fr. Murray, the Church of the Immaculate Conception "represents, to some extent, the systematization, the manifestation, the translation of the emerging consciousness of the people at the time it was built."[21] This emerging consciousness has gone through a number of changes in twenty-three years, and there is no unanimity in the community as to the precise message of the church. It is safe to assume that the Jesuit priests had hoped that in learning the language of Anishnaabe spirituality and helping to translate it into this space they might not only engage in the process of inculturation, but on a practical level, attract a larger congregation (or at least maintain membership). In fact, church attendance is extremely low and as the traditional ceremonies are revived and the *mide* society grows, the Christian congregation has decreased. Armstrong claims that the only time the church is full is on Christmas and at funerals. When I attended, in the summer of 1993, there were no more than one hundred people present at the only Sunday service and roughly two-thirds of the congregation were non-Natives.

In the skylight above the altar in the Church of the Immaculate Conception we see a traditional image of the Thunderbird manitou, standing in, parish publications contend, for the Dove of the Holy Spirit. Anishnaabe consultants, without exception, assert that the Thunderbird and Holy Spirit are distinct entities. It may be that when it was built the church reflected the spirit of a community that had just begun the process of remembering its traditional ways. Now that the traditions have regained prominence it would seem that many Anishnaabeg prefer to speak their spiritual symbols without translation. While I am not sure that I would agree with Kitty Bell that the Church has sought to appropriate and use the Anishnaabe symbols in order to continue the process of dispiriting traditionalists, I must acknowledge that integration in this context has limits. Some of those limits are purely individual—as in the case of the Armstrongs—but others are more communal. Judging by attendance and the reaction of the tourists who flock to it, the Church of the Immaculate Conception speaks most clearly to the *non*-Native Christians who now fill the services and whose faith is informed, and seemingly enriched, by the Anishnaabe experience. The Thunderbird, for them, may appear as another expression of the Holy Spirit who protects and guides those gathered in the circle of worship. For Native people, on the other hand, this symbol may gesture upward, outward, and back toward the natural world in which the traditional-ists find their own best path. Inculturation, syncretism, Christianization, and the Indianization of Christianity are issues that appear to be of more interest at present to scholars and theologians than to the Anishnaabe parishioners or tra-ditionalists of Manitoulin. For both Christian and non-Christian Anishnaabeg, the symbolism of the church may be not about identification with one religious system or another, but about identity itself. And the reclamation of Anishnaabe identity on Manitoulin is an ongoing journey, the character and outcome of which will only be determined by the Anishnaabeg themselves—perhaps in consensus, perhaps in factionalism—but always, on their own terms, in their own time, and in their own sense of place.

NOTES

1. Immaculate Conception Church, *Bekaadendan* (West Bay, Ontario, n.d.), 6–7.

2. See Kenneth Morrison, "Baptism and Alliance: The Symbolic Mediations of Religious Syncretism," *Ethnohistory* 37:4 (1990): 416–37.

3. R. G. Thwaites, ed., *The Jesuit Relations and Allied Documents* (Cleveland: Pagent Book Company), 11:89. See also John Steckley, "The Warrior and the Lineage: Jesuit Use of Iroquoian Images to Communicate Christianity," *Ethnohistory* 39:4 (1992): 478–509.

4. Thwaites, 11: 215.

5. Morrison, "Baptism and Alliance." See also Howard L. Harrod, "Missionary Life-World and Native Response: Jesuits in New France," *Studies in Religion* 13:2 (spring 1984): 179–92.

6. Thwaites, 5: 151. See also Kenneth Morrison, "Discourse and the Accomodation of Values: Toward a Revision of Mission History," *Journal of the American Academy of Religion* 53:3 (1985): 365–82.

7. Kitty Bell, personal communication, July 1988.

8. Raymond Armstrong, personal communication, August 1993.

9. John Paul II, "Address to the Native Peoples at Phoenix, Arizona, Sept. 14, 1987," *Origins* 17 (1987): 297. For a thorough review of contemporary Papal teachings on inculturation see Michael Stogre, *That the World May Believe: The Development of Papal Social Thought on Aboriginal Rights* (Sherbrooke QC: Editions Paulines, 1992), 209–45.

10. Kenneth A. David and John C. Boonstra, "Themes to Challenge the Mission of the Church," *International Review of Mission* 81:324 (1992): 600. "Mission as solidarity implies a commitment to the restoration of people's fundamental symbols of their own way of life . . . and to worship God using their own practices and celebrations."

11. On the specific issue of "Aboriginal Christology" see also Carl Starkloff, "Aboriginal Cultures and the Christ," *Theological Studies* 53 (1992): 288–312. "If and when distinctively cultural Christologies are formulated within a universal church community, it must clearly be Christian natives themselves who do it" (296–97).

12. Peter Schineller, S.J., "Inculturation and Syncretism: What is the Real Issue?" *International Bulletin of Missionary Research* (April 1992): 50–53.

13. *Ibid.*, 50.

14. *Ibid.*, 52–53.

15. George Tinker, "Spirituality, Native American Personhood, Sovereignty and Solidarity," *The Ecumenical Review* 44:3 (1992): 319.

16. Fr. Michael Murray, personal communication, August 1993.

17. *Ibid.*

18. Immaculate Conception Church, 2.

19. Armstrong, personal communication.

20. *Ibid.*

21. Murray, personal communication.

Nahuas and National Culture

A Contest of Appropriations

RICHARD HALY

Panian negin tet
nikehualtia notiopan
Upon this rock
I will build my church
　　　　Festival banner in the church of San Pedro y Pablo, Xaltipan, Puebla

Poor Mexico,
so far from God,
and so close to the United
States.
　　　　Porfirio Díaz, Mexican president, 1875–1911

The church is built of rough-cut blocks of gray limestone, mossy in places or marked with rust-like stains extending down from ferrous concretions embedded in the walls—bullets shot by the planet Venus, I've been told—but that would be another story. A low, red-tiled roof, likewise mossy, and two thick buttresses lend the church at Xaltipan a certain massiveness despite its small, chapel-like size. A bell hangs in a separate tower. The path down to Xaltipan is steep and stony. After walking a little over two hours, rounding the last turn, you see the church. Sunburst shapes, woven of hearts of palm, hang above open wooden doors. Fleshy red stalk-like orchids—more than four feet tall—flank them. There is a relatively new cement floor and no pews. Men in clean white shirts and short white trousers cluster on the left side, opposite the women who, in white shifts and blouses brightly embroidered at the neck and shoulders, with shawls, with beribboned lacy neck-garments, with multiple necklaces of red plastic coral, with brightly colored sashes, some with mirrors inset, sit or stand on a pile of wooden beams stored there. Dressed in red, green, white, and yellow satin, two groups of men from other villages perform ceremonial dances, each to separate accompaniments of a two-holed flute from which is suspended a tiny drum. Dogs, generic, skinny and yellow, weave in among them to the excited amusement of the children running in and out of the church. Other dancers of other dances—*negritos, santiagos, quetzales, vegas, huehuentones, migueles*—dance, or wait, or share cane liquor in front of the church. The trunk of a tall tree has been erected, and at the top—about 70 feet up—is a wooden frame with four ropes from which the flying dancers, the *voladores*, now dancing in the church, will spiral down. A man ignites skyrockets with a smoldering corn cob, and they burst above the church and can be heard all the way down at the river and in other outlying and even smaller settlements. Outside and inside the church, people are conversing as they usually do, quietly. Many watch intently these scenes that they have seen repeated year after year. Some are watching me. And I am looking at the altar where copal incense billows among the equally pungent flowers, the flickering candles, the hummingbirds and flowers rendered in beeswax, ears of maize, whispered prayers, and paper banners, one of which is inscribed: *Panian negin tet/nikehualtia notiopan*: "Upon this rock/I will build my church." It is eight in the morning on 29 June. This is the festival of Xaltipan's divine patrons, the *santos*, San Pedro and San Pablo.

Other years I might not have noticed the banner or thought much of it—if it was ever there—but this year, because an elderly Nahua woman teaching me of the saints in a neighboring church had explained the striated nimbus surrounding the body of the Virgin of Guadalupe not as light, but as cracks in the stone mountain wall from which she was emerging; and because don Prócoro Hernandez, a Nahua healer, had told me that the name of his community, Tecoltepec, meant "On-The-Stone-Ancestor-Mountain;" I had a new appreciation for the relations obtaining among saints and the landscape. San Pedro was the rock. And this was Xaltipan, meaning "In-The-Sand." Below here there is no rock for building, and churches are built of bamboo or cinder block. Beyond Xaltipan the mountains end, opening out onto river plains, the "hot country," a different landscape, a different economy, a different history.

In Mexico, as in the United States, a crucial issue facing indigenous peoples is their relationship to national culture. However, in Mexico, the dynamics of this relationship are significantly different, as Mexican national culture constructs an indigenous identity for its own ideological ends—those of nationalism. Nahua religious practices, as manifestations of Nahua epistemology and economy, conflict with those of national culture that frame an ideology of identity in terms of *mestizaje*,[1] a syncretism of Spanish institutions—Roman Catholicism, literacy, and constitutional government with indigenous *prima materia*. Outside of this paradigm the national culture is by and large unable and unwilling to recognize the authenticity of indigenous culture, while the indigenous perspective sees only the community-wide truth of its ancestral practices, never mind that some of these were also practices of Spanish ancestors.

From a nationalist perspective, Nahua culture, like indigenous culture in general, is a necessary, but not sufficient, condition for *mestizaje*. The same, of course, might be said of the other necessary-but-not-sufficient condition of *mestizaje*, the Spanish side. The nationalist perspective, however, acknowledges its Spanish roots as a viable, if not preferable, alternative to *mestizaje*; after all, Spain exists as a nation. To acknowledge indigenous nationhood within a paradigm of nationalism would be problematic, to say the least.[2] If mestizo national culture is founded on the principle of European institutions refining ("civilizing") what they considered indigenous raw ("primitive") material, that which is termed "indigenous" can never temper or refine Spanish institutions, as what is indigenous is, by nationalist definition, that which is to be refined by Spanish institutions. Nationalism represents this somewhat one-sided discourse as acculturation.

How then is indigenous culture—specifically the guarantor of its authority, i.e., religion—to survive in such a parlous state? In what follows, I argue that the nationalist perspective, with its relatively narrow focus on the public manifestation of national signs, can see only what its perspective permits: the public manifestation of national signs. From the perspective of nationalism, indigenous religion can be described only in terms of syncretism, a bastard and adopted (read illegitimate) *mestizaje* of Spanish Catholicism and preconquest practices. Even though formulated as syncretic and illegitimate, indigenous religion, to the degree that it is seen as a *mestizaje*, poses a challenge to the authority of the official *mestizaje* of nationalism. Moreover, nationalism is congenitally blind, not only to the legitimacy of "others" within the nation it creates, but its own epistemological and political roots, as well as to strategies by which "others" invest these signs with other meanings.

This article will demonstrate that the perspective of syncretism that has dominated the representation of indigenous religious practices misrepresents these practices, and that the Catholic practices performed by the Nahua are appropriations through which Nahua culture has been able to resist national culture. However, this is neither a case of "idols behind altars," nor one of public Catholicism and private indigenous practice. The epistemological quandary we are about to enter is much greater and more complex than either of these models. James Lockhart (1992:243) has observed, "A general principle of Spanish-Nahua interaction is that wherever the two cultures ran parallel, the Nahuas would soon adopt the relevant Spanish form without abandoning the essence of their own form." The same might be said of Mexican Nationalist-Nahua relations to the degree that these are Spanish signs and indigenous interpretations. Nationalists identify only the outward manifestations as more or less faithful performances of prescribed Spanish practices, while indigenous peoples make sense of these signs from their own, equally ethnocentric, points of view.[3]

Mexican Nationalism is a product of the social interactions which it claims to represent. A brief account of some of these will provide a context in which we can better appreciate the deep resonance of *mestizaje* as a syncretism of Spanish institutions and indigenous "raw material." The prototype of this formulation is the image of the Spanish conquistador Hernán Cortés and his indigenous interpreter and mistress, doña Malintzin, "La Malinche," whose offspring, Martín Cortés, the first "official" mestizo, was hanged for treason. While Hernán Cortés is in no way celebrated in Mexico, La Malinche remains a potent symbol of both betrayal—the "mother who gives one away"—and the victim, although recent North American scholarship has attempted to address the complexity and ambiguity of her position (Karttunen 1994). Unlike the British colonies in North America which were colonized primarily by families of English men and women—with the result that there was much less mixture of European and indigenous genes or cultures—New Spain, was colonized primarily by Spanish men who came from Spain in pursuit of their fortunes—an enterprise that often included marriage to indigenous women and the engendering of mestizo offspring. Criollos, the offspring of *Spanish* parents in New Spain, were a small (though powerful) minority.

While Spanish men sowed their seed in indigenous women of the New World, this land, unlike Asia—known for its production of coveted manufactured goods—or Africa—thought of as a source of labor—was considered primarily a source of raw materials—metals, animal and agricultural products. According to the eighteenth-century French naturalist Géorges Buffon, the very newness of the New World rendered it at once inferior and malleable, clay to be molded at the experienced hands of men of the Old World.

Yet, it was not the hands of Europeans that were to shape the future of New Spain as much as their ideas, new ideas of "natural rights" and of a "sovereign nation." However, unlike the struggles for independence in other Latin American countries, the Mexican War of Independence (1810–21) was not initiated by the Criollos, but as a social revolution undertaken by mestizos, indigenous peoples and mulattos. Ironically, what began as a social revolution was to end as a conservative *coup d'état*. Under the leadership of the priest Miguel de Hidalgo, and, later, a mestizo priest, José María Morelos, these groups attacked whites without distinction as to whether these were peninsulares, i.e., from Spain, or Criollos. At Chilpancingo, Morelos declared that Mexico's sovereignty lay in the "will of the people," calling forth pride in a Mexican, not a Spanish, past. Then, in 1820 as a new climate of liberalism prevailed in Spain, New Spain's peninsulars, fearful that this liberalism might threaten their considerable privileges, joined with the Criollos in taking it upon themselves to declare their independence from such a liberal monarchy in order to set up their own, *conservative,* monarchy. This situation led to a rapprochement between Criollos and mestizos and to the *Plan de Iguala* (1821), the first document of this monarchy with its Creole emperor, guaranteeing equal rights regardless of race (Keen and Wasserman 1984:156ff). Newly independent Mexico, following the intellectual currents of its time, adopted the Napoleonic code and a sense of nationalism from the French "Declaration of the Rights of Man and the Citizen" (1789) which held that "Law is an expression of the general will," a concept that was based neither on Locke nor on the separation of powers of English common law, but on the Enlightenment concept that, freed of "ignorance, forgetfulness, or contempt for the rights of man," the nation would spontaneously express a "general will" that was, by definition, incapable of oppression save against those who violated civic duty. This sovereign state, ruled by a newly created national group, recognized no law other than its own reason. And this reason was the nascent nationalism of "raw material"—here, the mestizos, mulattos, and indigenous peoples who began the war for independence—tempered by European institutions of church and government.

THE HERMENEUTICS OF NATIONALISM

If, as I am arguing here, Mexican nationalists consider the indigenous component of *mestizaje* grist for their ideological mill, what do they make of it? What forms does it take? When it remains "unprocessed" it is thought of as raw courage or, ironically, the endurance that comes from long suffering. In material terms, it is that which pertains to maize, particularly tortillas, though including other maize-based foods as tamales and atole. These foods are metaphors for nourishment, the hearth, mother love, and home. Through its association with mother love, the sense of endurance of long suffering is enforced, as "endurance of long suffering" is also a characteristic of a Mexican formulation of female gender.

As "other," indigenous religion is raw material awaiting the shaping of interpreters. I have argued elsewhere (Haly 1992) that interpretations such as those of the Mexican historian Miguel León-Portilla's influential *Aztec Thought and Culture: A Study of the Ancient Nahuatl Mind* (1963), though seminal works when they first appeared, now are strongly in need of revision. Even the ostensibly sympathetic interpretations of Andrés Segura, a self-proclaimed indigenous spiritual leader with a sizeable Chicano following, try to legitimize indigenous practices in European terms. Intending, no doubt, to highlight some Nahua contributions to contemporary culture and to point out that there is much to be learned from his culture, Segura (1989) claimed that such a prestigious organization as NASA was using maize to create a fiber that would withstand the extremely high temperatures of space travel—with the distinct implication that the Aztecs were aware of these putative properties of maize. In 1990 he interpreted a conjunction of three iconographic elements in the pre-Colombian pictorial manuscript *Codex Borgia* as evidence that the Nahua also had, or knew of, a "Trinity." While these cannot be regarded as serious claims in themselves, they are serious to the degree that they represent a conception of Nahua culture and religion as having value because they are legitimate in modern technological or Christian terms. However, such cultural nationalism is not unique to Segura's formulation of *lo indio*. In her book *Borderlands*, a widely read work on *Chicana* feminist/lesbian identity, Gloria Anzaldúa uses a Jungian inspired interpretation of the female Nahua divinity Coatlicue, "Her Skirt is Snakes," to make her own argument as to what it is to be Chicana and lesbian. Recent and equally ahistorical interpretations have been made of the Virgin of Guadalupe as well. I am not arguing here against academic freedom but for academic responsibility. The power of print is considerable, and when the people represented in that writing do not themselves have access to the medium—Nahua women, for instance—the danger of cultural imperialism always looms large. Our representations of indigenous peoples deny them a voice in their own behalf. But this is nothing new.

Further, one can make a case that interpreting indigenous practices through the Enlightenment category "religion" already creates a perspective on these practices that does not do them justice, in that this view sees indigenous religions as primarily a matter of belief, not of practice, an issue I will examine below. Among others, Stephen Toulmin's *Cosmopolis: The Hidden Agenda of Modernity* (1990), a recontextualization of the origins of Modernity—the Age of Reason—demonstrates that "belief" came to have a central role in our definition of religion in response to the issues raised as Catholics and Protestants slaughtered each other during the Thirty Year's War (1618–38). To focus on Nahua beliefs as characteristic of Nahua "religion" is thus both anachronistic and "anatopic."

Needless to say, I cannot claim to speak (or write) for the Nahua either. My method is to report my dialogues with Nahuas over the past twenty years, attempting to place our statements and questions in a context that makes sense to both of us. My interpretation of Nahua religious practices is an analysis of the relationships that Nahuas and I can recognize between practices and contexts.

Since 1975 I have focused my work primarily in the Nahuatl-speaking environs of Cuetzalan, in the Sierra Norte de Puebla, Mexico, a remote area that did not feel a strong Spanish or mestizo presence until around 1875 when mestizos and Italians moved into this humid cloud forest to clear land for the intensive cultivation of coffee. Prior to this period, Cuetzalan, such as it was, was subject to the famous, and distant, sixteenth-century center, San Juan de los Rios (today, dusty Libres), then, in the seventeenth century, to the smaller and closer head town of Tlatlauhquitepec and then, as more villages grew and came into their own, to nearer and smaller Zacapoaxtla. Although churches were built in Cuetzalan and neighboring San Miguel Tzinacapan in the latter half of the eighteenth century, Cuetzalan achieved the status of *municipio*, a district center, as its Porfirate architecture attests, only at the beginning of this century.

Bernardo García Martinez (1987) has examined the transformations of life in the Sierra as Nahua lands passed from indigenous religious forms of authority to secular Spanish forms and the indigenous adaptations of these. Not only are these dynamics interesting in that they are contemporaneous with the factors leading to the development of Mexican nationalism but many of them are today active social forms structuring Nahua religious practices. What follows is a brief account of these events based on García Martinez, James Lockhart's work with Nahuatl legal documents (1992), and my own inferences regarding these dynamics based on what is commonly held to be true of Nahua culture in general.

Prior to the Spanish conquest the Nahua in the Sierra Norte de Puebla lived spread over a land whose ownership was by and large communal. Leadership was lineage-based and the ruling lineage claimed responsibility for both agricultural and human fertility—as both the production of sustenance, *tonacayotl*, "that which pertains to radiance," and the animating entity of humans, *tonalli*, "radiance," derived from the rulers' ancestral relationship to the sun, *tonatiuh*, "it goes radiating." This ideology was embodied by the ruler whose blood possessed a particular "radiance," *tonalli*, giving him the right to rule. While all Nahuas possess *tonalli*, or a *tonalli*—radiance or soul in the form of an animal or meteorological phenomena—a ruler's *tonalli* was his "destiny," his unquestionable rights and obligations. It was his prestige, his soul, that distinguished him. Rulers were considered divine and were served by the labor and tribute of the common people. Labor and tribute were dedicated to the care of the divinity of the enduring corporate entity—rendered in a medium more durable than that of the ruler's human body, a figure of stone, or wood—the management of which was entrusted to members of the ruling lineage.

Since the same families held both religious and political office, the distinction between religious and political is probably an anachronism based on a Spanish model. This is an important point, as after the conquest the Spanish instituted their own form of local political government, the *cabildo*, to which the Nahua responded with a parallel religious hierarchy whose offices and functions later interpenetrated those of the secular *cabildo* (Lockhart 1992:40, 215). Thus the dual form of government of preconquest times was continued to some degree through the creative use of Spanish forms.

The institution of Spanish-style government took place simultaneously with the concentration, or *reducción*, of widely spaced indigenous communities into more easily managed towns. When the *reducciones* were first instituted, the title of "governor," *gobernador*, was given to the indigenous local lord. This office did not exist in the governments of mestizo towns. In some cases the creation of *reducciones* and the centralization of power led to greater popular representation than was accessible prior to the conquest. Importantly, the traditional ritual marriages of the local lords were supplanted by an electoral process, though it appears that new, non-noble dynasties soon developed based on a preconquest pattern and precedent. The Spanish conquest and the drastic decrease of the indigenous populations through epidemics provided opportunities—if not the outright necessity—for Indians of non-noble status to participate in governmental activities to a degree previously denied them.

However, if, owing to the absence of a nobility, a vacuum was created in the equation of noble indigenous blood with human and agricultural fertility, this *lacuna* was filled almost immediately: in the place of the ruler, the ancestor, the Sun, was set the image of the saint who was patron to the village. The *tonalli* formerly present in the body of the ruler and in the material representations of the ruler's legitimacy was transferred to the icon of a patron saint, fulfilling the same functions of fertility as it had in other forms prior to the Spanish invasion. This shift from the sanctity of noble ancestors to the sanctity of saints did not take place before 1580 in Central Mexico and much later in the Sierra Norte de Mexico. Thus the Nahua began to "serve the saints."

SERVING THE SAINTS

By the latter half of the eighteenth century Cuetzalan and San Miguel Tzinaca-pan, two Indian towns in the Sierra Norte de Puebla, had given over serving hereditary local lords and had begun the practice they continue today, that of "serving the saints." Saints, like ancestors, were imagined as the parents of their people and as the true owners of the unit's land (Lockhart 1992:237f). My use of this phrase comes from Lockhart who points out that service of the saints was a "universal imperative" and " 'to serve the saints' in a certain house was tantamount to saying 'to maintain residence there.' " If service of the saints replaced service of the lords, in what do these practices consist? The Nahuatl testaments examined by Lockhart state that their authors desired that their heirs serve the saints by sweeping for them as well as keeping them clean and provided with candles, flowers, and incense. In 1695 the phrase they used was based on the root *tequipanoa*, which to Franciscan friars in 1570 meant "to work," (Molina 1970). Today, in the Sierra Norte de Puebla, it is used by Nahua healers in a formula to make offerings to the earth, to greet the earth (because one greets with gifts), in order that the earth release the *tonalli*, the radiance or "soul" of a patient.[4] In this context it means "to maintain or nourish." *Tequipanoa* is part of a semantic complex including such meanings as "to hold office" and "to fulfill responsibilities" (Karttunen 1983:232), these having the implicit sense of "bearing tribute" (Molina 1970:105).[5] To "work," "maintain," "nourish," "fulfill responsibilities," or to "bear tribute," whether on behalf of saints or rulers, means that they are to be greeted, that is, provided with what they require. This is what "work" was before the introduction of wage labor. In the Sierra Norte de Puebla, *tequipanoa*, the work or tribute (*tequitl*) that was to be transported (*panoa*), is today a customary practice, simply *panoliz*, an expense (Toumi 1984).

Religion is production. Ritual is work. As the Spanish concentrated the Nahua population into Indian towns and the new religious hierarchy developed, the acceptance of a "cargo" or religious office was obligatory—under threat of arrest—and the *sine qua non* for advancement in the Spanish-style *cabildo*. Nahua spoke then of these obligations as they do today; holding office or fulfilling responsibilities are *burdens* that are borne on one's back. Eventually their weight bends one over, *coloa*, and one becomes a grandfather, an ancestor, a "bent-over-one," a *colli*.

People worked together. Brotherhoods, *cofradías*, were formed to sponsor public ceremonial devotions to local icons of divine lineage, i.e., saints, the Sacred Heart of Jesus, etc. Such events were funded by the "community chests," *cajas de communidad*, a Spanish institution, originally introduced into the Indian towns with the intention of storing in them any wealth left over after tribute had been paid. These community chests also were the result of an expanded use of money by the Nahua and contained money from the sale of cotton cloth and maize. The Spanish imagined that this surplus would be used for collective necessities, which is in fact the use to which they were put. However, Spanish and indigenous ideas of what "collective necessities" were differed considerably. "From the indigenous point of view . . . the good use of the collective patrimony was linked more to the fulfillment of ritual functions than to the accumulation of wealth" (García Martínez 1987:104). Local indigenous authorities had no qualms about levying further taxes on their own people, taxes unauthorized by their Spanish overlords, taxes that would be used to purchase ornaments for the local indigenous church, the home of the patron saint, and for grand displays of local identity in the form of village festivals. García Martinez (1987:108) remarks that these "festivities and celebrations were never controlled [by the Spanish] and remained subject to the requirements of the villages which generally spent—in lavish style—all their money without taking into account time or labor . . . From the Spanish perspective the community chests did everything except that for which they were intended: remedy the Nahuas' poverty."

While participation in the *cofradías* was voluntary, this was not the case with other religious cargoes or with the individual sponsorship of a saint's festival, a *mayordomía*. Today, this has changed as during the last thirty or forty years the religious cargoes and the sponsorship of a saint's festival have become voluntary. However, today, as then, the *mayordomía* of a principal saint involves an expense of literally a year's wages.

As Lockhart states, "the saints seem to have symbolized household identity and continuity" (Lockhart 1992:238), a continuity which, I argue, extended to the noble ancestors whom they replaced. Moreover, like their predecessors, saints own land. Nahua testaments record the transfer of particular plots of land to particular saints, who are to be served by the stewardship (*mayordomía*) of the living heirs (Lockhart 1992:239). This custom of giving land, mules, and other valuables to a saint under the stewardship of a family member was a set formula. However, it might also imply that some income realized by working the land or mule was offered to a *cofradías* associated with the saint. Thus, the saint is served. Accepting the custody of the saint is a commitment (*compromiso*) which the heir undertakes just as he or she might take on the sponsorship of a festival or participate for a number of years in one of the ceremonial dances dedicated to the saints.

If, as noted above, serving the saints in a certain place is synonymous with what it is to dwell there, this would imply a close relationship between "serving" and "dwelling," and likewise between "saints" and "places." It follows then, that if we wish to understand what it means to a Nahua to dwell in a certain place, we can examine the practices Nahuas perform in service of the saints, as well as the dynamics which obtain between saints and places. The relationship between saint and place is stated explicitly in the same sources which equated serving the saints with dwelling in a certain place, that is, Nahua testaments, an occurrence that is not, to my way of thinking, accidental. Nor do I think that the injunction to "serve the saints" which accompanies the transfer of property from generation to generation, is merely a pious formula. Rather, the testament is a form of contract established between the testator and the recipient of the testator's estate. Upon the death of the testator the heir is required to fulfill a number of obligations in order to render the inheritance valid, if not in a legal sense, at least in terms of maintaining prestige by showing proper respect for the dead. These obligations usually include such activities as offering Masses, candles, and incense in the name of the deceased. Land, houses, mules, and the images of the saints themselves were bequeathed with instructions that these be used in service of the saints. By establishing reciprocal obligations with one's heirs, the testators are, in effect, ensuring that they will be treated properly as they begin the process of becoming an ancestor. They thus request that the saints, "noble" ancestors, are treated properly as they, the testators, are soon to join them. Just as the ancestors have provided for the testator, the testator's children are now to keep his or her memory. Indeed, most every Nahua household altar is a tableau of images, those of saints and framed photographs of deceased family members, incipient ancestors.[6] Saints and ancestors do not have some mystical or transcendental power over people. Instead, their power resides in their ability to inspire human activities in their service—activities which, as we shall see below, have significant social consequences.

One of the injunctions to serve the saints asks that the saints remain where they are, that is, continuing their association with a certain place (Lockhart 1992:238). Such requests not only reinforce the inviolability of the activities stipulated in the testament, in that failure to carry them out would no longer merely be taking a person's lawful inheritance, but taking something that belonged to a being from an otherworld, a saint. At the same time, in the manner of a performative act, the injunction to "serve the saints" enforces the power of the place as a source of family *tonalli*, in that the injunction not to move the saints, the very rule, creates a link with the place that is, by definition, not to be broken. Saints assume local family power because of this injunction, the very power held by their noble preconquest predecessors. If they could be moved, what power could they have over a certain place? Who one is—one's background and one's presence—is associated with a place through one's relationship to a saint, and this relationship consists in performing the practices the saint requires. Thus do saints bind people to places.

SERVING THE SANTITOS IN SAN MIGUEL TZINACAPAN

Nahuas serve the saints in San Miguel Tzinacapan—San Miguel [of the] Bats by the Water—where, according to local accounts, San Miguel once killed a large snake, thereby making the place inhabitable.[7] As mentioned above, neighboring Cuetzalan, once a similar Indian town, became a predominantly mestizo settlement after 1875. Until its relatively recent access to national media, the most significant source of nationalist ideology in San Miguel was the mestizo culture of Cuetzalan—the local delegation of the long-dominant political party PRI (Partido Revolucionario Institucional) and a conservative

Church. Cuetzalan, at the end of the paved road, where Nahuas catch buses to Puebla or Mexico City in search of wage labor; where tourists come to visit the Sunday market; whose inhabitants call all Indian women "María" and men, "Miguel;" residence of the regions largest landholders, and the municipality to which San Miguel belongs, is regarded by most people of San Miguel with considerable ambiguity, and by many others with an only slightly concealed hostility. Serving the saints is a daily matter and an intrinsically local matter—indeed, dwelling in San Miguel Tzinacapan consists precisely in this. To some extent, San Migueleño identity is created in contrast to the Cuetzaltecan "other." This, despite the fact that mestizos of Cuetzalan share more culture with their Nahua neighbors than they do with many mestizos in other parts of Mexico. The friction between the two is the result of economic and political power translated into culturally marked terms: the political and economic hegemony enjoyed by Cuetzaltecos has been gained at the expense of the Nahuas—as *prima materia*: land and labor—consequently anything marked "*indio*" (Indian) is, by definition, inferior, or from the perspective of mestizo Roman Catholicism, "improperly understood." What follows is an account of the way things are understood in San Miguel Tzinacapan, a rough account of the differences between a Nahua way of serving the saints and mestizo Catholicism.

THE DOMAINS OF SAINTS AND ANCESTORS

Having equated saints with places, serving the saints, dwelling in a place— dwelling in the domain of the saints—involves three fields of action; *semantic fields*, which comprise the day-to-day making sense of the world; *saints' enclosures*, which include the church patio and household altars; and *maize fields*, the source of sustenance. Neither of these fields is more important than any other, as two always are necessary for the functioning of the third: a day-to-day understanding of the world and offerings to the saints and ancestors are necessary for the production of maize, just as the production of maize and a day-to-day understanding of the world is necessary to make offerings to saints and ancestors, while sustenance and offerings to saints and ancestors are necessary to make day-to-day sense of the world.

The Nahua world of San Miguel Tzinacapan is an integrated one. Upperworld (Nahuatl: *ilhuicac*), middleworld (Nah. *talticpac*), and lowerworld (Nah. *talocan*), are bound together by the necessary dialogue and exchange of *tonalli*, radiance, between them. *Tonalli*, the currency exchanged between worlds and times, has a number of meanings and forms. For the Nahua it is radiance, the light of day, as well as one's "fortune" or "destiny," one's lot in life (Molina 1970). It is also one's "lot" in the sense of a parcel of land. It is one's soul; it animates one. It is the story one tells oneself in order to get out of bed in the morning. *Tonalli* links one with the past, with the ancestors. It is spoken of as an "animal living on the mountain." This "radiance" is one's reputation, that which is said about one. If there is a great deal of this radiance then "reputation" becomes "fame," or *tleyotl*, "that which pertains to fire"; that is, something visible from afar though concentrated in a single place. From my perspective, since I cannot see or measure *tonalli*, I must take the Nahuas' word for it, that it exists. If this is all I have—their word for it—then *tonalli* can only be "the Nahuas' word for it," that is, *tonalli* is language: a story told by oneself or about oneself, a dream narrative, reputation, gossip, prestige, authority, the metaphor that links past to present. It is the work of humans to sustain themselves in this dialogue between upper and lower worlds, between saints and ancestors, sun and maize.

The domain of saints and ancestors is bounded by the semantic fields Nahuas use when speaking of their world. To speak of the world Nahuas use metaphors, occasionally as poetic devices, but always as epistemological constructs by which one thing is known in terms of another (Lakoff and Johnson 1980). Often their dialogue with the world includes ethnocentric interpretations of Christian signs. I was not, however, initially aware of this. During the first few years I spent working in the Sierra Norte de Puebla I labored under the mistaken perspective that as regards Nahua cultural practices there were two kinds: those that were Christian and those that were "survivals" of a preconquest culture. As I was then at work translating a collection of sixteenth-century Nahuatl lyrics, the *Cantares Mexicanos*, I had reasoned that perhaps some of the techniques and metaphors of the old lyrics were still alive in the orations of contemporary native healers. I was, therefore, plainly interested in the "survivals," and until one of the healers, don Pedro Toral, set me straight, I took the saints—never mind their local idiosyncrasies—as given, as Catholicism "imperfectly understood." I focused instead on the healers' formulation of the lower world, *Talocan*, reasoning that I might map this cosmology onto what was known from other sources about the preconquest Nahua cosmos. And indeed, in many instances there was a strong correspondence between the two; so strong in fact, that my success encouraged me to continue working with this perspective. I was, however, mistaken. Not about the correspondence between contemporary formulations of *Talocan* and preconquest ones, but about the role of the saints and of most everything I "knew" to be Christian.

THE DOMAIN OF OUR FATHER

Perhaps understandably enough I thought of Roman Catholicism as monolithic—this, after all, is what Catholicism teaches—the very word "catholic" attests its universality. I was aware of the doctrinal distinctions between Roman

Catholicism and the Byzantine Church as well as the social distinctions made among Irish, Polish, and Italian Catholics. Yet Catholicism itself, was, at its core, its essence, the same. Then don Pedro Toral taught me, unwittingly, to doubt, and I learned that local Catholicism has little to do with its national or universal representations. I had gone to don Pedro's home to tape a curing ceremony for a patient who had succumbed to the malady called *nemouhtil* in Nahuatl or *susto* in Spanish, meaning "fright," but entailing an understanding that the patient had "lost her *tonal*," her radiance, her soul. As I had learned from other healers, the ceremony would begin with the recitation of a number of "Christian prayers," in this case seven "Our Fathers." Even though these were recited in Nahuatl, they were nonetheless Christian prayers and not of any particular interest to me. I was waiting for the part that would follow, where the healer petitions the earth to release the patient's lost tonal; it was here that I might find among the "names of the earth" new old metaphors, more "survivals." I even toyed with the idea of pressing the pause button in my tape recorder so as to save batteries and tape.

Unlike many recitations of Christian prayers that I've heard, don Pedro Toral prayed fervently and relatively slowly as though cognizant of the import of the words he spoke: *Totatziné ipan in ilhuicac*, "Our Father, who art in heaven," and *ma titechmactilia in totaxcal*, "give us our tortilla [our daily bread]," and later, in his petition to the earth, the lower world wherein the lost *tonal* of his patient was captive, more "survivals." Afterward, I had some questions, but it was already noon and one of us had some other place to be. I asked don Pedro if I might return the next day to discuss with him what went on, and as he accompanied me out the doorway from the smoky darkness of his plank house, I remember shielding my eyes against the bright sun that broke through the branches of a zapote tree in the yard. Don Pedro said, "*quema, mozta, qualcan*, yes, tomorrow, early," as he extended his arm, white-shirted and thin, pointing toward the sun adding "*queman tanesic in totatzin dios*, when Our Father Dios appears," —meaning tomorrow morning. I continued blinking, though now from the sudden brightness of incredulity. It had dawned on me that the "Our Father" had another interpretation, one as thoroughly Nahua as I had previously imagined it to be thoroughly Christian. Don Pedro, having just referred to the sun as "Our Father Dios," recalled to me the prayers he'd recited an hour before. "Our Father, who art in heaven . . . give us our tortilla." Don Pedro, conservative Nahua that he was, heard in this what was commonsense to every Nahua: one prays to the sun for maize. From a Nahua perspective the Christian prayer said just that: "thy kingdom come, thy will be done, on earth as it is in heaven." My point here is simply the ethnocentric "invisibility" of this religious practice. Since Nahuas go about reciting the "Our Father" under the would-be paternal gaze of the visiting priest, lighting candles on the altar, offering ears of dried maize to the bloody image of Padre Jesus, "Father Jesus," I couldn't say whether they were or were not Christian. I recalled a passage I had read some years before in the *Chronicles of Michoacan* (Craine and Reindorp 1967) in which a sixteenth-century Franciscan vociferously objected to the "mockery" he saw in the indigenous practice of using tortillas for the Eucharist in their own "Mass." Perhaps, I thought, these Indians understood things perfectly. At any rate, I began to see things differently: using the language of Christianity, Nahuas went about their business of being Nahuas. As Nahua representations of the lower world, *Talocan*, could be mapped onto what we knew of preconquest cosmology, so too could the semantic fields of Christianity. Here, Our Father—the sun—has become the organizing principle and source of entailments—heat and light—by which a sacred authority and prestige of the upper world is managed in earthly, human terms. Having thus taken over the domain of the saints, the Nahua world was suddenly bigger, ironically victorious, and utterly vital.

THE DOMAIN OF THE HOLY TRINITY

While there are saints and other powerful beings in heaven, in the sky, their power and gravity resides in their interaction with the earth, with people on earth—a concern varying from the intimate presence or absence of the sun—the brute blood of the air, to that of the temporally and spatially remote threat of the perpetually hungry sources of cold, the unnamed stars. Not surprisingly, it is earthly doings—their own—that are important to the Nahuas in the Sierra Norte de Puebla. These mundane affairs are grounded in dialogues with the ancestors who are disembodied embodiments of the past in the present, the arbiters of order in the world. These dialogues take place on numerous occasions as Nahuas greet or feed the ancestors, the *tatitas, los abuelitos*, in dreams, or by offering incense, prayers, and flowers on household altars. These instances are recognitions of an implicit order that governs all daily practices, an order that enters the middle world, the present, from the lower world, the past, the Land of the Dead, another repository for the rules that make culture.

In the Sierra Norte de Puebla, Nahuas call the earth "the Holy Trinity," using the Spanish phrase "la Santísima Trinidad." They speak of the surface of the earth as a *comal*, an earthenware griddle on which tortillas are cooked, a metaphor parallel to that of their relation to upper world as "people [maize] increase their *tonalli*, their radiance [are cooked]." The three stones (*tenamaztli*) upon which the *comal* rests are the earth's bones and are its source of strength (Signorini and Lupo 1989).[8] This Santísima Trinidad, however, does not consist in the same three persons as the Roman Catholic trinity: the three stones are "Father and Mother Trinity" and "their child." The Santísima Trinidad, the earth, is a family, a perdurable arrangement of strict relations. Doña Guadalupe Vásquez and don Prócoro Hernandez, two of the healers with whom I worked, refer to Father Trinity and Mother Trinity as lords of the lower world, *Talocan Tata* and *Talocan Nana*, "*Talocan* Father" and "*Talocan* Mother" or *Talocan Toteizcalticatahtzin* and *Talocan toteizcalticanantzin*, "Our Honored Father/Mother Who Nurtures People," that is, as ancestors. The earth "as a family" is consistent with the associations of lineage and place found in both pre-Hispanic and contemporary sources in which the earth itself is animate, and like the sun, a source of *tonalli*.

There is an imperfect fit between this appropriation of a trinity and the patently pre-Hispanic and contemporary accounts of the four figures, *taloqueh*, who support the earth, at the center of which is the "Heart of the Mountain."[9] Don Prócoro spoke of them with the Spanish honorific, *don*, as "the earth, *talmanic*, don Martín, Manuel, Antonio, and Francisco," the names of the patron saints in the larger villages to the west, north, east, and south, respectively.[10] When planting maize, offerings are made to each of these in the shape of a cross. In the Sierra Notre de Puebla both accounts may be held by the same person without contradiction or conflict, a fact which, to me, indicates both the vitality of the Nahua cosmos, in that it is understood as "a way of talking about the world," and the use of metaphors in specific contexts to make sense in and of this cosmos. By using both metaphors, Nahuas are able to speak of two kinds of order on the earth: temporal order, by means of the "family" metaphor, and spatial order by means of the "four corners" metaphor. Both of these metaphors have further hierarchical entailments. In the "family" metaphor, the elder generation is ranked higher than the younger, and in the "four corners" metaphor, the eastern figure of the four is the eldest and therefore highest-ranked.

The Roman Catholic sign of the cross, crossroads, and crosses in general, should be added to this formulation, as these are understood as part of the semantic field of world-orderers. Crosses are beings who spread out, creating a center, or who stand at the corners communicating with worlds above or below as their location requires. Wherever two paths or roads join, it is common to find a shrine to the Holy Cross as a recipient of prayers to the twelve *hueyoh*, the "twelve great roads," that the traveler might not hunger nor thirst on the road.[11] According to doña Guadalupe, Jesucristo bearing the heavy burden of his cross during the Passion evokes images of the pains of being distant from one's community as well as those of the Mesoamerican metaphor of holding political or religious office—represented as "carrying a burden, or cargo." Jesucristo is the light of the sun, on earth, in the form of maize. His work, or office, is bearing this light (*tonalli*) to all four corners—the cross—the sacrifice of his blood—bearer of *tonalli*—and its resurrection from the earth in the form of his body—maize. Not only does this ancestral *tonalli* (of Jesucristo, son of the Eternal Father) make maize grow; it is also responsible for social order. That is, the *tonalli* transferred from ancestors to the living, in the form of social practices, is an absolute necessity for the cultivation of maize—a communal activity, and metaphorically, the cultivation of Nahuas themselves. Thus the earth has its order.

THE DOMAIN OF THE VIRGIN MARY AND OF HER-SKIRT-IS-JADE

Things that move like liquid, with liquid: water, menses, conception, childbirth, lightning, memory; these are the domain of the virgins; of "Her-Skirt-is-Jade," of "Mother Virgin Lightning Bolt," of the "Heart of Mary," of María, Malintzin, Ocotlán, of Rosa, Concepción, of Guadalupe, of Dolores, and Marta del Mar, among others. When don Prócoro petitions the four corners of the earth seeking the germination and protection of his maize, he asks that the Mother Virgin Lightning Bolt for her "sprout"—the lightning, the accompanying rain, and the maize—so that he might live. Again, it is the earth he is addressing—or more specifically, the mountains. Lightning and water come from within the mountains as they always do in Mesoamerica. Again, Nahuas in the Sierra Norte de Puebla share Roman Catholic icons with their mestizo neighbors, with, of course, their own local interpretations.

Like the "Eternal Father," the sun, and the "Holy Trinity," the earth, the identification of the Roman Catholic Virgin Mary with a Nahua counterpart is due to the Nahuas' ethnocentric interpretations of Catholic representations which parallel their own. Before the arrival of the Spaniards, lightning and water in mountains were the domain of *Chalchihuitl Icue*, "Her-Skirt-Is-Jade" or *Matlacueyeh*, "She-Has-A-Bluegreen-Skirt" in the case of the green slopes of the mountain watershed of the Tlaxcalla-Puebla high plains. Indeed, the Roman Catholic Virgin Mother Mary repeats—with her blue cape and her virginity—both the indigenous formulation of Chalchiuhuitl Icue's bluegreen shift and the sixteenth-century Nahua metaphor for a girl who is "still a maiden or virgin": *oc chalchiuhuitl*, "she is still jade," they said (Molina 1970:2:75). During the colonial period the mountain Matlacueyeh came to be called Malintzin, a Nahuatlization of "Honored Marina," [Malin(a)-tzin], later Hispanized as "Malinche." Today, in the *ranchería* Zoapilaco, "Place of the Girl's Water," about ten kilometers from Cuetzalan, there is a shrine to the patron saint, Malintzin, the patroness of waters. It is significant that the Nahuas in no way associate Malintzin with the complex figure of Malinche, Cortés' indigenous translator and mistress, herself the subject of much nationalist culture as the first mother—with first father, Conquistador Cortés—of the *raza cósmica*, "the cosmic race," *mestizaje*.

The Virgin Mary's association with pregnancy and childbirth is likewise another Nahua appropriation. Both conception and childbirth are translations of life from ancestors to the living, or more precisely, from ancestors living in the lower world to the Nahuas living in the middleworld, on the surface of the earth. Again, it was Chalchihuitl Icue, "Her-Skirt-Is-Jade," whom midwives petitioned to "cleanse the heart" of a newborn child as they cut the umbilical cord, and as they bathed the child on the day that the child was to receive his or her *tonalli*, one's radiance, or "soul" (Sahagún 1974–82). These acts of separation and subsequent incorporation depend on the liminal activity of "cleansing the heart," a transformation that enables the heart to record the ancestral information, the *tonalli*, that is to be inscribed upon it.

"Cleansing the heart" has its analogue in contemporary Nahua practices, beyond the obvious associations with Roman Catholic baptism. Before doña Guadalupe undertakes the restoration of a patient's lost *tonalli*, she prepares herself to dream, for it is in dreams that her own *tonalli* will enter the lowerworld, *Talocan*, to seek the lost *tonalli* of her patient. One day, as I was seeking information on possible mnemonic devices in Nahuatl oral transmission, I asked doña Guadalupe how she remembered everything, all the prayers and petitions she knew. I was amused and surprised as she told me she had a prayer (yet another) to help her remember everything. She prayed to "Our Great Mother," the Heart of Mary, (Corazón de María), thus: "Heart of Mary/Open me in the heart./Cleanse me in the heart./Clear for me my heart of hearts./So that all that I dream, I know./May I remember it all./May there be nothing that I might forget."[12] To remember then, depends on having one's heart "cleansed." Memory, particularly memory of ancestral relations—as imaged in dreams in the lower world—is a *habitus* of the heart. Just as ancestral relations are inscribed in the earth, the ability to remember them depends—from a Nahua perspective—on the purity of one's heart, though I would argue that the ability to remember ancestral relations is itself performative "proof" that one's heart is pure. The *tonalli* or soul that a child receives soon after birth is related to the child by "Her-Skirt-Is-Jade" via the midwife. If, at some point "in the middle way of our life" the *tonalli* or "soul" is lost, a ceremony, analogous to that of "baptism," is held, a healing ceremony, by which the *tonalli* is restored to the patient by the healer through the intercession of the "Heart of Mary." If the earth, the Holy Trinity, is, as we have seen, a record of the ancestral landscape, the volatility of this memory is imaged in water which has the metaphoric capacity to cleanse and erase, to spring from dark recesses and to return to them, to evaporate, to come upon one in a torrent, to reflect in stillness. Water is the "blood of earth" as don Miguel Cruz says; moving among ancestors, among mountains, from the Heart of the Mountain, from the Heart of Mary, She-Has-A-Bluegreen-Skirt.

Sometime after I had learned what Nahuas mean by the "Our Father," I was again recording curing ceremonies—this time however, paying more attention to the "Christian" elements. It was an unseasonably cold and misty March, and I had forced a Volkswagen down to the *ranchería* of Tzitzilan which, though somewhat below San Miguel Tzinacapan, was neither warmer nor less damp. Luis Juarez was about to perform a curing ceremony for a child who had lost his *tonalli*. Beginning with an offering of thirty Our Fathers (which I did not record), he would then offer thirty Aves Marías. Had I heard him right? Aves Marías? That is, not "Ave," *Hail*, Mary, but "*aves*," birds. In Spanish, a "Hail Mary" is an *avemaría*, one word. Don Luis recited these in Spanish. I later asked him if he knew this prayer in Nahuatl. He did not. This was important, as there is nothing in the Nahuatl version of the prayer—beginning, *cihuapillé*, "O young woman"—that could be interpreted as having anything to do with birds. Still, it was strange. What is this bird, "full of *gracia*" who is related somehow to the "blessed fruit of thy womb, Jesus"?

The bird is the Holy Spirit, the animal *tonalli* of Jesucristo. It's right there in the church, the fading chromo of the Sacred Heart of Jesus and "the dove descending breaks the air with wings of incandescent fire." Doña Guadalupe said, *Dios yetoc eyi tonal*, "God is three *tonalli*, God the Father, God the Son, God the Holy Spirit," though these are not the Holy Trinity discussed above. Rather, it is the last-named of these, the Holy Spirit, who cares for one's *tonalli*, one's soul or destiny and its manifestation in the world as an animal or as meteorological phenomena. And it is the Holy Spirit in the shape of a dove who transfers his divinity to the womb of the Virgin Mary, as do the Nahua ancestors their *tonalli* in any pregnancy. And the Virgin bears Jesucristo, maize. She is full of "gracia" as Nahuas and other Mesoamericans call maize, "*gracia*," grace. The Holy Spirit is the *tonalli* of Jesucristo. It is the Holy Spirit who, as tongues of fire, visits the apostles—all of them saints—after Jesucristo had returned to heaven, after which they begin to perform numerous baptisms, as though they now had the *tonalli*, the rights and obligations to communicate, to bestow membership in the community.

We have seen that God the Father is the sun, which means that Nahuas must relate to the sun as to a father, and to fathers as sources of heat and light. We have seen that the Holy Trinity is the earth, a family; that the Holy Cross is a means of relating people to each other and to maize, that the Virgin Mary and the Sacred Heart of Mary are life-giving, life-sustaining liquids, and that the Holy Spirit, the Ave María, the "Bird María," is a fluttering, hypostatization of the vibrant radiance of sunlight and maize. Yet it would be a mistake to think of these as anything like doctrines. They are not. They are living metaphors. Using the language of Roman Catholicism, Nahuas represent their relations in a world that is self-evident to all Nahuas: a world or worlds in which ancestors, the sun and earth, are the epistemological guarantors of such sense as the world makes. Whether don Prócoro addresses "Manuel Martín Antonio Francisco" as he prepares to plant his maize, while doña Guadalupe addresses San Isidro the Worker; whether don Pedro begins a ceremony with seven "Our Fathers" and don Luis, with thirty: these differences are not important.[13] While doña Guadalupe is always interested in what I know of the prayers of Miguel Cruz or of don Prócoro, puzzled as to why I want to know their ways in addition to her own, ready to belittle the power of these practices, contest their metaphors taken out of context (and this, despite the fact that all the ceremonies and explanations are, from my perspective, remarkably similar), it is not because these other ways are untrue or ineffective. Rather, it is because these other ways *are* true and effective that doña Guadalupe must contest them. It is not knowledge of Catholicism—in whatever form—that makes these people prestigious members of their communities, people with the power to heal. It is the prestige—the *tonalli*—they acquire by means of their ability to interpret the world in ways that are useful to family, ritual kin, neighbors, other Nahuas, that gives their words weight. Their representations, then, are products of their experience and that of their teachers, and there is no reason to expect that doña Guadalupe's way should be the same in every detail as that of don Prócoro. Thus the jealousy and competition among healers—for it is their prestige that heals, and their interpretive acumen gives them prestige.[14] The vitality of Nahua religion lies precisely here, in the competition engendered in making the world make sense. While Nahua religion changes, it is this ability to change—while claiming to remain the same—that makes it effective.

MAKING COMMONSENSE

Nahuas do not believe in ancestors any more than it can be said that we *believe* in our language. If I had been mistaken about the nature of the semantic fields which accompanied talk about saints, I later realized that I had been likewise mistaken in what I thought was the significance of such talk. I had the wrong idea about what knowledge or knowing was. Looking for "survivals" I had looked for "specialized" knowledge, something I thought would be distinct from the day-to-day, "sacred" not "profane," a private matter, even esoteric, something that Nahua healers had and I didn't have. And this latter formulation was, is, to some degree, true. But at the same time, such a perspective limited me to a description of knowledge that was private and intellectual, a knowledge that resembled the sort of learning universities used to encourage, "book learning"—a catalogue of what the Nahua know and, regarding religion, what the Nahua believe. Serving the saints had been an imported "belief system," not a collection of practices integrated with the service of ancestors, ensuring the social and material well-being of the community. Knowledge is in the practice of serving saints and ancestors. The degree to which anything one knows contributes to this task is the degree of its significance, the mark of its meaning.

Nowhere is this more explicit than in the form of knowledge distinctive to the Nahua healers with whom I worked; that is, in dreaming, an act that was private, mental, and raw material for interpretation *par excellence*, or so I thought. Nothing could have been further from the truth. Dreaming with the intention of divining the reason for the loss of someone's *tonalli* is a practice that distinguishes Nahua soul-loss, *nemouhtil*, from its mestizo counterpart, *susto* (Signorini and Lupo 1989:123). Dreams are symptomatic of both the cause and cure of soul-loss. Nahua people of San Miguel Tzinacapan say that dreams are one's *tonalli*, one's radiance, escaping the body during sleep, breaking free during coitus, or frightened out of one, to roam the lowerworld where it is subject to more powerful luminaries—saints, ancestors and other villagers. The lower world is the dwelling place of this ancestral radiance, the radiance that flowers in maize. *Tonalli* lost there can end up, as we say, "pushing up daisies."

As we have already seen, healers use their own *tonalli*—in dreams—to enter this world in search of the lost *tonalli* of their patients. The healers mediate between the patient and the gods, that is, the saints and ancestors, that is, between people and rules. By interviewing the patient or the patient's family, the healer learns (if he or she does not already know) what conflict oppresses the patient. The dream, then, though ostensibly diagnostic, is perhaps better understood as an authoritative confirmation of the symptoms. The many dreams I have heard recounted over the years all have remarkably similar plots—flight, loss, disorientation—and all are told in similar images, images which are, moreover, those of the innumerable stories told by the Nahua among themselves. In San Miguel the storytelling tradition rhymes with the dream-telling tradition, as if stories were "famous" dreams or dreams echoed the perpetual telling of these stories. At any rate, anyone who does not tell these stories, has heard them. The language of dreams is public, not esoteric. It is commonsense. Part of the work of the healer is in recounting and formalizing the conflict, placing oneself at the center of the conflict—the social conflict—which oppresses the patient, running the risk thereby, that mediation renders one vulnerable, makes one a target of the ill will or envy directed at and oppressing the patient. The ability to accomplish this, to "know how to go on" better than someone else, demonstrates the strength of the healer's *tonalli*, his or her prestige.

Not only were dreams not private, but the words of the petitions to the earth, which I had thought to be jealously guarded property of the healers, were communicated to me on numerous occasions by ten healers in the Cuetzalan area alone. I had expected "secret knowledge," but found, in fact, that many people know the words to the petitions—more so as these are not, for the most part, texts memorized verbatim but generated from a formula asking that such and such be done in exchange for this or that. Being asked on a number of occasions to perform the ceremony to restore a lost *tonalli*, I discovered that it was not the words of the petitions and prayers that had the power to cure. It is significant that my mediation was sought only in cases in which the person requesting my services wanted the ceremony performed without the patient knowing about it. This is, in itself, evidence of two aspects of Nahua religious practice: first, the Nahua faith in the power of the ceremony, that it could function unbeknownst to the patient—or victim—as what I was being asked to do was technically "witchcraft"; secondly, an awareness, despite the power of the ceremony in itself, of a social dimension of the ceremony: my status as an outsider assured that the request would not become public knowledge, a doubly important consideration since the very act of seeking help from outsiders could be interpreted as an act of distancing oneself from indigenous identity—an act likely to provoke precisely the kinds of sanctions which result in soul-loss (Hermitte 1964). Once when I declined—as I always did—to undertake a request to cure a woman of soul-loss, her husband, who had made the request, commented that despite my knowledge of the words and other aspects of the ceremony, "not everyone can heal." It followed that if everyone dreams, and everyone knows what the dream signs mean, and if many people know the petitions to the lower world, these are not what distinguish healers from those who cannot heal. That is, it was not any power inherent in the words that made them efficacious, but the social manifestation of the words, the power of the person who spoke them, that is, her authority, his prestige, the strength of that person's *tonalli*. And this prestige, the prerequisite for becoming a healer likewise depends not on one's personal knowledge, but on its public manifestation—a sign such as recovering from a life-threatening illness or a vision (to Nahua these are more or less the same thing), or one's continued association with a healer such that one acquires prestige (and knowledge) by consorting with the prestigious.

It is within this context, against this background, this understanding of Nahua knowledge, that the phenomena which comprise what it is to serve the saints make most sense. By serving the saints a person's public persona comes into being. In San Miguel Tzinacapan, where emphasis is placed on communal, that is, public, activity, the private sphere is regarded as dangerous, threatening, a source of envy and intrigue. Consequently, activities performed in private cannot be sources of prestige. At best such activities are sources of fear or awe. The contemporary Nahua religious practices outlined below are to be understood therefore as structures of common sense in San Miguel Tzinacapan, self-evident spheres of activity in which Nahuas go about the work of living and assuring themselves a future.

MY KIND OF TOWN

Serving the saints, for the more or less twenty-five hundred residents of San Miguel Tzinacapan, entails the performance of minimally twenty-eight festivals each year. And this figure does not take into account the events associated with baptisms, marriage, house roofings, and wakes.

In the table below we can see that the majority of the saints' festivals fall within three one-month periods: mid-March through mid-April (five festivals),[15] June (six festivals),[16] and December 8 to January 6 (six festivals), with another four festivals during a one-week period at the end of September and the first of October; all of which is to say, 64 percent of the festivals fall in three months, or 71 percent in three months and a week. This is significant not because the festivals are clustered around equinoxes and solstices, as they are for Roman Catholics whose calendar they follow, but because this arrangement means that there are up to three months between intensive festival activities, a period which is necessary, as I will argue in the next section, for the fulfillment of the reciprocal obligations into which participants in the festivals enter.[17]

Regarding the gender of the saints, the table shows that festivals celebrating male *santos* outnumber those honoring female *santos*, two to one (17:8). However, this is misleading in that of the seventeen festivals employing male images, eight of these celebrate various aspects of Jesucristo, who, one might argue, is something of a special case. If we accept this formulation, then male saints (nine) are hardly more celebrated than female saints (eight), an account that is strengthened by the fact that six additional festivals (the Holy Trinity and the Holy Family among them) celebrate both male and female divinities. Nonetheless, despite this apparent equality, festivals for female saints are consistently smaller in scale, requiring less investment on the part of their sponsors than those pertaining to Jesucristo or male saints. From the perspectives of the women who have interpreted the saints in the church to me, male saints are the focus of offerings regarding work and, to some degree, male activities such as fishing, planting, and traveling out of the community to work. Female saints, however, are the focus of offerings relative to a person's life at home: the Virgen de la Concepcíon, for giving birth; the Virgen de Ocotlán, to protect the virginity of young women; Santa Rosa and her sisters, Santas Veronica, Anna, and Teresa, to protect reputations by keeping girls "out of the street," that is, at home; the Virgen de los Dolores to guard the memory of the deceased.

TABLE 1 : Festival Cycle: San Miguel Tzinacapan, Puebla

DATE fiXed or moVeable		FESTIVAL	SEX		TYPE †		THE SAINTS' COFFERS 3 New Pesos = $1U.S.		
			M	F	L	W	1994	1991	+%
6.I	x	*Los Reyes	•	•	•	•	n/a	n/a	n/a
2.II	x	*Candelaria	•	•	•		n/a	n/a	n/a
19.III	x	San José	•		•		no data	12	n/a
7.IV	v	Virgen de Dolores		•	•		9	7	28.5
9.IV	v	San Ramos	JC		•		42	20.6	103.8
14.IV	v	Santo Entierro	JC		•		90	no data	0
16.IV	v	Ascensíon del Señor	JC		•		no data	9	n/a
3.V	x	Santa Cruz	•	•	•	•	10	10	0
15.V	x	San Isidro Labrador	•			•	20	no data	n/a
4.VI	v	Espirito Santo	JC		•		n/a	n/a	n/a
11.VI	v	Santísima Trinidad	•	•	•	•	20	10	100
15.VI	v	Santísima Sacramento	JC			•	80	80	0
23.VI	v	Corazón de Jesús	JC		•		20	10	100
24.VI	v	Corazón de María	•	•	•	•	4	2	100
24.VI	x	San Juan Bautista	•			•	25	15	66
29.VI	x	San Pedro	•			•	n/a	n/a	n/a
12.VII	x	Virgen de Ocotlán		•	•		20	5.1	292
16.VII	x	Virgen del Carmen		•	•		20	17	17.6
6.VIII	x	Padre Jesús Nazareno	JC		•		no data	30	n/a
30.VIII	x	Santa Rosa		•	•		21	16	31
29.IX	x	San Miguel Arcangel	•		•		30	20	50
29.IX	x	San Gabriel Arcangel	•		•		20	5	300
2.X	x	Angel Custodio	•	•	•		30	20	50
4.X	x	San Francisco de Asís	•			•	30	15	100
2.XI	x	Anima Sola	•	•	•		6	0	600
30.XI	x	San Rafael Pescador	•				25	21	19
8.XII	x	Virgen de la Concepción		•	•		35	6	483
12.XII	x	Virgen de Guadalupe		•	•		20	17	17.6
25.XII	x	Niño Dios	JC		•		40	20	100
27.XII	x	San Juan Evangelista	•			•	13	2.5	420
1.I	x	Sagrada Familia	•	•	•		n/a	n/a	n/a

*indicates a festival celebrated with no material representation of the associated "saint" in the church of San Miguel Tzinacapan.

Shading indicates a material representation of a "saint" in the church with no accompanying festival in San Miguel Tzinacapan.

JC indicates Jesucristo.

†indicates that the festival celebrates either rites of passage and attendant issues (L = life cycle) or events seen as directly related to the economic maintenance of the community (W = work).

TABLE 2 : Gender of Divinities and Number of Festivals

DIVINITIES	FESTIVALS
Jesucristo	8
Male Saints	9
Female Saints	8
Both	6

Jesucristo who, as maize, transcends gender, also has specific related functions which depend on the metaphor "humans are maize." From the women's perspective, not only is the Niño Jesús the "new corn," he is also a guardian of the tender *tonalli* of a newborn child. Padre Jesús, the fully ripe maize, is the recipient of offerings when a husband has mistresses, in order that the offending husband might break off that relationship. The Santo Entierro ["Holy Burial," Good Friday], the dried maize, is the object of offerings when a man beats his wife so that *ixpanoltia mocama*, "he is made to leave your bed." When a man dies, his widow will offer dried ears of maize at the Santo Entierro in the church. This equation of humans and maize also functions reflexively in that human actions, such as having mistresses or beating one's wife, cause problems with maize and one's children.

The resources in the saints' coffers are not reliable indicators of the relative richness or poverty of the associated festival. One cannot interpret the fact that thirty pesos accompany both the festival of San Miguel Arcangel and that of the Angel Custodio [Guardian Angel] as meaning that these festivals are in any way equivalent. They are not. The festival of San Miguel, the patron of the village—whose sponsorship is the means to the highest prestige—involves the feeding of hundreds of people, while that of the Angel Custodio may feed only thirty or forty people. Indeed, it is the number of people fed that determines the prestige of the festival's sponsor. Of course the sponsor (*mayordomo*) of the festival of San Miguel will spend more cash during the sponsorship than will his or her counterpart in a lesser festival, but the amount of money spent is, in effect, only tangential to the real work of the festival, in that money is used only where gifts are not.[18] The festival economy is not a cash economy. While money is used daily to make purchases within the village, it is gifts, not cash purchases, that provide the extraordinary quantities of everything, from food to skyrockets, consumed during a festival. If money is part of a festival, it, like the Spanish language, is used most in dealings with non-Nahuas, that is, to pay for Masses or the colored satin used in the dancers' costumes—services and goods available only from priests and other mestizos in Cuetzalan, the closest representatives of the national culture.[19] While a *mayordomo's* expenses may be considerable, these, in themselves are not what make the festival work.

What, then, are the monies in the saints' coffers, and what can they tell us? The funds in the saints' coffers are symbolic of the real expenses undertaken by a *mayordomo*. They are in no way intended to offset those expenses. Even the largest account, the ninety pesos associated with the festival of the Santo Entierro, is only a mere fraction of the real cost of the festival if all the pigs, turkeys, chiles, maize, cane liquor, colored satin, copal incense, and Masses were given a cash value. Rather, these accounts, small as they are, are symbolic gifts to the next *mayordomo*, a sort of last act performed by the outgoing *mayordomo* to further increase his prestige after the festival, when a new *mayordomo* will undertake the service of the saints. *Mayordomos* have told me with evident pride that they left more in these accounts than was given them on January 6 of the previous year when they received the saint's image in their homes and began to bear their burden, their cargo. In fact, the village records show not only the transfer of cash, but also that of "kilograms of paraffin" (that is, candles), as well as kilograms of beeswax, and copal incense — all of which increased or remained the same over the last five years. In San Miguel Tzinacapan the saints are well-served.

Local records also show that for the more than one hundred public festivals during the period 1991–94 no one person has sponsored more than one festival. This is not due to lack of interest. Despite the difficulty in acquiring the great quantities of goods necessary to feed large numbers of people — and the attendant risk of failure — and despite the fact that festival sponsorships (*mayordomías*) are the most serious public representation of oneself possible in the village and are voluntary, there is considerable competition for them and they are solicited well in advance.[20] The ideal Nahua of San Miguel Tzinacapan will hold seven *mayordomías* during adult life (that is, after marriage), a goal that is difficult though not beyond reach.

DOING THE WORK

Festivals are the primary means by which Nahuas order their world. They institutionalize the gods whose lives and works bring about solstices and equinoxes — naturalized prototypes for rites of passage in human and vegetable life. At these and other critical points, Nahuas order time and space by ordering relations with the guardians of these, the saints and ancestors. We have already seen that saints, ancestors, and places are alike in that their significance and their power depend on the presence of *tonalli*. Likewise, I have shown above that it is *tonalli* — as prestige or authority — that renders prayers, petitions, and ceremonies effective in dialogue with other *tonalli*-bearing beings; the saints and ancestors inherent in the earth. Festivals are the primary means by which Nahuas acquire (or create) *tonalli*. Festivals are performed to address the earth in a dialogue through which people produce sustenance and social order, maize and prestige.

Serving the saints is work, literally. A festival is no picnic. The energy expended by a *mayordomo* during the months of preparation for the festival plus that of the consumption of great quantities of sustenance on the festival day combine to produce something that the Spanish friars and cultural nationalists missed, seeing extravagance and excess where I see hard work. What do festivals produce? Functionalist answers include "social order," "solidarity," "corporate identity," "prestige," and a psychological or spiritual *je-ne-sais-quoi* that somehow satisfies the participants. While all of these may be true to some degree, the issue remains as to how this happens? William Blake claimed that "Prayers plow not. Praises reap not;" how then do the prayers and the praises, the dancing, the flowers, the incense, and the consumption of industrial quantities of food and drink, produce anything? The answer lies in the performative process of putting on the festival.

How does a *mayordomo*, with access to more or less the same resources as other Nahuas in San Miguel Tzinacapan, ever acquire sufficient sustenance to successfully sponsor a festival? Even though all Nahuas in San Miguel Tzinacapan do not have access to the same amount or quality of land, this is immaterial as even with the best parcels, the best seed, and the cooperation of the weather, one could not amass the sustenance necessary to feed so many in service of the saints. We can only imagine the difficulty of sponsoring a festival long ago when land was communal and access to personal resources was even more limited. The sustenance itself, the pigs, turkeys, chiles, and maize, also have their own reproductive cycles which make it unlikely that they will—like Jack's magic beans in the fairy tale—suddenly produce much more than they have in the past. Moreover, there is no means of storing surplus from one year to another. There is cash, but purchasing everything oneself would have to be a relatively recent phenomenon as San Miguel Tzinacapan itself has become significantly involved in a cash economy only within the last fifty years. Moreover, the proposition of a *mayordomo* purchasing everything for a festival by oneself, as it is unable to explain how festivals worked *before* the existence of a local cash economy, would indicate a radical break with the previous method, whatever it was. Cash, then, while offering no ready explanation as to how a festival works, has the additional disadvantage of rather limited historical relevance.

There is, however, another resource, shared by all Nahuas equally, a resource which, unlike animal husbandry or agriculture, can lend itself, if it pleases, to a sudden yield of sustenance. This, or rather, these are human resources:

tocnihuan, "our brothers," fellow San Migueleños, bearers of gifts. Herein lie both the latent authority of the ancestors and the potential prestige of a *mayordomo*: it is the work of a festival to incarnate this power and prestige in the participants, to strengthen one's *tonalli*. A *mayordomo* accumulates sufficient sustenance for a festival meal by participating at the festival meals of other *mayordomos* who, in order to sponsor a festival, have participated at the festival meals of yet other *mayordomos*. And so on. In other words, one gets things done the same way that one always does: one has what one has by having participated in communal labor, the clearing, planting, weeding, and harvesting of the field, which begins, significantly, with a ceremony directed at ensuring the success of the undertaking.

Participating at a festival meal means that one does not arrive empty-handed. In San Miguel Tzinacapan there is a minimum contribution for a couple attending a festival meal. A man makes a gift of tobacco, matches, and a bottle of cane liquor, none of which are produced in San Miguel and therefore must be purchased. A woman brings a straw bag, a *morral,* full of ingredients used in the festival dish, *mole poblano,* that is, "half an almud of maize [for tortillas], 125 g. chile seco, 250 g. chile ancho, one peso worth cloves, one peso cinnamon, 250 g. salt, 1/2 kg. tomato, 1 kg. sugar."[21] With the exception of clove, cinnamon, and salt, all these items are produced locally. As a couple arrives at the home of the *mayordomo* the man and woman usually separate, the man joining the men, and the woman, the other women, who are in the kitchen preparing the meal. As the woman enters the kitchen, the wife of the *mayordomo* notes the quantity and quality of the contribution. The quantities contributed are always greater than those their donors will consume. By these contributions the couple demonstrates that they have likewise given the time necessary to produce the gift, and that they are members of a network of responsible working people. On ceremonial occasions the public nature of giving intensifies as a person may be held publicly accountable for failure to participate (cf. Vogt 1976:111).

By having assisted at the festival meals of past *mayordomos,* the current *mayordomo* knows he can count on their presence and contributions, just as he can also rely on the contributions of those who would be *mayordomos* in the future. It is this network of exchanges that makes it possible to accumulate sufficient foodstuffs to feed a large group (cf. Monaghan 1990). At the end of a festival—sometimes after three days and nights of eating and drinking—one thing is clear: who participated and to what degree. All participants are aware of what they have contributed and to whom, and at whose expense they have eaten and drunk. The *mayordomo* is aware of the "unsolicited" contributions and of those who are "returning" his own prior prestations. And this is precisely the point. Festivals are vehicles through which people formalize relations to each other. The actual work of the festival is done in its performance: in order to serve the saints people must become indebted to each other. At the end of a festival everyone knows just where they stand relative to everyone else. Everyone is aware of their obligations and knows when and in what manner they are to be fulfilled—often in the next period of festival activity, perhaps just three months away. Moreover, this is public knowledge. As such, one faces public recognition of one's success or failure to fulfill one's obligations to other members of the community. Failure to fulfill these obligations entails a significant loss of social credit, or trust, the most viable "currency" in an environment managed by shared labor.

MYTHIC TIME AND THE PRI

Perhaps because we, along with Mexican Nationalists, "naturally" consider religious ceremonies as "sacred" events, it is common to focus on that which differs from "the profane." Ignoring what we might consider "preparatory" or "material" occupations, we focus instead on the spectacle of the ceremony, a procession or sacrifice on "spiritual" concerns, for example, as meaningful in themselves; understanding such practice as worship, referring to a God or gods somewhere "over there." Likewise, an act of prayer is commonly represented as "praying for something," and there is usually a "lag time" between "praying for something" and receiving it. This is not the case in Mesoamerican cultures, nor is it the case in the cultures of other Native Americans whose divinities are immanent.

The principle upon which festivals operate—the consumption of sustenance creates more sustenance—is a self-fulfilling prophecy. Not only is it the work of putting on the festival—the creation and/or affirmation of mutual debts—that accomplishes the festival's intent—the service of the saints—such practice is also instrumental in assuring that there will be a surplus of sustenance (people with mutual debts will work together), while it also provides a safe means to dispose of the surplus, which might otherwise create considerable social inequalities. Festivals produce prestige (*tonalli*) by the same rules that produce sustenance (*tonacayotl*). Their structure is that of an agricultural metaphor: a potential *mayordomo*, by contributing sustenance to another *mayordomo* at another festival, guarantees the return of sustenance at a later date. He is, in effect, planting his sustenance, to be harvested later, and consumed publicly at his own table. If we recall that in Mesoamerica "humans are maize" and the Nahua identification of the incarnation of Jesucristo as the "sun (the father) producing maize (the son)," we can appreciate how the dynamics of exchange in a festival work to make the truth of such claims appear self-evident.

Linking upper and lower worlds through obligations on the surface of the earth, festivals create a public sense of "being there." The people of San Miguel

Tzinacapan are themselves both the creators of this link and the link itself. Through the public performance of one's social obligations and the undertaking of new obligations, festivals create a structure which will constitute what it is to be, living, in and of that place, until the next ceremony is performed.[22] As festivals (re)enact ancestral structures, ensuring their continuity, past and future debts coalesce in a present charged with the immediate sense of destiny (*tonalli*). The "heat" and radiance created by the friction of gift exchange is proverbial among the Nahua of San Miguel Tzinacapan who say: "If you give someone food, you must not eat any of that which you gave, or your house might burn."[23] In the sixteenth century, the Franciscan friar Bernardino de Sahagún noted that for the festival dedicated to a divinity who apparently gave order to time and space, *Nappa teuctli*:[24] "it was as if one's debt were paid to the degree that one's goods, one's possessions were at hand . . . [One said:] 'may I not eat in vain, may I consume not in vain, may I use not for myself alone that which has benefited me. May there be eating, may there be drinking, may there be consumption of food; thereupon may our god Nappa teuctli dance.' " (1974–82:1:45f.)

Ordering the world means both *arranging* it and *commanding* it. There is, however, another side to the order festivals create—that of dissatisfaction with the order and potential disorder. The fact that everyone knows where one stands in relation to everyone else may be order, but it certainly does not follow that everyone is happy in their present situation. In fact, as festivals produce prestige, they are just as likely to produce envy, *nexicol,* among those who, for whatever reason, focus on themselves, putting their perceived private concerns before those of the perceived community.[25] This double role of the patron saint in creating prestige (and envy) and community (and outsiders) is evident in a prayer Doña Guadalupe taught me in response to my questions regarding the work of the saints. One prays to San Miguel Tzinacapan, who is both cause and cure, for protection against *talticpacnocniuh nexicol,* against the "envy of my earthly brother." Because the network of potential contributors to one's prestige is inherited from one's parents; that is, the ritual kin of one's parents are also one's own ritual kin, and the son of your father's *compadre* is likely to be your *compadre,* alliances—and feuds—last a long time. Nahuas' recognition of the importance of ancestors is quite explicit on this point. Despite their wrappings in the semantic fields of saints and ancestors, the stories they tell themselves of themselves—for prestige and its lack are stories—these are as perpetually up-to-date as they are perpetually and hotly contested.

In San Miguel Tzinacapan it is more accurate to speak of festivals creating communities, rather than a single community, as San Miguel has been divided into three *ad hoc* political groups since sometime around 1900 when four families, controlling most of the village's land, began to exclude two other families from communal activities. The third group was formed by another family that functioned as a mediator between the wealthy group of four families and the poor group of two. Around 1930, the poorer of the groups made a personal dislike political and, in post-revolutionary spirit, tried to bring about some land reform in order to break up the richer group's holdings.

The tension between the two groups continues. During the 1970s, the poorer group was active in the PPS (Partido Politico Socialista) and now many of them are no longer Catholics, (of any variety), having converted to various Protestant sects. While increasing the enmity between themselves and the richer group, who are extremist Catholics, these conversions also have placed further pressure on the mediators, as this group, now the only other group to participate in the festivals, practices a form of liberation theology. The mediating family has now evolved to include various organizations, among them, the powerful agricultural cooperative, Tosepan Titaneskej, "United We Will Win," and the CEPEC, the "Center for Studies and Promotion of Education in the Field." The richer group now includes six families and does not participate in the community work, the *faena*. From its traditional PRI and CNC stand, it has moved further to the right, to that of the ultra-right wing *indigenismo* ideology of the PRI's own *agents provocateurs*, the Antorcha Campesina. This last group, posing as violently anti-mestizo, infiltrates legitimate indigenous cooperatives and either paralyzes them by radicalizing and polarizing all issues or, with government support, kills its leaders. Moreover, this extremist Catholic group has close links to the mestizo government of Cuetzalan, including people who, knowing how to use the bureaucracy, hire themselves out to other people in San Miguel Tzinacapan to get things done. Presently this group is using PRI money from Cuetzalan in an attempt to control the festival of San Miguel, the largest and most important in the village, by offering assistance to *mayordomos* and others in return for their support. However, the frequency of festivals in San Miguel, in that their performance requires constant creation and renewal of mutual obligations, and the large numbers of people involved in the festivals, make it difficult for any one group to take power and maintain it for long—especially if that group is not responsive to the changing needs of the pueblo.

San Miguel Tzinacapan, literally at the end of the road, is metaphorically at a crossroads. Yet it has been at this dangerous center for a long time. One might even argue that the strength of the festival system is in its ability to create a "right direction" as people negotiate and renew alliances relative to their own economic situation as each new year comes around. Regarding nationalism, one of the problems of the relations between the religion of a national mestizo culture and that of an indigenous culture is that the indigenous religion functions as a local economy which, to remain local and viable, must at some point distinguish itself from that of the national culture: it cannot fully integrate into national culture without losing its identity. Thus the opposition in San Miguel Tzinacapan between the economy of the rich who receive money from the mestizo government thereby risking their autonomy, and the economy of the cooperatives who risk alienating the mestizo government thereby risking their autonomy, as "others" as *prima materia* in need of national culture's "civilizing influences."

While it appears that national culture has made inroads in San Miguel Tzinacapan via the Antorcha Campesina, one might also argue that this has strengthened resistance to national culture. At the time of this writing, the same may be said for all of Mexico, poised at an analogous crossroads between NAFTA and the armies of Walmart, and the indigenous forces of the Zapatista EZLN. I am reminded of a cold and rainy twentieth of November when I was surprised to see the groups of *quetzales* and *negritos* dancing in front of the church at San Miguel. The twentieth of November was not, after all, a religious festival but a *national* holiday celebrating the slight and unassuming Francisco Madero's opposition to the "reelection" of the dictator of thirty-odd years, Porfirio Díaz. "We are celebrating," I was told, "because a long time ago on this day San Miguel killed the Devil." So far from God and so close to the United States; work, greet, offer, nourish: the saints are in their houses—who will feed them?

NOTES

1. While the nineteenth-century origins of Mexican nationalism were based on racial distinctions, I use the term *mestizaje*, "crossbreeding," in a cultural, not racial, sense following Signorini and Lupo (1989:20f.). Nahuas are people whose first language is Nahuatl. They may or may not dress distinctly from Spanish speakers, and their way of life—domestic, ceremonial, and work habits—is likewise distinct from those of monolingual Spanish speakers.

2. This is not meant to imply that ideology is the driving force in nationalist politics. Land and other economic considerations are always at issue. My point is to show how nationalism functions to create a state in which legitimate difference (indigenous nationhood) must remain unrecognized or be recognized only as illegitimate difference (indigenous materia prima), i.e., subject to change at the behest of the state.

3. Manuel Gándara (1992) argues that Mexican "official archaeology" was one of the purveyors of this nationalism. The same might be said of an "official ethnography" or an "official history," if by "official" we mean that which propounds the views of indigenous culture or the past favorable to the Partido Revolucionario Institutional (PRI)—the Mexican political party in power for the past seventy-five years, responsible for much of the development of Mexican Nationalism.

4. The full formula is: *Nican nimitzaxcatiliti nehin motahpalol/para tehua xicmahce-hua,/tehua ximotamaca,/ tehua ximotequipano,/ tehua ximoamiccehui. Amo ximoamic-cehui ica notalticpac icnitzi,/ amo ximahcehua notalticpac icnitzi,/ sino que yehua nehin*

ica mitzyolohpachoa,/ yehua nehin motahpaloh mitzaxcaltilia. [trans. Here I am going to make you owner of this offering [greeting], for you that you may eat, that you may feed yourself, *that you may nourish yourself,* that you may slake your thirst. Don't slake your thirst with my little earthly brother [the patient], don't eat my little earthly brother, instead with this he pleases you [greets you], he makes you owner of this offering [greeting]. "Formula for an offering/greeting to the Earth" (Signorini and Lupo 1989).

5. These definitions depend on whether the Nahuatl root is accompanied by reflexive or various object prefixes.

6. Those altars that have saints images and no photographs of deceased family members have been, in my experience, those of the poorest households, that is, those which cannot afford photographs. However, in these households the saints' images, also for economic reasons, are more likely to have been carved by family members themselves, who when deceased, are remembered through the saint.

7. In San Miguel saints are generally referred to as "*santitos,*" and ancestors, "*abueli-tos,*" "little [or dear] grandparents." The diminuitive ending "*-ito*" may be a calque of the honorific "*-tzin*" in Nahuatl. It denotes both intimacy and respect. The translation "Bats by the Water" follows local accounts which derive Tzinacapan from *Tzinaca(tl)* "bat," and *apan* "by the water, resulting in Tzinacaapan. The translation "By the Bats," *Tzinaca(tl)-pan* is also possible. Prócoro Hernandez, Tecoltepec, Mpo. de Cuetzalan, Pue., personal communication, 24 August 1991.

8. For further discussion of bones as the source of life in Mesoamerica see Haly 1992.

9. These beings are like the Maya *chac* who also have an upperworld correspondence with the "Four Fathers of the Land" whom I have elsewhere identified with four of the stars of the constellation Cygnus which is directly overhead at midnight on the Maya New Year (17 July), thereby joining space with time. Cf. Haly, *On Becoming a Mountain,* in preparation.

10. These are San Martín Tuzamapan, Reyes de Vallarta, San Antonio Rayón, and San Francisco Cuetzalan. On other occasions don Prócoro spoke of a "flowering tree" at the center of this cross which put forth different colored blossoms in each of the four directions. This was, he said, a metaphor for the work of the healer who puts forth roots (prayers) in each of the four directions of the lowerworld in order to bring the water (the lost *tonalli*) up through his trunk and make it bloom (restore the lost *tonalli* to the patient). While the names vary (the late Doña Rufina Manzano and her pupil the late Doña Guadalupe Vásquez spoke of "Jose María Sacramento, Jose María Trinidad, don Juan Manuel Martin, and don Juan Manuel Antonio"), I have never in my work with ten healers in this area heard any Nahuatl names for these beings.

11. Crossroads are dangerous in many cultures as places which combine both external influences with the act of decision-making. The Huasteca Nahua, using grains of maize to divine the origin of a disease, relate grains fallen in form of a cross to a disease from a crossroads (Sandstrom 1991:235). The practices associated with the cross-shrines at crossroads has, incidentally, a pre-Hispanic counterpart as seats or thrones were placed

at each crossroads. No one was permitted to sit in these places as they were reserved for the guarantor of all legitimate social order, the ruler, or the deity Tezcatlipoca. Like the cross-shrines, these were kept covered with boughs. These *momoztli*, as they were called, represent the omnipresence of legitimate order at center of crossroads, an order which they enforce by the proscriptive practices associated with this place: that no one might place themselves in this source of order (Torquemada [1615] 1969).

12. *Corazón de María. / Xinechyoltapo. / Xinechyolchipahua. / [Xi]nechchipahuili noyollotzin. / Mah nochi in tein . . . / Nochi in tein sueño nicmati. / Mah nochi nicmati. / Mah nochi maj nochi niquilnamiqui. / Mah amo tej niquilcahua.*

13. These different practices may be attributed to the fact that don Prócoro lives in the lowlands, the "hot country," where two crops of maize are produced each year, while doña Guadalupe lives at an elevation of two thousand feet higher, yielding one maize crop per year, a crop which is sown around mid-March, a date that coincides with that of San Isidro the Worker, March 15.

14. I have argued elsewhere that the restoration of one's soul once lost—manifest as a loss of social credit—is accomplished by two primary aspects of the healer's art: (1) recounting a diagnostic dream which gives the patient the "otherworld reason" for his/her malaise and (2) the patient's going into debt to with a person of high prestige, the healer, offers the chance of restoring the patient's social credit in the eyes of the villagers who have sanctioned the patient for failure to act as his/her social status requires.

15. In 1995, this period began with the festival of San Isidro Labrador on 15 March, and ended with Easter Sunday, 16 April. However, as most of the festivals in this period are part of the Easter cycle and are moveable feasts, this period can also be much shorter—on occasion only nine days long, when Easter Sunday falls on the second day of Spring, 23 March.

16. I include the festival of Santos Pedro and Pablo (29 June) as part of this period even though it is not celebrated in San Miguel Tzinacapan. It is, however, celebrated in Xaltipan and attended by a significant number of people from San Miguel, among them the mayor and his officers.

17. Of course the Roman Catholic calendar often follows that of its own pre-Christian predecessors, who ordered time in equinoxes and solstices in ways similar to those of the pre-Hispanic (and thus pre-Christian) Nahuas.

18. *Mayordomos* are usually male, though in 1992 a woman, a widow, was the sponsor of the festival of San Miguel.

19. It is arguable that the predominance of red, green, white, and yellow in the satin costumes of many of the groups of ceremonial dancers is due to the fact that these are also the colors of the Mexican flag, and thus the colors most readily available in stores; while these colors are also those that Nahuas associate with the four directions and with the colors of maize.

20. Being "solicited well in advance" also gives the prospective *mayordomo* more time to prepare for the festival.

21. Elena Islas et al., San Miguel Tzinacapan: personal communication April 1994.

22. To address or greet ancestors in the earth by means of a festival was once a slightly more transparent enterprise as Nahuas in the Sierra Norte de Puebla, prior to adopting the Spanish surnames of a mestizo boss (*patrón*) or *compadre*, were addressed by terms relating to that which grew in the places where they lived. Some of these names are still in use today. Miguel Cruz is locally known as Miguel Papata, "Miguel By-the-Banana-Trees." Adriana Xilot, Adriana "New Corn"; and Hilario Chilar, Hilario "Chile Patch," are additional examples.

23. *Komo jkón titeuantik teyisá amo uel tej tikuas teyin titeuantik. Uelis tatas nochan.* Eliseo Zamora Islas, personal communication, San Miguel Tzinacapan: April 1994.

24. *Nappa Teuctli* means "Four Times Lord." As each Nahua year was "borne" by a figure in a different quarter of the world, "Four Times Lord" implies "Four Places Lord." I understand this deity as the god in the center of the world orderers, a "Heart of the Sky" corresponding to the "Heart of the Mountain." *Nappa Teuctli* may be identified with the center star in the constellation "Cygnus."

25. The Nahuatl *nexicoliztli*, envy, has its root in *xictli*, navel, with apparent reference to self-centeredness and lineage.

REFERENCES

Craine, Eugene R., and Reginald C. Reindorp, eds. 1967. *Chronicles of Michoacan.* Norman: University of Oklahoma Press.

Gándara, Manuel. 1992. *La arqueología oficial mexicana: Causas y efectos.* Colección Divulgación, México DF: Instituto Nacional de Antropología e Historia.

García Martinez, Bernardo. 1987. *Los Pueblos de la Sierra: El poder y espacio entre los indios del norte de Puebla hasta 1700.* Mexico: Centro de Estudios Históricos. El Colegio de México.

Haly, Richard. 1992. "Bare Bones: Rethinking Mesoamerican Divinity." *History of Religions*: 269–304.

———. 1994. "How Doña Guadalupe Restores a Soul: Reciprocity, Status, and the Mesoamerican Landscape." Paper given at regional meeting of AAA/NEAA, 7–9 April, SUNY Geneseo, New York.

Hermitte, M. Esther. 1964. "Supernatural Power and Social Control in a Modern Mayan Village." University of Chicago.

Karttunen, Frances. 1983. *An Analytical Dictionary of Nahuatl.* Austin: University of Texas.

———. 1994. *Between Worlds: Interpreters, Guides, and Survivors.* New Brunswick NJ: Rutgers University Press.

Keen, Benjamin, and Mark Wasserman. 1984. *A Short History of Latin America*, 2nd ed. Boston MA: Houghton Mifflin.

Lakoff, George, and Mark Johnson. 1980. *Metaphors We Live By*. Chicago IL: University of Chicago Press.

León-Portilla, Miguel. 1963. *Aztec Thought and Culture: A Study of the Ancient Nahuatl Mind*. Trans. Jack Emory Davis. Norman: University of Oklahoma Press.

Lockhart, James. 1992. *The Nahuas After the Conquest*. Stanford CA: Stanford University Press.

Molina, Alonso de. 1970. *Vocabulario en lengua castellana y mexicana y mexicana y castellana*. Ed. Miguel León-Portilla. Mexico: Editorial Porrúa.

Monaghan, John. 1990. "Reciprocity, Redistribution, and the Transaction of Value in the Mesoamerican Fiesta." *American Ethnologist* 17:758–74.

Sahagún, Bernardino de. 1974–82. *Florentine Codex: General History of the Things of New Spain*. Trans. Arthur J. O. Anderson and Charles E. Dibble. Salt Lake City: School of American Research and University of Utah Press.

Sandstrom, Alan R. 1991. *Corn is Our Blood: Culture and Ethnic Identity is a Contemporary Aztec Village*. Norman: University of Oklahoma Press.

Signorini, Italo, and Alessandro Lupo. 1989. *Los Tres Ejes de la Vida: Almas, Cuerpo, Enfermedad entre los Nahuas de la Sierra de Puebla*. Xalapa, Mexico: Universidad Veracruzana.

Torquemada, Fray Juan de. 1969 [1615]. *Monarquía Indiana*. Ed. Miguel León-Portilla. Mexico: Editorial Porrúa.

Toulmin, Stephen. 1990. *Cosmopolis: The Hidden Agenda of Modernity*. New York: Free Press.

Toumi, Sybille. 1984. *Vocabulario Mexicano de Tzinacapan-Sierra Norte de Puebla*. Vol. supplément 3 au n:9 d'amerindia. Paris: A.E.A.

Vogt, Evon Z. 1976. *Tortillas for the Gods: A Symbolic Analysis of Zinacanteco Rituals*. Cambridge MA: Harvard University Press.

HISTORICAL REFLECTIONS 3

Repatriating the Past

Recreating Indian History

CLARA SUE KIDWELL

When Jesse Jackson visited the Hopi reservation in 1985 during the course of his campaign for the presidency of the United States, he gave a stirring speech on behalf of his Rainbow Coalition. The Hopi people listened politely, and Jackson moved on. A short while later, at one of the Hopi ceremonies, a new clown appeared in a large orange Afro wig and a pin-striped suit and proceeded to do a Hopi version of Jackson's speech, complete with cadence and rhythm.

Hopi clowns play a crucial role in ceremonials, mimicking strangers and members of other tribes. They reverse the normal order of things to provoke laughter but they also reinforce, by their perversity, norms of behavior. The Jackson clown helped the Hopi deal with the process of history. He was the means to integrate an event of historical importance into the Hopi understanding of the world and the rhythm of their own lives.[1] When clowning became part of Hopi culture cannot be determined from written records. It might be discovered from archaeological records. It is certainly of prehistoric origin, but it becomes a part of a distinctively Hopi sense of history.

The Hopi, in their villages in the Southwest, have a different sense of history than do other Americans. Their lives are more tied to cycles of nature in a ceremonial cycle that they have preserved with fierce determination throughout the twentieth century. Many Indian people on reservations, particularly those located in remote, rural areas throughout the western United States, share a similar awareness of the physical cycles of seasons, marked by both economic activities such as farming and cattle raising and by social/ceremonial activities such as pow-wows and sun dances. According to the 1990 census, almost half of the Indian people in the United States lived in rural areas.[2]

In the course of the historical experience of Indian-white contact and conflict, much has been lost by tribal people—population, language, traditional knowledge, and material objects that passed into the hands of missionaries, travelers, explorers, and military men. Bishop Diego de Landa burned the sacred books of the Maya in 1562, deeming them signs of heathenism.[3] An

Iroquois wampum belt created to signify an agreement between the Iroquois and George Washington found its way into the collection of the State Museum of New York at Albany.[4] Although wampum belts and Mayan codices are both tangible records of human events, Europeans could not read them, and since Indians did not produce written documents, the stuff of history, they have been deemed "prehistoric."

Indian people have lost much of their history to museum collections. Colonial Indian agents, missionaries, and traders acquired objects from Indian people and carried them back to Europe. Remarkable collections of Indian artifacts reside in museums in Germany, Spain, and England. They are remarkable because they represent some of the oldest evidence of artistic and cultural products of Native people in the Americas.

Also in museums, however, are the human remains of many Indians. In 1867 George Otis, the curator of the Army Medical Museum in Washington DC, issued a call to field physicians for Indian specimens. In 1868 U.S. Army Surgeon General Joseph Barnes directed army doctors in Indian country to collect more Indian skulls, and Otis arranged to give the Smithsonian Institution any burial goods found with those skulls. Military men collected skulls from battlefields, and sometimes from graves, and sent them to the U.S. Army Medical Museum for study aimed at determining patterns of human evolution. The bones were eventually sent to the Museum of Natural History at the Smithsonian Institution where they became the basis for further research in the name of science.[5]

In Nebraska, the state historical society collections contained approximately five hundred sets of Pawnee skeletal remains. When the Pawnee tribe laid claim to the remains, the historical society resisted, maintaining that it had legal possession of them. Following a lengthy dispute between the tribe and the society, the Nebraska legislature passed a repatriation law, and the historical society returned the remains to the tribe in May of 1989.[6]

In 1986 a group of Southern Cheyenne people discovered that a number of remains of their ancestors were in the Museum of Natural History at the Smithsonian Institution. Unable to obtain the remains by request to the museum, they pursued a legislative remedy that culminated in the passage of two pieces of legislation in 1989 and 1990, the National Museum of the American Indian Act (NMAI, P.L. 101-185) and the Native American Graves Protection and Repatriation Act (NAGPRA, P.L. 101-601, November 16, 1990).[7]

These acts have given tribal people the opportunity to reclaim the remains of their ancestors and their sacred and patrimonial material culture that now reside in museums. The first, the National Museum of the American Indian Act, applies to the Smithsonian Institution in Washington DC. It provided for the transfer of the Heye Foundation collection, one of the world's largest and most comprehensive collections of Indian artifacts and photographs of Indians, to the Smithsonian, and it mandated that human remains and certain classes of Indian material culture held in the Smithsonian be returned to tribal groups. The Native American Graves Protection and Repatriation Act extended the general principles of the NMAI Act to all repositories of Indian material that receive federal funding.

The repatriation legislation is a significant assertion of tribal sovereignty, the rights of Indian people to reclaim things that are essential to their identity and history. It also presents an irony of history—that traditional attitudes toward property and personal possessions, attitudes that generations of missionaries, federal agents, and military personnel strove to change, have now been codified within the federal legal system, with requirements for evidence as proof of ownership.

In traditional tribal societies, people may own their private possessions—clothing, utensils, domestic animals—but the cultural property—things used in ceremonies that promote the well-being of the tribe—belong to all the people. They cannot be sold by a single individual nor bought by people outside the tribe. The concept of communal property is embedded in American law in the idea of a corporation, but there individuals retain rights to buy and sell shares to people outside the corporation. The repatriation legislation acknowledges the inviolability of ongoing, corporate holding of property. It also acknowledges that there is continuity in Indian cultures. Legal constructs such as federal recognition demonstrate that cultural groups can change and adapt to new circumstances without losing their identities as tribal groups.[8]

The basic requirement for a valid claim is that a tribe must establish cultural affiliation with the materials they claim. Cultural affiliation is defined as "a relationship of shared group identity that may be reasonably traced historically or prehistorically between a present-day Indian tribe or Native Hawaiian organization and an identifiable earlier group."[9] For relatively recent materials, the requirement should be easy to establish. Museum records will generally contain information on when, where, and from whom materials were collected. For older material, and particularly for pre-European contact material, the documentation is much more problematic. Early museum collectors were often not as concerned with provenance as with the artistic or aesthetic qualities of the material, and documentation of acquisition is often very sketchy.

For the most ancient material, which generally comes from burial sites excavated by archaeologists, and from cultures that predate European contact, the documentation is particularly problematic. Archaeologists have debated the origins of American Indian tribes, although the most generally accepted theory in the archaeological community is still the Bering Straits theory, which says that Indians migrated from Asia across a land bridge between Asia and North

America that appeared intermittently anywhere from fifty thousand to one hundred thousand years ago during the advance and retreat of glaciers during a series of climatic changes. Waves of people following large game animals moved across the Straits to populate the Americas.

A Lakota scholar, Vine Deloria Jr., who has studied tribal traditions and scientific evidence, has challenged this theory, citing tribal traditions of emergence into this world from worlds below, or from the sky above. He has questioned the validity of the Bering Strait theory by challenging the reliability of scientific carbon dating techniques. He suggests that Indians might have originated in the Americas and moved northward.[10]

The issue of cultural affiliation of prehistoric material with contemporary tribes raises interesting questions for historians, who must interpret oral traditions of the distant past, for archaeologists, who must interpret relationships of material objects and human remains, and for anthropologists, who must look for evidence of cultural continuity in the midst of significant cultural change.

The repatriation laws establish property rights within the American legal system, but they also constrain the rights of tribes by defining certain categories of property to which they have rights. NAGPRA establishes human remains, associated funerary objects, unassociated funerary objects, sacred objects, and cultural patrimony as categories and defines those categories in the language of the act. The NMAI Act requires the Smithsonian to inventory all Indian human remains and Indian funerary objects in its possession or control and "using the best available scientific and historical documentation, identify the origins of such remains and objects." Upon request from tribal members "culturally affiliated" with the remains, the Smithsonian shall return them and associated objects to the tribe.[11]

Historical proof of cultural affiliation is dealt with in different ways in the legislation. In NAGPRA, "cultural affiliation" is defined as "a relationship of shared group identity which can be reasonably traced historically or prehistorically." The law thus maintains the language of periodization—history and prehistory.[12] NAGPRA does not address directly what constitutes the historical evidence that can establish cultural affiliation. The federal regulations that clarify the language of the act list "geographical, kinship, biological, archeological, anthropological, linguistic, folklore, oral tradition, historical, or other relevant information or expert opinion" as examples of such evidence.[13]

The Board of Trustees of the National Museum of the American Indian used the mandate of the NMAI legislation to write an extensive policy statement to implement the spirit of the law. Under the section of its policy concerning "Burden of Proof," the policy states that "lineal descent, tribal affiliation, and/or cultural affiliation" may be established by a requesting party "through evidence of geography, descent, kinship, archaeology, anthropology, linguistics, folklore, oral tradition, historical patterns of ownership and/or control, and other relevant information or expert opinion."[14] The National Museum of Natural History in the Smithsonian chose to follow the language of NAGPRA in carrying out its return of human remains.

The Larsen Bay case demonstrates the complications that repatriation raises for archaeologists, historians, and anthropologists. What happens when a Native people's sense of their own history differs from the views of non-Native scientists?

During field work on Kodiak Island, Alaska, from 1932 to 1936, Aleš Hrdlička, an archaeologist working for the National Museum of Natural History, excavated the Uyak Site, a village that covered several acres and included houses and middens and a cemetery. It had been occupied for approximately 3000 years before its abandonment about 1500 A.D. Hrdlička collected 756 sets of human skeletal remains, 144 items buried with them, and thousands of other artifacts, which he sent to the museum in Washington.[15]

In 1987 the contemporary Aleut community of Larsen Bay, Alaska, presented the Museum of Natural History with a claim for repatriation of these remains. The people of Larsen Bay based their claim for cultural affiliation on their own traditions and their physical proximity to the site of the remains. The scholarly community of archaeologists and physical anthropologists, however, was divided in their opinions as to whether the contemporary Larsen Bay community was directly descended from the individuals whose graves Hrdlička had excavated. The interpretation of the evidence from the site was made particularly difficult given the crudeness of Hrdlička's excavation techniques, which often disturbed strata, and his record keeping techniques.[16]

The time depth of the site, the historical records from Russian contact, the debates among archaeologists concerning the physical continuity of human population at the site, and the present location of the Larsen Bay community near the site show how various archaeological and historical sources can be read to determine continuity of human activity from earliest occupation to the present. The crucial issue for repatriation, however, is cultural continuity.

The Larsen Bay site contained three archeologically defined sites: the Ocean Bay Tradition (4000–2500 B.C.), Old Koniag (2500–1500 B.C.?), Kachemak (1500 B.C.–1100 A.D.), Koniag (1100–1763 A.D.), and Historic Koniag (1763–present).[17] The physical evidence from the sites indicates cultural change from the Old Koniag to the Kachemak traditions, but archaeologists continue to debate the continuity of culture from the Ocean Bay and Koniag traditions to the contemporary Larsen Bay community. There has been a vigorous debate among archaeologists (based on material culture) and physical anthropologists (based on analysis of skulls and teeth) about the continuity of the population on the site.[18] The crux of the debate is whether cultural and physical evolution was taking place on the site over time or whether earlier populations were displaced by later immigrants who came to Kodiak Island and decided it was a good place to settle. One author noted both the dilemma of the scientist and the nature of evidence: "A recent trend in south Alaskan studies takes prehistory beyond the study of artifacts and the level of historiography by looking for patterns of social, political and economic development shared between prehistoric cultures over extensive expanses of the North Pacific Coast."[19]

The resolution of the Larsen Bay claim was not left, however, to the decision of scientists, nor to the advisory committee composed of Indian and non-Indian experts on history and culture that the Smithsonian had established under the NMAI legislative mandate. The advisory committee was to be the decision making body in cases where Indian claims to cultural affiliation were in question, but in the summer of 1991, Robert Adams, secretary of the Smithsonian, decided, upon the basis of reports from two archaeologists, that the Larsen Bay community had rights to the remains in question based on cultural affiliation.[20]

The Larsen Bay case indicates the problems associated with a legalistic and scientific approach to the matter of repatriation. The scientific evidence of archaeology is not always clear cut about the evolution or movement of human populations in the distant past. The legal requirement for proof of cultural affiliation can be interpreted broadly or narrowly. The final decision rendered by Secretary Adams was based upon the contested report of two experts, and it circumvented the more elaborate decision making process provided by the legislation. It was a decision made on moral and political grounds rather than purely objective, scientific grounds. Indeed, those latter grounds did not exist and may never be established.

There will be many disagreements in the academic world of archaeologists on matters of cultural affiliation, and Indian tribes will not always find sympathetic audiences for their claims. The legal language of the NMAI Act and NAGPRA encodes the idea of scientifically objective truth, which is the reason Indian remains were originally collected.

A number of tribes have begun to make statements concerning their own history and culture to support potential repatriation claims. In 1993 Vernon Maysayesva, chairman of the Hopi tribe, addressed a letter to museums throughout the country asserting the tribe's cultural affiliation with paleo-Indian, Hohokam, Mimbres, Anasazi, Salcedo, and Mogollon cultures in the Southwest.[21] The Zuni have declared their affiliation with Anasazi and Mogollon sites throughout the northern corner of Arizona and New Mexico.[22] The O'odham have asserted their claims to Mogollon material.[23]

These assertions challenge archaeologists to clarify their analysis of data from widespread sites throughout the Southwest to determine affiliation between those sites and contemporary tribes. Tribes must prepare for negotiations among themselves over whose beliefs and traditions best fit with archaeological data and written historical records to support their claims. As repatriation legislation has given tribes the rights to property and the power to define the materials that fall within the legally defined categories of objects subject to repatriation, tribes have gained the power to reclaim not only objects but their own sense of history.

For Native people, the repatriation legislation gives them both the right and the responsibility to define their own history. As Rennard Strickland has observed, "The Native community acting under NAGPRA has a compelling duty and a tremendous responsibility. The tribe is the only unit with the ability to obtain the historical facts and interpret their cultural meanings relating to the return of sacred objects, objects of cultural patrimony, and unassociated funerary objects."[24]

Given the legislated rights of Indian people to establish their rights to cultural property, what is the historian to make of the assertion by a member of a contemporary Lakota community that "Everything that we made was sacred"? Ethnographic records indicate patterns of individual ownership of personal property and use in ways that had no particular sacred connotations.

The League of the Haudensaunee has issued a general statement about their attitudes concerning the false face masks, examples of which exist in many museum collections. The statement asserts that all masks are sacred and thus could not be sold by their makers, declaring that "There is no legal, moral or ethical way in which a medicine mask can be obtained or possessed by a non-Indian individual or an institution, in that in order for a medicine mask to be removed from the society it would require the sanction of the Grand Council of Chiefs. This sanction has never been given." The assertion denies the personal motives of tribal members who sold masks in the past and those who still sell masks.[25] For the historian, the discrepancy between evidence of personal intent in the form of sales records and the written declaration of the League raises questions about values of historical "truth."

The repatriation of objects from museum collections raises numerous issues for people working in the institutions that have based their activities on the lives, knowledge, and material culture of Native people. For anthropologists and archaeologists, repatriation represents a potential threat to the body of information about material culture in museums that has been a basis for scholarly activity. There is still a significant amount of resistance to repatriation policies within the academic community. The return of human remains to Native tribes is perceived as the loss of scientific knowledge.[26]

For archaeologists, however, repatriation policy represents a way to assert the importance of archaeological research in establishing the historical continuity between Native cultures before European contact and those thereafter. The distinction between prehistory and history begins to blur. For historians, repatriation poses challenges to notions of historical objectivity and presents new bodies of information, including oral traditions presented by contemporary Native people, that must be assessed and interpreted in light of written documents.

For those of us who are ethnohistorians, the tradition and methods of the field arose out of the work of anthropologists and historians whose testimony before the Indian Claims Commission from the late 1940s through the 1970s helped to establish aboriginal and historical occupation and use of land by Indian communities.[27] The collaboration between Indian tribes and scholars that arose from that work remind us how archaeologists, anthropologists, and historians today can participate in the process of establishing the evidence of cultural affiliation demanded by repatriation laws. The process of repatriation will offer new opportunities to learn from Native communities about their histories and to integrate the work of academic scholars with that of Native historians.

NOTES

1. Alfonso Ortiz, personal communication, Chicago IL, 13 June 1990; Louis A. Hieb, "Meaning and Mismeaning: Toward an Understanding of the Ritual Clown," in *New Perspectives on the Pueblos*, ed. Alfonso Ortiz (Albuquerque: University of New Mexico Press, 1972), 165–96.

2. According to the 1990 census there were 2,015,143 people identifying themselves as American Indians, Eskimos, or Aleuts. Of those, 437,771 resided on reservations or on Indian trust land. See U.S. Department of Commerce, Economics and Statistics Administration, Bureau of the Census, *1990 Census of Population, Social and Economic Characteristics, American Indian and Alaska Native Areas*, 1.

3. Michael D. Coe, *Breaking the Maya Code* (New York: Thames and Hudson, 1992), 100–101.

4. Peter and Jill Furst, *North American Indian Art* (New York: Rizzoli, 1982), 220.

5. Jack F. Trope and Walter R. Echo-Hawk, "The Native American Graves Protection and Repatriation Act: Background and Legislative History," *Arizona State Law Journal* 24, no. 1 (spring 1992): 40–41; Robert E. Bieder, "The Representations of Indian Bodies in Nineteenth-Century American Anthropology," *American Indian Quarterly* 20, no. 2 (spring 1996): 173–74.

6. James Riding In, "Without Ethics & Morality: A Historical Overview of Imperial Archaeology and American Indians," *Arizona State Law Journal* 24, no. 1 (spring 1992): 30; H. Marcus Price III, *Disputing the Dead: U.S. Law on Aboriginal Remains and Grave Goods* (Columbia: University of Missouri Press, 1991), 83–85; Robert M.

Peregoy, "Nebraska's Landmark Repatriation Law: A Study of Cross-Cultural Conflict and Resolution," *American Indian Culture and Research Journal* 16:2 (1992): 139–95.

7. Price, *Disputing the Dead*, 38–43, 54–59.

8. See James H. Merrell, *The Indians' New World: Catawabas and their Neighbors from European Contact through the Era of Removal* (Chapel Hill: University of North Carolina Press for the Institute of Early American History and Culture, Williamsburg VA, 1989) for an excellent study of cultural adaptation and persistence. James Clifford provides a thought provoking case study of contemporary tribal identity in "Identity at Mashpee," chap. 12 in *The Predicament of Culture: Twentieth-Century Ethnography, Literature, and Art* (Cambridge: Harvard University Press, 1988), 277–346.

9. *"Native American Graves Protection and Repatriation Act* Regulations; Final Rule," 43 CFR Part 10, *Federal Register* December 4, 1995, section 10.14.c.

10. Vine Deloria Jr., *Red Earth, White Lies: Native Americans and the Myth of Scientific Fact* (New York: Scribner, 1995), 155, 177, 246–48, 251.

11. Public Law 101-185, An Act to Establish the National Museum of the American Indian within the Smithsonian Institution, and for other purposes, Nov. 18, 1989, 103 Stat. 1336, Sec. 11, (a)–(d).

12. Public Law 101-601, An Act to Provide for the Protection of Native American Graves, and for other purposes, Nov. 16, 1990, 101st Congress, 25 USC 3001, Sec. 2,(2).

13. NAGPRA: Final Rule, Section 10.14.e.

14. Collections Policy, National Museum of the American Indian, appendix A, National Museum of the American Indian Policy Statement on Native American Human Remains and Cultural Materials, in *Mending the Circle: A Native American Repatriation Guide* (New York: American Indian Ritual Object Repatriation Foundation, 1996), 129–33.

15. William W. Fitzhugh, foreword to *Reckoning With the Dead*, ed. Tamara L. Bray and Thomas W. Killion (Washington DC: Smithsonian Institution Press, 1994), viii.

16. Stuart Speaker, "The Red, Black, and Blue: Context and Mortuary Data at Larsen Bay, Kodiak Island," in *Reckoning With the Dead*, 55–60.

17. Don E. Dumond, "The Uyak Site in Prehistory," in *Reckoning With the Dead*, 45.

18. G. Richard Scott, "Teeth and Prehistory on Kodiak Island," in *Reckoning with the Dead*, 73; Donald W. Clark, "Still a Big Story," in *Reckoning With the Dead*, 146.

19. Clark, "Still a Big Story," 146.

20. Fitzhugh, foreword, vii.

21. Vernon Maseyesva, Chair, Hopi Tribe, to Mr. Ray Gonyea, Director of Repatriation, National Museum of the American Indian, undated [1994].

22. Deborah L. Nichols, Anthony L. Klesert, and Roger Anyon, "Ancestral Sites, Shrines and Graves: Native American Perspectives on the Ethics of Collecting Cultural Properties," in *The Ethics of Collecting Cultural Property*, ed. Phyllis Mauch Messenger (Albuquerque: University of New Mexico Press, 1989), 32.

23. Personal statement by Mr. Joe Joaquin, representative of the O'Odham, at

a repatriation workshop held by the National Museum of the American Indian in Tucson, Arizona, August 24, 1993. Archaeologically, the O'Odham are associated with the Hokokam prehistoric culture. See George J. Gumerman and Emil W. Haury, "Prehistory: Hohokam," in *Handbook of North American Indians: Southwest*, vol. 9, ed. Alfonso Ortiz (Washington DC : Smithsonian Institution, 1979), 76.

24. Rennard Strickland, "Implementing the National Policy of Understanding, Preserving, and Safeguarding the Heritage of Indian Peoples, Sacred Objects, and Cultural Patrimony," *Arizona State Law Journal* 24 (spring 1992): 189.

25. Haudenosaunee, October 18, 1993. Statement issued by Hoaudenosaunee, Onondaga Nation, Hemlock Road, Box 319B, via Nedrow, New York, 13120.

26. Clement W. Meighan, "Another View on Repatriation: Lost to the Public, Lost to History," *Public Historian* 14, no. 3 (summer 1992).

27. Helen Hornbeck Tanner, "Erminie Wheeler-Voegelin (1903–1988), Founder of the American Society for Ethnohistory," *Ethnohistory* 38, no. 1 (winter 1991): 58–72.

Purity and Pollution

Unearthing an Oppositional Paradigm in the
Study of Cherokee Religious Traditions

MARY C. CHURCHILL

Without doubt, anthropologist Charles Hudson should be included among the most important twentieth-century scholars of Native Americans of the Southeastern United States.[1] His *Southeastern Indians* is considered an important if not *the* standard reference in the study of Southeastern American Indians.[2] While he covers many Southeastern indigenous nations in this book, he most thoroughly discusses the Cherokees. Despite the work's prominence, however, its interpretation of the religious traditions of Southeastern American Indians generally and Cherokees specifically is problematic. In particular, Hudson's approach relies on the binary opposition of purity versus pollution. Before I turn to my analysis of *The Southeastern Indians* itself, though, I will begin with some introductory remarks about the role of this book in the study of Cherokee religious traditions and will survey the academic regard for it generally.

At present, there are no comprehensive treatments of Cherokee religious traditions. This situation has arisen not because of a lack of interest or paucity of sources, however. For instance, the work of James Mooney of the Bureau of American Ethnology, which emphasizes the Eastern Cherokee but also includes the Western Cherokee, is generally regarded as the most important scholarship on Cherokee religious traditions. In particular, his "Myths of the Cherokee" is an often-cited source, though his "Sacred Formulas of the Cherokees" contains information scholars find invaluable for the study of Cherokee traditions as well.[3] Also significant are the publications of Cherokee scholars Jack Frederick Kilpatrick and Anna Gritts Kilpatrick. Their works, including *Friends of Thunder, Walk in Your Soul,* and *Run Toward the Nightland,* constitute the backbone of the study of Oklahoma Cherokee sacred ways.[4] Raymond D. Fogelson's treatment of Cherokee conjury and witchcraft also is notable.[5] So, too, is his work on the conception of Cherokee power.[6] To this list could be added more recent articles by Alan Edwin Kilpatrick and Lee Irwin.[7] The works of several other scholars could be mentioned as well. Fogelson notes, however, that "despite the fact that a bewildering amount has been published about Cherokee spiritual beliefs and practice, no satisfactory general synthesis of Cherokee religion exists."[8] We find this same assessment echoed ten years later in William L. Anderson's 1988 survey of the literature.[9] The situation remains essentially unchanged today.

In the absence of such a treatment, Hudson's *Southeastern Indians* serves as an important overview of Cherokee religious traditions, especially as they are thought to have been lived and practiced prior to significant European contact.[10] While Hudson describes the book as a "comprehensive introduction" to the Native Americans of the Southeast, including the Cherokees, Choctaws, Chickasaws, Creeks, Seminoles, Catawbas, Timucuas, Caddos, and many others, Fogelson and Walter L. Williams have noted its emphasis on the Cherokees in particular.[11] Hudson himself acknowledges that his chapter on the Southeastern Indian belief system relies "almost exclusively" on sources concerning the Cherokee.[12] His chapter "Ceremony" draws on Cherokee materials as well. Even though the book concerns the Southeastern Indians in general, its emphasis on the Cherokees makes it an important resource for Cherokee studies.

In regard to the academic assessment of *The Southeastern Indians*, it is important to note that this work has been not only included in bibliographic surveys of Southeastern Indian and Cherokee sources and reviewed in journals but also praised for its contribution to the study of Southeastern Indians in general. Cherokee legal scholar Rennard Strickland in his review of literature on the Cherokees regarded Hudson's *Southeastern Indians* as a "significant and impressive new study" in 1977.[13] In his 1978 bibliographic survey of Cherokee research, Fogelson referred to *The Southeastern Indians* as "the best recent synthesis of the [Southeastern culture] area."[14] Additionally, Williams's "Cherokee History: An Analysis of Recent Studies" included discussion of this work.[15] Elsewhere, Williams and Thomas R. French referred to Hudson's *Southeastern Indians* as an "excellent synthesis."[16] James H. Howard wrote that the work is "a real blockbuster, certainly the best summary treatment of the Native Americans in what is now known as the American South which has appeared to date," and he noted Hudson's strength in covering the Southeastern belief system.[17] Meanwhile, the scholar considered by some as the most knowledgeable of the literature on Native American religious traditions, Åke Hultkrantz, acclaimed *The Southeastern Indians* as an "excellent book" on the Southeastern Indians.[18] And in a 1979 review, Michael A. Lofaro touted *The Southeastern Indians* as "a landmark in the study of the native people of the American South," concluding that the book will "serve as a standard reference for many years to come."[19]

It appears that Lofaro's prediction has come true. For instance, John James Collins relied on *The Southeastern Indians* in his overview of American Indian religious traditions, *Native American Religions: A Geographical Survey*, as did

Denise Lardner Carmody and John Tully Carmody in their survey, *Native American Religions: An Introduction*.[20] In the study of Cherokee religious history, William G. McLoughlin cited Hudson's book as well, characterizing it as a "fine study of the Southeastern Indians."[21] In *The Cherokees and Christianity*, McLoughlin even cited Hudson's use of the idea of purity.[22] Theda Perdue, a historian of Southeastern Indians, also relied on Hudson's purity versus pollution interpretation in her discussion of cultural traditions in *Nations Remembered: An Oral History of the Cherokees, Chickasaws, Choctaws, Creeks, and Seminoles in Oklahoma, 1865–1907*.[23]

Since the publication of *The Southeastern Indians* in 1976, Hudson's interpretation of Southeastern Indian culture has continued to make its way into print. For instance, his *Elements of Southeastern Indian Religion* was published in 1984.[24] Hudson also wrote the entry, "North American Indians: Indians of the Southeast Woodlands," for *The Encyclopedia of Religion*.[25] This encyclopedic passage appeared two years later as a selection in the edited volume, *Native American Religions, North America*.[26] Hudson's *Southeastern Indians*, along with these later works, has served and continues to serve as an important academic articulation on Southeastern Indian religious traditions in general and Cherokee sacred ways in particular.

Part of Hudson's contribution to the study of Native American religious traditions is the regard he has for the sacred ways of the Southeastern indigenous peoples. Calvin Martin noted the "humane" quality of *The Southeastern Indians*.[27] Hudson himself says, "I assume that the beliefs of the Southeastern Indians ought to be taken seriously."[28] And despite his grasp of the literature on the Southeastern Indians and the length of the book itself—more than 575 pages—Hudson considers *The Southeastern Indians* more of a beginning in the study of this area. The book is, in his words,

a comprehensive introduction to the native people of the Southeastern United States. It is comprehensive in that it traces the main outlines of their prehistory, social institutions, and history, but it is introductory in that I have not entered into fine points of interpretation. More than any of the native people in North America, the Southeastern Indians have been victims of scholarly neglect; and above all I have wanted to bring them to life, to sketch them boldly and vividly. The intricacies of specialist uncertainties would have blurred the images I have sought to make plain. Hence this book is more the first word on the subject than the last word.[29]

Since 1975, when Hudson wrote those initial words of *The Southeastern Indians*, academic vocabularies have been influenced by a burgeoning interest in cultural criticism and have increasingly come to include new terms, such as "postcolonialism," "hegemonic discourse," and "standpoint epistemology." In the context of cultural criticism and the critical studies movement, academics from all disciplines more and more engage in conversations that inquire about the assumptions and implications of scholarly endeavors. They speak about "intricacies of specialist uncertainties" and "blurred images" and try to find or make meaning in ways probably foreign to a Hudson of twenty years ago. It is in the context of this critical conversation, then, that I respond to Hudson's "first word."

My intention in this dialogue of sorts is to examine some of the concepts that underlie Hudson's interpretation of Southeastern Indian religious traditions generally and those of the Cherokees specifically. Although Hudson states that the organizing principles of the Southeastern Indian belief system were opposition, purity, balance, and analogy, a close reading of the book reveals his emphasis on two of these elements, opposition and purity.[30] As I shall demonstrate, Hudson's interpretation of Cherokee traditions in particular relies on both of these concepts.

In Hudson's interpretive paradigm, oppositional elements are separated from one another by means of boundaries. While these elements may merely differ from each other, conflict or antagonism can characterize their relationship as well. The central opposition that informs Hudson's *Southeastern Indians* is the dichotomy between purity and pollution, wherein purity is connoted positively and pollution negatively. For Hudson, purity is associated with order and the maintenance of boundaries between different categories, while pollution entails chaos and the mixing of categories or the crossing of categorical boundaries. In order to explicate Hudson's interpretation, I will begin with his portrayal of the Cherokee cosmos and its components.

According to Hudson, the Cherokee cosmos is ordered by fundamental categories. Describing the cosmos, Hudson writes,

In the beginning, just two worlds existed: the Upper World and the Under World. This World, the world on which the Indians lived, was created later. The Upper World epitomized order and expectableness, while the Under World epitomized disorder and change, and This World stood somewhere between perfect order and complete chaos.[31]

According to this portrayal, the Upper World and the Under World are in an oppositional relationship, while This World, the earth, occupies a middle space between them.[32] This World resembles the Upper World in many ways, while the Under World features inversions of This World.[33] Floating on a body of water, the earth is suspended from four cords, one at each cardinal direction. These cords extend upward to the sky vault, consisting of solid rock. These four cords have oppositional significance as well. According to Hudson,

The Cherokees attached much significance to the four cardinal directions, associating each of them with a series of social values. Actually, these seem to have been two sets of opposites. In one opposition, the east was the direction of the Sun, the color red, sacred fire, blood, and life and success; its opposite, the west, was associated with the Moon, the souls of the dead, the color black, and death. In the other opposed pair, the north was associated with cold, the color blue (and purple), and trouble and defeat; while its opposite, the south, was associated with warmth, the color white, peace, and happiness.[34]

Just as the worlds and directions are classified, Hudson notes three categories of beings: humans (Hudson's "men"), animals, and plants. While plants are often allies with humans, opposition characterizes the relationship between humans and animals. As Hudson states, "Men and animals were opposed to each other, with enmity existing between them."[35] Within the classification of humans, gender was subject to categorization as well. "One of the fundamental categories of opposition in Southeastern thought," Hudson writes, "was the man/woman dichotomy."[36] In this dichotomy, men and women are understood to be radically different from each other.[37]

The Cherokees recognized, however, that certain beings cross the boundaries between categories or incorporate elements from one or more categories. For instance, bridging the boundary separating humans from animals, bears are considered four-footed animals, yet they sometimes walk on two feet like humans. The bat also mixes elements from more than one category of animals. Within the animal category are three subgroups: in Hudson's words, "the four-footed animals, epitomized by the deer; the birds, who because of flight were associated with the Upper World, and who were epitomized by the bald eagle; and thirdly, vermin, such as snakes, lizards, frogs, fish, perhaps insects, and other animals associated with the Under World and epitomized by the rattlesnake."[38] Bats have four feet, so they belong to the category of four-footed animals, yet unlike most four-footed animals they can fly. Hudson refers to beings that cross categories or incorporate elements from more than one category as "anomalies and abominations."[39] Hudson considers the Cherokee being known as the *Uktena*, for example, to be anomalous and abominable. The *Uktena* has the characteristics of a serpent (Under World), a deer (This World), and a bird (Upper World).[40] It is often depicted as a snake-like being with antlers and wings.

As anomalies, those beings that cross boundaries or mix categories are abnormal or deviant and hence abominable to the Cherokees, according to Hudson. Consistent with Hudson's interpretation of Cherokee traditions, anomalies violate the purity of categories that is necessary for the maintenance of an orderly existence. For Hudson, this order is paramount in the Southeastern Indian religious system. As he puts it, "If there is a single word which epitomizes the Southeastern Indian belief system, it is 'order.' "[41] As pollutants of cosmic purity, anomalies therefore entail the greatest "abomination," cosmic chaos.

Hudson's use of the oppositional paradigm is central not only in his characterization of the Cherokee cosmos, but also in his interpretation of Southeastern American Indian religious traditions overall. Using the language of purity versus pollution, Hudson offers explanations, for example, of Southeastern Indian ceremonialism:

The Southeastern Indians' concern with maintaining purity and avoiding pollution, [was] a concern, in fact, that was so extreme that it strikes us as having been almost obsessive. Quite simply, purity was maintained when separation was successful, and pollution occurred when separation failed. Much of the ceremony of the Southeastern Indians can be understood as a means of maintaining separation and as a means of overcoming pollution when separation failed.[42]

Hudson extends this generalization to particular Southeastern Indian rituals, most notably the Green Corn ceremony and the ritual—there and in other ceremonial contexts—of "going to the water."[43] The Green Corn ceremony or "busk" was a common "first-fruits" rite throughout much of the Southeast. Hudson describes it as "an important vehicle in the Indians' quest for purity[,] . . . a means of purifying their social order."[44] Included in this "purifying," for example, are the separation of women and men and the resolution of offenses. In the particular case of the Green Corn ceremony, an essential element is the sacred fire. At the Green Corn, for instance, the ceremonial fire is rekindled, and from this new fire, all hearths in the community are relit and renewed. According to Hudson, the sacred fire is "the principal symbol of purity" among the Southeastern Indians.[45]

Hudson also interprets the Southeastern Indian ritual of "going to the water" in terms of purity versus pollution. Hudson writes that "one of the principal ceremonial means of overcoming pollution in the Southeast was by bathing in creeks and rivers. . . . By overcoming pollution, bathing was believed to increase longevity."[46] He adds that going to the water at daybreak was "especially purifying."[47] It should be noted here, however, that this ritual resembles dunking more than bathing, as in this description of a communal "going to the water":

Soon after sunrise, all repaired to the river, and at the direction of the priest, all waded into the river, the men above, and the women and children below, all having their clothes on. Then standing with their faces toward the east, all plunged entirely under water, seven times, with their heads towards the east. All the children plunged also, and mothers plunged their infants seven times.[48]

The occasion of going to the water varied among the Cherokees. In addition to the communal rites, families went to the water at dawn and after the burial of a relative, and the practice was used in private rituals involving a curer and a patient.

In light of Hudson's application of the oppositional model to Cherokee cosmological and ceremonial conceptions, it should come as no surprise to find the discourse of purity versus pollution in his characterization of other elements of Southeastern Indian traditions. In particular, I cite the example of menstruation, a subject that will reappear later in my analysis. Historically, the Cherokee had specific ways of treating people who were bleeding. Menstruating women and warriors returning from battle, for instance, were separated from others in the community and the community separated from them. In the case of menstruation, it has been proposed in the literature that this separation was due to female "impurity" during this time. Hudson himself offers this same explanation:

Women, perhaps because of their procreative powers, were particularly likely to cause pollution, and they had to take special care when they menstruated and when they were pregnant. A menstruating woman possessed an especially powerful female nature, and she was forbidden to do anything that might cause a man to be polluted by it.[49]

The insight of anthropologist Mary Douglas is especially helpful for understanding how menstruation could be interpreted as polluting. She explains:

Any structure of ideas is vulnerable at its margins. We should expect the orifices of the body to symbolize its specially vulnerable points. Matter issuing from them is marginal stuff of the most obvious kind. Spittle, blood, milk, urine, faeces or tears by simply issuing forth have traversed the boundary of the body. So also have bodily parings, skin, nail, hair clippings and sweat.[50]

Like the anomalous beings who cross cosmological boundaries, menstruation exhibits this phenomenon of boundary crossing as well. In so doing, menstruation also poses a threat to the order valued by Southeastern Native Americans, according to Hudson.

Before discussing the problematic nature of Hudson's interpretation in general, I think it is important to recognize that in articulating his purity/pollution model of Southeastern Indian and Cherokee religious traditions, Hudson was not alone in his thinking, however. In the next section, I propose how he probably arrived at his interpretive paradigm.

The paradigm of purity versus pollution advanced by Hudson has its roots in both the historical and ethnographic documentation he had available to him and the theoretical approach he employed. As I shall demonstrate, Hudson's *Southeastern Indians* is a more recent articulation of what might be understood as a "given fact" of Southeastern Indian religious traditions—the importance of maintaining purity and eliminating pollution. An examination of the works underlying *The Southeastern Indians*, therefore, is useful for illuminating Hudson's interpretation of Cherokee religious traditions.

Concerning historical and ethnographic sources on the Southeastern Indians, Hudson notes that "although we shall be forever in the dark about some details, enough information was collected by early observers like John Lawson, James Adair, and William Bartram and by anthropologists like James Mooney and John R. Swanton to allow us at least to reconstruct the outlines of the Southeastern belief system."[51] In the works of these individuals and those they in turn cited, the use of *purity* and *pollution* and closely related terms in the discussion of Southeastern or Cherokee religious traditions is apparent. While I will not treat each of the works by Lawson, Adair, Bartram, Mooney, and Swanton, I will cite examples to demonstrate the discourse of purity versus pollution in their work.

Among the earliest sources on the Southeast is John Lawson's *A New Voyage to Carolina*, printed in 1709.[52] Lawson had been appointed nine years earlier by the Lords Proprietor to survey interior Carolina.[53] While it appears that he did not have direct contact with the Cherokees in particular, he occasionally spoke of Southeastern native "purgations." Lawson wrote, for instance, that "the Savage Women quit all Company, and dress not their own Victuals, during their Purgations."[54] While he did not specify what he meant by "purgations" in this case, it was a practice among various Southeastern Indians to separate individuals from the community and the community from them at particular times. The return of war parties was an occasion for this separation, as were menstruation and childbirth. Lawson also referred to what appears to be an initiation process for youths as "their time of Purgatory."[55] Moreover, he regarded the drinking and vomiting of a particular "*Yaupon* or Tea" as "purging."[56] Even though Lawson does not appear to have reported on the Cherokees specifically, it is important to realize that Hudson used as a source of background information a work that employed ideas of purgation in describing Southeastern Indian traditions.

Another source on which Hudson relies is James Adair's *History of the American Indians*.[57] Adair was a non-Indian trader who lived among the Southeastern Indians, engaging in commerce with the Cherokees in 1736 and among the Chickasaws in 1744.[58] Hudson notes that it is on Adair's work that scholars depend for much of the knowledge on Southeastern Indians.[59] Swanton and Fogelson have also recognized the importance of Adair's work.[60] Adair's discussion of ceremonialism and various conditions of individuals features the language of purity versus pollution. His use of these ideas most likely arises in part from his belief that Native Americans were descendants of the "Israelites."[61] Indeed, his *History of the American Indians* is an extended argument supporting this contention. Adair was not alone in his interest in the Hebraic origins of the Indians. Tracing American Indian heritage back to biblical roots was not an uncommon practice. It is featured, for instance, in the reflections of the Reverend Daniel S. Butrick, a nineteenth-century missionary to the Cherokees.[62]

In describing the Green Corn ceremony, for example, Adair made reference to the central plaza as a "holy square," from which the "impure" were excluded.[63] Adair related the ceremonial drink of this rite (often referred to as the "black drink") to purification as well, noting that "the religious attendants boil a sufficient quantity of button-snake-root, highly imbittered, and give it round pretty warm, in order to vomit and purge their sinful bodies. Thus they continue to mortify and purify themselves, till the end of the fast."[64] Adair's interpretation of another ritual, that of "going to the water," not only demonstrates his use of the idea of purity in Cherokee ritual but also suggests that his word choice may have resulted from his effort to offer convincing evidence for his proof of the Cherokee's Semitic origins:

The Hebrews had various Ablutions and Anointings, according to the Mosaic ritual—and all the Indian nations constantly observe similar customs from religious motives. Their frequent bathing, or dipping themselves and their children in rivers, even in the severest weather, seems to be as truly Jewish, as the other rites and ceremonies which have been mentioned. . . . After bathing, they return home, rejoicing as they run for having so well performed their religious duty, and thus purged away the impurities of the preceding day by ablution.[65]

Adair also characterized people in various states as "impure." For instance, wounded warriors remained in a special "hut" during their "impurity."[66] Other sources of impurity included the dead, particular foods, adultery, and childbirth.[67] Menstruation could also foster a "most horrid and dangerous pollution." As Adair wrote:

The Indians have customs consonant to the Mosaic Laws of Uncleanness. They oblige their women in their *lunar retreats*, to build small huts, at as considerable a distance from their dwelling-houses, as they imagine may be out of the enemies reach; where, during the space of that period, they are obliged to stay at the risque [*sic*] of their lives. Should they be known to violate that ancient law, they must answer for every misfortune that befalls any of the people, as a certain effect of the divine fire; though the lurking enemy sometimes kills them in their religious retirement. Notwithstanding they reckon it conveys a most horrid and dangerous pollution to those who touch, or go near them, or walk anywhere within the circle of their retreats; and are in fear of thereby spoiling the supposed purity and power of their holy ark, which they always carry to war.[68]

Here Adair appears to oppose the "impurity" of contact with or proximity to a menstruating woman with the purity and power of the Cherokee "ark." Adair expressed this opposition between "impure women" and the sacred again, this time in terms of sin and holiness:

Should any of the Indian women violate this law of purity, they would be censured, and suffer for any sudden sickness, or death that might happen among the people, as the necessary effect of the divine anger for their polluting sin, contrary to their old traditional law of female purity. . . . At the stated period, the Indian women's impurity is finished by ablution, and they are again admitted to social and holy privileges.[69]

In sum, these examples from Adair's *History of the American Indians* demonstrate again the appearance of the discourse of purity versus pollution in a source utilized by Hudson.

But there is more. In addition to Adair, Hudson includes the naturalist William Bartram in his list of "early observers" of Cherokee culture. Fogelson affirms that Bartram's *Travels Through North and South Carolina, Georgia, East and West Florida, the Cherokee Country, the Extensive Territories of the Muscogulges, or Creek Confederacy, and the Country of the Chactaws* [sic] and his "Observations on the Creek and Cherokee Indians" are "important firsthand accounts."[70] In *Travels*, published in 1791, Bartram made reference to purity in two particular instances. When speaking of the busk (Green Corn ceremony), Bartram described the preparation of the sacred fire:

On the fourth morning, the high priest, by rubbing wood together, produces new fire in the public square, from whence every habitation in the town is supplied with the new and pure flame.[71]

In the second example, Bartram concluded his discussion of the busk by noting that at the end of the ceremony, visitors from nearby join town members in the celebration. These visiting friends have "purified and prepared themselves," according to Bartram.[72] While there are only two references to purity in this discussion, it is clear that Bartram's understanding of the ceremony was influenced by ideas of purity, especially when we consider his description of the preparation and early stages of this rite. Bartram wrote,

When a town celebrates the busk, having previously provided themselves with new cloaths [sic], new pots, pans, and other household utensils and furniture, they collect all their worn-out cloaths and other despicable things, sweep and cleanse their houses, squares, and the whole town, of their filth, which with all the remaining grain and other provisions, they cast together into one common heap, and consume it with fire. After having taken medicine, and fasted for three days, all the fire in the town is extinguished. During this fast they abstain from the gratification of every appetite and passion whatever.[73]

In his description of the ceremony, he appears to be speaking of the Creeks, although this is not certain. Even if he had been focusing on the Creek version of the ritual, the Cherokee ceremony was very similar, especially in the features Bartram mentioned. Bartram was in all likelihood familiar with the Cherokee version, based on his "Observations on the Creek and Cherokee Indians," to which I turn next.

While Bartram referred to Southeastern Indian purity in his *Travels*, he himself did not use this language in his "Observations." Nevertheless, the work merits inclusion in this list of sources on which Hudson had to draw for reasons that will become apparent. In a prefatory note to the manuscript, Ephraim George Squire, an archaeologist and ethnologist, described the extant history of the document and the process by which he brought it out of obscurity.[74] Apparently written by Bartram in 1789, the manuscript came to be published in the 1853 issue of *Transactions of the American Ethnological Society*. Squire, himself knowledgeable about the Southeast, wrote supplementary notes to the manuscript, which were published with Bartram's account.[75] Bartram himself made no reference to purity in his "Observations," however. It is only in Squire's supplementary notes to Bartram's manuscript that this language is found. Squire wrote, for example, that the Southeastern Indians had a series of "peculiar observances" that included "purifications, dances, and sacrifices."[76] In addition to this and another instance of Squire's own use of the language of purity, Squire included in the supplemental notes information from Adair's *History of the American Indians* that mentioned the purification associated with the taking of the Southeastern Indian bitter herb drink.[77] More importantly, however, Squire quoted from John Howard Payne's unpublished manuscripts.[78] A well-known writer, Payne made several trips to the South in the 1830s, collecting information on Cherokee history. Among his papers were copies of official Cherokee documents; information from his interviews with Cherokees; and correspondence with missionaries, most notably Reverend Butrick of the American Board of Commissioners of the Foreign Missions.[79] Relying on Payne's papers, Squire mentioned purification preceding the Green Corn ceremony, for example.[80] The discourse of purity is therefore present in Bartram's *Travels* as well as in Squire's supplementary notes to Bartram's "Observations."

The pattern, moreover, continued. Approximately a century later appeared works by ethnologist James Mooney, among them "The Sacred Formulas of the Cherokees" and "Myths of the Cherokee."[81] Many scholars consider the latter work especially valuable in studying Cherokee traditions.[82] Mooney's approach combined field research with comparative analysis. In *The Southeastern Indians*, Hudson relied on Mooney's writings, which include the notion of purity as well. In "Myths of the Cherokee," for instance, Mooney indicated that purification was part of the preparation for the Green Corn ceremony:

> In former times the annual thanksgiving ceremony of the Green-corn dance, preliminary to eating the first new corn, was the most solemn tribal function, a propitiation and expiation for the sins of the past year, an amnesty for public criminals, and a prayer for happiness and prosperity for the year to come. Only those who had properly prepared themselves by prayer, fasting, and purification were allowed to take part in this ceremony, and no one dared to taste the new corn until then.[83]

Mooney also wrote of "going to the water" as purification, and he told that such a purificatory practice was necessary before hearing very sacred stories.[84] It is true Mooney attempted to separate obvious European elements from Cherokee myths in his writings, but this did not prevent him from employing the idea of purification to a limited degree.

Mooney was known for his field work among the Cherokee. However, he still consulted other written sources in preparing his works. Among them was Adair's *History of the American Indians*, which, as I have shown, employed notions of purity.[85] Mooney also relied on writings by Squire and John Haywood. Squire, who supplemented Bartram's "Observations," also wrote *The Serpent Symbol, and the Worship of the Reciprocal Principles of Nature in America*, which Mooney cited on several occasions in "Myths of the Cherokee."[86] Moreover, Mooney actually relied in part on *The Serpent Symbol* for Squire's summarization of and quotations from the Payne manuscripts.[87] Citing *The Serpent Symbol*, Mooney wrote that Payne

> makes the kindling of the new fire a part of the annual spring festival. At that time, says Payne, "the altar in the center of the national heptagon [i.e., townhouse] was repaired. It was constructed of a conical shape, of fresh earth. A circle was drawn around the top to receive the fire of sacrifice. Upon this was laid, ready for use, the inner bark of seven different kinds of trees. This bark was carefully chosen from the east side of the trees, and was clear and free from blemish." After some days of preliminary purification, sacrifice, and other ceremonial performances, the day appointed for the kindling of the new fire arrived.[88]

Again referring to Payne, but not quoting him, Mooney wrote that "after some days of preliminary purification, sacrifice, and other ceremonial performances, the day appointed for the kindling of the new fire arrived."[89]

A review of the John Howard Payne Papers does reveal Payne's own use of the discourse of purity versus pollution.[90] In volume 1, for instance, Payne wrote, regarding the treatment of children in preparation for "priesthood," "On the approach of the regular monthly disqualification of the mother for coming into contact with holy things, she delivered her infant to his grandmother, or some aged matron, for the protection of his purity."[91] More explicitly, in the Payne papers, there was the observation:

Females during their monthly courses were unclean. Anciently they had tents by themselves, some distance from the house. No one must touch them, or anything that they touched. At the end of seven days they purified themselves by plunging entirely seven times in running water. They then put on clean clothes, and returned to the house and associated with the other members of the family.[92]

Payne also wrote of a ceremony, which he referred to as the "Propitiation or Cementation Festival," in which a ceremonial leader, praying, "implore[d] that the people might be cleansed from all the pollutions and impurities of the year preceding."[93] At the completion of this ceremony, remarked Payne, "The people retired, free, as they supposed, from all pollution. The Cherokees were considered purer, immediately after this Festival, than at any other time."[94]

It should be noted that among Payne's papers were letters sent to Payne from Butrick, who also employed the language of purity versus pollution. According to the Reverend Worcester Willy, another missionary among the Cherokees, Butrick spent the last ten years of his life, "writing, with the purpose, as he said, to show that the Indian is somebody. He wrote trunksfull of manuscripts on Indian antiquities and Indian languages. He spent much time in comparing these languages with the Hebrew. He became convinced that they are all of Hebrew origin."[95] Of all the missionaries among the Cherokees, noted McLoughlin, Butrick was "the most indefatigable" in showing that the Cherokees were descendants from the "Lost Tribes of Israel."[96] As McLoughlin wrote, Butrick's "fascination with the Semitic origins of the Cherokee people led him to undertake intensive research into their customs, sacred myths, and religious rituals," including firsthand study.[97] In addition to the missionary's own research, Adair's *History of the American Indians* was almost certainly available to Butrick as well.[98] Butrick's "A few promiscuous comparisons between Indian & Jewish Antiquities" is suggestive of Adair's arguments on the Hebraic origins of Native Americans.[99] In Butrick's writings to Payne, he used the language of purity. For example, Butrick wrote,

With regard to their manner of warfare the Cherokees and Creeks & probably most of the tribes greatly resembled each other. They had a high priest for the wars, and soldiers, on enlisting, came under his immediate direction and tuition. He, by various means, purified & prepared them for the conflict. None must have any farther [*sic*] intercourse with women till the war was concluded.[100]

Butrick also mentioned that some Cherokees wore their old clothing when ceremonially "going to the water." When these clothes floated away, "the impurities of the last year" went with them.[101]

My tracing of these citations illustrates that Hudson had in Mooney's "Myths of the Cherokee" not only the example of Mooney's own use of the language of purity but also further illustrations of this discourse in Mooney's quotations and summarization of the words of others on whom he relied. Thus, while Mooney himself apparently did not directly rely on the Payne Papers themselves or the Butrick letters in them, the ideas of purity versus pollution nevertheless made their way into "Myths of the Cherokee" and hence into the interpretive paradigm of Hudson's *Southeastern Indians*.[102]

Mooney used other sources as well in describing Cherokee traditions. In his publications, Mooney also quoted the writing of John Haywood, author of *The Natural and Aboriginal History of Tennessee*.[103] Haywood was probably best known for his legal career in North Carolina and Tennessee. He practiced law and became a supreme court justice in both states.[104] In "Sacred Formulas of the Cherokees," Mooney wrote that Haywood

also mentions the veneration which [according to Haywood] "their physicians have for the numbers four and seven, who say that after man was placed upon the earth four and seven nights were instituted for the cure of diseases in the human body and the seventh night as the limit for female impurity."[105]

This quotation is only one example of the discourse of purity versus pollution employed by Haywood. He mentioned "ceremonies of purification" and referred to the black drink as "their purifying *beloved* physic."[106] Beyond that, he noted the practice of moving the body of someone who had died at home outside "for fear of pollution."[107]

It appears that Haywood himself was not only knowledgeable about Southeastern American Indians but also familiar with works by others on the same subject. He mentioned Adair's study of the Southeastern Indians and noted that the remnants of ceremonies in his (Haywood's) own time confirmed Adair's earlier representations of them.[108] Mary U. Rothrock, in her annotations to Haywood's work, noted that part of Haywood's chapter on the Cherokees

is similar to, and possibly based upon, James Adair's attempt to identify the American Indians with the "lost tribes" of Israel. . . . Much of the material in this section is similar to the writings of Daniel Sabin Butrick, missionary to the Cherokee in the early 19th Century. . . . It is possible that Haywood was acquainted with Butrick and discussed these matters with him as well as with educated Indians like Charles Hicks.[109]

Whether Haywood merely perpetuated Adair's or Butrick's ideas, arrived at his own interpretations, or employed some combination of the two, he nevertheless perpetuated the language of purity versus pollution in writing about South-eastern Indian religious traditions. In using Haywood as a source, Mooney carried on this characterization of Cherokee religious traditions. Either directly or indirectly, therefore, Mooney relied on the work of several others—Adair, Squire, Payne, Butrick, and Haywood—in discussing Cherokee traditions. In turn, Hudson imported the discourse of purity versus pollution from their writing into his own.

John R. Swanton's work was yet another source that Hudson had at his disposal in writing *The Southeastern Indians*. Still, despite the stature of Swanton in the field of Southeastern Indian studies, his "Indians of the Southeastern United States" did not treat the Cherokees in much detail.[110] In this book, Swanton did not use terms like *purity* and *pollution* to describe Cherokee traditions. However, he did quote Charles Hicks and Charles Lanman who both used this language. Swanton cited Hicks, a Cherokee chief, as stating,

> The doctors among the Cherokee suppose that cures are to be made in 7 nights of the different disorders which the human body is subject to. During these cures the doctors are remarkably strict to keep out of the house where the patient lies such persons as have handled a dead body, women, &c. for it is held among the Cherokees that these persons are impure until bathing in the water of the seventh night in the morning. Some changes have of late taken place—instead of seven, four nights are now deemed sufficient.[111]

Swanton also reprinted a passage from Lanman's "Green-Corn Ceremonies of the Cherokees."[112] Lanman included this chapter in his *Adventures in the Wilds of the United States and British American Provinces*, which he described as "a kind of Cyclopedia of American Scenery and Personal Adventure, and of Traveling Incidents."[113] Quoting Lanman, Swanton wrote:

> The ruling men [calendar keepers] of the tribe have signified to their people that the period for planting corn has arrived, and that they must gather themselves together for the purpose of submitting to the annual ceremonies of purification. For doing this they have a double object: they would, in the first place, expunge from their bodies every vestige of all the colds and diseases with which they may have been afflicted during the past winter; and, in the second place, they would propitiate the Great Spirit, so as to secure his blessing upon the crops which they are about to deposit in the ground.[114]

Swanton's "Indians of the Southeastern United States" therefore made readily available additional illustrations of purity versus pollution language in impor-tant but relatively obscure sources.

These several examples illustrate the discourse of purity versus pollution in the works of those Hudson considers important for the reconstruction of the belief system of Southeastern American Indians. It is not surprising therefore that Hudson himself uses this discourse in his own interpretation of these traditions in *The Southeastern Indians*. Nor is this all that needs to be said. In addition to the accounts that Hudson used or considered important, he employed theoretical conceptions drawn from the work of Mary Douglas. Her *Purity and Danger: An Analysis of the Concepts of Pollution and Taboo* thoroughly compounded his emphasis on purity versus pollution. Hudson only cites her work a few times, it is true, but the imprint of her theoretical apparatus nonetheless marked his discussion of Southeastern Indian religious traditions. Douglas argued in *Purity and Danger* that

ideas about separating, purifying, demarcating and punishing transgressions have as their main function to impose system on an inherently untidy experience. It is only by exaggerating the difference between within and without, above and below, male and female, with and against, that a semblance of order is created.[115]

In discussing this practice of creating and seeking order, she employed conceptions of "dirt" — "matter out of place" — and classification or "positive structure."[116] The anomalous and the ambiguous contravene the order that is inherent in classification.[117] While Douglas did acknowledge that dirt could be "creative," and that "eliminating it is not a negative moment, but a positive effort to organize the environment," she generally characterized dirt negatively.[118] She suggested that dirt is, in her words, "normally destructive," and "rejected from our normal scheme of classifications"; it "offends against order."[119] In *The Southeastern Indians*, Hudson's interpretation of purity and pollution clearly resembles that of Douglas. As in *Purity and Danger*, Hudson uses the idea of categorization and characterizes pejoratively (as "abominable") that which does not fit into categories. Thus, for Hudson, the Southeastern Indians were concerned with "maintaining purity and avoiding pollution."[120] Impurity was to be "overcome."[121] Generally ceremonies were "means of keeping their categories pure and of ridding them of pollution after it occurred."[122]

Douglas's understanding of purity versus pollution was no doubt influenced, at least in part, by the thought of anthropologist Claude Lévi-Strauss. The dichotomy of purity versus pollution reflects one of Lévi-Strauss's main concerns; that is, binary opposition. He drew on the work of linguists Ferdinand de Saussure and Roman Jakobson in articulating his "structuralist" approach.[123] Lévi-Strauss relied on Saussure's idea that language is a system of signs. A linguistic sign is binary, consisting of the "signifier" (a sound, image, or object, etc.) and the "signified" (concept). Moreover, according to Saussure, if a concept is part of a system, this concept is defined by contrasting it to other elements in the system, not by referring to the concept's own content. Definition is therefore a process of contrast. Extending these ideas, but applying them to the social level, Lévi-Strauss argued that culture and society are outward projections of inward mental structures and that cultural elements gain significance through differentiation.

Lévi-Strauss utilized Jakobson's contention that the human mind interprets sounds as bundles of binary oppositions; for instance, the mind distinguishes between the phoneme /p/ in *pin* from the phoneme /b/ in *bin*. The /p/ phoneme is unvoiced while the /b/ phoneme is voiced. As such, this pair is one example of approximately thirty distinctive figures of language.[124] Thus, for Lévi-Strauss, human beings naturally formulate cultural constructs out of binary oppositions in the mind. Such pairs are noticeable at the social and cultural level in myth, kinship relations, and the organization of communities, for instance. Therefore, the binary opposition of purity versus pollution in Hudson's *Southeastern Indians* is reflective not only of Douglas's but also of Lévi-Strauss's use of the conception.

To sum up, this demonstration of the sources—documentary and theoretical—that influenced Hudson directly or indirectly is important for several reasons. Tracing the use of *purity* and *pollution* and related terms in these accounts reveals that Hudson was not alone in his use of this discourse to interpret Cherokee religious traditions. He more than merely replicated the interpretation offered in his sources, however. He lent validity, in the twentieth century, to an understanding of Southeastern Indian traditions that originated at least two centuries earlier and that, by virtue of its age alone, should have been interrogated more thoroughly. Perhaps Douglas's twentieth-century articulation of a theory of purity and pollution and Lévi-Strauss's structuralism quelled any suspicions Hudson may have had.

Any response to Hudson, then, actually addresses a dominant theme running through central Southeastern sources. Similarly, because Douglas's work has been so influential in the study of this theoretical area, a criticism of Hudson's *Southeastern Indians* actually challenges an important academic conception of purity and pollution as well. My response to Hudson therefore entails an expanded dialogue not only with Hudson but also with those whose wrote works on which Hudson drew directly or indirectly either for information or theory.

With this sketch of Hudson's oppositional model and its antecedents in mind, I now turn to the problematic nature of his interpretive paradigm. Recall that in interpreting Southeastern Indian ritualism, Hudson argues that Southeastern Indian ceremony can be understood as a way of "maintaining purity and avoiding pollution" and of "maintaining separation and . . . overcoming pollution when separation failed."[125] Elsewhere he uses different language to restate the same idea: "If there is a single word which epitomizes the Southeastern Indian belief system, it is 'order,'" writes Hudson.[126] In light of these points and of discussion earlier in this analysis, it is possible to state that the aim of Cherokee traditions, according to Hudson, was therefore two-fold: restore and maintain purity (order, separation, clear categorical boundaries) and avoid and overcome pollution (chaos, boundary crossing, categorical fuzziness). In this paradigm, maintaining purity, order, separation, and clear categorical boundaries are the objectives and are therefore connoted positively whereas pollution, chaos, boundary crossing, and categorical fuzziness, which are to be avoided and even eliminated, are connoted negatively. At first glance, this interpretation appears logical and plausible. It reflects, however, an incomplete portrayal of Cherokee religious traditions.

Interestingly, Hudson himself includes information in *The Southeastern Indians* that contradicts his interpretation of these traditions. To begin this explanation, I return to the subject of anomalies, "beings which fell into two or more of their categories," according to Hudson.[127] He cites as an example of an anomaly the *Utkena* because it has the characteristics of a serpent, which belongs to the Under World; a deer, which belongs to This World; and a bird, which belongs to the Upper World. Hudson refers to such anomalous beings as "abominable" detested and loathsome. They are the pollutants in a system of purity, the chaos in a system of order. Yet Hudson points out the particular value of such anomalous beings:

The Southeastern Indians were particularly interested in anomalies and abominations. . . . These anomalies and abominations were singled out for special symbolic values, and they played important roles in their oral traditions.[128]

He indicates that bear, owl, and cougar—as anomalous beings—were held up as "special animals" with "special meaning."[129] These animals in one way or another defied the Southeastern system of categories. Hudson suggests that they were special because "they shored up the integrity of their classification system."[130] There is another reason—in my opinion, a more important reason—why these beings were considered special to Southeastern Indians, however. Hudson also indicates that the especially anomalous beings, the *Uktena* and Water Cougar, were "objects of fear and power" to the Southeastern Indians. He notes that "the *Uktena* was feared as an anomalous monster, but . . . the Cherokees seized upon that which was most horrible as an important source of power."[131] Though the Uktena was considered "abominable," according to Hudson, other evidence indicates that it was valued as well. Hudson himself notes the positive value of the Uktena's crystals:

Like most of the Indians of the Southeast, the Cherokees believed that their priests and conjurers were able to see into the future by gazing into certain crystals. According to Cherokee oral tradition, the most powerful crystal of all was the *Ulunsuti* (literally 'transparent'), the crest that blazed on an Uktena's head. One had to risk one's life to obtain one of these, but it was thought to be worth the risk. Inferior crystals could be had from the mere scales of an Uktena.[132]

Here, then, is where Hudson's interpretation breaks down. Hudson's oppositional paradigm forces him to imply that the Southeastern Indians, in assigning positive value to purity, order, and the maintenance of categories, therefore had to assign the opposite (negative) value to that which polluted, contravened order, and crossed boundaries. On the contrary, *Uktena* was positively valued, though it fell into more than one category and was feared.

Hudson had apparently failed to realize that Douglas has revised the theory of pollution she presented in *Purity and Danger*. In 1975, one year before the publication of *The Southeastern Indians*, there appeared in print, "Self-Evidence," a chapter of *Implicit Meanings: Essays in Anthropology*,[133] wherein Douglas wrote:

In *Purity and Danger*, I supposed that the Hebrew response of rejecting anomaly was the normal one. I argued that to classify is a necessary human activity and that there is a universal human tendency to pass adverse judgment on that which eludes classification or refuses to fit into the tidy compartments of the mind. A too facile solution. I failed to exploit the full interest of the contrast between my fieldwork in the Congo and my library research in the Bible. For the Lele, many anomalies are auspicious and they religiously celebrate the most anomalous of all, which carries defining marks of land and water creatures, humans and animals, the pangolin or scaly ant-eater. On the other hand on this showing, every anomaly conceived according to the Biblical classification of nature is a defiling monster.[134]

Therefore, for the revised Douglas, beings that straddled categories could be considered favorable or horrifying, depending on the context.[135] It is important to note here Douglas's assumption that a Western, in this case Judaic, conception of pollution was the "normal" one. When she reconsidered her non-Western example, however, her assumption merited revision.

Douglas's revision points to one of the dangers of using pollution theory, especially a theory informed largely by Western conceptions. Thomas Buckley and Alma Gottlieb in *Blood Magic: The Anthropology of Menstruation* articulate this danger in the case of menstrual blood as a "pollutant":

The very power of pollution theory, coupled with Western societies' own codings of menstrual blood as a pollutant, has perhaps created "dirt" where none previously existed, or existed only for some people and/or in some contexts in a given culture. The elegance of pollution theory itself can thus manufacture the illusion of overwhelming negativity in symbolic systems where menstruation may be coded ambiguously or even positively.[136]

In developing the purity versus pollution paradigm as a central element of *The Southeastern Indians*, Hudson therefore does not adequately elaborate on the positive implications of "pollutants." While he does mention benefits that resulted, in the case of the *Uktena*, from obtaining a crystal, the stress on the avoidance and elimination of "pollution" negates the reality that contact with "abominations and anomalies" was an unavoidable part of life and that for the well-being of the community such contact was necessary and sought after for the spiritual power it could bring. Instead of being opposed to the sacred, "anomalies" were sources of access to it.

Hudson's treatment of purity and pollution as oppositional also presents difficulties. Underlying Hudson's paradigm of opposition is the concept of dualism. The idea of dualistic structures as fundamental may be a truth in classic Western thought, but it is problematic when assigned to Cherokee religious traditions. A Western philosophical understanding of dualism includes the notion of "irreducible difference"; hence, the definition of the term as "any system of thought which divides everything in some way into two categories or elements, or else derives everything from two principles, or else refuses to admit more or less than two substances or two kinds of substance.[137] Historians and phenomenologists of religion may be familiar with these meanings, especially the definition of derivation from two principles, since dualism also refers to the binary causal principles that underlie the world's existence.[138] The term itself, according to Mircea Eliade and Ioan P. Couliano, was coined in 1700 C.E., to describe the "Iranian doctrine of the two spirits" and has been found relevant to various religious traditions, including Zoroastrianism, Gnosticism, and Manichaeism, and to the philosophy of Plato.[139] Eliade and Couliano have defined dualism most simply as "*opposition of two principles*," and they added that "this implies a judgment of value (good *versus* bad) and the establishment of a polarity at all levels of reality: cosmological, anthropological, ethical, and so on."[140] Some important Western binary oppositions, according to Vincent M. Colapietro, include: "matter/spirit; body/soul; emotion/reason; outward sign/inward meaning; exterior/interior; surface/depth; margin/central; appearance/reality; representation/presence; artificial/natural (nomos/physis)."[141] In common usage, *opposition* denotes, "resistance, antagonism," "the state of being hostile or in conflict or disagreement," and "contrast or antithesis."[142]

The concept of binary opposition has come to be questioned for several reasons, a few of which I will describe here. First, its accuracy for describing non-Western and/or non-masculine traditions and experience has been denied. In regard to Native American cultures, for instance, Joseph Epes Brown, a scholar known for his work on the Lakota, has noted the inadequacy of dualism for representing their traditions:

Unlike the conceptual categories of Western culture, American Indian traditions generally do not fragment experience into mutually exclusive dichotomies, but tend rather to stress modes of interrelatedness across categories of meaning, never losing sight of an ultimate wholeness.[143]

Feminist historian Joan W. Scott has argued that "fixed oppositions conceal the extent to which things presented as oppositional are, in fact, interdependent."[144] Scott's point is illustrated in the work of Patricia Hill Collins. In *Black Feminist Thought*, Collins looked to the experience of African Americans, especially Black women, to point out that dualism does not describe the complexity of their lives. As she put it, "Being Black encompasses *both* experiencing white domination *and* individual and group valuation of an independent, long-standing Afrocentric consciousness."[145] Collins noted that Black women's "both/and conceptual orientation," in contrast to the Western "either/or" orientation, stems from the experiences of Black women as simultaneously African American, female, and, in many cases, poor.[146]

Another problem with oppositional constructs lies in the hierarchies implicit in their formulations. The first term of a binary is usually considered superior while the second term is inferior. Relying on Jacques Derrida, Scott wrote that the interdependence of terms in a binary is "hierarchal with one term dominant or prior, the opposite term subordinate and secondary. The Western philosophical tradition, he argues, rests on binary oppositions: unity/diversity, identity/difference, presence/absence, and universality/specificity. The leading terms are accorded primacy; their partners are represented as weaker or derivative."[147] Therefore, in the binary oppositions purity/pollution, order/chaos, and bound by categorical boundaries/crossing categorical boundaries, superior status and positive connotation are implied in the first term of each binary and the opposite meanings suggested in the second term.

In addition to these particular criticisms, "master theories" and what was once considered certain have been undermined by modern and postmodern thought generally. In these approaches, for instance, determinism has given way to indeterminacy, univocalism to polyvocality, objectivity to partial perspectives, unity to montage, and canonical interpretations to postcolonial ones. In the age of "blurred images," the definite relation established in binary opposition and the particular meanings of elements within binaries are suspect.

As a consequence of Hudson's interpretative paradigm of purity versus pollution, one comes away with at worst an inaccurate understanding of Cherokee religious traditions and at best a partial one. There is evidence to the contrary that Cherokee traditions could be more accurately interpreted in terms of an indigenous-based model of complementarity rather than opposition. Some theorists argue that partial interpretations may be all that any critic has. If this is the case, then our future as scholars lies in the restoration and maintenance of dialogue, not only with other academics but also with members of native communities, especially elders and religious practitioners. Dialogue could be an important means through which partial perspectives are transformed into more complete understandings.

NOTES

For their insightful comments and suggestions on this manuscript, I wish to thank Paula Gunn Allen, Inés M. Talamantez, Catherine L. Albanese, and Marcia Westkott.

1. Hudson (1976).

2. Hudson (1976).

3. Mooney (1900, 1891).

4. Kilpatrick and Kilpatrick (1964, 1965, 1967).

5. Fogelson (1975).

6. Fogelson (1977).

7. Kilpatrick (1991); Irwin (1992).

8. Fogelson (1978: 35).

9. Anderson (1988: 17).

10. Hudson portrays Southeastern Indian traditions both, as he says, synchronically and diachronically (1976: vii-viii). His synchronic treatment reflects what would be considered "traditional" or "pre-contact" indigenous ways of life in the Southeastern United States, although written documentation of these traditions does not often appear until the eighteenth and nineteenth centuries. While Hudson tries to represent seventeenth-century traditions in his synchronic discussion, it should be noted that he inevitably draws on "post-contact" sources, however. His synchronic segment constitutes the central chapters of The Southeastern Indians, and it is before and after these chapters that Hudson historically frames Southeastern Indian traditions. The first diachronic chapter concerns Southeastern prehistory and early European exploration. He ends the book with his second diachronic chapter, which explicitly addresses post-contact ways of life through the mid to late twentieth century. Because of this structure, Hudson discusses "traditional" ways of living in the past tense, which conceals the continuity of some traditions into the present day. To avoid this inaccuracy, I prefer to use the present tense in speaking about Native Americans, but because my purpose here is not to argue this particular issue with Hudson, I will often use the same tense Hudson uses in discussing Southeastern Indian traditions.

11. Hudson (1976: vii); Fogelson (1978: 7); Williams (1979: 348).

12. Hudson (1976: 14).

13. Strickland (1977: xxi).

14. Fogelson (1978: 7).

15. Williams (1979: 348).

16. Williams and French (1979: 211).

17. Howard (1977–78: 373–74).

18. Hultkrantz (1990: 170).

19. Lofaro (1979: 91, 93).

20. Collins (1991); Carmody and Carmody (1993).

21. McLoughlin (1984: 5, 6, 21–23; quoted passage appears on page 6); McLoughlin (1994: 159–60, 323 n. 37).

22. McLoughlin (1994: 159).

23. Perdue (1980: 85–86; 116 n. 10).

24. Hudson (1984).

25. Hudson (1987: 485–90). This work, along with Hudson's *Elements of Southeastern Indian Religion* (1984), was noted in Hultkrantz's review of the literature on Native American religious traditions in the 1980s; see Hultkrantz (1990: 170).

26. Hudson (1989: 139–46).

27. Martin (1978: 1076).

28. Hudson (1976: viii).

29. Hudson (1976: vii).

30. Hudson (1976: 350).

31. Hudson (1976: 123, 125).

32. Hudson (1976: 136).

33. Hudson (1976: 127).

34. Hudson (1976: 132).

35. Hudson (1976: 128).

36. Hudson (1976: 319).

37. Hudson (1976: 259).

38. Hudson (1976: 128).

39. Hudson (1976: 139, 148).

40. Hudson (1976: 144).

41. Hudson (1976: 121).

42. Hudson (1976: 317).

43. The phrase "Green Corn ceremony" or "Green Corn feast" is generally found in the literature on the Cherokees. Relying on historical documents, William Harlen Gilbert Jr. (1943: 326–27) noted that the Cherokee ceremonial cycle actually featured two such rites. One of them, which Gilbert referred to as the "Preliminary Green Corn Feast," occurred in August, while the other, the "Green Corn Feast," followed the preliminary ceremony by about forty to fifty days. These rites corresponded with the life cycle of corn, the preliminary Green Corn ceremony occurring when the corn was young and first fit to eat and the "Green Corn" proper taking place when the corn matured and hardened, usually in mid to late September. It is not always possible to determine to which of these ceremonies an observation refers, though it is important to note that the rites resembled each other, according to Gilbert.

44. Hudson (1976: 367).

45. Hudson (1976: 126).

46. Hudson (1976: 324).

47. Hudson (1976: 345).

48. Payne (n.d., 4: 215).

49. Hudson (1976: 319).

50. Douglas (1966: 121).

51. Hudson (1976: 121).

52. Lawson (1709).

53. Lefler (1967: xi).

54. Lawson (1709: 197).

55. Lawson (1709: 241).

56. Lawson (1709: 229; Lawson's italics).

57. Adair (1775).

58. Williams (1930: viii, ix).

59. Hudson (1976: 436).

60. Swanton (1946: 831); Fogelson (1978: 12).

61. Adair (1775: 14).

62. McLoughlin and Conser (1994: 134; 321 n. 6). Depending on the source one uses, Butrick's name appears as Butrick or Buttrick.

63. Adair (1775: 108).

64. Adair (1775: 108).

65. Adair (1775: 126).

66. Adair (1775: 131).

67. Adair (1775: 130, 132, 136–45, 244).

68. Adair (1775: 129–30; Adair's italics).

69. Adair (1775: 130–31). The term *sin* appears in other comments Adair made about Cherokee religious traditions as well. For instance, he associated taking the "black drink" and "going to the water" with the cleansing or washing away of sin: "At the end of this notable religious dance, the old beloved, or holy women return home to hasten the feast of the new sanctified fruits. In the mean while [*sic*], every one at the temple drinks very plentifully of the Cusseena and other bitter liquids, to cleanse their sinful bodies; after which, they go to some convenient deep water, and there according to the ceremonial law of the Hebrews, they wash away their sins with water" (1775: 103–4). Adair even referred to one of the Green Corn ceremonies as "the grand festival of the annual expiation of sin" (1775: 105). Interestingly (and problematically), although writing in the late twentieth century, Hudson uses the term *sin* in *The Southeastern Indians*, albeit irregularly. He writes, for example that "sin and impurity were serious matters among the Southeastern Indians. They affected not only the well-being of the sinner, but of his entire community and society as well" (Hudson, 1976: 174).

70. Fogelson (1978: 12); Bartram (1791; 1853: 1–81). Swanton (1946: 831) also noted that Bartram's works are among the best published sources of Cherokee ethnology.

71. Bartram (1791: 399).

72. Bartram (1791: 399).

73. Bartram (1791: 399).

74. Squire (1853a: 3–7).

75. Squire (1853b: 59–81). For information on Squire, see Bieder (1986: 104–45).

76. Squire (1853b: 72).

77. Squire (1853b: 73).

78. Squire (1853b: 74–77).

79. McLoughlin (1984: 355–56). McLoughlin noted the importance of these papers for their information on early Cherokee national affairs and culture. Payne also authored "The Ancient Cherokee Traditions and Religious Rites" (1849).

80. Squire (1853b: 75).

81. Mooney (1891, 1900).

82. Fogelson (1978: 8–9); Swanton (1946: 831).

83. Mooney (1900: 423).

84. Mooney (1900: 230, 431, 492).

85. Mooney (1900: 459–60, 476).

86. Squire (1851); Mooney (1900: 436, 440, 442, 502–3).

87. In "Myths of the Cherokee" (1900) Mooney did not cite the John Howard Payne Papers directly, although he did cite, on 502, Payne's "The Green-Corn Dance" (1862), an account of a Creek Green Corn Ceremony.

88. Mooney (1900: 502; Mooney's brackets); Squire (1851: 116).

89. Mooney (1900, 502).

90. Hudson does not cite the John Howard Payne Papers in *The Southeastern Indians*, so it is unclear if Hudson himself directly read these manuscripts. Nevertheless, the language in the Payne Papers is additional evidence of purity/pollution discourse in important sources on Native Americans in the Southeastern United States, and, of course, through Mooney, Hudson was conversant with the basic outline of the Payne model.

91. Payne (n.d., 1: 38).

92. Payne (n.d., 3: 76).

93. Payne (n.d., 1: 56, 62).

94. Payne (n.d., 1: 69).

95. Indian Chieftain (1884: n.p.).

96. McLoughlin (1994: 141).

97. McLoughlin (1994: 141).

98. Rothrock (1959a: 424–25 n. m).

99. Payne (n.d., 4: 253–61).

100. Payne (n.d., 4: 29).

101. Payne (n.d., 4: 183).

102. Mooney (1900: 428, 436–37, 478, 502) did, however, cite *Antiquities of the Cherokee Indians*, a collection of Butrick's notes published by the Indian Chieftain (1884).

103. Haywood (1823). Swanton (1946: 831) also considered this work valuable for Cherokee ethnology.

104. Rothrock (1959b: xi–xv).

105. Mooney (1891: 322); Haywood (1823: 263).

106. Haywood (1823: 231; Haywood's italics).

107. Haywood (1823: 233).

108. Haywood (1823: 230–31).

109. Rothrock (1959a: 424–25 n. m).

110. Fogelson (1978: 7–8); Swanton (1946).

111. Swanton (1946: 768–69); Hicks (1818: 1). This quotation appeared in "Manners & Customs of the Cherokees," a submission by Calvin Jones to the editor of the *Raleigh Register and North-Carolina Gazette*. Jones indicated that this "notice" was drawn up by Charles Hicks.

112. Lanman (1856: 2: 424–28). Lanman noted that this account is based to a great degree on information from Preston Starritt of Tennessee (2: 424).

113. Lanman (1856: 1: iii).

114. Swanton (1946: 769; my brackets); Lanman (1856: 2: 424–25).

115. Douglas (1966: 4).

116. Douglas (1966: 2–4, 35, 159).

117. Douglas (1966: 35).

118. Douglas (1966: 2, 159).

119. Douglas (1966: 2, 36, 159).

120. Hudson (1976: 317).

121. Hudson (1976: 317).

122. Hudson (1976: 121).

123. Leach (1987: 55–56).

124. Leach (1987: 55–56).

125. Hudson (1976: 317).

126. Hudson (1976: 121).

127. Hudson (1976: 139).

128. Hudson (1976: 139).

129. Hudson (1976: 148).

130. Hudson (1976: 148).

131. Hudson (1976: 166).

132. Hudson (1976: 166–67).

133. This chapter first appeared as the Henry Myers Lecture, which Douglas had given before the Royal Anthropological Institute in 1972 (Douglas: 1975, vii).

134. Douglas (1975: 284–85).

135. Douglas (1975: 282–83).

136. Buckley and Gottlieb (1988: 32).

137. Hall (1989: 84).

138. Bianchi (1987: 506).

139. Eliade and Couliano (1991: 95–96).

140. Eliade and Couliano (1991: 95; Eliade's and Couliano's italics).

141. Colapietro (1993: 53).

142. *The Oxford Encyclopedic English Dictionary*, 1991 ed., s.v. "opposition."

143. Brown (1982: 71).

144. Scott (1988: 37).

145. Collins (1990: 27; Collins's italics).

146. Collins (1990: 29).

147. Scott (1988: 37).

REFERENCES

Adair, James. 1775. *History of the American Indians*. London: Edward and Charles Dilly. Reprinted as *Adair's History of the American Indians*. Samuel Cole Williams, ed. [No city] TN: National Society of Colonial Dames in America, 1930. Reprinted as *Adair's History of the American Indians*. New York: Promontory Press, n.d. (Page references are to the Promontory Press edition.)

Anderson, William L. 1988. "The Direction of Cherokee Research." *Native Press Research Journal* 7 (spring): 17–28.

Bartram, William. 1791. *Travels Through North and South Carolina, Georgia, East and West Florida, the Cherokee Country, the Extensive Territories of the Muscogulges, or Creek Confederacy, and the Country of the Chactaws* [sic]. Philadelphia: James and Johnson. Reprinted as *Travels of William Bartram*. Mark Van Doren, ed. New York: Dover Publications, 1955. (Page references are to reprint edition.)

———. 1853. "Observations on the Creek and Cherokee Indians." *Transactions of the American Ethnological Society* 3:1–81.

Bianchi, Ugo. 1987. "Dualism." In *The Encyclopedia of Religion*. Vol. 4, Mircea Eliade, ed. New York: Macmillan. 506–12.

Bieder, Robert E. 1986. "Ephraim George Squire and the Archaeology of Mental Progress." In *Science Encounters the Indian, 1820–1880: The Early Years of American Ethnology*. Norman: University of Oklahoma Press. 104–45.

Brown, Joseph Epes. 1982. *The Spiritual Legacy of the American Indian*. New York: Crossroad.

Buckley, Thomas, and Alma Gottlieb, eds. 1988. *Blood Magic: The Anthropology of Menstruation*. Berkeley: University of California Press.

Buttrick [Butrick], Daniel Sabin. 1884. *Antiquities of the Cherokee Indians.* Vinita, Indian Territory: Indian Chieftain.

Carmody, Denise Lardner, and John Tully Carmody. 1993. *Native American Religions: An Introduction.* New York: Paulist Press.

Colapietro, Vincent M. 1993. *Glossary of Semiotics.* New York: Paragon.

Collins, John James. 1991. *Native American Religions: A Geographical Survey.* Vol. 1, *Native American Studies.* Lewiston NY: Edwin Mellen Press.

Collins, Patricia Hill. 1990. *Black Feminist Thought: Knowledge, Consciousness, and the Politics of Empowerment.* London: Unwin Hyman. Reprint, Perspectives on Gender, vol. 2. New York: Routledge, 1991. (Page references are to reprint edition.)

Douglas, Mary. 1966. *Purity and Danger: An Analysis of the Concepts of Pollution and Taboo.* London: Routledge & Kegan Paul. Reprint, London: Ark Paperbacks, 1988. (Page references are to reprint edition.)

―――. 1975. *Implicit Meanings: Essays in Anthropology.* London: Routledge & Kegan Paul.

Eliade, Mircea, and Ioan P. Couliano. 1991. *The Eliade Guide to World Religions.* New York: HarperCollins.

Fogelson, Raymond D. 1975. "An Analysis of Cherokee Sorcery and Witchcraft." In *Four Centuries of Southern Indians.* Charles M. Hudson, ed. Athens: University of Georgia Press. 113–31.

―――. 1977. "Cherokee Notions of Power." In *The Anthropology of Power: Ethnographic Studies from Asia, Oceania, and the New World.* Raymond D. Fogelson and Richard N. Adams, eds. Studies in Anthropology. New York: Academic Press. 185–94.

―――. 1978. *The Cherokees: A Critical Bibliography.* Newberry Library Center for the History of the American Indian Bibliographical Series. Bloomington: Indiana University Press for the Newberry Library.

Gilbert, William Harlen, Jr. 1943. "The Eastern Cherokees." Smithsonian Institution *Bureau of American Ethnology Bulletin 133.* Anthropological Papers, no. 23. Washington DC: Government Printing Office.

Hall, Roland. 1989. "Dualism." In *The Concise Encyclopedia of Western Philosophy and Philosophers.* J. O. Urmson and Jonathan Rée, eds. Rev. ed. London: Unwin Hyman. 84–85.

Haywood, John. 1823. *The Natural and Aboriginal History of Tennessee.* Nashville: George Wilson. Reprint, Mary U. Rothrock, ed. Jackson TN: McCowat-Mercer, 1959. (Page references are to reprint edition.)

Hicks, Charles. 1818. "Manners & Customs of the Cherokees." *Raleigh Register and North-Carolina Gazette,* 6 November.

Howard, James H. 1977–78. Review of *The Southeastern Indians,* by Charles Hudson. *American Indian Quarterly* 3 (winter): 373–75.

Hudson, Charles. 1976. *The Southeastern Indians.* Knoxville: University of Tennessee Press.

———. 1984. *Elements of Southeastern Indian Religion*. Iconography of Religions, section 10. Leiden: E. J. Brill.

———. 1987. "North American Indians: Indians of the Southeast Woodlands." In *The Encyclopedia of Religion*. Vol. 10, Mircea Eliade, ed. New York: Macmillan Publishing. 485–90.

———. 1989. "The Southeast Woodlands." In *Native American Religions, North America: Religion, History, and Culture, Selections from "The Encyclopedia of Religion."* Lawrence E. Sullivan, ed. New York: Macmillan Publishing. 139–46.

Hultkrantz, Åke. 1990. "A Decade of Progress: Works on North American Indian Religions in the 1980s." In *Religion in Native North America*. Christopher Vecsey, ed. Moscow: University of Idaho Press. 167–201.

Indian Chieftain. 1884. Preface to *Antiquities of the Cherokee Indians*, by Daniel Sabin Buttrick. Vinita, Indian Territory: Indian Chieftain.

Irwin, Lee. 1992. "Cherokee Healing: Myth, Dreams, and Medicine." *American Indian Quarterly* 16 (spring): 237–57.

Kilpatrick, Alan Edwin. 1991. " 'Going to the Water': A Structural Analysis of Cherokee Purification Rituals." *American Indian Culture and Research Journal* 15, no. 4: 49–58.

Kilpatrick, Jack F[rederick] and Anna G[ritts] Kilpatrick. 1964. *Friends of Thunder: Folktales of the Oklahoma Cherokees*. Dallas: Southern Methodist University Press.

———. 1965. *Walk in Your Soul: Love Incantations of the Oklahoma Cherokees*. Dallas: Southern Methodist University Press.

———. 1967. *Run Toward the Nightland: Magic of the Oklahoma Cherokees*. Dallas: Southern Methodist University Press.

Lanman, Charles. 1856. *Adventures in the Wilds of the United States and British American Provinces*. 2 vols. Philadelphia: John W. Moore.

Lawson, John. 1709. *A New Voyage to Carolina*. Vol. 2, *A New Collection of Voyages and Travels*. John Stevens, ed. London: n.p. Reprint, Hugh Talmage Lefler, ed. Chapel Hill: University of North Carolina Press, 1967. (Page references are to reprint edition.)

Leach, Edmund. 1987. "Structuralism." In *The Encyclopedia of Religion*. Vol. 14, Mircea Eliade, ed. New York: Macmillan Publishing. 54–64.

Lefler, Hugh Talmage. 1967. Introduction to *A New Voyage to Carolina*, by John Lawson. Hugh Talmage Lefler, ed. Chapel Hill: University of North Carolina Press.

Lofaro, Michael A. 1979. Review of *The Southeastern Indians*, by Charles Hudson. *Journal of American Folklore* 92 (January–March): 91–93.

Martin, Calvin. 1978. Review of *The Southeastern Indians*, by Charles Hudson. *The Journal of American History* 64 (March): 1075–76.

McLoughlin, William G. 1984. *Cherokees and Missionaries, 1789–1839*. New Haven: Yale University Press.

———. 1994. *The Cherokees and Christianity, 1794–1870: Essays on Acculturation and Cultural Persistence*. Walter H. Conser Jr., ed. Athens: University of Georgia Press.

McLoughlin, William G., and Walter H. Conser Jr. 1994. "Christianity and Racism:

Cherokee Responses to the Debate over Indian Origins, 1760–1860." In *Cherokees and Christianity*, 129–51.

Mooney, James. 1891. "The Sacred Formulas of the Cherokees." *Seventh Annual Report of the Bureau of American Ethnology, 1885–86*. Washington DC: Government Printing Office. Reprinted in *Myths of the Cherokee and Sacred Formulas of the Cherokees*. Nashville: Charles and Randy Elder, 1982. (Page references are to reprint edition.)

———. 1900. "Myths of the Cherokee." *Nineteenth Annual Report of the Bureau of American Ethnology, 1897–98*. Part 1. Washington DC: Government Printing Office. Reprinted in *Myths of the Cherokee*. (Page references are to reprint edition.)

Payne, John Howard. n.d. Papers. 14 vols. Typescript. Ayer Collection. Newberry Library.

———. 1849. "The Ancient Cherokee Traditions and Religious Rites." *Quarterly Register and Magazine* December: 444–50. (Ayer Collection, document 6815, Newberry Library.)

———. 1862. "The Green-Corn Dance." *The Continental Monthly* 1 (January): 17–29. Reprinted as "The Green Corn Dance." John R. Swanton, ed. *Chronicles of Oklahoma* 10 (June 1932): 170–95. (Page references are to the original edition.)

Perdue, Theda. 1980. *Nations Remembered: An Oral History of the Five Civilized Tribes, 1865–1907*. Westport CT: Greenwood Press. Reprinted as *Nations Remembered: An Oral History of the Cherokees, Chickasaws, Choctaws, Creeks, and Seminoles in Oklahoma, 1865–1907*. Norman: University of Oklahoma Press, 1993. (Page references are to reprint edition.)

Rothrock, Mary U. 1959a. Annotations of *The Natural and Aboriginal History of Tennessee*, by John Haywood. Mary U. Rothrock, ed. Jackson TN: McCowat-Mercer.

———. 1959b. "John Haywood, Historian of the Western Country." In *Natural and Aboriginal History of Tennessee*. xi–xxvii.

Scott, Joan W. 1988. "Deconstructing Equality-Versus-Difference: Or, the Uses of Poststructuralist Theory for Feminism." *Feminist Studies* 14 (spring): 33–50.

Squire, E[phraim] G[eorge]. 1851. *The Serpent Symbol, and the Worship of the Reciprocal Principles of Nature in America*. American Archaeological Researches, no. 1. New York: George P. Putnam. Reprint, Millwood NY: Kraus Reprint, 1975. (Page references are to reprint edition.)

———. 1853a. Prefatory note to "Observations on the Creek and Cherokee Indians," by William Bartram. *Transactions of the American Ethnological Society* 3: 3–7.

———. 1853b. Notes to "Observations on the Creek and Cherokee Indians," by William Bartram. *Transactions of the American Ethnological Society* 3: 59–81.

Strickland, Rennard. 1977. "In Search of Cherokee History: A Bibliographical Foreword to the Second Printing" [of] *A Political History of the Cherokee Nation, 1838–1907*, by Morris L. Wardell. Norman: University of Oklahoma Press. Original edition, Norman: University of Oklahoma Press, 1938.

Swanton, James. 1946. "Indians of the Southeastern United States." Smithsonian Institution *Bureau of American Ethnology Bulletin* 137. Washington DC: Government

Printing Office. Reprinted as *The Indians of the Southeastern United States*. Washington DC: Smithsonian Institution Press, 1979. (Page references are to reprint edition.)

Williams, Samuel Cole. 1930. Introduction to *Adair's History of the American Indians*, by James Adair. Samuel Cole Williams, ed. Reprint, New York: Promontory Press, n.d. (Page references are to the reprint edition.)

Williams, Walter L. 1979. "Cherokee History: An Analysis of Recent Studies." *American Indian Quarterly* 5 (fall): 347–54.

Williams, Walter L., and Thomas R. French. 1979. "Bibliographic Essay." In *Southeastern Indians Since the Removal Era*. Walter L. Williams, ed. Athens: University of Georgia Press. 211–41.

Kiowa Religion in
Historical Perspective

BENJAMIN R. KRACHT

When the missionaries came to the Kiowas, we already knew how to pray to
God; we knew how to do it before they brought us that book [the Bible].
Alice Palmer, Kiowa elder, February 20, 1987

Religiosity best describes Kiowa religious practices.[1] Colleagues and students
who have accompanied me to Kiowa country have been impressed with the
piety and devoutness of the Kiowa, and often have been emotionally affected
by observing the Kiowa at prayer.[2] Pulitzer prize-winning author and poet,
N. Scott Momaday, best recounts Kiowa prayer in a description of his deceased
grandmother, Aho.

I remember her most often at prayer. She made long, rambling prayers out of suffering
and hope, having seen many things. I was never sure that I had the right to hear, so
exclusive were they of all mere custom and company. The last time I saw her she prayed
standing by the side of her bed at night, naked to the waist, the light of a kerosene
lamp moving upon her dark skin. Her long black hair, always drawn and braided in
the day, lay upon her shoulders and against her breasts like a shawl. I do not speak
Kiowa, and I never understood her prayers, but there was something inherently sad in
the sound, some merest hesitation upon the syllables of sorrow. She began in a high and
descending pitch, exhausting her breath to silence; then again and again — and always
the same intensity of effort, of something that is, and is not, like urgency in the human
voice. Transported so in the dancing light among the shadows of her room, she seemed
beyond the reach of time. [Momaday 1987 {1969}:10]

The literature describing Native American belief systems has devoted little
attention to the emotive experiences of prayer. Åke Hultkrantz (1989:8) briefly
describes Indian prayers as "deeply emotional cries for help and sustenance,"
and notes that an increasing number of people are attracted to the "experiential
religious emotions" of American Indian religions (Hultkrantz 1990:168). In

236

the classic monograph, *The Peyote Cult*, Weston LaBarre (1938:50) specifically mentions that Kiowa elders often pray during peyote meetings "with tears running down their cheeks, their voices choked with emotion. . . . The tone is of a poor and pitiful person humbly asking the aid and pity of a great power."

Like many people who have observed the Kiowa at prayer, I have been greatly affected by "experiential religious emotions." Though describing such subjective experiences has been counter to ethnographic writing, some contemporary ethnologists contend that such encounters represent valid anthropological data (Goulet 1994:18–19; see Young and Goulet 1994). Having written an ethnohistoric/symbolic-based dissertation on Kiowa religion (Kracht 1989), I believe that the movement toward "experiential anthropology" transforms the ethnographic text from merely paying lip service to people's beliefs — "well . . . if they believe in it, it must work for them" — to a narrative that says, "yes, there is something here." The purpose of this essay is to delineate Kiowa belief and ritual symbolically and experientially.

The following is an ethnohistoric description of Kiowa belief systems, divided into four parts: the prereservation period, 1832–1869[3]; the reservation period, 1869–1901; the postallotment period, 1901–1945; and the modern era, post 1945. Major trends in Kiowa religion are delineated, followed by my interpretation of Kiowa belief systems today.[4]

THE PRERESERVATION PERIOD: 1832–1869

Central to Kiowa cosmology was the concept of *dwdw* "power," a spirit force permeating the universe, including the earth, sun, moon, sky, planets, stars, mountains, rivers and streams, plants, and animals.[5] The Kiowa believed that these entities possessed souls, or spirits manifested through natural phenomena like thunder, lightning, whirlwinds, and tornados, or they assumed bird or animal guises. All spirits possessed *dwdw* according to a hierarchial scheme: predators were more powerful than their prey, and "powers from above" had stronger *dwdw* than earthly animals; it follows that Sun was stronger than Eagle which was stronger than Buffalo. The Kiowa people prayed to a multitude of spirit powers for long and prosperous lives (LaBarre et al. 1935; LaBarre 1935; Kracht 1989:80–81).

Dwdw only was available to a handful of male power seekers who had successfully supplicated the spiritual forces during vision quests. Since power was not easily obtainable, *dwdw* was restricted to the *ondedw* "rich" families comprising approximately ten percent of the Kiowa population. Hence personal power and the tribal medicine bundles were kept intact through the inheritance pattern of *wde* "favorite child," transference from father to son. The *ondedw* upperclass was structured around several families that kept their power intact.

Despite this stratification, lower status individuals could purchase *dwdw* by becoming apprentices to men of power; however, power obtained through the vision quest was stronger — and rarer — than inherited or purchased power (LaBarre et al. 1935; LaBarre 1935; Mooney 1891–1904; Kracht 1989:102–3).

Individuals inheriting or purchasing *dwdw* still had to undergo the vision quest under the tutelage of a man of power, whose *doi* "medicine" was painted on a circular war shield. Clad in a breechcloth and moccasins, with a buffalo robe draped around his shoulders, hair side out, and armed with a long-stemmed, black stone pipe and tobacco pouch, the initiate took the shield up into the Wichita Mountains or to an isolated spot and fasted with it under his head so he could learn about the shield keeper's power. Upon reaching the predetermined destination, the power seeker ascended to the highest possible elevation — the higher the elevation, and the closer to the "spirits which travel in the air," the better — and sat down on a bed of sage, facing east. After offering tobacco to the spirits, the initiate loaded the pipe, lighted it, then smoked, praying and crying to the spirits for their compassion. Fasting, smoking, and praying continued for up to four days, or until the supplicant received a vision. On the fourth day, a friend or relative came to bring him back to the village. Upon his return, no one asked the power seeker whether he had received a vision, nor did he volunteer any information. If successful, he painted a shield with the symbols of his newly acquired power, and waited for his *dwdw* to manifest itself. Conversely, if an individual lied about having *dwdw*, misfortune — possibly death — would beset him (LaBarre et al. 1935; LaBarre 1935; Mooney 1891–1904; Kracht 1989:105–7).

Successful vision seekers obtained *dwdw* related to curing power or war power. These realms of power were generally mutually exclusive: one either became a great warrior or a great curer, though some curers were also great warriors. War power, often related to Sun, represented a warrior's *doi* "medicine," or protection, whereas curing power provided "doctoring" medicine in addition to personal protection. Moreover, curers could accumulate specific types of power. For example, it was not unusual for a curer to stanch battlefield wounds and to be equally gifted at administering febrifuges to break fevers. Life was more difficult for a curer because of the responsibilities and restrictions accompanying his power; his life typically involved a stringent set of prohibitions placed on his doctoring medicine, such as avoiding certain animal foods — bears, moles, or fish — or animal parts — brains or marrow. Kiowa men possessing either type of *dwdw* were highly respected for their powers. Certain curers were sought out for their gifts of healing, although some were feared as sorcerers, particularly since the Kiowa believed that all medicines had good and bad uses. Great warriors often became leaders of the different hunting bands (LaBarre et al. 1935; LaBarre 1935; Kracht 1989:108–10).

Like other Plains tribes, Kiowa social organization was characterized by sodalities that cross-cut kinship ties: shield and warrior societies, medicine or curing societies, and religious "priesthood" societies. Men with war and curing power were recruited into the first two organizations, whereas *ondedw* men who inherited the eleven tribal medicine bundles belonged to the priestly societies. The most powerful Kiowa curers, the buffalo doctors, belonged to the Buffalo Medicine Lodge, an elite group of medicine men who inherited or bought their positions. Mooney reconstructed the formation of this society between 1750 and 1770, when the original ten buffalo shields were made. Buffalo doctors were best known for their ability to treat wounds incurred from combat (Kracht 1989:108; Mooney 1891–1904).

Eleven men owned the tribal medicine bundles, the *Zaide Thali* "Half Boy" bundles (Ten Medicines), and the *Taime* Sun Dance bundle. The keepers of the Ten Medicines, *doidoga* ("medicine," "taking care," LaBarre called them "priests"), were distinguished from curers in that they evoked spiritual assistance to help sick people, as opposed to the technological healing techniques of the shaman. The ten *Zaide Thali* keepers assembled to pray for the welfare of the tribe, and the *Taimek'i* ("*Taime* keeper") was the "high priest" of the Sun Dance. All together, the eleven tribal bundle keepers evoked spiritual assistance for individual and tribal affairs, performing sacred rituals which maintained psychological and social stability within the Kiowa tribe (LaBarre 1935; Kracht 1989:145).

Zaide Thali keepers were "supposed to be very peaceable, pleasant, non-truculent, obliging, [and] patient," although some were renowned warriors, like *Set'angya* "Sitting Bear," who was killed by white soldiers near Fort Sill in 1871. The keepers settled disputes within the villages, and prayed for the well-being of the tribe. When feuds or squabbles arose, someone was dispatched to find the nearest keeper, who filled his long-stemmed pipe with tobacco and departed. Arriving at the scene of the argument, the keeper lighted the pipe, then offered it to both parties, who smoked and established an agreement. The pipe was never refused, because it was believed that tobacco smoke carried prayers to the spirits in the sky; hence the spirit world witnessed the forged peace. Importantly, the keepers always prayed to the bundles for the protection and good health of the tribe. People brought gifts to the bundles along with prayer requests for sick family members (symbolically, an offering to one bundle represented all ten). The first thunder in the spring—the beginning of the new year—was the best time to pray to the medicines (LaBarre et al. 1935; LaBarre 1935; Kracht 1989:150–54).

Taime, the Sun Dance icon, became the focal point of traditional Kiowa religious beliefs during the Sun Dance. This icon, placed at the western side of the Sun Dance lodge, symbolized Sun, and mediated between the people and Sun power. During the Sun Dance, *Taime* bestowed the Kiowa people with good fortune (Scott 1911:351). There were several *Taime* images in the nineteenth century; some were captured by the Osage and Ute, given back, lost, or re-created. Hence there is some confusion surrounding the differing *Taime* effigies (cf. Scott 1911:349–50; Mooney 1979 [1898]:240–41, 301–5, 322–23). There were three shield societies that participated in the Sun Dance with their "dream" shields, which were inspired by war power visions obtained by the founders (Kracht 1989:210–21).

The Sun Dance, the most important Kiowa dance, unified the tribe socially and spiritually. When pledged, the dance was held between mid June and late July (contrary to stereotypes, it was not an annual dance, see Mooney [1979]). Socially, the Sun Dance marked the only time the Kiowa bands, as well as the Plains Apache, coalesced in a single encampment; the success of the ritual was contingent on collective cooperation. On a spiritual level, Sun, the life-giving power of the universe, possessed the strongest *dwdw*, symbolizing life itself. Sun gave power directly to the buffalo, on which the Kiowa depended, so that Sun was the father of Buffalo and the Kiowa. Sun gave the Kiowa war power, affiliated with *Taime*, the Sun Dance effigy. The Kiowa Sun Dance, then, was replete with Buffalo, Sun, and *Taime* symbolism. The Sun Dance was a renewal ceremony where people prayed for the spiritual and physical well-being of their families. Importantly, the men who endured the fasting and dancing ordeal of the four-day dance ensured that their pitiful condition strengthened their prayers, thereby bringing good fortune in the future (LaBarre et al. 1935; Kracht 1989:258–59).

THE RESERVATION PERIOD: 1869–1901

The Medicine Lodge Treaty, negotiated in October 1867, and ratified by Congress in 1868, marked the beginning of the end for the Kiowa and neighboring Southern Plains tribes—Cheyenne, Arapaho, Plains Apache, and Comanche—in that it precipitated dramatic and destructive political, economic, and social change among these tribes (Mooney 1979 [1898]:182).[6] It provided for the construction and garrisoning of Fort Sill, the military base of operations where the Kiowa and Comanche bands surrendered during the winter of 1874–75 after a war of attrition (see Mooney 1979 [1898]:211–15; Nye 1983:229–31). After May 1875, the Kiowa could not hunt off the reservation without a military escort (Mooney 1979:339), and by 1881, the Southern Plains herds were all but extinct. The Kiowa became dependent on the federal government for subsistence (Kracht 1989:447–49).

Provisions of the Medicine Lodge Treaty to "civilize" the Southern Plains tribes through education and religious training were implemented in 1869, when President Grant turned the management of reservation life over to the Board of Indian Commissioners, consisting of many Christian denominations. The Orthodox Friends (Quakers) assumed control of the Central Superintendency which included the Kiowa reservation. By 1880, when the Quakers withdrew from the Central Superintendency, they had established an Indian school at Fort Sill, and provided religious services for the nearby Indian agency. For the next ten years, several mission societies unsuccessfully attempted to Christianize the "wild blanket Indians" of the Kiowa Reservation (Kracht 1989:627–28).

The Dawes Act (General Allotment Act) of 1887 inspired several Protestant and Catholic organizations to petition the Department of the Interior for permission to construct missions at the Kiowa Reservation. The first missionary to arrive in the fall of 1887 was the Rev. John J. Methvin of the Home Mission Board of the Methodist Episcopal Church, South. He was followed by the Rev. George W. Hicks of the American Baptist Home Mission Society, and Lauretta E. Ballew of the Territorial Baptist Convention. Their limited success establishing missions in Kiowa country prompted further missionization by the Reformed Presbyterian Church of North America, the Catholics, and the Presbyterians. By 1901, nineteen churches boasted a membership of 448 Kiowa, Comanche, and Plains Apache Indians, and mission societies operated four of the seven Indian schools on the reservation (White 1888; Kracht 1989:627–28, 638, 1035).

With exceptions, the missionaries encountered resistance and gained few converts in the nascent years of missionization. Nevertheless, their persistence and perseverance to convert the Indians won the respect of some Kiowa people. Those Kiowa who converted to Christianity were attracted to the consistency and good works of the missionaries and field matrons who helped them make the transition from tipis to houses; they showed the Kiowa how to can fruits and vegetables, and how to sew quilts and clothing. Notable among the missionaries was Isabel Crawford of the American Baptist Home Mission Society. Crawford lived in the Saddle Mountain Kiowa community from 1896 to 1906, where she held prayer services and gospel meetings, cooked, cleaned, administered to the sick and dying, and provided funeral services (Corwin 1958:49–50, 1968:49–50; Crawford 1915:16; 239–40; Kracht 1989:660–72). Years later, after her death, her body—by her request—was brought to the Saddle Mountain cemetery for interment. Her tombstone reads: "I dwell among my people."

Another attractive feature of the missionaries was their connection to major power sources: *Dwk'i* "God" and Jesus. Missionaries like Crawford convinced Kiowa proselytes that the Christian God could heal the sick and that the deceased went "to live with Jesus." Kiowa converts readily accepted the latter concept and believed that their recently deceased children were in Heaven with

Jesus, as evidenced by a Kiowa woman's testimony: "It is true that Jesus has our children and this makes me try so hard to follow him" (Crawford n.d.:15). Perhaps the willingness to accept the Christian concept of continuity after death hinged on the high infant mortality rates among the Kiowa, Comanche, and Plains Apache in the 1890s, in addition to epidemics such as smallpox and measles that swept through Indian communities. For instance, the measles epidemic of 1892 killed about three hundred reservation children (Methvin n.d.:79). Jesus was not perceived as a personal spirit power, but as a guardian spirit available to everyone. Instead of helping certain people with *dwdw*, Jesus was believed to protect everyone from harm. The missionaries thus presented Jesus as a positive spirit force, as opposed to Satan, a negative spirit force. One Kiowa lamented that Satan sent a tornado to destroy his home because he did not follow the "Jesus road" (Crawford 1915:145; Kracht 1989:699–702). It is apparent that the missionaries played into traditional Kiowa beliefs by casting Jesus and God as positive, and Satan as negative; hence the analogy to good and bad medicine. Moreover, the Kiowa concept of *Dwk'i* as a personified creator probably came about due to Christian influence, as happened among many other tribes (cf. Steinmetz 1990:40).

Not everyone, of course, converted to Christianity during the reservation period. Peyote, the divine cactus, had been used in religious ceremonies by the Kiowa and Comanche as early as 1870. Several important works trace the origin and diffusion of the Southern Plains peyote rite that began on the KCA Reservation (see LaBarre 1938; Slotkin 1975 [1956]; Anderson 1980; Stewart 1987). Peyote, Lophophora williamsii, a small, green, spineless cactus indigenous to the Rio Grande River region adjacent to the current Texas-Mexico boundary, grows in single or small clusters of "buttons" attached to a taproot. The plant produces religious visions (Schultes 1937:132–34). Sources vary concerning peyote's diffusion to southwestern Oklahoma, but Omer Stewart (1987:47–51) believes that the nascent Southern Plains peyote rite originated with the Coahuiltecan-speaking Carrizo, spread to the Lipan Apache, who introduced it to Kiowa-Comanche war parties trekking into Mexico in the mid–nineteenth century.

LaBarre's collaborators believed that the peyote ritual was received from the Mescalero Apache sometime around 1870, but the earliest remembered peyote meeting occurred in the summer of 1885. By 1887, the peyote ceremony was firmly entrenched among the Kiowa (LaBarre 1935). In his 1886 annual report, Kiowa agent Lee Hall noted the use of peyote "which they eat, and it produces the same effect as opium, putting them to sleep for twenty-four hours at a time." Hall wanted the Indian Office to declare peyote contraband (Hall 1886; see Stewart 1987:128), as did Special Agent E. E. White two years later (White 1888). Ignorance and intolerance towards peyote by Anglo-Americans led to a vigorous anti-peyote campaign that lasted for fifty years (Kracht 1989:859; see Stewart 1987). During this period, James Mooney was one of the few non-Indian peyote advocates; his rapport with Kiowa peyotists gained him access to a peyote meeting in the summer of 1891 that he documented with his new Kodak camera, making him the first non-Indian to chronicle the Kiowa-Comanche rite (Stewart 1987:34–36; Moses 1984:182–84).

Sankadote, Apekaum, and Zempadlte were identified as the proselytizers who in 1885 introduced to the Kiowa the ritual they had learned from the Comanche. During the initial meeting, the Sons of the Sun, a Kiowa contingent opposing new religious practices, threw a rotten bear's head into the tipi to break up the meeting. Despite some initial opposition, a new group sprang up among the Kiowa, the Twelve Disciples of Peyote, who pledged allegiance to the peyote religion. Little Bow, Botone, and Red Buffalo were among the charter members. Peyote meetings were conducted in a canvas tent with a fire in the middle and a crescent-shaped earthen altar on the west side. Beginning at sunrise and continuing until evening, when a meal was consumed, the ceremony, conducted "like [a] Quaker meeting," consisted of testimonies and preaching. By 1891, the ritual had evolved into the Kiowa-Comanche crescent moon peyote ceremony attended by Mooney, then later by LaBarre and other non-Indians. The crescent moon rite continues today with few changes (LaBarre 1935; LaBarre et al. 1935; Kracht 1989:749–51).

Kiowa peyote meetings, pledged to celebrate birthdays, recovery from illness, or for doctoring, began about 9 P.M. (typically on a Saturday). A great deal of personal preparation occurred before arriving at the tipi set up by the Roadman, or leader of the rite (LaBarre 1938:45, 112n). Each person wore his (at this time, the participants were men) finest buckskin, feathers, and decorative paint (Stewart 1987:37). The meetings were conducted in a canvas tipi—the opening faced the east—set up in the afternoon by the sponsor's female kinfolk, and where the crescent moon altar had been constructed. It was the sponsor's obligation to provide the peyote for the meeting, the ritual food and meal that would be prepared by his female kinfolk. The Roadman brought the ritual paraphernalia: the peyote staff, water drum, drumstick, gourd rattle, eagle-bone whistle, cedar incense, altar cloth, and feathers for doctoring (LaBarre 1938:43–45; Kracht 1989:751–52).

Peyote meetings were all-night prayer meetings. The participants sat cross-legged around the perimeter of the tipi facing the fire, the Roadman sat at the west end of the tipi, to his immediate right sat his drummer, and to his left sat the Cedar Man, if needed. North of the door sat the Fireman, whose responsibility was to keep the fire in the center of the tipi burning, and to let people in and out during the night. The meeting began when the Roadman placed his Father Peyote (a large peyote button) on the crescent moon altar, then arranged his ritual paraphernalia close to him. Lighting a Bull Durham cigarette rolled in corn husks signified the beginning of the ritual smoke where everyone smoked and prayed to the peyote power and to *Domdwk'i* "earth-creator," explaining the purpose of the meeting. After the opening prayers, cedar was sprinkled in the fire to purify the lodge, and the participants rubbed sage into their bodies. After the cedar incense blessing, peyote buttons were passed around for individual consumption (LaBarre 1938:45–49; Stewart 1987:37).

The Opening Song was started by the Roadman who held his staff at arm's length and shook his gourd rattle, accompanied by the drummer. After four completions of the Opening Song, they exchanged instruments, sang four more peyote songs, then the staff, gourd rattle, and water drum circulated clockwise around the tipi for the duration of the meeting, marked by praying and peyote songs. A short break occurred at midnight, preceded by the Midnight Water Song. Any doctoring occurred after the break. The meeting continued until dawn, when the wife of the sponsor was summoned to bring in the ritual pail of water for everyone's first drink of water since midnight. The four Morning songs signified this part of the ritual. The rest of the meeting was informal, in that the participants walked outside to stretch and smoke cigarettes, or they might lounge inside the tipi and listen to quasi-sermons given by the Roadman or other elders. Afterward, ritual pails of water, parched corn, fruit, and meat were brought into the tipi, while the Roadman sang the last four songs, including the Quitting Song. The ritual meal was consumed, then the men napped in the shade while the women took down the tipi. At noon a meal prepared by the sponsor's womenfolk was consumed, then everyone went home early Sunday afternoon (LaBarre 1938:49–53; Stewart 1987:38–39).

The peyote religion may have become attractive to the Kiowa after 1885 because of the demise of the Sun Dance religion. By the 1880s, the Southern Plains bison herds were extinct, and the Sun Dance became difficult to conduct because the *Taime* priest could not obtain the buffalo bull hide for the altar post in the Sun Dance arbor. In addition, the cessation of raids into Texas, Mexico, and New Mexico, and the surrender of the Kiowa at Fort Sill in the winter of 1874–75 signified the end of Kiowa war power. The Sun Dance, deeply steeped in Sun, Buffalo, and war power symbolism, became impractical. As they prepared for the 1890 Sun Dance, rumors of army patrols in the area compelled the Kiowa to abandon the dance midway through the construction of the Sun Dance arbor. Hence the interrupted dance was called "sun dance when the forked poles were left standing" (Mooney 1979 [1898]:347, 352–59). The Sun Dance was never performed again (Kracht 1992:458, 1994:327).

The demise of Sun Dance in the 1880s was concomitant to two failed attempts by Kiowa prophets to revive the vanished buffalo herds. In the summer of 1882,

Pa-tepte (Buffalo-bull-coming-out) recounted a vision in which he brought the bison back to the earth's surface since the Kiowa believed that Anglos were holding them underground to exterminate the Indians. Pa-tepte felt that his *dwdw* could restore the herds. Given some hope, people brought Pa-tepte offerings of blankets, horses and money. By the summer of 1883, the buffalo still had not returned, and the "buffalo prophet" got sick and died during the winter of 1883–84; the Kiowa believed his death was attributed to lying about his medicine powers (Mooney 1979 [1898]:349–50; LaBarre 1935; Kracht 1989:738–41). In the spring of 1887, another prophet, Pa-ingya (In the Middle) promised the return of the buffalo. Setting up camp among Lone Wolf's band on Elk Creek at the western end of the reservation, Pa-ingya prophesied that whites and Indians living like whites would be destroyed by his Whirlwind and Fire power. Among his followers were the Sons of the Sun, those who opposed peyote and other new religions. In the summer of 1888, Pa-ingya announced that the Kiowa should congregate at his Elk Creek encampment. Those who did not join the camp would perish. The Kiowa peoples assembled at Elk Creek waiting for old lifeways to be restored became terrified when troops from Fort Sill were reported in the vicinity. Moreover, Pa-ingya's powers did not revive the buffalo, so the majority of the Kiowa returned home discouraged. Despite these setbacks, Pa-ingya still maintained a small following, including the Sons of the Sun (Mooney 1979 [1898]:220, 356–57; Nye 1983 [1937]:269; LaBarre et al. 1935; LeBarre 1935; 1935; Kracht 1989:741–43).

The summer of 1890 witnessed the last attempted Sun Dance and the introduction of the Ghost Dance to the Kiowa. Having heard of the Paiute prophet Wovoka's prophesy, Poor Buffalo and a Kiowa delegation visited the Cheyenne and Arapaho at the Darlington Agency, witnessed the dance, then brought it to the Anadarko Agency, where the Wichita, Caddo, Kiowa, and others gathered for their biweekly rations. The dance took hold and the largest Ghost Dance in Kiowa history was held in October 1890 at the mouth of Rainy Mountain Creek near present-day Mountain View, Oklahoma. A'piaton ("Wooden Lance"), was interested in the Ghost Dance, particularly the doctrine proclaiming that Indians would be reunited with deceased relatives, since he had recently lost a child. Money was collected to send A'piaton to visit Wovoka to further investigate the new religion. In September, A'piaton traveled north to Pine Ridge Reservation and visited Lakota Sioux proselytes who encouraged him to visit Wovoka in Mason Valley, Nevada. Upon meeting the "messiah," A'piatan learned that he was not omniscient because he needed an interpreter to communicate, and could not resurrect his child. A disappointed A'piatan stopped at Fort Hall, Idaho, and sent a telegram to Anadarko stating Wovoka was a fraud. On February 19, 1891, A'piatan arrived at the Anadarko Agency and gave a stirring speech against the Ghost Dance. Many discouraged people broke down and cried as they left Anadarko. The 1890–91 Ghost Dance lost most of its momentum (Mooney 1991 [1896]:907–14; Kracht 1992:459).

The Ghost Dance resurfaced in 1894 through the efforts of Setzepetoi (Afraid-of-Bears), a blind clairvoyant who attracted new followers by inducing trances where the supplicants visited deceased relatives in the spirit world. Importantly, the revived Ghost Dance symbolized stasis in a world that was rapidly changing. Adherents of the Ghost Dance opposed "progress" on the KCA Reservation, e.g., wearing "civilized" clothing, improving land by building houses and fences, and attending Christian services. The so-called Jerome Agreement of 1892 (see Clark 1994) precipitated such opposition to progress, because the KCA Indians were now subjected to the allotment that they bitterly fought for the next nine years. On August 6, 1901, the "opening" of KCA lands for homesteading caused the KCA Indians to lose most of the 2.8 million acre reservation in exchange for individual 160-acre allotments. Confinement on a reservation, impending allotment, and pressures from missionaries and Indian agents to become "civilized" symbolized the end of freedom, causing many Kiowa to flock to the Ghost Dance (Kracht 1992:470, 1994:328).

THE POST-ALLOTMENT PERIOD: 1901–1945

The Ghost Dance movement had a strong following the first two decades of the twentieth century, especially among the Kiowa deemed the most incorrigible by the Indian agents, missionaries, and the newly Christianized Kiowa. In particular, Ghost Dance participants supported war dancing and other forms of ceremonial song and dance, and were identified as the "dance crowd." Afraid-of-Bears told Isabel Crawford that: "He [God] gave the Book [Bible] to the White People . . . but he gave to the Indians the dance road and told us to hold on to it tight till He came back to earth with our dead and our buffalo" (Crawford 1915:28). Dancing was an integral part of the ceremony to help achieve the trances that allowed the participants to visit their deceased relatives (Kracht 1989:815). Ghost Dance followers also identified with the tribal medicine bundles, shamans, and the nascent peyote rite. In 1910, it was estimated that one-half of the Kiowa were involved in the peyote religion, and it is possible that peyote was consumed during Ghost Dance meetings (Crawford 1915:26–28).

At the turn of the century, the Ghost Dance faction—allied with peyotists and dance enthusiasts—challenged the power of the missionaries and the Christianized Kiowa. Afraid-of-Bears even proclaimed the second coming of Jesus Christ, stating to Crawford that he was coming to Saddle Mountain at noon on July 15, 1904, accompanied by buffalo (Crawford 1915:230–32). It appears that the Ghost Dance was developing into a syncretic religion that blended together elements from Christianity, peyotism, and indigenous tribal beliefs. A Baptist missionary likened the Ghost Dance to "a crude form of Spiritualism" (Gassaway 1913), and another perceived it to be "an inclusive religion" that worshiped "the Indian medicine man" and "all the old Kiowa medicine bags" (Treat 1914). Syncretisms in the Ghost Dance ritual—references to the Great Father, Jesus, the Bible, an altar constructed of a cross and cedar tree, and possible peyote use—suggest that the Kiowa incorporated concepts that best fit their needs. Given the aboriginal belief that *dwdw* or power could be accumulated, it seems logical that similar power sources were represented in the Ghost Dance. The Kiowa did not have to commit to any one religion, and they sought *dwdw* wherever they could find it (Kracht 1992:462–63).

During this period of religious diversity represented by the Ghost Dance, peyotism, Christianity, and indigenous beliefs founded in tribal and personal bundles, *dwdw*, shamans, and prophets, the fact that the Ghost Dance leaders challenged Christians is analogous to rivalry between shamans displaying their powers. Moreover, many Kiowa individuals shuffled back and forth between religions during the post-allotment period, depending on the circumstances. Crawford wrote that a Kiowa man quit the church, "took the feather" and joined the Ghost Dance because the missionaries preached against peyote (Crawford 1915:230–31). In 1927, Kiowa Jim Tongkeamah, a peyotist and "dance road" enthusiast, lost a son, who, before death, incurred a near-death experience in which he claimed to have entered Heaven; he begged his father to convert to Christianity. Kiowa Jim converted not only because of his son's vision, but because the Indian peyote doctors failed to save him. The Tongkeamahs became members of Saddle Mountain Baptist Church (Pewo 1994). There are many family stories about back and forth conversions.

Agent C. V. Stinchecum launched a campaign to eradicate the Ghost Dance when he took over the Kiowa Superintendency on April 1, 1915. Threatening to withhold per-capita payments—interest payments on trust monies from the sale of the KCA Reservation—from the participants, Stinchecum convinced the leaders to stage a "picnic" instead of the annual July 4 Ghost Dance. In 1916, dances occurred on scattered allotments, compelling Stinchecum to generate a blacklist of seventy-nine Kiowa individuals who had attended the dances. Through such tactics, the Ghost Dance ended, although other forms of dancing continued as surreptitious events (Kracht 1992:464–70, 1994:327–31). Significantly, many former Ghost Dance members became Christians after 1917, and by 1922, approximately one-third of the Kiowa had converted to Christianity (Beaver 1988:453).

Several of the Kiowa elders I interviewed suggested that many of the Ghost Dance participants were confused by rapid cultural change, and that the dance provided temporary solace as the Kiowa transformed from hunters and gatherers into Christians and peyotists. Christian syncretisms in the ceremony suggest that the Ghost Dance was a Kiowa interpretation of Christianity. Ghost Dance songs and Kiowa hymns composed during that era are very similar, as are the very emotional prayers. Perhaps one reason for abandoning the Ghost Dance and embracing Christianity for some was an admission that the latter had the stronger *dwdw* (Kracht 1992:470–71).

Between 1917 and 1945, there were only seven Christian community churches —four Baptist, three Methodist—in Kiowa country, and none in Anadarko and Carnegie, the most populous towns. "Six miles from a church was as good as fifty." Yet elders who remember this era speak fondly of week-long camp meetings and revivals, camping near the churches for up to a month during the Christmas season, and the baseball leagues. In areas where there were no churches, prayer meetings and church services were held in homes or makeshift army tents. Altogether, Kiowa elders recount pleasant memories of much socializing and feasting at these events (Kracht 1987:710–11, 913–14, 918–19, 1994:328).

Christianity, nevertheless, did not dominate the religious scene, for peyotism, chartered in 1918 as the Native American Church, had a strong following. By the time LaBarre studied the peyote religion in 1936, some changes had occurred in the crescent-moon rite: Women could attend meetings, and doctoring ceremonies sometimes occurred shortly after the Morning Song (LaBarre 1938:51–53). At one time, peyote had been incompatible with traditional beliefs, but LaBarre found that in comparison with the Ten Medicines and personal bundles, the peyote rite was perceived as a more recent power source (LaBarre 1935; Apekaum 1937:66–68). Although some Kiowa became adherents of one religion over another, there were many who easily walked more than one "road." For example, bundle keepers attended peyote meetings, as did Christians. Analogous to nineteenth-century beliefs in the accumulation of powers, some Kiowa interpreted that religions were not necessarily mutually exclusive (Kracht 1989:777).

THE MODERN ERA: SINCE 1945

As Kiowa warfare in the nineteenth century was based on *dwdw* obtained from Sun, Kiowa veterans returning from World War II—and later wars—also felt personal power came from peyote, God, or the Ten Medicines. Several stories I have collected relate how soldiers consulted one or more of these power sources before going overseas, and many who returned back to their Kiowa people believed their religious beliefs kept them alive. John Tsatoke (Hunting Horse), a World War II veteran, vowed that if he came back alive, he would become a

Christian and pledge his life to God. While serving in General Patton's Ghost Corps, Tsatoke helped liberate a Polish prison camp and a Jewish concentration camp. Upon his return, he dedicated himself "to labor for the Lord" (Tsatoke 1987). When he died in 1989, he had served the Methodist Church for more than 30 years, working his way up from unpaid volunteer to minister (Kracht 1989:895, 912–13).

Gus Palmer, another World War II veteran, first entered the peyote tipi in 1928 when he was nine years old, and sat between his mother and father. By the time the war broke out, he was very knowledgeable about the crescent moon rite. In 1944, Palmer volunteered to serve in the Air Force. Before leaving, his father-in-law, Henry Oliver Tanedooah (Medicine Bird), a prominent peyote Roadman, sponsored a tipi meeting to send him off protected by prayers. After midnight, Tanedooah and the other elders presented him with a peyote button to take into combat as a "shield." His mother sewed it into a little beadwork pouch that he wore attached by a chain to his dog tag. Palmer flew eighteen missions over Germany in a B-17 bomber, including the big air strike over Berlin, and returned unscathed to Carnegie. Once a fellow soldier asked if he could have his own peyote charm, but Palmer said that his fetish covered everyone in the plane. Upon his return, a peyote meeting was held to give thanks. To this day, Palmer, a Roadman, claims that the magical power God bestows in peyote, a "beautiful medicine," was solely responsible for his combat success (Palmer 1987; Kracht 1989:930–31).

After the war, several new churches appeared in Kiowa country as Christianity became widespread. Economic changes, however, affected attendance. More and more people now worked for cash wages, as opposed to the post-allotment era, when families lived off per capita payments and land leases to non-Indian ranchers. Large families affected land inheritance patterns in that numerous heirs inherited parcels of land owned by the original allotees; hence harder economic times implied that people no longer had the leisure time to camp at the churches for weeks at a time. Working people could not afford the luxury of long camp meetings (Stumblingbear 1987). In addition, after the war, there were few monolingual Kiowa speakers left, and the younger people discontinued the practice (Amauty 1987). While conducting fieldwork in 1987, I counted about sixteen Kiowa-oriented churches, primarily Baptist, Methodist, and the more recent Pentecostal. Even though there are more churches today, the Kiowa population has grown substantially. On the surface, it appears that most of today's Kiowa are Christians, but in name only. Even the largest community church I attended averages at most two or three dozen members on any given Sunday. In 1987, Ware's Chapel (Methodist) claimed 450 members. On Palm Sunday, there were 33 adults and 13 children in attendance (Kracht 1989:917–21). In June 1985, the six Kiowa Methodist churches were represented by 1,167 members, but only averaged 199 church participants each Sunday. Only 17 percent of all active church members attended church on any given Sunday (Gomez 1985:91–92).

If most Kiowa are Christians—as I have found they claim—then where are all the people on Sunday? There are several answers. First, it is important to note that the Native American Church has some parallels with the Christian churches including inadequate representation among younger people. Today, there are few young people entering the ministry, and many of the Kiowa ministers are retiring. There will be no Kiowa ministers in a few years if this trend continues. Some of the elders I have talked to blame weekend powwows as a distraction taking young people away from the church. Every weekend there is a powwow in Oklahoma, so those who take the "powwow highway" are too busy to attend church services or even peyote meetings. Similar to the findings of Jerrold Levy (1958:38–39), some Kiowa Roadmen have told me that the youth do not take the peyote religion seriously. Some elders I spoke with claim that powwows serve as a religion for the youth. In other words, powwows have replaced going to church or attending peyote meetings. Another factor is that many younger people have moved away from southwestern Oklahoma since World War II in order to find employment (Kracht 1989:934, 920–22). Even though many Kiowa are not active Christians or peyotists, they share in common a spirituality that unites all of these religions.

Kiowa religion today is represented by a syncretic collage of peyotist, Christian, and traditional symbols. Even though some Christians oppose peyote and think that the Ten Medicines and other bundles are icons of the past, and some peyotists shun Christian events, most of the Kiowa individuals I know respect the diversity of religious beliefs among contemporary Kiowa peoples. Perhaps "respect" best describes how the Kiowa perceive religion. They commonly believe that they are praying to *Dwk'i* "God," regardless of what form of religious expression they employ. All the elders I have interviewed emphasized the importance and power of prayer, whether it comes from a tipi meeting or a family prayer meeting where different denominations and even peyotists are present. Several elders have pointed out that the Kiowa believe in praying to God in a pitiful manner, so, like in former times, they cry while they pray (Kracht 1989:925–26). Having witnessed many prayers, I find it difficult to express my emotions, or subjective experiences, other than to say I have been profoundly affected; Kiowa prayers are very moving.

Perhaps the best way to summarize contemporary Kiowa beliefs is to relate personal anecdotes about my fieldwork, thereby elucidating experiential subjective experiences. I first met Clifton Tongkeamah in May 1983, but it took about two years for him to accept me, and I was subjected to my fair share of "ethnographic tests." One day in the fall of 1985 he "adopted" me: "Ben, I'm old enough to be your father, so I take you for my son." We did a lot of things together: traveled to powwows in Texas and Oklahoma, attended Kiowa dances in Carnegie and Anadarko, and drank beer at Indian bars in Dallas. Through my father, I learned much about Kiowa belief systems beyond what was available in books: that bear meat is taboo because the Kiowa are brothers and sisters to the bear; that the swpodl "owl," is feared because it is the messenger of death; that the khomtho "ghost," like the owl is potentially bad, and that encountering a ghost or owl can cause one's face to twist (an explanation for Bell's Palsy, a small stroke that causes tension in the facial muscles); and that whirlwinds represent wandering ghosts that are to be avoided. We also discussed the fact that the Ten Medicines and the Taime bundle are still around, and even though inheritance patterns have broken down, and the whereabouts of some of the bundles are unknown to most people, they are still consulted with prayer requests. I also learned that the Kiowa, like many Indian peoples in Oklahoma, burn cedar in purification "smoking" ceremonies; for instance, a medicine man can be consulted to "smoke" a house after the death of a close relative. The idea is that cedar removes bad feelings and influences. Since our initial conversations, I have discussed these topics with other Kiowa collaborators.

My Kiowa father died on May 3, 1993. Early that morning, I woke up from a dream that he was in; I had never dreamt about him before. Later that day, I received the phone call that he had passed away about the time that I had my dream. The next day I drove west through Anadarko to Fort Cobb to Carnegie to Mountain View to the wake at Rainy Mountain Kiowa Baptist Church. As I approached the church, driving through the mesquite shrub-covered prairie north of the Wichita Mountains, a huge dust devil blew across the field. I felt this was symbolic of his spirit traversing the plains, since he had always talked about the freedom his people once enjoyed while roaming about this sun-parched land. During the service a series of thunderstorms came through and rocked the church but did not interrupt the prayers and Kiowa hymns that were offered. That night as I drove back to my motel room in Anadarko, it rained sideways and I became disoriented, even though I knew where I was. Then, the lightning illuminated the sky and I espied the threadlike rope of a tornado hanging from an overhead cloud. I said a verbal prayer for safety, then said: "Well father, we've been through many adventures before, so we might as well do it one more time." I stopped at a bar in Fort Cobb and drank two beers, probably because he would have suggested that course of action. Two weeks after the funeral I spoke with my adopted mother, Betty Tanedooah Tongkeamah, and she informed me that a week before Clifton's death, they stayed in a motel in Anadarko, and she was awakened in the middle of the night by an owl hooting outside the window.

Immediately, she prayed to *Dwk'i* that nothing would happen to Cliff—he was chronically ill—but she knew deep down that he was going to die soon. That is the Kiowa way.

Despite religious diversity among the Kiowa, they will continue to offer their prayers for the people of their tribe, for the nation, and for the world. The Kiowa will always invoke *Dwk'i* through tearful, pitiful, invocations. *Dwdw* is still around, it merely assumes different guises. The Kiowa will always be a deeply spiritual people.

NOTES

1. This article is dedicated to my deceased adopted Kiowa father, Clifton Tongkeamah, his wife, my adopted mother, Betty Tanedooah Tongkeamah, and my deceased adopted grandparents, Weiser and Henrietta Tongkeamah. I will miss them until we meet again. I would also like to thank all my Kiowa friends—too numerous to name—who have helped me over the years; they know who they are. I would like to give my friend Bryan "Jake" Chanate special recognition for reading this text and helping me where my father left off. Aho. As always, I am responsible for all interpretations and mistakes in this text.

Several funding agencies made my research possible, and I wish to thank them: Northeastern State University, Faculty Research Council; the D'Arcy McNickle Center for the Study of the American Indian, Newberry Library; the American Philosophical Society; the Whatcom Museum of History and Art; the Institute for the Study of Earth and Man, Southern Methodist University; and the Smithsonian Institution.

2. Today, over four thousand Kiowa reside on scattered allotments north of Lawton, Oklahoma and the Wichita Mountains. Anadarko, Carnegie, Fort Cobb, Mountain View, Gotebo, Hobart, and Lone Wolf are the principal Kiowa towns in southwestern Oklahoma. Over six thousand Kiowa peoples live outside of Kiowa country in other Oklahoma communities, or in urban areas like Dallas, Texas, Washington DC, and Los Angeles, California.

3. The dates given for the prereservation era, 1832–69, coincide in part with Mooney's calendar history of the Kiowa, which he reconstructed back to the winter of 1832–33. Although one could determine several dates as the onset of the reservation period, I choose 1869 since that was the year Fort Sill was established near present day Lawton, Oklahoma (see Nye 1983 [1937]:100ff.).

4.Several important sources have been consulted for this project. Foremost are thirteen hundred pages of typewritten fieldnotes compiled by William Bascom, Weston LaBarre, Jane Richardson, Donald Collier, and Bernard Mishkin in the summer of 1935 under the auspices of the Santa Fe Laboratory of Anthropology directed by Alexander Lesser. The fieldnotes—cross-interviews with approximately twenty elders—providing a wealth of information about the horse and buffalo days of the nineteenth century (LaBarre et al. 1935), are housed along with Weston LaBarre's handwritten fieldnotes

(LaBarre 1935) in the National Anthropological Archives, Smithsonian Institution. I consulted these sources in the summer of 1987 along with James Mooney's "Kiowa Heraldry Notebook" (1891–1904).

In the summer of 1987 I also consulted sources in the United States National Archives, filed under Bureau of Indian Affairs, Record Group 75 (RG 75). Within this record, I used a collection entitled "General Records of the Kiowa Indian Agency, Anadarko, Oklahoma, 1907–1939," consisting of correspondence between the Indian Office and the Kiowa Agency, and individuals affiliated with affairs in Kiowa country. Letters were primarily written by missionaries and Indian agents in regard to Kiowa dances and religious gatherings, and are topically arranged according to a decimal-subject classification scheme. Principal topics of this collection include category 062 "Feasts-Fiestas-Festivals," category 063 "Dances," category 126 "Liquor Traffic-Cocaine-Drugs-Mescal," category 810 "Teaching and Training-School Curriculum," category 816 "Religious Training," category 816.2 "Missions, Missionaries, and Churches," and category 820 "Pupils." Microfilm rolls also were examined at the Newberry Library, the Oklahoma Historical Society, and the Federal Record Center, Fort Worth, Texas.

Other sources include newspaper clippings, unpublished manuscripts in the possession of Kiowa friends, and various primary and secondary sources. Field data are derived from participant-observation at Kiowa-sponsored powwows, warrior society dances, church services, funerals, and other public and private events, and interviews with Kiowa elders, ministers and Roadmen.

5. In Kiowa, w represents the low back vowel in "caught."

6. The Medicine Lodge Treaty established what became known as the KCA (Kiowa, Comanche, and [Plains] Apache) Reservation, sometimes referred to as simply the Kiowa Reservation. The Indian agency, originally near Fort Sill, then moved to Anadarko in 1878, was referred to as the Kiowa Agency. In 1901, after application of the Allotment Act, the former KCA Reservation was called the KCA Jurisdiction.

REFERENCES

Amauty, Billy. 1987. Taped interview with Ben Kracht, 14 April.

Anderson, Edward F. 1980. *Peyote: The Divine Cactus*. Tucson: University of Arizona Press.

Apekaum, Charlie. 1937. "The Autobiography of a Kiowa Indian." Transcribed and edited by Weston LaBarre. Ms. Washington DC: National Anthropological Archives, Smithsonian Institution.

Beaver, R. Pierce. 1988. "Protestant Churches and the Indians." In *Handbook of North American Indians, Volume 4, History of Indian-White Relations*. Edited by Wilcomb E. Washburn. Washington DC: Smithsonian Institution Press. 430–58.

Clark, Blue. 1994. *Lone Wolf v. Hitchcock: Treaty Rights and Indian Law at the End of the Nineteenth Century*. Lincoln: University of Nebraska Press.

Corwin, Hugh D. 1958. *The Kiowa Indians: Their History and Life Stories.* Guthrie ok: Private.

——. 1968. "Protestant Missionary Work among the Comanches and Kiowas." *The Chronicles of Oklahoma* 46(1):41–57.

Crawford, Isabel. n.d. *From Tent to Chapel at Saddle Mountain.* Edited by Mary G. Burdette. Chicago: The Woman's Baptist Home Mission Society.

——. 1915. *Kiowa: The History of a Blanket Indian Mission.* New York: Fleming H. Revell Company.

Gassaway, B. F. 1914. Letter to Kiowa Superintendent Ernest Stecker, 6 June. Washington dc: National Archives Record Service [hereafter nars], document filing number 91980-1914-063K[iowa].

Gomez, Evaline, ed. 1985. *Oklahoma Indian Missionary Annual Conference 1985 Journal.* Anadarko ok: Oklahoma Indian Missionary Conference, United Methodist Church.

Goulet, Jean-Guy. 1994. "Dreams and Visions in Other Lifeworlds." In *Being Changed: The Anthropology of Extraordinary Experience.* Edited by David E. Young and Jean-Guy Goulet. Ontario, Canada: Broadview Press. 16–38.

Hall, Lee. 1888. Letter written to Indian Commissioner Oberly, August 18, 1888. *Annual Report of the Commissioner of Indian Affairs.* Washington dc: Government Printing Office.

Hultkrantz, Åke. 1989. "The Religious Life of Native North Americans." In *Native American Religions: North America.* Edited by Lawrence E. Sullivan. New York: Macmillan Publishing Company. 3–18.

——. 1990. "A Decade of Progress: Works on North American Indian Religions in the 1980s." In *Religion in Native North America.* Edited by Christopher Vecsey. Moscow: University of Idaho Press. 167–201.

Kracht, Benjamin R. 1989. "Kiowa Religion: An Ethnohistorical Analysis of Ritual Symbolism, 1832–1987." Ph.D. dissertation. Anthropology Department, Southern Methodist University.

——. 1992. "The Kiowa Ghost Dance, 1894–1916: An Unheralded Revitalization Movement." *Ethnohistory* 39(4):452–77.

——. 1994. "Kiowa Powwows: Continuity in Ritual Practice." *American Indian Quarterly* 18(3):321–48.

LaBarre, Weston. 1935. "Spiral Notebooks." Ms. Washington dc: National Anthropological Archives, Smithsonian Institution.

——. 1938. *The Peyote Cult.* Yale University Publications in Anthropology, No. 19. New Haven ct: Yale University Press.

LaBarre, Weston, Jane Richardson, Donald Collier, William Bascom, and Alexander Lesser. 1935. "Notes on Kiowa Ethnography." Ms. Washington dc: National Anthropological Archives, Smithsonian Institution.

Levy, Gerrald. 1958. "Kiowa and Comanche: A Report from the Field." *Anthropology Tomorrow* 6(2):30–44.

Methvin, John J. n.d. *In the Limelight, or History of Anadarko [Caddo County and Vicinity from the Earliest Days]*. Anadarko OK: N.T. Plummer Printing Company.

Momaday, N. Scott. 1987 [1969]. *The Way to Rainy Mountain*. Albuquerque: University of New Mexico Press.

Mooney, James. 1991 [1896]. *The Ghost-Dance Religion and the Sioux Outbreak of 1890*. Lincoln: University of Nebraska Press.

———. 1979 [1898]. *Calendar History of the Kiowa Indians, Seventeenth Annual Report of the Bureau of American Ethnology, 1895–96*. Washington DC: Smithsonian Institution Press.

———. 1891–1904. "Kiowa Heraldry Notebook: Descriptions of Kiowa Tipis and Shields." Ms. Washington DC: National Anthropological Archives, Smithsonian Institution.

Moses, L. G. 1984. *The Indian Man: A Biography of James Mooney*. Urbana: University of Illinois Press.

Nye, Wilbur S. 1983 [1937]. *Carbine and Lance: The Story of Old Fort Sill*. Norman: University of Oklahoma Press.

Palmer, Gus. 1987. Taped interviews with Ben Kracht, 19–20 February.

Pewo, Levina Tongkeamah. 1994. Taped interview with Ben Kracht, 18 May.

Schultes, Richard Evans. 1937. "Peyote and Plants Used in the Peyote Ceremony." *Harvard University Botanical Museum Leaflets* 4(8):129–52.

Scott, Hugh Lenox. 1911. "Notes on the Kado, or Sun Dance of the Kiowas." *American Anthropologist* N.S. 13(3):345–79.

Slotkin, James S. 1975 [1956]. *The Peyote Religion: A Study in Indian-White Relations*. New York: Octagon Books.

Stewart, Omer C. 1987. *Peyote Religion: A History*. Norman: University of Oklahoma Press.

Steinmetz, Paul B. 1990. *Pipe, Bible, and Peyote among the Oglala Lakota: A Study in Religious Identity*. Knoxville: University of Tennessee Press.

Stumblingbear, Richard. 1987. Taped interview with Ben Kracht, 9 April.

Treat, Harry H. 1914. Letter to Superintendent Stecker, 6 June. NARS 91980-1914-063K.

Tsatoke, John. 1987. Taped interview with Ben Kracht, 30 April.

White, E. E. 1888. "Special Agent E. E. White to Indian Commissioner John D. C. Atkins, August 18, 1888. *Annual Reports of the Commissioner of Indian Affairs*. Washington DC: Government Printing Office.

Young, David E., and Jean-Guy Goulet, eds. 1994. *Being Changed by Cross-Cultural Encounters: The Anthropology of Extraordinary Experience*. Ontario, Canada: Broadview Press.

The Shaker Church and the
Indian Way in Native
Northwestern California

THOMAS BUCKLEY

The Indian Shaker Church originated on Puget Sound in 1882 and was brought into Native northwestern California in 1926.[1] Outsider scholars have often reduced it to the status of a minor "crisis cult" or "revitalization movement," as opposed to a real—that is, "traditional"—Indian religion. Reports that California Shakers rejected all indigenous ceremonialism as "sinful" and anti-Christian while asserting that the new religion was a purely Native way, best closed to non-Indians, appeared to support this view (Barnett 1957: 142–43). While converted elders quietly defended the Church as a "continuation" of traditional ways (in Gould and Furukawa 1966: 59), they seemed, to some, to be deluding themselves in a struggle to maintain their Indian identities while becoming pseudo-Christians. But even outsiders do well to listen closely to what the elders say and to think long on it, as local people well know.

The notion that the Shaker Church is a "continuation" of an authentic Indian spirituality—an "evolution" of it, as a Church member said to me in 1978—rings false only as long as we view modern Native American history in terms of polarities—Indian/Christian, traditionalist/Shaker, this faction/that faction, and the rest (as anthropologists once did habitually). Perhaps it helps to view Native/European as the typal opposition, of which all the others are tokens, and to remember that it was, first, racist Europeans who insisted on its validity? But this, too, is over simple: the Indian Shakers themselves have insisted on a rigid us/them, inside/outside dichotomy (Gould and Furukawa 1966: 57–64), whether such oppositional dualism was "traditional" or the result of acculturation to "European" modes of thought (e.g., Buckley 1984).

Something more complex may be going on here, revealed in part by the powerful reemergence of indigenous ceremonialism that has occurred in northwestern California as elsewhere in Indian Country during the past two decades. The contemporary emergence of forms of religious life that non-Indian anthropologists and Native people alike once viewed as utterly gone should alert us to the possibility that, yes, innovations like the Shaker Church have indeed been continuations of Native traditions, and that—perhaps more difficult to see—reemergent traditions are themselves continuations or evolutions of modern innovations like the Shaker Church. That is, theoretically, that such seemingly diametrically opposed tokens are better understood as emergent processes co-participating in a historical and spiritual dialogue.

SURVIVAL

The Indian peoples of northwestern California—Tolowas, Yuroks, Karuks, Wiyots, Hupas and others—underwent their first massive encounters with Euroamericans beginning in 1850. Suddenly, in the first few months of that year, news of a gold strike on the Trinity River brought an estimated ten thousand fortune seekers into the Klamath River drainage. It was the beginning of what Indian people came to call, variously, "the end of the world," "the time when the stars fell," and "the end of Indian time."

It has been hard for Indian people in that region (as virtually everywhere else in the United States) in the hundred and forty years since. A short time ago a friend remarked about young men on the Hoopa Valley Indian Reservation, "Well, there are two ways for Indian men to save their lives these days, Christianity and the Indian Way, and that's it." I don't think that she was over-dramatizing. Impressionistically at least, without the support and discipline of a religious practice, life for these men—and women—tends to be rough and, tragically often, short. Fortunately, if my friend is correct, there is a lively and diverse assortment of Christian congregations in the region, and there has also been a considerable renaissance in traditional Indian religious practices, gathering momentum steadily since the late 1960s.

Not that "the Indian Way" disappeared entirely after 1850, but it had indeed "gone underground for awhile," as a Hupa-Yurok ceremonial doctor put it in 1976. Most strikingly, the re-emergence of the Indian Way has manifested in the regeneration of the complex system—including religious, social, economic, and political dimensions—that the anthropologist A. L. Kroeber called "the World Renewal Cult" and that he deemed moribund and nearly extinct by the 1940s (Kroeber and Gifford 1949).

RESISTANCE TO CHRISTIANITY

Today, the northwestern California Indian Way tends to be construed by participants as exclusive of Christian belief and practice, and individuals following it tend, in many cases, to forcefully reject Christianity as un-Indian. Anti-Christian sentiment, found especially among the upper ranks of these somewhat stratified societies from which the spiritual elite has always tended to come, can be traced back to the earliest years of contact.

Presbyterian missionaries came to the Hoopa Valley in 1873 and had extended their evangelical efforts outwards, up and down the Klamath and along the various forks of the Trinity River, by the 1890s. Conversions were few, however, and seem to have been restricted to mixed-blood Indians who were, at that time, marginal to both Indian and non-Indian societies and thus had little to lose in moving even farther from the moral center of elite Native society. By contrast, the Native elites did not seek parity with the increasingly oppressive whites, who dominated northwestern California after the end of armed Indian resistance in 1867, through conversion to Christianity. Between 1870 and 1890, for instance, Wolf Morris, a Polish-Jewish trader dealing in dentalium shells with Yurok and Tolowa customers, found it advantageous to stress the fact that he, like his high-status potential customers, was *not* a Christian (Pilling 1970: 4; cf., Pilling and Pilling 1970: 103). No full-blooded Yurok Indian is known to have converted to Christianity before the end of the First World War.

There were, it should be mentioned, some notable Native efforts to secure religious tolerance and respect from non-Indians through *apologia* cast as comparisons of traditional belief systems to Christianity. Thus, by 1900, the Yurok trickster-creator Wohpekumew was being called "God," in English, by certain Yuroks in an effort to increase cross-cultural understanding (Kroeber 1976: 420). This mythical equivalence has been reiterated throughout this century and still is popular today. A contemporary Yurok intellectual and religious activist suggests that the first Yurok Indian to compare the licentious Wohpekumew to God was perhaps acting in the spirit of a trickster himself. But there are other possibilities.

The comparison was at least in part based on an interesting similarity: Wohpekumew tried to kill his Immortal son, Kapuloyo, imprisoning him high in a tree and blinding his own grandson, Kewomer. Wohpekumew did not try to sacrifice Kapuloyo and Kewomer to save humanity, however, but to facilitate his own seductions of women. Happily, Kapuloyo resurrected himself by his own wits and restored Kewomer's sight. Together they went to the spirit world, abandoning Wohpekumew (Kroeber 1976).

While the Wohpekumew/God equivalence may have reflected some Yuroks' perceptions of the darker similarities of the two myths (cf. Bakan 1968: 96–128), the crucifixion of Christ has not, historically, had much resonance for Yurok people inclined toward traditional ways, or for their like-minded neighbors — Hupa, Karuk and Tolowa Indians. A late Yurok Indian doctor told me in 1978,

Now Christianity . . . If an Indian had a brand new pair of hundred dollar boots and cut off his foot with his axe, he'd throw those boots away because they had blood in them and weren't any good. We throw away whatever has blood in it because it's spoiled. But Christians have this cross where they killed Jesus, which is covered with blood, and they fool with it and wear it around their necks, and that's no good. [fieldnotes, 1978.]

In light of such strongly held views, Indian efforts at rapprochement through creating intercultural equivalences, as in identifying the trickster-creator Wohpekumew with "God," the hero Pulekukwerek with Christ, or in calling the indigenous mythic Immortals "angels," seem at best half-hearted (cf. Thompson 1916).

Despite all such resistance, be it softly apologetic or harshly anti-Christian, Christianity has indeed made inroads into the staunch religious conservatism of a region where cultures are epitomized by the social and spiritual elites. The Presbyterian Church is a central feature of Indian religious life at Hoopa today, a hundred and seventeen years after it was established. Other churches came much later, but remained in the area as well. By 1928 the Four Square Gospel Church at Klamath was attracting Yurok members, the Baptists were active in Requa, and at least one Yurok woman had become a Pentecostal Christian (Pilling 1970: 5). Today there are Assembly of God Churches in Hoopa, on the Yurok Reservation at Weitchpec and at Pecwan, in Karuk country at Orleans, and so on; Mormon, Seventh Day Adventist, various fundamentalist Protestant churches as well as Roman Catholic missions—including the Mission of Blessed Kateri Tekakwitha (the Algonquin-Mohawk saint) at Hoopa—all attract significant Indian congregations. Traveling revivalists, especially those offering to heal, do a lively business in the area as well.

Still, the rise of these congregations during the past sixty years should not obscure the continuing tensions and occasional conflicts between Christian and traditional ways. Christian preachers and parishioners alike have castigated indigenous beliefs and practices as heathen delusion, going so far as to urge the burning of traditional dance regalia and accusing medicine people of deviltry. Traditionalists, on the other hand, have accused the Christians of being "superstitious" in their rejection of "spiritualism."

The Indian Shaker Church, a syncretic sect perceived by its members as a special religious dispensation intended by God for Indians alone, has sought since 1926 to mediate this rift that dates back to the earliest years of contact in northwestern California precisely by incorporating indigenous religious elements: what critics of Christianity refer to as spiritualism. I turn now to the Shaker Church, examining its teaching and its history as well as its degree of success in this effort.

SHAKER SYNCRETISM

In 1882, John Slocum, a Nisqualy Indian from Puget Sound, "died." He revived, and then once again died, his spirit ascending to Heaven where he was instructed by "an angel of God." He came back into his body, awoke, and instructed those about him in the new religion that God had revealed to him through His angel.

Slocum's experience was coherent with the Prophet Dance pattern of coastal Washington and the Plateau, and it also showed the considerable influence of both Protestant and Catholic missions in the Puget Sound area. In brief, as God's agent, John Slocum taught that there are:

good things in Heaven. God is kind to us. If you all try hard and help me, we will be better men on earth. . . . They know in Heaven what we think. When people are sick we pray to God to cure us. We pray that he takes the evil away and leave the good. [This is the] good road for us to travel. . . . do good and sing good songs . . . Christ said he sends power to every believing soul on earth. [Slocum, in Slagle 1985: 354.]

This teaching was augmented by John Slocum's wife, Mary, who discovered that the power of the "Spirit of Christ" (Smith 1954: 121) manifested in her own body as light trancing and physical trembling—"the Shake" through which she could heal. The Shake has been viewed widely by anthropologists as a reembodiment of the indigenous Salishan concept of "power," particularly as it once pertained to "shamans" (Smith 1954: 121). "Shaman," however, has never been a viable term for most Native people on the Klamath River. Yuroks, for instance, once called their most powerful healers kegey (Buckley 1992). Today, the spiritual heirs of these "sucking doctors" are usually called "Indian doctors," and—as Smith suggested would be the case—the recent history of these Indian doctors has been richly intertwined with that of the Shaker Church.

John Slocum incorporated his wife Mary's innovation of the Shake into his own teaching and instructed his followers to build him a church at Mud Bay, Washington, where their joint revelations might be put into formal practice by a congregation. The Indian Shaker Church was organized as an association in 1892 and incorporated in 1910 (Slagel 1985: 353). The wooden church itself was illuminated by copious candles. Services focused on Christian worship as well as singing and dancing to the accompaniment of handbells, which supported the converted in light trancing. Preaching stressed the importance of "like-mindedness," among the congregants, and a famous song instructs:

Make all one mind
and Jesus will help you. [In Valory 1966a: 76.]

The unity of the congregation against the forces of evil outside the church was paramount, and this like-mindedness reinforced the Shake, which empowered congregants to heal, prophesy, trace lost objects, and cast out evil. Healing focused both on individuals and on the world at large. Shakers prayed for the end of war and a return to world balance and harmony, when the necessary and rigid inside/outside dichotomy would be outmoded.

The new syncretic church spread widely in the Pacific Northwest. In 1926 Jimmy Jack, a Yurok Indian, brought the Shaker dispensation to the Lower

Klamath River. There was a barn there owned by the Gensaw family that was being rented out by a foster daughter, the late Florence Shaughnessy, for use as a dance hall. Jimmy Jack rented this barn at the beginning of September for the first Shaker meeting in California. Fifty years later, Mrs. Shaughnessy, a Yurok Indian, gave this account:

> Jimmy Jack from old Klamath went up to Siletz in Oregon, and he married a Siletz woman. The Shakers were there, and they wanted to come down here, so Jimmy Jack brought them. They asked me if they could use the big barn where I used to have my dances, so I let them. They had the whole place full of white candles, and it was quite beautiful. They all started dancing in there and ringing their bells. People kept pouring in until the hall was full, and people kept coming and crowded all around the place in front of the door. It was packed. There were commercial fishermen on the river and they heard bells ringing and they all came in too, because they'd never heard anything like those bells at Requa.
>
> I went with my mother. She asked me to take her and we stood in that crowd outside. But this woman who was dancing inside saw us and she came out, and she touched my mother and said, "You are in terrible trouble; come inside." But my mother said, "Flo, take me home. I feel so weak." So I walked her back, and she was trembling and shaking and she could hardly stand and walk. And that woman was right: two or three days later my mother was found, drowned. Strange things happen. Perhaps she should have listened. [fieldnotes, 1976.]

At first, Shakers, as had the Presbyterians before them, mainly converted people marginal to respectable Yurok society: half-bloods, the illegitimate and the very poor. For instance, despite his strong efforts Jimmy Jack was unable to convert the influential Requa traditionalist and spiritual leader Robert Spott. Spott attended Shaker meetings out of politeness, as he did Baptist services. At one point, Jimmy Jack touched him, transmitting the Shake to him as the Siletz woman had done to Florence Shaughnessy's mother. But Spott refused to convert, even after this experience, on the grounds that the Shakers were Christians and thus un-Indian (Barnett 1957: 76–77, 272–74).

Jack continued to seek such conversions, however, knowing that the Church could gain a solid foothold in the region only with the support of influential people like Spott. While Robert Spott's sister, Alice, was helpful but ambivalent, other Yurok women of high repute did eventually convert wholeheartedly.

Since the 1880s and '90s, Yurok candidates for the traditional doctoring vocation of *kegey* had increasingly failed to gain their powers in the mountain sacred sites and were unable to demonstrate these powers in the requisite *remohpoh*, "Kick Dance," or "Doctor Dance," put up in the riverine village sweat houses (Buckley 1992). Nonetheless a number of women who had been spiritually called, while failing to gain full standing as *kegey*, achieved some recognition as clairvoyants and healers. Several of these women lived on the lower Klamath in the villages near Johnson's Landing. They began, by 1930, to find a new context for legitimacy as Indian doctors in the Shaker Church, whose dancing they claimed as a substitute for the older, non-Christian *remohpoh*. Although some of the very few old-time *kegey* who survived disparagingly referred to these new healers as "half doctors," the younger Yurok Indian doctors soon virtually controlled the Shaker Church established at Smith River, twenty-five miles north of Requa, in Tolowa territory.[2] The participation of these powerful Yurok women inspired the conversion of highly respected Tolowa religious people, including the influential Sam Lopez. With this impetus, other important conversions were achieved, including that of Woodruff Hostler, a Hupa Indian. In 1932 Jimmy Jack cured another Hupa, John Charlie, who, giving up all traditional ways and selling all of his family's dance regalia, established a church at Hoopa. Other churches were eventually established at Johnsons and at Jimmy Jack's hometown of Klamath, both in Yurok territory.

Despite its increasing strength, the Shaker church in California was rife with dissention and controversy almost from its inception, and this conflict centered, generally, on issues of Indian identity. In 1933, the Church in northwestern California was riven by "Bible controversy." "Book" congregations argued for the use of the Bible in services; "Shake" advocates insisted that God intended the Bible for white people only, and not for Indians who received the Holy Spirit directly, through the Shake.

A second focus of controversy was ownership of traditional dance regalia and participation in pre-Christian dances, such as the child-curing Brush Dance. Some Shakers argued that traditional dancing was of the devil and all regalia must be destroyed if individuals were to be cured, wars ended, and the world saved. Others declared that this was an individual matter and that the Church could not dictate individuals' religious lives. Nonetheless, some converts were accused of "backsliding" when they insisted on their right to participate in both Shaker meetings *and* in Brush Dances: taking part in "outside" activities, they weakened "like-mindedness" and threatened the "inside," the church.

From one point of view, particularly strong among Smith River Shakers, the Shake was a "continuation" of the old Indian Way, completely Indian but also obviating earlier traditional practices. It was on the strength of this sentiment that the anthropologists Richard Gould and Theodore Furukawa wrote, in 1964, that, "it is our tentative prediction . . . that the Indian Shaker Church will provide the most tangible focus for the identity of the 'Indian' in the face of white American culture in this area of northwestern California" (Gould and Furukawa 1964: 67).

However, many Indian people continued to agree with, for instance, the Hupa traditionalists who hold that dancing in the traditional Brush, Deerskin and

Jump Dances makes folks more Indian, more "real," or *xoche*. As a person dances through the night in the Brush Dance, for example, he becomes more and more "real" and more and more "Indian" until, in the last dance shortly after dawn, he is once again completely *xoche*: real, pure, beautiful, balanced—Indian (Lee Davis, personal communication, 1989). The notion was recently reiterated by a Karuk ceremonial singer and dancer, Julian Lang, who said that, in displaying regalia and dancing in ceremonies like the world-renewing Jump Dance:

[t]he whole idea of displaying that stuff is to spark people inside so . . . if that power is in there sleeping inside them . . . in the ceremony you're waking up those people, that power inside the people, so when that wakes up and looks at that stuff and it sees all that kinship, pretty soon it wants to go into that stuff again and it wants to participate in that stuff, and it turns the people back into Indians. [Taped interview, 1988.]

By 1965, with the passing of the first generation of converts including, pertinently, most of the Indian doctors, the Shaker Church was already losing significant membership. Sam Lopez, the Tolowa spiritual leader, was drifting away, moving towards the Bible-oriented Four Square Gospel Church. Others, were attempting to keep a foot in both camps, Shaker and traditional. Most church members, however, while accepting Shakers' attendance at other Christian church services, firmly rejected Shaker participation in traditional dances or the participation of those committed to the older Indian Way in Shaker meetings. Complex negotiations of membership and identity occurred, as when the late Ella Norris, Yurok-Tolowa, moved to the Four Square Gospel Church both as an adherent to Biblical teaching and because Church members did not object to her participating in Brush Dances.

Thus, while Gould and Furukawa wrote in 1964 of the Shaker Church as the probable focus of Indian identity in northwestern California in the future, in 1966 Dale Valory confidently described the Shaker Church as having already reached its peak and beginning to ebb (Valory 1966: 67). In fact none of the three, all graduate students in anthropology at Berkeley in the mid-1960s, were entirely correct. Twenty-six years after Gould and Furukawa wrote, the Shaker Church has neither ebbed to insignificance nor does it form a primary religious focus for Indian identity today: not, at least, for the majority of the most visible and influential religious people in northwestern California.

RESURGENCE OF THE INDIAN WAY

Among these people, often the modern descendants of the old "high families," another option has all along been open, that of denouncing Christianity altogether, as had their lineal ancestors in the nineteenth century and before the 1920s. This option became more attractive as the 1960s wore on and became the

1970s, a time that saw, in northwestern California as in much of Indian Country, a concerted effort among many to renounce the ways of the dominant society and return to "Indian" traditions. This renaissance was most evident among younger Indian people, but was certainly not limited to them.

Along with a burst of new enthusiasm for the Brush Dance, the 1960s also saw a profound regeneration of interest in the far more portentous Jump and Deerskin Dances at Hoopa, under the leadership of the elder Rudolph Soctish. In the 1970s Karuk Indians, led by another elder, Shan Davis, revived their equally solemn New Years "World Making," *pikiawish*, at Katimin, on the Klamath River. By the 1980s, Yuroks, under the guidance of the elders Dewey George and Howard Ames, both of whom trained in the sweat house at Pecwan in the 1930s, restored the Jump Dance at Pecwan. Slightly later in that decade, Tolowa Indians led by a protege of Sam Lopez were beginning to revive their own world renewal dance at Smith River.

In the 1980s, as younger men took over from elders who were rapidly passing away, almost as a group, the anti-Christian sentiment which had long been a feature of "high" or elite thought, came increasingly into prominence among, especially, Indian religious activists in their thirties and forties and now responsible for most of the formal traditional leadership positions in the region: the "dance makers," "medicine men," singers and dancers, feasting "fire owners" and so on. Such sentiment extended naturally to the Shakers, who tend to be seen more simply as "Christians."

By 1989 Loren Bommelyn, a charismatic and respected craftsman and teacher who is an excellent singer as well, had come to regard anti-Shaker sentiment as counterproductive. At a large intertribal gathering in Arcata in the fall of 1989 he introduced an evening of singing by a dozen of the most noted Yurok, Karuk, Hupa and Tolowa Indian singers, old and young, with an impassioned plea for religious tolerance of the Shakers by those following both Christian and Indian Ways. He said that he himself was no longer a Shaker but that he fully respected the Church as an authentic Indian religious expression and urged others to do the same, opening the evening's singing with a solo Shaker invocation of remarkable beauty and power. It was a brave, virtuoso move on his part, before an audience of three hundred or so people, many well known for their anti-Christian sentiments, and his words and song were greeted with silent appreciation and respect.

Despite Valory's pessimism in 1966, Shakers remain a strong presence in the religious life of the region, even now attracting younger men and women who, for whatever reason, do not find the traditional Indian Way satisfying. To an extent, perhaps, the continuing vitality of the Church is due to the resolution of the Bible controversy in 1984. This long-standing dispute caused schism among the various churches in the region and was not fully resolved until 1984 when Harris Teo, the Bishop of the Indian Shaker Church in California, stated categorically that "Bibles were not to be used or directly quoted in any Shaker church" (in Slagle 1985: 354). Shakers have also survived through becoming less rigidly opposed to members' participation in the Brush Dance and other Indian doings, or to members' ownership of traditional dance regalia. The once heretical participation in Indian dances by prominent Shakers came slowly and however reluctantly to be accepted by many. Most today are willing to grant the membership far more personal autonomy and discretion than was once the case. People tend to work out their own solutions to the cultural conflicts posed by Shaker and traditional involvements. For example, a well-known Hupa-Yurok artist, widely recognized as among the finest living makers of traditional dance regalia, an inspired and proselytizing Shaker, will not himself dance in any of the rituals for which he makes such fine regalia.

If the Shakers have become more tolerant of multiple religious commitments among their members, the same cannot, I think, be said of the traditionalists, particularly the younger ones now ascendant in the so-called (by Kroeber) "world renewal cult." Observation suggests that those coming into leadership positions in the big dances are increasingly clear—as their efforts become increasingly secured—in their rejection of the Shakers as religiously un-Indian. On the last day of the ten day Jump Dance at Pecwan in 1986, for instance, a "dance maker" refused to permit a Shaker to lead a Shaker prayer in the dance pit, saying that the dance was an Indian, not a Christian, occasion.

These things are serious matters in riverine northwestern California. They become the source of endless gossip and often become what people talk about for the two years until the next dance, when something new and equally scandalous may come up. I relate such sensitive matters only to support my conclusion that the Indian Shaker Church, while it continues to exist and even to attract new converts, has largely failed as a mediation of mainstream Christianity and the Indian Way. Indeed, the kind of syncretic fusion that it enabled—a revolutionary response to dispossession and white oppression—itself became a new old way, a "traditional" way that younger neo-traditionalists, like the dance makers at Pecwan and at Hoopa, putatively returning to the old old way, now reject as old-fashioned and reactionary. However, while the Indian Way is on the upsurge once again in Native northwestern California, as a Yurok acquaintance said of his peers, "We may be Indians, but we all die Christians." Shaker and other Christian practitioners have become the most widely accepted and appreciated purveyors of funeral rites, whatever the spiritual commitments of the deceased and his family—much as, in Japan, Buddhist priests have come to be known for the mortuary services that they provide bereaved families that are, at best, only nominally Buddhist (Chadwick 1994).

Despite the broad acceptance of Christian burial services, the broader pattern that I have been narrating reflects a widespread, national movement toward retribalization and the reclamation of purely local cultural and spiritual traditions in lieu of continuing in the development of pan-Indianism, as offered by the Shaker and the Native American Churches. The dialectic between two sets of oppositions—being "Indian" as opposed to "non-Indian," and being Yurok or Hupa, say, as contrasted with "Native American"—is a newly dynamic one. The Shakers are rejected by the new traditionalists not simply in continuance of perennial anti-Christian sentiment among the religious elite, but also in defense of purely local religious knowledge and practice, as distinct from pan-Indianism.

T. T. Waterman, a Berkeley anthropologist of the Kroeber era, made the astute observation in 1924 that "the shake religion of Puget Sound," with its heavy "shamanistic" content, was most appealing to Indians whose indigenous religious practices were still strong; that is, where traditional doctoring was still practiced. Waterman further observed that it was this purely indigenous component of the new Christian sect that attracted influential traditionalists—like, slightly later, the Yurok Indian doctors (Waterman 1924).

There is a mild irony here. The Shaker Church was most successful in converting those who were most confident in traditional spiritual practices and who were most resistant to mainstream forms of Christianity, such as Presbyterianism in the Hoopa Valley. It offered an acceptable compromise at a time when, despite strong commitment to the Indian Way, that Way seemed to be in need of updating, in keeping with the radically changed circumstances of post-invasion northwestern North America that, for example, mitigated against the Yurok Indian doctors gaining the traditional sucking doctors' full powers. The adaptation of Christian belief to Indian purpose among the California Shakers provided a means of "vitalization," in Marian Smith's insightful terms (Smith 1954: 122): of adapting still strong cultures to current circumstances, rather than of "revitalizing" moribund cultures (cf. Wallace 1956).

Be this as it may, the Shaker Church comprised a powerful vehicle of acculturation to non-Indian beliefs—especially, to hierarchical, oppositional dualism as found in mainstream Christianity and in such Shaker polarities as inside/outside, Heaven/earth, Shake/devil, and other such dichotomies. And it is such acculturation that has been resisted by the newer generation of traditional practitioners, with their more self-consciously holistic world views (cf. Buckley 1984). The process amounts to a dialogue with a by-now familiar structure.

Edward Bruner has examined the nature of ethnographies of North American Indians and found them to be "narratives" that we anthropologists share with the putative objects of our studies. Bruner claims not only that non-Native anthropologists and non-anthropologist Natives tell each other stories, but that we coauthor the stories that we each tell: stories that emerge dialogically from our interactions (Bruner 1986).

Bruner argues that, up until the 1960s, Indians and anthropologists shared a narrative of Indian history that was structured by a scenario of past glory, tragic defeat, current cultural fragmentation, and eventual assimilation. Our coauthored story changed, he says, in the 1960s to follow a different scenario: past glory, oppression, current resistance, eventual resurgence. In fact, Bruner concludes, both stories are true and both are oversimplifications. Our histories are codeterminous and dialectical, rather than mono-causal and linear. A degree of assimilation, he argues, both gave Indian people the means of physical survival and, eventually, a profound commitment to resist further assimilation. This resistance both ensures cultural survival and brings the self-confidence and firmness of identity that allow communities to accept further, moderate degrees of change. So the two varieties of narrative both witness, Bruner concludes, codetermined processes in post-contact Native American history.

From this perspective the Shaker church has afforded the Indian people of northwestern California a holding action. That is, its voicing of Biblical Christianity was, of course, a (contested) means of ideational assimilation to non-Indian intellectual and spiritual culture, but the Church also served as a vehicle for the preservation and transmission of indigenous doctoring traditions in changing circumstances, as its pan-Indianism was both a source of cultural loss, through amalgamation, and of preservation of Indianness, through the Church's insistence on the "like-mindedness" of congregants and its inside/outside, us/them dualism.

Ironically, the success of the Indian Shaker Church in northwestern California in these particular directions has ultimately led to its own seeming decline. It has preserved an Indian focus that ultimately emerged in resistance to the Christian context within which it was preserved, in a new expression of old anti-Christian feeling, and in a return from pan-Indian engagement to localized, non-Christian religious practice. If the Shake was a "continuation" of the Indian Way, as the most respected members of the Church have always claimed, then, too, the resurgent local Indian Way must be viewed as a "continuation" of the Shake.

"And so it goes," as the anthropologically trained fabulist Kurt Vonnegut Jr. is fond of writing. I have reached the end of my story but not, I think, the end of the dialogic process that is its subject. In the past, anthropologists have written confidently about the imminent demise of Yurok Indian culture (Kroeber and Lévi-Strauss, in Valory 1966b), about the disappearance of "American Indians" and their replacement by "Indian Americans" in Native northwest California (Bushnell 1968) and, as we have seen above, about replacement of earlier Native spiritual identities with that of the Shakers. All of these predictions have been wrong and now, for my own part, I would not hazard a guess as to just where the process I have examined leads next. I tend to agree with the contemporary Onondaga Turtle Clan chief Oren Lyons when he says of non-Indians, "as long as the Indian nations exist, so will you. But when we are gone, you too will go" (1981: 93). In the meantime, mainstream Christianity, the Indian Shaker Church, and the Indian Way continue to coexist in Native northwestern California, however contentious such pluralism occasionally may be.

NOTES

1. This paper was originally presented at Dartmouth College as a part of the 1990 Edward and Molly Scheu Native American Studies Symposium on Native Americans and Christianity. Research incorporated was funded, in 1988, by the Phillips Fund of the American Philosophical Society and by the Jacobs Fund of the Whatcom Museum Foundation. My thanks to Mr. and Mrs. Scheu and to these two helpful organizations for their support, to Professor Sergei Kan of Dartmouth for his comments, and to Dr. Lee Davis.

2. The English term "half doctor" alluded to the fact that, although the new doctors had been spiritually called and trained, they had not capped their training by passing an "examination" in the mountains, nor had they danced the Doctor Dance in their villages. Thus they had done only half of what was traditionally required—as a person who married without the exchange of full bridewealth was once said to be "half married."

REFERENCES

Bakan, David. 1968. *Disease, Pain and Sacrifice: Toward a Psychology of Suffering.* Chicago: University of Chicago Press.

Barnett, Homer G. 1957. *Indian Shakers: A Messianic Cult of the Pacific Northwest.* Carbondale: Southern Illinois University Press.

Bruner, Edward M. 1986. "Ethnography as narrative." In *The Anthropology of Experience.* Ed. Victor Turner and Edward M. Bruner. Urbana: University of Illinois Press. 139–55.

Buckley, Thomas. 1984. "Yurok speech registers and ontology." *Language in Society* 13(4): 467–88.

———. 1992. "Yurok doctors and the concept of 'shamanism.'" In *California Indian Shamanism.* Ed. Lowell John Bean. Menlo Park CA: Ballena Press. 117–62.

Bushnell, John. 1968. "From American Indian to Indian American: The changing identity of the Hupa." *American Anthropologist* 70: 1108–116.

Chadwick, David. 1994. *Thank You and OK! An American Zen Failure in Japan.* New York: Penguin.

Gould, Richard A., and Theodore Paul Furukawa. 1964. "Aspects of ceremonial life among the Indian Shakers of Smith River, California." *Kroeber Anthropological Society Papers* 31: 51–67.

Kroeber, A. L. 1926. "The law of the Yurok Indians." *Atti del Congresso Internazional degli Americanisti*. Roma. 2: 511–16.

———. 1976. *Yurok Myths*. Berkeley: University of California Press.

Kroeber, A. L., and E. W. Gifford. 1949. "World renewal: A cult system of native northwest California." *Anthropological Records* 13(1): 1–155.

Lyons, Oren. 1981. "Our mother earth." *Parabola* 6(1): 91–93.

Pilling, Arnold R. 1970. "The ethnography of Christian and/or historical Indian burials (Yurok Indians of northwestern California)." Paper presented at the Meeting of the Society for Historical Archaeology. Toronto.

Pilling, Arnold R., and Patricia L. Pilling. 1970. "Cloth, clothes, hose and bows: Nonsedentary merchants among the Indians of northwestern California." In *Migration and Anthropology: Proceedings, 1970 Annual Spring Meeting of the American Ethnological Society*. Seattle: University of Washington Press. 97–119.

Slagle, Allogan. 1985. "Tolowa Indian Shakers and the role of prophecy at Smith River, California." *The American Indian Quarterly* 9(3): 353–74.

Smith, Marian W. 1954. "Shamanism in the Shaker religion of northwest America." *Man* 54: 119–22.

Thompson, Lucy. 1991. *To the American Indian: Reminiscences of a Yurok Indian Woman*. Berkeley: Heyday Books. [1916]

Valory, Dale Kieth. 1966a. "The focus of Indian Shaker healing." *Kroeber Anthropological Society Papers* 35: 67–111.

———. 1966b. "Humanity, what is it? An interview with Claude Lévi-Strauss." *Kroeber Anthropological Society Papers* 35: 41–53.

Wallace, A. F. C. 1956. "Revitalization movements: Some theoretical considerations for their comparative study." *American Anthropologist* 58(2): 264–81.

Waterman, T. T. 1924. "The 'Shake Religion' of Puget Sound." *Smithsonian Institution Annual Report for 1922*: 499–507.

Intertribal Traditionalism and the Religious Roots of Red Power

JAMES TREAT

Most so-called serious historians have seen a different Sixties than did many of the participants. Rejecting the counterculture and the hippies as a clownish sideshow, and the drug scene as an embarrassment, they have zeroed in on what appears in hindsight to have been really important, the political side of the decade's experience: the dramatic free speech, civil rights, antiwar, black power, and other protest and revolutionary movements.

    Robert S. Ellwood, *The Sixties Spiritual Awakening*

Every time I come up here it seems like I've been in hell all my life and I'm coming into some sort of utopia. . . . This convention might not mean we'll have more food on the table, but it does mean spiritual revival for Indians. Man can't survive on bread alone.

    Clifton Hill, Creek Centralization Committee

As word spread that Tadodaho had died, tribal people throughout the Iroquois confederacy mourned the loss of their leader and quietly speculated on the selection of his successor. It was the fall of 1968, a time of rising conflict with colonial powers, and many Iroquois traditionalists hoped their new "chief of chiefs" would be both wise and strong, able to defend their land and sovereignty against unrelenting encroachments. Long-standing tradition required that a confederacy council of hereditary chiefs—who governed under the watchful eyes of the clan mothers—select a new leader from among the Onondagas, the keepers of the fire. The waiting finally ended on December 7, when the council chiefs announced that fifty-three-year-old Leon Shenandoah had been installed as Tadodaho of the confederacy. Known as a humble man who supported his large family by working as a custodian at nearby Syracuse University, Shenandoah inaugurated his tenure by promising to be true to his traditional name, which can be translated as "Unfinished Business."[1]

    Only eleven days later, Mohawk activists blockaded the international bridge at Cornwall Island to protest Canada's aggressive violations of the 1794 Jay Treaty, which guaranteed Native people free passage and trade across the Canada-U.S. border. The influential Mohawk periodical *Akwesasne Notes* was born in the midst of this struggle, and the highly publicized—and ultimately successful—blockade generated a heightened sense of political consciousness in other Iroquois communities and among Native people across North America. Unlike his predecessor, who had preferred the religious aspects of Tadodaho's leadership responsibilities, Shenandoah did not shy away from this conflict and quickly distinguished himself as one who recognized the need to assert both the spiritual prerogative and the political authority of his office.[2]

A number of Iroquois leaders had already been urging the council chiefs to convene an intertribal gathering of traditionalists where they could discuss common concerns and develop a sense of solidarity. The Cornwall Island controversy brought the need for such a meeting into sharp relief, and on January 5, in one of his first official acts as Tadodaho, Shenandoah announced that the confederacy would host the hemispheric "super-council" during the summer of 1969. "We'll be discussing the warning signs of disaster and ways to prepare ahead," he explained to local reporters. "We don't know definitely what we'll talk about. That is why we will gather." A headline in the *Syracuse Post-Standard* called the Iroquois "disturbed" and their planned gathering a "pow-wow," but Shenandoah objected to these demeaning characterizations. "We're not calling it a powwow. It's a meeting," he insisted in an interview several weeks later, "to discuss plans for uniting all our people for action. We have to plan ahead for our future." He even suggested that the council chiefs might invite other Native communities to join the confederacy, which could expand to include as many as one hundred tribal nations spanning the continent. "They are interested. There has been preliminary discussion. They may come into the confederacy."[3]

Initial plans called for a four-day meeting at the Tonawanda Seneca reservation beginning August 16, an automobile caravan across upstate New York, and another four-day meeting at the Onondaga reservation, ending August 24. A joint Seneca-Onondaga planning committee formed and invitations were mailed to more than a hundred tribal communities throughout North, Central, and South America. *Akwesasne Notes* published a handwritten advertisement in their March issue encouraging "Native Aboriginals of the Americas" to attend the "Unity Convention" and billing it as "one of the largest Indian meetings of our times." Shenandoah anticipated that hundreds of delegates would attend the gathering. "It could be one thousand," he predicted. "We're just beginning our plans for uniting all of our people for action."[4]

Another *Akwesasne Notes* advertisement four months later reflected growing interest in the convention. Traditionalist men and women from a number of tribal communities—Algonquin, Cheyenne, Chipewyan, Cree, Hopi, Muscogee, Nisqually, Salish, Seminole, Shoshone—had already committed to attend, and the schedule had been extended to include meetings farther north at the Akwesasne Mohawk reservation and the Maniwaki Algonquin reserve. The political situation was little changed; although the Cornwall Island blockade had succeeded in forcing Canada to recognize Native rights to free passage and trade across the Canada-U.S. border, Shenandoah and other Iroquois leaders still faced ongoing disputes involving their lands, schools, and sacred wampum belts. Convention organizers hoped to address these and other political issues but were even more concerned to foster the cultural survival of tribal communities. Activities planned for the gathering included traditional feasts, social dancing, discussion of prophecies, and handicraft trading. Local leaders in the four host communities kept busy organizing the free food, firewood, and camping space that would be provided to delegates.[5]

On the fifteenth day of August, old cars and pickup trucks bearing battered license plates from the four directions—Washington, Oklahoma, Massachusetts, Ontario, and points beyond—began pulling into the camping grounds at Beeman Logan's place on the Tonawanda Seneca reservation. Respected elders and spiritual leaders, medicine men and women, young people and small children unloaded themselves and set up tents and tipis, anticipating the momentous events that would begin unfolding the next morning.[6]

TRADITIONAL MOVEMENT

Like all human communities, Native people in the Americas have always recognized the cultural continuities that mark collective experience, those idiosyncratic beliefs and practices identifiable as "tradition." Of course, any living cultural tradition is also a dynamic process, an indeterminate body of knowledge whose specific content is ever evolving in accordance with environmental and social circumstances. Even the very notion of a "traditional" identity has emerged, in the aftermath of European imperialism, as a common Native tradition, a convenient strategy for tagging the factionalism provoked by assimilationist aggression. Intertribal "traditionalism" was born in colonial-era experiments in military alliance, retreated underground during the repressions of republican expansionism, and has flourished in the postwar period as a distinctly postcolonial phenomenon.

Iroquois protests against violations of their sovereign rights, like their leadership in promoting intertribal solidarity, began decades before the confederacy chiefs agreed to sponsor the 1969 unity convention. In 1926 Tuscarora chief Clinton Rickard led a group of traditionalists in founding the Indian Defense League of America to protect Native political interests on both sides of the

Canada-U.S. border. They organized an annual "Border Crossing Celebration" at Niagara Falls (an event that continues today) to call attention to their rights under the Jay Treaty and other international agreements, and in the years that followed they also lobbied against the Indian Reorganization Act and other assimilationist schemes hatched in Washington and Ottawa. Rickard had volunteered for service in the Philippines during the Spanish-American War and later fought the 1924 Indian Citizenship Act; in 1940 he opposed the enforcement of the military draft in tribal communities and encouraged those who wanted to volunteer their services during the Second World War to enlist as "alien non-residents."

In 1948 an Indian Defense League delegation visited the United Nations headquarters in New York City, where they reported on treaty violations and requested assistance in their struggles with Canadian and American authorities. The downstate pilgrimage became an annual event and two years later the *New York Times* covered their visit, though reporters were more impressed by the delegates' feathered headdresses and beaded buckskin jackets than by their petition for membership in the international body. The accomplishments of the Indian Defense League figure prominently in Rickard's autobiography, *Fighting Tuscarora*, which concludes with an emphasis on the need for intertribal solidarity: "The one message I wish to leave with all my people everywhere," he wrote, "is to work for unity. If we do not all work together, if we are divided, then eventually we face the danger of being destroyed. . . . I want to see Indians help themselves, carry on their own affairs, and be independent. This we can do if we all pull together."[7]

The postwar period also saw the emergence of a traditionalist faction among the Hopis in the desert Southwest. In a 1947 kiva meeting at Shungopavi village, clan leaders discussing an ancient prophecy concerning a "gourd full of ashes" concluded that it had been fulfilled by the dropping of the atomic bombs on Hiroshima and Nagasaki two years earlier. Several interpreted this development as a sign that the end of the present world is near and that they should now share their religious teachings with non-Hopis, and more meetings and discussions followed. In 1948 Shungopavi hosted an important four-day conference of village chiefs and clan leaders, the first such meeting in decades, at which they discussed strategies for revitalizing Hopi ceremonial traditions. They also laid plans for disseminating their apocalyptic message to the outside world by appointing four interpreter-spokesmen, including Thomas Banyacya. Born into the churchgoing Jenkins family at Moenkopi, Banyacya had been one of the first Hopis to attend college and later worked in the Bureau of Indian Affairs for a few years. He eventually grew disillusioned with the American way of life and served as an interpreter in 1941 when Hotevilla clan leaders Dan Katchongva and James Pongonyuma testified on behalf of several Hopi traditionalists who had refused the military draft. Attaching himself to Katchongva, Jenkins soon replaced his Anglo surname with an initiation name used in one of the kachina societies.

Hopi elders met again at Shungopavi for four days in March of 1949, where they drafted a letter to President Truman from the "Hopi Indian Empire" enumerating their concerns regarding Hopi sovereignty and American policy in an era of Cold War. Warning the U.S. leader about a coming judgment day in this, "the most critical time in the history of mankind," they asked both the American people and "our own people, American Indians," to "give these words of ours your most serious consideration. Let us all re-examine ourselves and see where we stand today." During the next several years Hopi traditionalists sent additional letters to various government officials protesting federal policies, asserting Hopi autonomy, and threatening to take their complaints to the United Nations. In 1953 clan leader Andrew Hermequaftewa recorded the traditionalists' version of Hopi history in a short manifesto titled "The Hopi Way of Life Is the Way of Peace," which was published in pamphlet form and circulated widely. Banyacya, meanwhile, had begun touring the country as a missionary of Hopi prophetic apocalypticism.[8]

Katchongva and other traditionalist leaders traveled to Washington in May of 1955 and visited the commissioner of Indian affairs, persuading him to convene hearings on Hopi grievances. The hearings were held at Keams Canyon during the last two weeks of July; the traditionalists made their case, but Hopis representing other political and religious persuasions were also allowed to participate in the proceedings and no consensus emerged. Unable to supplant these other Hopi voices or to dislodge the tribal council, Katchongva and his colleagues instead sought out like-minded leaders in other Native communities. The Hopi traditionalists adopted an intertribal orientation in 1956 by hosting two important gatherings at Hotevilla: the "Meeting of Indian Brothers" brought together traditionalist leaders from other tribal communities, while the "Meeting of Religious People" welcomed both Native and non-Native participants. Katchongva, Hermequaftewa, and others delivered lengthy speeches describing Hopi origins and prophecies. The Great Spirit gave each tribal community their homeland and "life plan," Katchongva explained in one of his orations, and "we must never lose faith" or "we will once again destroy both life and land." Warning his listeners to be prepared for the coming day of purification, he argued, "It is up to the Hopi and other religious organizations not to participate in war." "I am sure," Katchongva concluded, "that all other Indian people on this land know these same teachings." In the years to come Hopi traditionalists would be among the most vocal opponents of various development projects—such as the infamous strip-mining operation at Black Mesa—approved by the tribal council.[9]

Many Americans remember the fifties as a period of expansive prosperity, but few also recall the intense exploitation of natural resources that facilitated consumer extravagance. Iroquois communities endured repeated assaults on their lands and sovereign powers during the fifties, the most severe of which were the massive hydroelectric projects imposed on the Allegany Seneca and Tuscarora reservations and the Saint Lawrence Seaway project that stripped land from the Mohawk reserves at Akwesasne and Caughnawaga. Although the Iroquois ultimately lost each of these battles, their spirited resistance caught the attention of the media and inspired Native people elsewhere. The dramatic protests that began in 1958 over the construction of a reservoir at Tuscarora were led by Clinton Rickard's son William along with John Hewitt and Wallace "Mad Bear" Anderson, though Anderson quickly preempted the other leaders and dominated media accounts of the nonviolent "stand-ins."

Miccosukees threatened by similar development pressures in the Everglades heard about the Tuscarora conflict and later that year invited Anderson to meet with them and other southeastern traditionalist leaders, where they resolved to form an intertribal alliance of Native people in the Americas. Traditionalists in the Far West also became more active during this period, coordinating efforts with their eastern counterparts through Rickard's Indian Defense League and through the League of North American Indians, an intertribal political organization led by Cherokee Frank Tom-Pee-Saw. Hopi traditionalists at Hotevilla village hosted another "Meeting of Religious People" in 1958 as well.[10]

The year 1959 witnessed a number of important events in the rise of traditionalist activism and intertribal cooperation. In March Iroquois traditionalists occupied the band council headquarters at the Six Nations reserve on the Grand River for a week, until they were evicted by Canadian Mounties. One week later an intertribal delegation of more than one hundred traditionalists traveled to Washington, where they delivered a petition protesting Canadian and American policies and demanded the removal of the commissioner of Indian affairs. Thirty-six of these men and women then met with the Miccosukees in the Everglades and together laid plans for organizing a "United Indian Republic" that would eventually apply for membership in the United Nations. In May a delegation of Hopi traditionalists including Katchongva and Banyacya went to New York City, where their request to address the United Nations assembly was denied; instead, they met with Iroquois traditionalists at Onondaga before returning home. In July Pit River leader Ray Johnson died in Washington while picketing the Bureau of Indian Affairs over his tribe's land claim, so Anderson organized an intertribal caravan and carried Johnson's body home to northeastern California in a rented trailer. The League of North American Indians continued to enlist grassroots activists and published a periodical titled *Indian Views* to disseminate the traditionalist perspective.[11]

By 1960 traditionalists from Iroquois, Hopi, and other tribal communities had established an intertribal network spanning the continent and had laid the political and religious foundations for the broad Native activism that would follow over the next decade. Intertribal contacts among traditionalists intensified during the early sixties. Clinton Rickard, now in his eighties, enjoyed a reputation as an elder statesman among traditionalists and was visited at his home by tribal contingents from near and far. His son William, who had experienced a spiritual awakening during a two-week stay with the Hopis, developed a close friendship with Banyacya. In 1961 William was invited to serve on the steering committee for the American Indian Chicago Conference and emerged as that historic event's most forceful voice of nationalist dissent. Clinton's daughter Karen also attended the Chicago conference and several months later was one of the founding members of the National Indian Youth Council.

Hotevilla village hosted several more gatherings of "Indian Brothers" and "Religious People" during this period and welcomed both groups at a combined meeting in 1963. The League of North American Indians convened a "Grand Spiritual and Temporal Council" in June of that year, with about five hundred traditionalists from thirty-five tribes attending the event. The Committee for the Great Council Fire, led by Ojibwa Francis Le Quier, issued a statement to "chiefs and Spiritual Leaders of the Indians of the North and South American Continents," proclaiming: "This is the day when all tribes shall come together and be one nation. This is the day when all the nations shall come together and be one world. . . . This is the day of the Great Justice." In Los Angeles a group called the Native American Movement proclaimed itself the "spiritual descendant" of earlier intertribal alliances (such as those led by Popé, Tecumseh, and Wovoka) and announced the "reawakening" and "revival" of Native cultural traditions.[12]

By the midsixties these and other traditionalist initiatives had coalesced into the traditional movement, an amorphous network of Native groups and individuals. Developing in the context of nation-state policies aimed at extinguishing tribal land claims, disestablishing tribal governments, and relocating tribal people to urban environments, the traditional movement was intertribal and transnational, nationalistic and populist, intergenerational and prophetic. As the growing consciousness that would soon be labeled "Red Power" gathered momentum, Native activists formed a multitude of local, regional, national, and international organizations that built on these pioneering efforts.

UNITY CONVENTION

William Rickard had been a central figure in the Tuscarora resistance since 1957 and within several years had become one of the most influential young leaders in Indian country. His untimely death in 1964 was a major loss both for his own people and for the expanding intertribal network of traditionalists, and Native periodicals as far away as the Pacific Northwest published his obituary. During the early sixties Rickard had served as president of the League of North American Indians; after his death Alfred Gagne, an old friend of the Rickard family, assumed leadership of the organization and broadened its scope, renaming it the League of Nations, Pan-American Indians. Gagne worked to protect Native political rights, sponsoring meetings and lobbying the U.S. Congress, and he supported the growing interest in intertribal solidarity by cooperating with various traditionalist leaders, especially Tonawanda Seneca chief Beeman Logan.[13]

As the traditional movement grew stronger, political protests over fishing rights by tribal communities in the Pacific Northwest generated a new round of media attention to Native issues. The involvement of the National Indian Youth Council in these "fish-ins" beginning in 1964 signaled a militant turn for that organization and reflected the increasingly varied forces that could be brought to bear on local conflicts. Logan and Gagne, meanwhile, began strategizing ways to bring together their many traditionalist colleagues in hopes of presenting a united front against territorial and assimilationist intrusions. Undoubtedly inspired by the intertribal religious gatherings first held at Hotevilla a decade earlier, they and other Iroquois leaders eventually settled on the idea of hosting a "unity convention" at the end of the summer of 1967. Logan and other Tonawanda Seneca chiefs volunteered their longhouse as a site for the gathering. Traditionalist leaders throughout North America soon received letters and telephone calls inviting them to participate, while local organizers began preparing to host a large and diverse group of people.[14]

Some 175 delegates from more than fifty tribal nations turned out for the gathering during the last week of August, where they socialized, shared traditional foods and dances, listened to mythic and prophetic teachings, and discussed strategies for surviving the continuing invasion of the Americas. Iroquois and Hopi leaders took the lead during the proceedings, with Hopi elders recounting their warnings about the impending destruction of the "Fourth World" and Iroquois chiefs offering their "Great Law of Peace" as a model for regenerating social and environmental relations. One delegate who took these teachings to heart was Clifton Hill, leader of the Creek Centralization Committee in eastern Oklahoma. Like most participants, he understood this gathering to be a fundamentally religious event. "Our movement was ignited," he later wrote, "by inspiration of the Great Spirit. . . . We Traditionalists have acted as a messenger from the Great Spirit to interpret the meaning of our Indian customs, languages, prophecies, and treaties." Intent on perpetuating Native communities through both intertribal and transnational solidarities, these traditionalist men and women defied the cultural pressures and political powers modern nation-states were exerting on them by collectively affirming the value and priority of their indigenous religious traditions.[15]

Perhaps even more significant than the week-long convention was the cross-country motorcade that followed. While most participants packed up and headed for home after closing ceremonies, Logan, Gagne, and others—including Logan's assistant "Mad Bear" Anderson and Hopi spokesman Thomas Banyacya—arranged what they called the "North American Indian Unity Caravan." On the second day of September five carloads left the Tonawanda Seneca reservation for a pilgrimage across North America. Traveling through the Great Lakes region, the group was joined by a Canadian contingent at Whitefish Bay and then continued westward along the Canada-U.S. border. The caravan met with other traditionalists along the way and invited many to join them as they worked their way toward a large powwow at the Hoopa Valley reservation on the West Coast. Returning home by way of the Southwest, caravan leaders planted sacred stones at key points on their circular path as they disseminated their message of apocalypse, natural law, and intertribal solidarity. Nearly two dozen tribal communities had hosted the unity caravan by the time it completed its transcontinental journey. Health problems prevented Hill from participating in the caravan, but he considered it to be a very important development in the traditional movement. "I rejoice when I think of the American Indian Caravan," he wrote. "The Almighty, the Great Spirit, watched and cared for them til they completed the circle. The world was shown that there are yet faithful Indians with a burning desire to stand and represent their people at whatever cost—their livelihood, their homes, loved ones." The caravan also inspired longtime Mohawk activist Ernest Benedict to found the North American Indian Travelling College, with the goal of providing cultural and educational resources to isolated tribal communities while promoting intertribal understanding and unity.[16]

The year 1967 was a watershed in modern American history. As protest strategies shifted from civil disobedience to power politics, a spirit of revolution intensified America's many social contradictions, from military escalation in Southeast Asia to antiwar mobilization in North America, from the "summer of love" for middle-class hippies to the "long hot summer" in urban ghettos. In his study of "the sixties spiritual awakening," Robert Ellwood has interpreted American religion during this period in light of the modern/postmodern debate, arguing that "the modern age in America died, and the new postmodern era was born, in July 1967," a month before tribal traditionalists gathered at Tonawanda. According to Ellwood, sixties spirituality emphasized nonconformity, freedom, relevance, and the natural world, which suggests the decade "may have been not so much an aberration as a restoration" of a classically

American tradition. "In a certain sense," he concludes, "the characteristic sixties religious style was like a recovery of the more fluid, sentimental, charismatic, psychic, magical, communalistic, and righteous-prophetic style of the first decades of the Republic, perhaps especially the 1840s and 1850s, the 'sentimental years' and the heyday of the covered-wagon Western migration."[17]

While many observers have styled modern Native communities as exotic subcultures or denizens of the counterculture, a more historically informed (and less colonial) perspective would recognize the priority of indigenous tradition—call it anteculture. "The new Indian is a religious man," wrote journalist Stan Steiner in his noteworthy 1968 book *The New Indian*. "Land is the measure of life. In his view of the land the tribal Indian denies the values placed on it by the white society. His own values are to him more eternal and essential to the human spirit, having existed before the advent of the barbed wire and commercial fence." As the traditional movement found expression in the institution of the unity convention and caravan, traditionalist leaders measured the land according to spiritual values and forged a communal refuge from the barbs of commerce. They pursued a vision of earthly existence that negates colonial borders and transcends tribal boundaries—the precarious fusion of old and new, of stability and disruption, that is named by the paradoxical juxtaposition "traditional movement."[18]

INDIAN TERRITORY

Inspired by his experiences at the convention and by the rousing mission of the caravan, Clifton Hill returned to his Creek Nation home and worked to spread the gospel of intertribal unity. He was well suited for the task, a Baptist minister fluent in the Muscogee language and active in grassroots political organizing. Born and raised in the small town of Okemah, he had worked as a field hand and also earned some money in the boxing ring as a heavyweight prizefighter. Hill eventually followed his father's footsteps into the ministry and settled in Okmulgee, the Creek Nation capital, where he and his wife, Betty, raised three sons. For many years he served the Baptist church there and in the surrounding Creek communities as preacher, teacher, and itinerant evangelist, establishing a reputation as a prophetic leader devoted to the spiritual—and material—welfare of his people. He also traveled to Washington to testify in congressional hearings on behalf of Creek land claims.[19]

In the spring of 1965 Hill and other traditionalists formed the "Creek Centralization Committee" to advocate for tribal self-determination. The constitutional government of the Creek Nation had been forcibly dissolved by an act of the U.S. Congress in 1906, and since that time the office of principal chief had been filled by puppet leaders appointed by the U.S. president. Meeting in Okmulgee, the committee drafted a new constitution with by-laws and elected Hill as their leader. "All the Creek Centralization Committee desires is a voice in their own affairs and a working, representative government," he explained shortly after the meeting. "We have been fifty-eight years without representation and we do not want a drugstore Indian for a chief. We want a free election, a free voice, just like any other tribe." Hill was especially annoyed by appointed officials who took credit for federally funded projects that provided little relief to poverty-stricken traditionalists: "Why in the SAM HILL do we say we want to help the Indians but we want so much of the Indians' money to programize and so much money for tourists attraction. So much for this and so much for that. Then give the Indians a tiny drop of their own money. This is what some people call helping them. BIG DEAL." Hill also accused various bureaucratic personnel of trying to sabotage the committee's work by threatening supporters with the loss of tribal services.[20]

In January of 1967 the Creek Centralization Committee launched a pair of weekly radio programs in the Muscogee language, broadcast at midday over KOKL in Okmulgee, with Hill serving as programmer and host. A thirty-minute program on Sundays featured announcements, music, and a "non-sectarian" sermon, while a fifteen-minute program on Wednesdays was devoted to news items affecting Hill's Creek and Seminole listeners. His reputation and influence as a traditionalist leader continued to grow, and later that year he was visited by Stan Steiner, who was busy gathering information for his forthcoming book on the "new" Indians. Hill struck Steiner as a prophet, perhaps even a messiah, who drew on tribal traditions and biblical narratives in fashioning a "dirt-farm, grass-roots, backwoods movement" that might just lead his people into a new age of prosperity. Hill likened his effort to that of the biblical David and the legendary Robin Hood, doing battle with a bureaucratic Goliath in order to redistribute economic resources. "I always tell my people we are like little David in the Bible," he explained. "Poor, but stands for justice. . . . Lots of these Indians, they were looking for a man with great intelligency, vast amounts of money, a very educated man. They were always looking for someone like that. That's why I tell my people the story of little David." He continued: "I see myself as a Robin Hood. I take from the rich. And give it to the poor. That's what we need, a Robin Hood type. That's how I see myself." Hill envisioned a day when traditionalists would no longer be dominated by colonial authorities or by "mixed-bloods and educated Indians" and would have control over their own destinies. "Love is what combined our organization, not money or intelligency, but love of the poor. I am proud of being poor. . . . The day of the poor will come. Long as there's breath flows through my veins, long as I am alive, I am going to try to spearhead that. I don't know how in the world I will. But I will."[21]

Hill and his supporters in the Creek Centralization Committee were not the only eastern Oklahoma traditionalists organizing during the sixties. Among the Cherokee neighbors to the northeast, community leaders began meeting in the fall of 1965 to discuss infringements on their culturally indispensable—and treaty-guaranteed—fishing and hunting rights. A loosely knit confederation of traditionalist settlements emerged from these discussions, which they named the "Five County Northeastern Oklahoma Cherokee Organization." Frequent meetings during the months that followed raised a number of pressing issues, including fraudulent land sales, disputes over taxation, discrimination in health care and social services, and administrative neglect. The organization also quickly issued a "Declaration" outlining their concerns. "We meet in a time of darkness to seek the path to the light," it began. "We come together, just as our fathers have always done, . . . We stand united in the sight of God, our creator. We are joined by love and concern for each other and for all men. . . . We offer ourselves as the voice of the Cherokee people." Enumerating a series of changes necessary to insure the survival of the traditional Cherokee way of life, the manifesto concluded: "In the vision of our creator, we declare ourselves ready to stand proudly among the nationalities of these United States of America." A year later Secretary Andrew Dreadfulwater, a respected Keetoowah ceremonial leader and dedicated Baptist layman, was elevated to chairman of the traditionalist group, which he soon renamed the "Original Cherokee Community Organization."[22]

Dreadfulwater and the Original Cherokee Community Organization were joined by Hill and the Creek Centralization Committee in June of 1967 to protest the opening of "Cherokee Village," a tourist attraction built by the tribal government as the first phase of a "Cherokee Cultural Center." Promoted as an authentic reconstruction of a typical eighteenth-century Cherokee settlement, the marketable caricature featured actors wearing yarn wigs and vinyl buckskin costumes living in crude mud huts; anthropologists disputed this primitivist portrayal of "red cave men" and Cherokee traditionalists dubbed it "the zoo." Politicians and developers promised menial jobs for unemployed Cherokees, though local motel and restaurant owners seemed to be the project's most enthusiastic supporters. The National Indian Youth Council also participated in what was billed as the first picket line in Cherokee history, financing leaflets that explained to visitors why the village was opposed by traditionalists, who "teach our children of the days when our prosperous nation had a constitutional government, fine schools, and financial solidity. Can you imagine how it pains us to be presented to you as unlettered savages?" The three groups sponsoring the protest joined forces "to denounce this 'Cherokee Village' as an indignity and a cruel misuse of our living heritage."[23]

In August Hill and other Creek and Cherokee traditionalists traveled to the Tonawanda Seneca reservation for the 1967 unity convention and also met the caravan when it passed through eastern Oklahoma several weeks later. Encouraged by the new sense of intertribal solidarity generated by these events, Hill and Dreadfulwater offered to host another intertribal gathering the following summer. The Creek Centralization Committee and the Original Cherokee Community Organization agreed to cosponsor the "National Aboriginal Traditional Convention" and scheduled the meeting for the first week in June of 1968. Hill's ailing mother offered her forty-acre allotment near Okemah as a gathering site, which she envisioned as "a central meeting place of traditional Indians in the United States and Canada and Mexico, where they could come and exchange their views, prophecies, and medicine and be helpful one to another as the Great Spirit dictates." Hill published an open invitation to the convention in the widely read periodical *Indian Voices* and offered for sale two booklets, titled "A Portion of Indian History, Part I: American Traditional Movement" and "The Whiteman's Climaxing and Crumbling Power Structure." Proceeds from the sale of both were earmarked for building arbors and bathrooms and providing meals at the convention. In April Hill and Thomas Banyacya made presentations at an international conference on education and culture in Chicago, where Hill endorsed a policy of cultural pluralism and self-determination: "We must recognize each other's common and basic spiritual nature, taking into account all of our variety and sameness. Each people thus can contribute to one another's spiritual and material well-being."

Delegates from sixty-five tribes throughout North America attended the 1968 unity convention on the Hill family allotment, some of them arriving in vehicles bearing bumper stickers that read "I Support the North American Indian Unity Caravan." During the week-long gathering they discussed religious traditions and debated political strategies while enjoying the hospitality of their Creek and Cherokee hosts. In the end, they joined hands in a ceremonial embrace and then went their separate ways, looking forward to another opportunity for fellowship with their traditionalist kin.[24]

INTERTRIBAL CONFEDERACY

Iroquois traditionalists who attended the eastern Oklahoma gathering returned home to the turmoil of border conflicts and a change in leadership during the fall of 1968. These external and internal political developments generated increasing interest in pursuing intertribal unity through the traditional movement, which soon gained the support of Leon Shenandoah and the council chiefs. After months of planning and preparation, Beeman Logan opened the 1969 unity convention by welcoming the assembled delegates to the Tonawanda Seneca reservation. It was the morning of August 16; the military establishment had landed their Eagle near the Sea of Tranquillity less than a month earlier, and an army of baby boomers massed at Woodstock were engaged in their own variety of high-altitude exploration while Logan made his opening remarks. "The first step is to unite Indians and then bring them to understand each other," he explained, in a more down-to-earth vein. "We don't understand each other any more. Many of us are enemies. And it is because of the white man. He has separated us so we cannot communicate. . . . Once the Indian begins to understand himself and other Indians, the problems they thought existed between them will disappear." Logan was also intent on stimulating the revival of cultural and religious traditions and led an afternoon thanksgiving ceremony, part of the ancient Iroquois ceremonial cycle.[25]

The convention met for four days at Tonawanda "in an atmosphere of a large family gathering," as one local reporter described it. Only Native people were allowed to attend formal sessions each morning, though the public was invited to participate in dancing and other social activities during the afternoons and evenings. Initial discussions made it clear that almost every reservation community represented at the convention was embroiled in some type of conflict involving land rights or cultural freedoms, and traditionalist leaders were quick to point out the importance of both for the survival of tribal religious traditions. Speakers also expressed concern over the policies of the U.S. Department of the Interior and its Bureau of Indian Affairs. The most controversial item on the agenda, however, was the growing influence of the Red Power movement, a new presence on the Native political landscape. Three Native activists from New York City made impassioned speeches describing their newly formed "Pipe-Tomahawk Clan," an intertribal organization modeled after the Black Panthers.

Most convention participants were reservation traditionalists and showed little interest in the militant tactics advocated by these young urban radicals. Expounding on their Great Law of Peace, Iroquois leaders encouraged all people to pursue nonviolent strategies in protecting the earth and its inhabitants. "My religion and upbringing would not allow me to fight as a militant," confessed Tom Porter, a Mohawk delegate. These traditionalists may have been pacifist, but they were not passive. Porter proposed an intertribal demonstration spanning the continent, a collective act of civil disobedience capable of shaming the Canadian government into responsible behavior. "There are custom houses from the Atlantic to the Pacific, and there are Indians on both sides of the border from the Atlantic to the Pacific," he reminded those present. "We should pick one day during which Indians would take carloads of groceries and challenge every Canadian custom house along the border. What we would do is get arrested."[26]

Several hundred people representing some forty-five tribal nations had arrived at Tonawanda by the time they broke camp on August 20, when the convention caravaned to the Onondaga reservation for another four-day gathering. Shenandoah welcomed his traditionalist colleagues to the Iroquois capital, encouraging them to consider the possibility of joining an expanded confederacy under his leadership. Picking up their discussion of political relations with the United States, delegates issued a statement on August 22 calling for the immediate removal from office of Interior Secretary Walter Hickel and urging tribal leaders to resist any and all federal initiatives until he was gone. A former governor of Alaska, Hickel "destroyed the faith of all Indians toward the U.S. Department of the Interior by his high-handed, inconsiderate and illegal theft [of Alaska Native] tribal lands, rivers, hunting and fishing rights, timber, oil, gas and mineral resources, [and] has declared that he is against Indian people returning to their reservations once they have left them, thereby making the Native American a vagrant in his own country." Calling Hickel "one of the most dangerous men to have jurisdiction over the lands, waters, air and natural resources of the United States, the resolution warned Americans that "he will destroy the sources of life not only for you, but, even more important, the sources of life of your children and grandchildren. . . . He will destroy the very air you breathe in the name of progress. . . . His policies are flagrant violations of the natural laws of our creator, the giver of life." The next day convention delegates issued another statement, this one condemning the death sentence given by a South Dakota judge to Thomas White Hawk, a Rosebud Sioux university student convicted of killing an elderly white businessman. The White Hawk case had become "a symbol to all American Indians of the widespread discriminatory treatment of Indians in the legal systems of most states. Without reference to guilt or innocence, we protest this flagrant injustice, all too typical of the double standard of justice, one for whites and one for Indians, in local courts."[27]

As the Onondaga gathering drew to a close, Shenandoah announced that the unity convention was "coming along well" and that Maniwaki Algonquin traditionalists had expressed interest in joining the Iroquois confederacy. On August 25 convention participants formed another caravan and moved north to the Akwesasne Mohawk reservation, site of the Cornwall Island bridge blockade eight months earlier. Unhappy with media coverage of the convention and concerned about the intrusive presence of reporters at their meetings, delegates decided to bar the non-Native press and issue regular news releases summarizing their deliberations. Animated sessions in the longhouse ensued, debating treaty rights and tribal sovereignty, social problems and natural law, cultural traditions and spiritual revival. At the end of the first day of the Akwesasne gathering, delegates issued a statement addressing the border crossing dispute: "The imposed border that has been recently and illegally created by the United States and Canada has caused grave hardship and has divided our families and has always disrupted our spiritual, traditional way of life. This denies us our religious freedom." The statement also pledged support for Iroquois efforts to negotiate a peaceful resolution with Canadian and American authorities.[28]

In response to requests from the media, convention leaders agreed to hold a press conference. "Society has become sick," spokesman "Mad Bear" Anderson told reporters. "Democracy has failed and Communism will fail too. The only sanity left in the world is the unspoiled spiritual nature of the Indians. . . . Indians will reign supreme again on this continent. We will not always be squashed and Indians are already showing their strength. It's happening so fast, it's hard to keep up with." As one of the Akwesasne hosts, Porter also served as a spokesman and consented to an interview with a Canadian television station, which quizzed him on the goals of the unity convention. Another Mohawk, delegate Mike Mitchell, tried to assure bewildered reporters that the intertribal gathering of traditionalists was "both spiritual and political." Clifton Hill seemed to be enjoying the hospitality of his Akwesasne hosts, though local newspapers used his offhand remarks to portray their reservation neighbors as prosperous compared to other tribal communities, a timeworn strategy for displacing colonial guilt. "Every time I come up here it seems like I've been in hell all my life and I'm coming into some sort of utopia," Hill was quoted as saying. "[Akwesasne] Indians are wealthy people compared to us. . . . Our area is the most poverty-stricken in the United States and it's getting worse. There are hundreds of Indians suffering from acute malnutrition. We hear others talk of poverty, but they haven't had a taste of what we have."

Although local media outlets clearly were interested in convention proceedings and eagerly excerpted comments made by designated spokesmen and other male participants, reporters were not very adept at rendering a demographically accurate portrait of the event. A large photo in the *Massena (NY) Observer* featured Glenna Shilling, a twenty-two-year-old photography student from the Rama Chippewa reserve, but the "many Indian women" described in the caption as being present were otherwise ignored in newspaper accounts of the unity convention. Such obvious gender bias, a familiar failing of the documentary record, certainly does frustrate any historiographical effort that aspires to a balanced representation of personalities and voices.[29]

The three-day council ended on August 28 with a "Joining of the Hands" ceremony. Many considered the Akwesasne gathering to have been the best part of the convention yet, with new tribal delegations joining the group and momentum continuing to grow. As participants prepared for one more caravan, to the Maniwaki Algonquin reserve north of the Canada-U.S. border, Porter and Hill summed up the proceedings. "Our spiritual leaders have given us tranquillity," Porter said. "Indians are not an aggressive people. We believe in equality and brotherhood and peace." Hill agreed: "This convention might not mean we will have more food on the table, but it does mean spiritual revival for Indians. Man can't survive on bread alone."[30]

Canadian border agents quickly realized they were outmatched when a lengthy intertribal motorcade rolled across the Cornwall Island bridge on the morning of August 29, refusing to pay the toll. The caravan arrived at Maniwaki later that day and set up camp for a three-day gathering over the Labor Day weekend, the last stop of the convention. Hundreds of people representing more than seventy-five tribal nations were now present and meetings were moved from the longhouse to a mammoth tent to accommodate the growing throng. Open discussions addressed the suffering caused by boarding schools, unemployment, and alcoholism, and a lively debate over police brutality and militant activism focused on the problem of violence. "The violence is already here!" cried Rose Ojek, an Ojibway from Upper Slave Lake. "There are young Indians in Alberta who are going to burn the schools and the churches. They're not criminals in their hearts, but one of them says he's going to get a huge Caterpillar tractor and go to High Prairie and bulldoze the liquor store, pretend he's drunk. The police arrest them when they get drunk; a girl was arrested for that, and when her brother tried to touch her hand, that she was reaching out of the police car, they arrested him, too, and he got six months! I can't stand it when I hear of talking peace!" Although they disavowed violence, traditionalist leaders did pledge their support for Kahn-Tineta Horn, a young Mohawk woman facing trial on charges related to the Cornwall Island bridge blockade. Delegates also expressed concern over the Canadian government's recent "White Paper" proposing terminationist and assimilationist policies toward tribal communities. They invited Prime Minister Pierre Trudeau to join them for a traditional feast of corn soup and roast beaver with beans baked in sand, but he kept busy vacationing in Europe instead.[31]

The 1969 unity convention drew to a close in formal ceremonies on the first day of September. Convention delegates and other participants had spent over two weeks together, covering some five hundred miles as they caravaned through a pair of colonial nation-states in order to visit four welcoming reservation communities. From the four directions they had come—Algonquin, Penobscot, and Narragansett; Seminole, Creek, and Cherokee; Carib and Nahuatl; Apache, Navajo, Hopi, and Zuni; Shoshone, Washo, and Chumash; Nisqually, Walla Walla, Salish, Blackfeet, and Cheyenne; Chipewyan and Cree; Ojibwa, Winnebago, Potawatomi, and Ottawa; Seneca, Cayuga, Onondaga, Oneida, Mohawk, and Tuscarora—hundreds of men, women, and children united in a traditional circle of politics, prophecy, and peace.

Iroquois activists, inspired by the 1969 unity convention, soon organized a communications collective called "White Roots of Peace" to promote the cause of intertribal solidarity on a year-round basis. In September a dozen traditionalist apostles led by Tom Porter left Akwesasne for a two-month tour of the West Coast, visiting reservation communities, urban centers, college campuses, churches, and prisons. Their public programs typically included traditional music and dancing, thanksgiving prayers, teachings on the Great Law of Peace, and a film documenting the Cornwall Island bridge blockade. *Akwesasne Notes* reported that the itinerant troupe interacted with more than ten thousand people—both Native and non-Native—and was especially active in the San Francisco Bay Area, appearing at the Indian centers in San Francisco and Oakland and meeting with Native students at nearby universities. Porter and company stayed with Richard Oakes, an Akwesasne Mohawk attending San Francisco State University, for two weeks; they made a powerful impression on him and other young activists when they spoke to newly formed ethnic studies classes there and at the University of California in Berkeley. The group eventually left the Bay Area for other engagements, but not before they had stimulated a heightened sense of cultural pride and political power among a number of these energetic urban leaders, who organized themselves as "Indians of All Tribes" and began plotting a takeover of the abandoned prison on Alcatraz Island. White Roots of Peace was on the way home to Akwesasne by the first weekend in November; only one week later Indians of All Tribes laid claim to Alcatraz. "The Rock" was occupied again on November 20 and would remain under Native jurisdiction for nineteen months.[32]

The surprising and highly publicized occupation marked the beginning of a new era in Native activism. Over the next decade many other urban organizations and reservation communities initiated their own occupations and protests, exploiting the media's appetite for confrontational drama, though these radical actions were often trivialized by a consuming audience more interested in images than issues. The militant leaders of the American Indian Movement seized upon this public preference for style over substance and rose to prominence as the most memorable advocates of Red Power. As Robert Ellwood has demonstrated for sixties historiography in general, most historical accounts of intertribal activism during this period have "seen a different Sixties" than did many of its Native participants, in part because "the long-term impacts of spiritual movements are less easily read in the morning headlines than those of political movements." While retrospective studies typically emphasize "the political side of the decade's experience," first-hand reports on grassroots organizing often suggest that "what was really going on was not political but religious or spiritual revolution."

Reservation traditionalists, following the lead of the Onondagas, continued to organize during the early seventies by holding their annual unity conventions/caravans. In 1970 gatherings were hosted by traditionalists among the Creeks, Rosebud Sioux, and Tulalips. At the conclusion of the Tulalip convention in the Pacific Northwest, several dozen people caravaned down the coast to Alcatraz, where they conducted a religious ceremony in support of the occupation. In the summer of 1971 the unity caravan visited eight tribal communities on both sides of the Canada-U.S. border and also stopped at several urban Indian centers along the way. Young militant activists gradually began turning to their traditionalist elders for guidance and support; the twelve-month period beginning in June of 1972 proved to be one of the most dramatic years in the history of modern intertribal activism.[33]

The summer opened with two unity conventions hosted by Penobscot and Creek traditionalists, which were followed by the most extensive caravan yet during the months of July and August. Traditionalists gathered on the fourth of July for a youth convention at the Cattaraugus Seneca reservation, then departed on a cross-continent pilgrimage including more than two dozen scheduled stops, with various tribal delegations joining the caravan at points along the way. A week-long convention near the La Jolla reservation in southern California launched a series of unity meetings throughout the Southwest, including one with Mormons in Salt Lake City. But the movement's peaceful reputation was tarnished when caravan participants and members of the American Indian Movement protested the presence of non-Native visitors at a Hopi snake dance, disrupting the ceremonies and provoking a violent confrontation with Shungopavi villagers. The 1972 caravan ended quietly back in the Iroquois homeland with conventions at the Six Nations and Kahnawake reserves, as summer heat gave way to the calm of autumn.[34]

During the third week of August, while the unity caravan was embroiled in controversy on the Hopi reservation, a group of reservation residents along with members of the American Indian Movement who were gathered at the Rosebud Sioux reservation began discussing the idea of a mass demonstration converging on the U.S. capital. Plans for the cross-country "Trail of Broken Treaties" were finalized by the end of September, and the large caravan arrived in Washington a month later, guided by spiritual leaders and armed with a twenty-point proposal for policy reform. Plans originally called for political negotiations as well as daily activities modeled after the unity conventions: speeches, discussions, ceremonies, and social events in the evenings. Organizers, however, had failed to arrange accommodations for the nonviolent delegation—now several hundred members strong—and within a day local riot police had provoked a confrontation with restless activists, which quickly escalated into an occupation of the Bureau of Indian Affairs headquarters. Protesters agreed to vacate the building a week later, leaving behind a disturbing scene of destruction, a symbolic massacre of bureaucratic proportions. The following February, members of the American Indian Movement joined Oglala Lakota traditionalists at the Pine Ridge reservation, where they occupied the hamlet of Wounded Knee. The militarized standoff lasted more than two months, and its denouement in early May of 1973 marked another turning point in the complex evolution of contemporary Native activism.[35]

Annual unity conventions and caravans had ceased by the midseventies, but the traditional movement lived on in local and regional cultural gatherings and in the global political arena, where traditionalist activists pursued self-determination by testifying before various international tribunals. If intertribal traditionalism failed to effect substantive changes in the political status of traditionalist factions among North America's Native communities, it did achieve some measure of success at facilitating "spiritual revival for Indians." Like many religious movements, the most enduring legacy of the traditional movement can be found in the lives of those who participated in it. Aside from these personal considerations, the movement's greatest heuristic significance may be its witness to the unqualified compatibility between "traditionalism" and "activism," between religious commitment and political praxis, articulating cultural identity as a seamless garment of spiritual and social existence.

NOTES

1. "George A. Thomas Dead at 57, Chief of Iroquois Confederacy," *New York Times*, 24 October 1968, 47; Charles Barney, "Pow-wow Planned by Disturbed Indians," *Syracuse Post-Standard*, 6 January 1969; William N. Fenton, "The Funeral of Tadodaho: Onondaga of Today," *Indian Historian* 3 (spring 1970): 43–47, 66; Laurence M. Hauptman, *The Iroquois Struggle for Survival: World War II to Red Power* (Syracuse NY: Syracuse University Press, 1986), 216–17; Leon Shenandoah, foreword to *White Roots of Peace: The Iroquois Book of Life*, ed. Paul A. W. Wallace (Santa Fe NM: Clear Light Publishers, 1994), 9–15; Doug George-Kanentiio, "Tadodaho," *News from Indian Country*, 15 September 1996, 18A; "Iroquois Gather to Remember Their Spiritual Leader," *Ojibwe News*, 4 October 1996, 2; "In Memoriam Leon Shenandoah: 'A Champion of Indian Rights,'" *Native Americas* 13, no. 2 (1996): 13.

2. Hauptman, *Iroquois Struggle for Survival*, 148–49, 216.

3. "Conference of Indians Called by Area Band in Sequel to Dispute," *Akwesasne Notes* 1, no. 2 (February 1969), first published in *Cornwall (ON) Standard Freeholder*, 23 December 1968; Barney, "Pow-wow Planned"; "Western Hemisphere Meeting of Indians Called," *Akwesasne Notes* 1, no. 3 (March 1969): 14; Herbert G. Pelkey, "Iroquois

Plan Big Meeting for Summer," *Akwesasne Notes* 1, no. 4 (April 1969), first published in *Flint (MI) Journal*, 16 February 1969; Hauptman, *Iroquois Struggle for Survival*, 216.

4. Barney, "Pow-wow Planned; "Plan to Attend!" *Akwesasne Notes* 1, no. 3 (March 1969): 14.

5. Pelkey, "Iroquois Plan Big Meeting"; Gene Goshorn, "Chief Shenandoah Opposes School Integration Proposal for Indians," *Syracuse Herald-Journal*, 5 June 1969; "Indian Unity Convention," *Akwesasne Notes* 1, no. 7 (July 1969): 48; Hauptman, *Iroquois Struggle for Survival*, 218–21.

6. "Plan to Attend!"; "Indians Gather to Form Own Policy, Exchange Views on Minority Plight," *Akwesasne Notes* 1, no. 8 (September 1969): 1.

7. A. M. Rosenthal, "Indian Tribesmen Call at U.N. in Vain," *New York Times*, 9 May 1950, 10; "Iroquois See Vishinsky in Annual U.N. Protest," *New York Times*, 24 October 1950, 9; Elizabeth Chidester Duran, "Clinton Rickard: Chief of the Tuscaroras — Grand President, Indian Defense League of America," *Contemporary Indian Affairs* 1, no. 1 (spring, 1970): 34–48; Jack Forbes, "The New Indian Resistance?" *Akwesasne Notes* 4, no. 3 (late spring 1972): 21; Barbara Graymont, ed., *Fighting Tuscarora: The Autobiography of Chief Clinton Rickard* (Syracuse NY: Syracuse University Press, 1973), 13, 52–53, 75–78, 125–27, 131–32, 161–62; Laurence M. Hauptman, *The Iroquois and the New Deal* (Syracuse NY: Syracuse University Press, 1981), 17, 181; Hauptman, *Iroquois Struggle for Survival*, 5–6, 205–7; Joane Nagel, *American Indian Ethnic Renewal: Red Power and the Resurgence of Identity and Culture* (New York: Oxford University Press, 1996), 160–61; Bill Michelmore, "Keeping Up Tradition," *Niagara Falls (NY) Gazette*, 19 July 1998, 1B.

8. "Hopi Claim Religion Is Bar to Service," *Arizona Republic*, 24 May 1941, 10; Hopi Indian Empire, "Letter to President Harry Truman," in *The Invention of Prophecy: Continuity and Meaning in Hopi Indian Religion* by Armin W. Geertz (Berkeley: University of California Press, 1994), 441–46; "Letter to the Commissioner of Indian Affairs," in *Pages from Hopi History* by Harry C. James (Tucson: University of Arizona Press, 1974), 102–5; Andrew Hermequaftewa, "The Hopi Way of Life Is the Way of Peace," in *Red Power: The American Indians' Fight for Freedom*, ed. Alvin M. Josephy Jr. (New York: McGraw-Hill, 1971), 41–51; Frank Waters, *Book of the Hopi* (New York: Ballantine Books, 1963), 387–95; Earl Shorris, *The Death of the Great Spirit: An Elegy for the American Indian* (New York: Simon and Schuster, 1971), 122–26; Richard O. Clemmer, *Continuities of Hopi Culture Change* (Ramona CA: Acoma Books, 1978), 70–76; Geertz, *Invention of Prophecy*, 139–43, 261–63; Thomas E. Mails and Dan Evehema, *Hotevilla: Hopi Shrine of the Covenant* (New York: Marlowe and Company, 1995), 284–87.

9. Clemmer, *Continuities*, 72, 83; Geertz, *The Invention of Prophecy*, 143–47, 400–403.

10. "Indian League Elects," *New York Times*, 25 June 1956, 14; "Tribe on Wrong Trail," *New York Times*, 19 November 1958, 39; Edmond Wilson, *Apologies to the Iroquois* (New York: Vintage Books, 1960), 137–68, 270–72; Forbes, "New Indian Resistance?" 22; Graymont, *Fighting Tuscarora*, 138–52; Vine Deloria Jr., *Behind the Trail of Broken Treaties: An Indian Declaration of Independence* (New York: Delta Books, 1974), 20–

21; Clemmer, *Continuities*, 84; Hauptman, *Iroquois Struggle for Survival*, 85–178; Jack Forbes, telephone conversation with author, 1 April 1998; Steven Crum, telephone conversation with author, 2 June 1998; Jack Forbes, letter to author, 20 July 1998.

11. "Indians Seize Control of Tribes, Set Up Own Regime in Canada," *New York Times*, 6 March 1959, 8; "One Hundred Indian Raiders Move In on Capital," *New York Times*, 19 March 1959, 35; "Chiefs Back Plan to Unite Indians," *New York Times*, 2 April 1959, 25; Lawrence Fellows, "Grim Omen Sinks in U.N. Channels," *New York Times*, 6 May 1959, 2; "Impasse Persists at U.N. on Friendly Warning of War," *New York Times*, 8 May 1959, 4; Wilson, *Apologies to the Iroquois*, 260–64; Roy Bongartz, "Do These Indians Really Own Florida?" *Saturday Evening Post*, 1 February 1964, 62–65; Bongartz, "The New Indian," *Esquire*, August 1970, 107–8; Forbes, "New Indian Resistance?" 22; Hauptman, *Iroquois Struggle for Survival*, 172, 207–8.

12. Sunbird, Report on Preliminary Eastern Seaboard Conference at Haverford College, Haverford PA, 8–11 April 1961, American Indian Chicago Conference Manuscripts, Box 2, "East Regional Meeting," National Anthropological Archives, Smithsonian Institution, Washington DC; "Board of Directors of the National Indian Youth Council," *Aborigine* 1, no. 1 (1961): iii; "Indian Chiefs Meet for Grand Council," *New York Times*, 23 June 1963, 13; "Francis Le Quier (Ojibwa), Chairman, Committee for the Great Council Fire, 1963," in *The Indian in America's Past*, ed. Jack D. Forbes (Englewood Cliffs NJ: Prentice-Hall, 1964), 72; "The Native American Movement, 1963," in Forbes, *The Indian in America's Past*, 72; Karen Rickard, "Letter to the Editor," *Indian Voices*, April 1964, 12; Robert C. Day, "The Emergence of Activism as a Social Movement," in *Native Americans Today: Sociological Perspectives*, ed. Howard M. Bahr, Bruce A. Chadwick, and Robert C. Day (New York: Harper and Row, 1972), 514–30; Forbes, "New Indian Resistance?" 22; Graymont, *Fighting Tuscarora*, xviii; Clemmer, *Continuities*, 84; Hauptman, *Iroquois Struggle for Survival*, 208–14; Robert K. Thomas, "The Indian Ecumenical Movement: A Grassroots Religious Movement" (lecture delivered at Vancouver School of Theology, Vancouver BC, 21 July 1986); Robert Paul Brown, " 'The Year One': The American Indian Chicago Conference of 1961 and the Rebirth of Indian Activism" (M.A. thesis, University of Wisconsin, 1993), 23–24; Forbes, letter to author.

13. William Rickard, *Report of Land Grab Attempt on the Tuscarora Indian Reserve by the New York State Power Authority* (Niagara Falls NY: Indian Defense League of America, 1959); William Rickard to Anita de Frey, 17 April 1961, American Indian Chicago Conference Manuscripts, Box 2, "East Regional Meeting," National Anthropological Archives, Smithsonian Institution, Washington DC; League of Nations Pan-American Indians, "Civil Rights and the Indians," *Indian Voices*, February–March 1966, 23–24; Vine Deloria Jr., *Custer Died for Your Sins: An Indian Manifesto* (New York: Avon Books, 1969), 25; Graymont, *Fighting Tuscarora*, 154–56; Hauptman, *Iroquois Struggle for Survival*, 161–63, 177, 209–14.

14. Clifton Hill, "Traditional Indians More Active Than Ever," *Indian Voices* winter 1968, 3; American Friends Service Committee, *Uncommon Controversy: Fishing Rights*

of the Muckleshoot, Puyallup, and Nisqually Indians (Seattle: University of Washington Press, 1970), 108–13; James S. Olson and Raymond Wilson, *Native Americans in the Twentieth Century* (Urbana: University of Illinois Press, 1984), 160; Hauptman, *Iroquois Struggle for Survival*, 214.

15. Hill, "Traditional Indians More Active"; Clifton Hill, "Creek Leader Issues Invitation to Meeting," *Indian Voices*, winter 1968, 30–31; *The Great Law of Peace of the Longhouse People* (Mohawk Nation via Rooseveltown NY: *Akwesasne Notes*, [1971?]); Harold Courlander, *The Fourth World of the Hopis* (New York: Crown Publishers, 1971).

16. " 'Mad Bear' Anderson Leads California 'Unity' Trek," *Niagara Falls (NY) Gazette*, 3 September 1967, 1-C; Hill, "Traditional Indians More Active"; Hill, "Creek Leader Issues Invitation," 30–31; "Indian Travelling College No Longer Dream but Reality," *Akwesasne Notes* 1, no. 6 (June 1969); Deloria, *Custer Died for Your Sins*, 117, 242; Vine Deloria Jr., "This Country Was a Lot Better Off When the Indians Were Running It," *New York Times Magazine*, 8 March 1970, 54; Hauptman, *Iroquois Struggle for Survival*, 216, 222; Doug Boyd, *Mad Bear: Spirit, Healing, and the Sacred in the Life of a Native American Medicine Man* (New York : Simon and Schuster, 1994), 28, 31, 65.

17. Robert S. Ellwood, *The Sixties Spiritual Awakening: American Religion Moving from Modern to Postmodern* (New Brunswick NJ: Rutgers University Press, 1994), 185, 331–36.

18. Stan Steiner, *The New Indians* (New York: Dell Publishing Co., 1968).

19. Clifton Hill, "Creek Leader Makes Policy Statement," *Indian Voices*, December 1965, 16–17; Steiner, *New Indians*, 110–15; "Council Candidates," *Muscogee Nation News*, 1989; "Obituaries," *Muscogee Nation News*, December 1990, 11; Jean Chaudhuri and Richinda Sands, "Letter of Thanks," *Muscogee Nation News*, December 1990, 11.

20. Angie Debo, *And Still the Waters Run: The Betrayal of the Five Civilized Tribes* (Princeton: Princeton University Press, 1940), 63–65; "Creek Tribe Fights for Elected Tribal Government," *Indian Voices*, June 1965, 3–4; Hill, "Creek Leader Makes Policy Statement," 16–17; Steiner, *New Indians*, 206.

21. "New Indian Language Program on the Air," *Indian Voices*, December 1966–January 1967, 19; Steiner, *New Indians*, 5–6, 84, 92, 110–15; Vine Deloria Jr., "Religion and Revolution Among American Indians," *Worldview* 17, no. 1 (January 1974): 13.

22. Harry Wilensky, "Cherokee Group on Hunting Laws Warpath over Oklahoma," *Indian Voices*, August 1966, 26–27; "Cherokee Advocate to Be Revived," *Indian Voices*, December 1966–January 1967, 5–6; "New Indian Language Program"; Steiner, *New Indians*, 1–16; Sol Tax and Robert K. Thomas, "An Experiment in Cross-Cultural Education, 1962–1967: Report of the University of Chicago," in *The Study of the Education of Indian Children, 90th Congress, 1st and 2nd sessions, February 19, 1968, Twin Oaks, OK*, ed. Special Subcommittee on Indian Education, U.S. Senate Committee on Labor and Public Welfare (Washington DC: USGPO, 1968), 949–50; Peter Collier, *When Shall They Rest? The Cherokees' Long Struggle with America* (New York: Holt, Rinehart and Winston, 1973), 141–44; Albert L. Wahrhaftig and Jane Lukens-Wahrhaftig, "New Militants or

Resurrected State? The Five County Northeastern Oklahoma Cherokee Organization," in *The Cherokee Indian Nation: A Troubled History*, ed. Duane H. King (Knoxville: University of Tennessee Press, 1979), 230–38; Kenneth Fink, "A. Dreadfulwater: In Memoriam," *Interculture* 17, no. 4 (October–December 1984): 25.

23. "First Cherokee Picket Line Surprises Village Guests," *Indian Voices*, winter 1968, 13–15; Wahrhaftig and Wahrhaftig, "New Militants," 238.

24. Hill, "Creek Leader Issues Invitation," 30–31; "Rolling Thunder Speaks," *Akwesasne Notes* 1, no. 6 (June 1969): 36–38; Clifton Hill, "A Petition to the Education for Mankind Conference, Chicago, IL, April 1968," in "At the Fork in Our Trail," by Stand Middlestriker [Robert K. Thomas], [1977?] (National Indian Youth Council, Albuquerque NM, photocopy), 211–12; Thomas Banyacya, "A Message to the Education for Mankind Conference, Chicago IL, April 1968," in Middlestriker, "At the Fork in Our Trail," 213–14; Deloria, *Custer Died for Your Sins*, 25, 117.

25. Mike Power, "1,000 at Parley Light Pipe of Unity," *Akwesasne Notes* 1, no. 8 (September 1969): 5; Hauptman, *Iroquois Struggle for Survival*, 216–17.

26. Power, "Pipe of Unity," 5; "6 Indian Nations Gather in Effort to Save Lands," *Akwesasne Notes* 1, no. 8 (September 1969): 5; "Iroquois Will Rule Land Again Indians Told," *Akwesasne Notes* 1, no. 8 (September 1969): 6; "Mohawk Indian Wants to Fight against Customs with Groceries," *Akwesasne Notes* 1, no. 8 (September 1969): 5; Charles Russo, "Unity Hope of Indians," *Syracuse Herald Journal*, 20 August 1969.

27. Russo, "Unity"; Michael O'Toole, "Indian Unity Weighed," *Syracuse Post-Standard*, 22 August 1969; "46 Indian Tribes Ask Hickel Ouster," *New York Times*, 24 August 1969, 87; Charles Russo, "Indians Find Theme Accord," *Syracuse Herald American*, 24 August 1969; Michael O'Toole, "Indians Issue Protest, End Council on Unity," *Syracuse Post-Standard*, 25 August 1969; Dick Macdonald, "Enforce Law Fairly—Indians," *Akwesasne Notes* 1, no. 8 (September 1969): 4; Gerald Vizenor, "Thomas White Hawk," in *Crossbloods: Bone Courts, Bingo, and Other Reports* (Minneapolis: University of Minnesota Press, 1990), 101–51.

28. O'Toole, "Indians Issue Protest"; "Indians Gather to Form Own Policy"; Leonard H. Prince, "Indians Protest Curb on Travel Freedom between U.S.-Canada," *Akwesasne Notes* 1, no. 8 (September 1969): 4, first published in *Massena (NY) Observer*, 28 August 1969.

29. "Indians Gather to Form Own Policy"; Prince "Indians Protest Curb," 4; "St. Regis Is Paradise Says Oklahoma Indian," *Akwesasne Notes* 1, no. 8 (September 1969): 5; "Chiefs Gather in Longhouse: Hope to Improve Indian Life," *Akwesasne Notes* 1, no. 8 (September 1969): 6.

30. Prince, "Indians Protest Curb," 4; "St. Regis Is Paradise"; "Indians Plan Unity Ceremony," *Akwesasne Notes* 1, no. 8 (September 1969): 5.

31. Macdonald, "Enforce Law Fairly"; Roy Bongartz, "The New Indian," 107–8, 125–26.

32. John Lawson, "Iroquois Leader Seeking Better Deal for Indians," *Akwesasne Notes* 1, no. 9 (October 1969); "White Roots of Peace," *Akwesasne Notes* 1, no. 9 (October

1969); Troy R. Johnson, *The Occupation of Alcatraz Island: Indian Self-Determination and the Rise of Indian Activism* (Urbana: University of Illinois Press, 1996), 40–41, 51; "An Interview with Tommy Porter," in *People of the Seventh Fire*, ed. Dagmar Thorpe (Ithaca NY: Akwe:kon Press, 1996), 38; Steve Talbot, "Indian Students and Reminiscences of Alcatraz," in *American Indian Activism: Alcatraz to the Longest Walk*, ed. Troy Johnson, Joane Nagel, and Duane Champagne (Urbana: University of Illinois Press, 1997), 105–6; Luis S. Kemnitzer, "Personal Memories of Alcatraz, 1969," in *American Indian Activism*, 116–17.

33. Macdonald, "Enforce Law Fairly"; "Indian Land Calendar," *Akwesasne Notes* 2, no. 4 (July–August 1970): 47; "North American Indian Unity Convention," in *The Way: An Anthology of American Indian Literature*, ed. Shirley Hill Witt and Stan Steiner (New York: Alfred A. Knopf, 1972), 229–31, first published in *Indian Magazine*, [1970?]; "Indian Land Calendar," *Akwesasne Notes* 3, no. 3 (April 1971): 3; "Indian Land Calendar," *Akwesasne Notes* 3, no. 5 (June 1971): 3; "Indian Land Calendar," *Akwesasne Notes* 3, no. 6 (July–August 1971): 3; Hauptman, *Iroquois Struggle for Survival*, 217; Rex Weyler, *Blood of the Land: The Government and Corporate War Against First Nations*, rev. ed. (Philadelphia: New Society Publishers, 1992), 43–44; Ellwood, *Sixties Spiritual Awakening*, 7–8; Johnson, *Occupation of Alcatraz Island*, 137–38.

34. "Indian Land Calendar," *Akwesasne Notes* 4, no. 2 (early spring 1972): 3; "Traditional Indian Unity Caravan," *Akwesasne Notes* 4, no. 3 (late spring 1972): 3; "Traditional Indian Unity Caravan," *Akwesasne Notes* 4, no. 5 (early autumn 1972): 8; Louis Hall, "Longhouse News: Caughnawaga's First Traditional Indian Unity Convention Held," *Akwesasne Notes* 4, no. 5 (early autumn 1972): 32; Vine Deloria Jr., "The Theological Dimension of the Indian Protest Movement," *Christian Century*, 19 September 1973, 913; Harry C. James, *Pages from Hopi History* (Tucson: University of Arizona Press, 1974), 218–20.

35. "'Trail of Broken Treaties' Caravan Moves on Washington D.C.," *Akwesasne Notes* 4, no. 6 (late autumn 1972); Richard La Course, "The Beginning of the Trail," *Akwesasne Notes* 5, no. 1 (early winter 1973): 3; *Trail of Broken Treaties: B.I.A. I'm Not Your Indian Anymore* (Mohawk Nation via Rooseveltown NY: Akwesasne Notes, [1973?]); *Voices from Wounded Knee, 1973: In the Words of the Participants* (Mohawk Nation via Rooseveltown NY: Akwesasne Notes, 1974); Paul Chaat Smith and Robert Allen Warrior, *Like a Hurricane: The Indian Movement from Alcatraz to Wounded Knee* (New York: New Press, 1996), 139–68.

Freedom, Law, and Prophecy

A Brief History of Native American
Religious Resistance

LEE IRWIN

In August 1978, the American Indian Religious Freedom Act (AIRFA) was passed by Congress as a guarantee of constitutional protection of First Amendment rights for Native Americans. This act was passed as an attempt to redress past wrongs by the federal government or its agents. That history of legal suppression was due to "the lack of a clear, comprehensive and consistent Federal policy [which] has often resulted in the abridgement of religious freedom for traditional American Indians." The summary text of this act states:

Henceforth it shall be the policy of the United States to protect and preserve for American Indians their inherent right of freedom to believe, express, and exercise the traditional religions of the American Indian, Eskimo, Aleut, and Native Hawaiians, including but not limited to access to sacred sites, use and possession of sacred objects and freedom to worship through ceremonials and traditional rites.[1]

It is perhaps hard for those unfamiliar with the history of Native American religious oppression to realize that in our own lifetimes it continues to be difficult or impossible for Native Americans to freely practice their religions. The suppression of those practices has been pervasive to such a degree that AIRFA has proven to be insufficient to grant the freedom that many Native Americans feel is necessary for the complete affirmation of their respective religious identities.

What is the background that necessitated AIRFA and what directions have issues of religious affirmation taken since this act became law? Perhaps the most suppressive laws regarding religious freedom were those promulgated by the Bureau of Indian Affairs for the Indian Courts, known as the Indian Religious Crimes Code. These laws were first developed in 1883 by Secretary of the Interior Henry Teller as a means to prohibit Native American ceremonial activity under pain of imprisonment. Teller's general guidelines to all Indian agents ordered them to discontinue dances and feasts as well as instructing them to take steps with regard to all medicine men, "who are always found in the anti-progressive party . . . to compel these impostors to abandon this deception and discontinue their practices, which are not only without benefit to them but positively injurious to them."[2]

Religious offenses on the reservations were later codified by the Commissioner of Indian Affairs, Thomas J. Morgan, in 1892 in his "Rules for Indian Courts," whereby he established a series of criminal offenses aimed at Native American religious practices. He wrote:

Dances — Any Indian who shall engage in the sun dance, scalp dance, or war dance, or any similar feast, so called, shall be guilty of an offense, and upon conviction thereof shall be punished for the first offense by with holding of his rations for not exceeding ten days or by imprisonment for not exceeding ten days; for any subsequent offense under this clause he shall be punished by withholding his rations for not less than ten days nor more than thirty days, or by imprisonment for not less than ten days nor more than thirty days.

Medicine men — Any Indian who shall engage in the practices of so-called medicine men, or who shall resort to any artifice or device to keep the Indians of the reservation from adopting and following civilized habits and pursuits, or shall use any arts of conjurer to prevent Indians from abandoning their barbarous rites and customs, shall be deemed guilty of an offense, and upon conviction thereof, for the first offense shall be imprisoned for not less than ten days and not more than thirty days: Provided that, for subsequent conviction for such offense the maximum term or imprisonment shall not exceed six months.[3]

These laws not only abrogate First Amendment rights in a conscious and well-documented policy of religious oppression, they also reveal a systematic attempt on the part of highly placed government officials to stamp out Native American religious practices. They also represent a determined policy to reconstruct Native religions in conformity with dominant Protestant majority values in a myopic vision of what constitutes "civilized" religious behavior. Such policy is found consistently in the Annual Reports of many commissioners of Indian Affairs from the creation of the office in 1832 through the appointment of John Collier in 1934.[4]

These oppressive policies can be traced through the writings of not only the Indian commissioners and other heads of state who managed Indian affairs such as various secretaries of state (after 1849) as well as various secretaries of war (1824–48), to an even earlier policy, that of the 1819 Indian Civilization Fund Act, the primary intent of which was to create a fund to reform and "civilize" Indian peoples in accordance with alien cultural norms imposed on them by a conquering majority.[5] Where this proved impossible or undesirable, the Indian Civilization Act also called for the more insidious policy of Indian removal, generally to the west and thus away from encroaching Euroamerican settlement. The mandate for determining Indian affairs by government officials can be further traced back to the 1783 First Continental Congress Indian Proclamation which says, "The United States in Congress assembled have the sole and exclusive right and power of regulating trade and managing all affairs with the Indians."[6] This set in place the legal precedent by which Indian peoples were denied religious freedom, imposing exclusively non-Native standards of legitimacy. Pushing back even further, it is significant that in the United States Constitution only five words can be found that refer to any Native peoples, these words involving only trade and taxation agreements.[7]

What strategies have Native peoples followed in responding to this crushing onslaught against their spiritual lives, goods, and diverse religious practices? In general, there has been a range of strategies in a spectrum between two major alternatives: accommodation or resistance. As Gregory Dowd has argued, the late 1700s and early 1800s was a period of resistance by Native people against Anglo-American settlement, a time of "widespread intertribal activity" in which various Native peoples sought to solve the challenges of cultural and political encroachment while also being deeply influenced by events affecting other tribes.[8] On the religious front, some groups, like the Cherokee and other southeastern peoples, tried to accommodate the new way of life introduced by settlement, taking up Anglo farming as well as taking a receptive interest in the teachings of Christianity. Significantly, the strategy of accommodation often was promoted by those in upper echelon leadership roles (like John Ross among the Cherokee) who often had diminishing contact with the most traditional ways of life as a result of intermarriages, exposure to Anglo-European education, or wealth accrued through non-Native economic practices.[9]

However, this strategy of accommodation proved to be primarily a one-way accommodation; that is, while Native groups struggled to adapt or accommodate the invading Anglo-Europeans, this accommodation was rarely if ever reciprocated. Such one-way accommodation often proved fatal, such as in the Cherokee case when, after many years of often successful adaptation and conformity to alien values and lifeways, they were forced off their lands through the greed and racist mentality of the Georgia legislature that revoked their political rights after gold was discovered on Cherokee lands. The federal government then forced Cherokees to take the Trail of Tears in the fateful winter of 1838 when so many Cherokee people died.[10] Thus the strategy of accommodation has its own tragic history and has largely been nonreciprocal, often resulting in a subordination of Native concerns to those of the dominating political hierarchies on state and federal levels.

Over against the strategy of accommodation is the resistance or revivalist movements that increasingly emphasized the importance of traditional Native values, indigenous religious orientations, and the need to abandon all dependency on non-Native goods or ideas. Often, the origins of this resistance came from a variety of Native religious leaders who emphatically called for an assertion of Native beliefs and practices as an affirmation of intrinsic, inherited spiritual values and as a rallying cry for the preservation of the many diverse paths found in Native religious life. At the extreme pole of this response, "nativistic" came to mean not a return to the past in an ideal or artificial, utopian sense, but a preservation of core indigenous values and beliefs as a basis for cultural survival, a survival that might include a diverse synthesis of alternative religious ideas or practices. This affirmation was strengthened by the emergence of a significant number of prophetic spiritual leaders whose visionary experiences confirmed and celebrated Native religious orientation as a primary source of empowerment for resisting colonial advancement. In many cases, this prophetic leadership was forced to advocate a militant resistance and a strategy of complex alliances, often turning hostile in the face of non-Native aggression while also rejecting any form of unilateral, submissive accommodation.[11]

Examples of this prophetic leadership are many, extending from coast to coast in the wake of increasing patterns of political and cultural domination. The corrosive effects of trans-Appalachian conflicts through the forced migrations of east coast indigenous peoples, the uninhibited spread of the rum and whiskey trade, and various Anglo-European armed conflicts (and later American military aggression) all contributed to a necessarily defensive stance on the part of Native peoples.[12] A responsive religious leadership began to emerge among Native peoples in the form of empowered individuals whose messages were oriented to more apocalyptic visions in which non-Native aggressors would be defeated, destroyed, or pushed back depending on the degree to which Native peoples could re-affirm traditional values corrupted by colonial advancement.

As early as 1752, Munsee religious leader Papounhan received a vision while mourning the death of his father that he should lead the Munsee people in a restoration of their Native traditions that had been nearly lost as a result of European contact.[13] The Delaware prophet Neolin, in the 1760s, was one of four such prophetic leaders who arose to reaffirm through personal visions the importance of traditional religious values and in fact influenced Pontiac's resistance during his so-called "conspiracy" of 1763. In 1776, Wangomen, another Delaware prophet, also advocated a return to Native values and religion. He condemned a number of Euroamerican practices such as slavery and the use of alcohol and tried to lead the Delaware to a renewed affirmation of traditional Delaware values.[14] Around 1800, Handsome Lake, a Seneca prophet, perhaps a bit more of an accommodationist, received a religious revelation that combined elements of Christianity and core Senecan religious practices. Preaching the Gaiwiio or Good Word, Handsome Lake led the Iroquois in reorganizing their economic, social, and religious lives along lines that combined traditional Iroquois religious practices and beliefs with elements from Christianity.[15]

By the early 1800s on the Northwest Coast, many such prophetic and charismatic figures appeared in a sequence of revitalizing spiritual movements, all advocating a new rebirth of older religious patterns as a means for the affirmation and survival of indigenous tribal identities. The Spokane leaders Yurareechen (Circling Raven), the Flathead leader Shining Shirt, and the Umatilla religious leader Dlaupác, all preached the importance of preserving indigenous traditions. Dlaupác predicted ominous and apocalyptic scenarios in the wake of the arrival of Euroamerican settlers, including a prediction of the complete destruction of the Indian way of life as well as the destruction of the world through flood or fire.[16] In the east, prior to 1812, Tenskataaw (Open Door), the Shawnee prophet and brother of Tecumseh, sparked the first intertribal confederacy that united many thousands of diverse Native peoples around a religiously motivated resistance movement. Tenskataaw emphasized a return to indigenous values as a result of a visionary journey he had during a near death experience. He condemned intermarriage and all contact with Europeans and urged a return to traditional communal values. He traveled extensively throughout the tribes with his message of spiritual and political renewal.[17] Around this same time Hildis Hadjo (or Josiah Francis), the Creek Prophet, also led a movement that combined resistance to Anglo-European ways with a return to Native values in the face of cultural erosion.[18]

Throughout the nineteenth century, revitalization movements continued along the front of advancing Anglo-American settlement, as tribal displacements made life increasingly more difficult and bitter for Native peoples. In 1820, Yonaguska (Drowning-Bear), a Cherokee prophet, as a result of a visionary experience at the age of sixty, promulgated traditional Cherokee values, promoted antialcoholism, and resisted removal talk, emphasizing the need to retain ancestral ties to the Blue Ridge mountains as intrinsic to Cherokee spiritual life.[19] In 1832, Kenekuk, a Kickapoo spiritual leader, led the Kickapoo to Illinois when they were displaced by settlers as a result of the 1832 Indian Removal Act promulgated by Andrew Jackson. While Kenekuk assimilated some features of Christianity into his teachings, he also emphasized the maintenance of core Kickapoo religious values and practices as essential for Kickapoo survival. The Kickapoo under his leadership resisted standardized education and land division, refused to learn English, and engaged in Kickapoo dances and singing during religious ceremonies.[20] In the mid-1850s, other Nativistic religious movements in the Northwest were underway, led by Smohalla, the Wanapam dreamer-prophet and Washani religious revitalizer. Smohalla's teachings, which emphasized a return to Native traditions and the abandonment of alien goods and ideas, acted as a catalyst for tribal confederation during the Yakima Wars of 1855–56 against Anglo-American encroachment and government plans to confine the Northwest peoples onto small and inadequate reservations. Those who kept the old Washani spiritual ways would be resurrected after death and their traditional world would be restored to them.[21] Smohalla, like many other *yantcha* or "spiritual leaders" of the Northwest emphasized non-violence and peaceful co-existence with non-Natives (as did Kenekuk and Drowning Bear) while still seeking to return to older ways and indigenous spiritual values.

From this period forward, many such prophetic movements arose, all emphasizing Native values and traditional religions, with varying degrees of accommodation with Christian beliefs—but all stressing the importance of a return to basic core values and indigenous practices. The culmination of this movement, what Leslie Spier has called the Prophet Dance tradition, was transmitted by the 1860s dreamer-prophet, Wodziwob, a Paiute of central California, to Tavibo, the father of the Nevada Paiute, Wovoka, the visionary founder of the Ghost Dance of 1889. Again, this visionary history of spirit dancing became a rallying cry for many different Native peoples throughout the Great Plains area, illustrating the intertribal effects of Native prophetic movements and their often unifying character. Many different tribes sent representatives to meet with Wovoka who then instructed them in Ghost Dances rites. These rites were then transported back to the Plains tribes as a revelation of greatest import—the practice of the dance was to result in the return of the old way of life now rapidly diminished, a return of the buffalo, and the expulsion of Anglo-Americans from Native lands.[22] The tragic consequence of the Lakota practice of this dance resulted in the U.S. Army's slaughter of eighty-four men, forty-four women, and eighteen children at Wounded Knee, in December 1890. The victims of this massacre are buried in a mass grave on the Pine Ridge reservation. This site, a stain on the American national conscience, continues to be a historic monument of the tragic and aggressive assault on Native religious life. Even though the Ghost Dance continued sporadically, as among the Kiowa, the unprovoked destruction of the Lakota people as they attempted to arbitrate their rights to practice Native religions, had a shocking, suppressive force on all Native religious practices.[23]

It is around the time of the events at Wounded Knee that the most suppressive measures against Native religions were promoted through the "Rules of Indian Courts" instigated by Commissioner Thomas J. Morgan, nominal head of the BIA under the Secretary of the Interior. Morgan also wrote in his 1889 Annual Report:

The Indians must conform to "the white man's ways," peaceably if they will, forcibly if they must. . . . The tribal relations should be broken up, socialism destroyed, and the family and the autonomy of the individual substituted. The allotment of lands in severalty, the establishment of local courts and police, the development of a personal sense of independence and the universal adoption of the English language are the means to this end.[24]

A similar Canadian law also was promoted, the 1884 Canadian Indian Act that made Native potlatch or giveaways illegal and participants subject to a misdemeanor and imprisonment from two to six months. Similarly repressive laws were introduced and approved by the Canadian legislature in 1895, 1914, and 1933.[25]

The darkest and most difficult times for the practice of Native religions and ways of life was the post–Civil War period up to the mid-twentieth century. During this period Sun Dancing and other such rites were made illegal, suppressed by government Indian agents as "barbaric and uncivilized." In accordance with the Grant Peace Policy, the Board of Indian Commissioners was formed in 1869. Their first report noted that the duties of the board were "to educate the Indians in industry, the arts of civilization, and the principles of Christianity." This board was given joint control with the secretary of the interior over congressional funds appropriated for dealing with the Indian agencies. Christian missionaries of all denominations were given government support for the founding of missions on Indian reservation land on seventy-three agencies. In 1872, Commissioner of Indian Affairs Walker reported that agents from the most Protestant denominations were appointed "to assume charge of the intellectual and moral education of the Indians thus brought within the reach of their influence."[26] During this time, Native children were forcibly shipped to Christian missionary schools where they were denied the rights to speak Native languages, to wear Native clothing, or to practice any form of Native religion.[27] Missionary zeal specifically targeted Native religions as the bane of all civilized Christian ideology. Subsequent missionary activities caused "fractions, feuds and schisms, discredited popular leaders and imposed new ones on the Indians and in scores of ways undermined and weakened the unity of the tribes."[28] Indian ceremonies were banned, religious practices disrupted, and sacred objects destroyed or confiscated.

Some renewal movements did continue, such as the turn of the century Four Mothers Society of the Natchez-Creek based on a return to the old Southeast ceremonial tradition. Membership in the Four Mothers Society linked traditional full-bloods from the Natchez, Creek, Cherokee, Choctaw, Chickasaw, and Seminole in Oklahoma. In 1900 there was a resistance to allotment led by the Creek spiritual leader Chitto Harjo (Crazy Snake), who formed a Chitto or Snake Society, members of which were dedicated to preserving the old Creek spiritual way and to resisting political encroachment. In 1902 Redbird Smith, breaking away from the Four Mothers Society, led a renewal of the Oklahoma

Cherokee Ketoowa or Night-Hawk Society and laid out a traditional ceremonial ground on Blackgum Mountain. This effort established a new sacred fire from which twenty-two more traditional fires were started spreading a traditionalist spiritual movement among the older Cherokee population.[29] In the Northwest, in 1910, the Nisqually John Slocum established the Shaker Church in Olympia, Washington. As a result of a visionary experience, Slocum and his wife promoted a religious movement that brought together Native people from many different tribes throughout the Northwest and California in a synthesis of prophetic Native indigenous beliefs and reinterpreted Christianity.[30] In 1918 the Native American Church (NAC) was legally incorporated in Oklahoma in resistance to congressional efforts to make possession and transportation of peyote illegal, though seventeen states passed laws making the use of peyote illegal.[31]

During the early twentieth century, however, Native religious reaffirmation movements tended to decline as indigenous peoples struggled to survive under the appalling and oppressive political circumstances. In 1906, the Act for the Preservation of American Antiquities (APAA), while making it a criminal offense to appropriate, excavate, injure, or destroy historic or prehistoric ruins or monuments or objects of antiquity located on lands owned or controlled by the U.S. government, also defined dead Indians or Indian artifacts as "archaeological resources" and converted these persons and objects into federal "property," thereby further depriving Native peoples of the right to dispose of their dead or to maintain possession of sacred objects as reservation lands were under federal jurisdiction.[32]

Indian religions, many still espousing a commitment to Native religious practices, went underground, into the Kivas, out of sight, into the back hills and hidden valleys of the reservations. Many religious leaders still refused to accommodate the larger cultural imperium. In 1934, John Collier was appointed as the Commissioner of Indian Affairs and the Indian Reorganization Act was passed. This act ended allotment, allowed for the appointment of Native people to the BIA without civil service requirements, and encouraged the formation of tribal governments—but only with a written constitution and accompanying by-laws approved by the Department of the Interior. Secretary of the Interior Harold Ickes approved of Collier's BIA Circular 2970 titled "Indian Religious Freedom and Indian Culture," which was sent to all agencies and stated that "no interference with Indian religious life or ceremonial expression will hereafter be tolerated." This circular represents the government's first specific policy statement made to protect Native American religious rights.[33]

Still, the long history of religious oppression was by no means ended as government policy and legislation continued to undermine the solidarity and cohesion of reservation life. In 1940 the Fish and Wildlife Service of the

Department of the Interior "issued regulations restricting the taking, possessing and transporting of bald and golden eagles or their parts" as a result of the Bald (and later Golden) Eagle Protection Act. This made the use of eagle feathers a federal offense and individual spiritual leaders and traditional practitioners were persecuted under this act.[34] Displacement from reservation lands in the mid-1950s to forced relocations in urban environments, as epitomized by the 1954 Mennominee Termination Act, further added to disorientation and spiritual loss as many families were paid to move into large cities where promised job opportunities and employment failed to materialize. Thousands of indigenous people found themselves alienated from reservation life, living in "red ghettos" where crime, poverty and alcoholism escalated to extreme proportions.[35] In 1959, a court case between the Native American Church and the Navajo Tribal Council resulted in a ruling from the Tenth Circuit Court of Appeals that "The First Amendment applies only to Congress. . . . No provision in the Constitution makes the First Amendment applicable to Indian nations nor is there any law of Congress doing so." This decision severely limited the freedom and legal rights of Native peoples to seek redress from religious oppression or discrimination.[36] As late as 1971, Sun Dancers were being arrested on Pine Ridge by tribal police because the tribal judge issued an injunction against Sun Dancing.[37]

The first contemporary resistance movement came with the formation of yet another Nativistic survival movement, this time led by younger Native American political activists, in the form of the American Indian Movement (AIM). In 1968, George Mitchell and Dennis Banks (Chippewas) founded AIM in Minneapolis in an attempt to force better treatment for inner-city Native peoples harassed constantly by police and other city officials. Shortly thereafter, Clyde and Vernon Bellecourt (Chippewa) and Russell Means (Oglala) joined AIM and, in 1969, AIM members joined with other Native peoples in the occupation of Alcatraz Island as "Indian land" in the first public re-affirmation of Red Power since Wounded Knee. In August 1972, AIM members went to the Lakota Crow Dog Sun Dance at Pine Ridge where traditional spiritual leaders gave their support to the movement. The "spiritual rebirth" of Indian rights was affirmed as a union between traditional religious and political leaders espousing a revival of Native identity and a rebirth of Native religious practices as a means for political empowerment. AIM became the spearhead in the effort to secure tribal rights, authentic religious practices, and governmental redress of past wrongs and oppression. Increasing confrontations between AIM leaders and non-Native authorities, as well as opposition from government-supported tribal leaders at Pine Ridge, resulted in numerous shoot-outs and yet another battle and standoff at Wounded Knee (Feb–May 1973) as AIM members confronted state and federal authorities. While no redress was given after AIM members and tribal religious leaders surrendered at Wounded Knee (562 were arrested, yet only fifteen were found guilty of a crime), from this time forward visible redress of Native rights begins to surface in government policy.[38]

In 1973, all attempts at tribal termination officially ended; in 1974 the Indian Self-Determination and Education Assistance Act (ISDEAA) authorized the secretary of the interior to implement "an orderly transition from federal domination of programs for and services to Indians to effective and meaningful participation by Indian people in the planning, conduct, and administration of those programs and services." This act allowed for contracts and grants to train Native people to operate programs they might want to take over in full, as well as for the disbursement of funds more directly to reservation populations and the election of Native peoples to official positions within governmental institutions and programs.[39] In 1978, the Indian Child Welfare Act assured that there will be no more governmentally enforced education or the "forcible and systematic transferring of care of Indian children to non-Natives through compulsory boarding schools and adoption to non-Natives."[40] And in 1978, the American Indian Religious Freedom Act (AIRFA) was passed.

In 1979, the Archaeological Resources Protection Act (ARPA) attempted to redress the 1906 Act for the Preservation of American Antiquities by ruling that permits must be obtained for excavations of sites more than one hundred years old, that consent must be obtained for any work on tribal Indian lands by tribal landowners, and that work on public lands held to be sacred by any tribes requires those tribes to be notified before any permits are granted. However, human remains on federal lands are still "archaeological resources" and "property of the United States" which, if excavated under federal permit, can be "preserved by a suitable university, museum or other scientific or educational institution."[41] This act still undercuts the rights of Native peoples to claim legitimate control over ancestral dead territorially identified as under federal jurisdiction and inhibits religious claims about how those ancestral dead (now or previously unearthed) should be treated.

In 1987, the National Park Service issued a policy statement in response to AIRFA, to explore means for integrating the needs of Native religious practitioners into park resource management. The statement clearly says that Native religious claims "must be within the bounds of existing legislation as well as NPS rules and policies" thereby subordinating Native religious needs and practices to pre-existing government regulations.[42] Also in 1987, the Iroquois Recognition Bill was passed "to acknowledge the contribution of the Iroquois Confederacy of Nations in the development of the United States Constitution and to reaffirm the continuing government-to-government relationship between tribes and the United States established in the Constitution." In 1989, the National Museum of the American Indian Act (NMAIA) provided for the repatriation of

Native human remains collected by the Smithsonian Institution to American Indian tribes upon tribal request. The Smithsonian must inventory and, where possible, identify its collection of remains (18,000), notify appropriate tribal groups, and return them if the tribes requests—Blackfeet reburial of 16 ancestral remains occurred in 1989; and 700 remains presently are being returned to Kodiak Island cemetery.[43] Previous to this, in the 1980s, the Denver Art Museum returned War Gods to the Zuni; the Heard Museum in Phoenix returned Kiva masks to Hopi elders; the Wheelwright Museum returned 11 medicine bundles to Navajo; the State Museum of New York in Albany returned 12 wampum belts to Six Nation Confederacy and a clan bundle to the Hidatsa; the Boston Peabody Museum returned the sacred pole (plus 270 other artifacts) to the Omaha; and many others have made nominal returns as well. But many museums and institutions have ignored requests. For example, the Iroquois request for return of all their sacred masks has not been met.[44]

In 1990, Native American Grave Protection and Repatriation Act (NAGPRA) was passed. This act protects Indian gravesites from looting and requires repatriation of all culturally identifiable tribal artifacts. According to the act, museums must inventory collections and notify tribes of their holdings. Legal procedures are established for reclaiming artifacts, though claimants must meet strict legal tests.[45] However, NAGPRA does not apply to state land or private property. By 1991, thirty-two states had laws that dealt with reburial and repatriation of ancestral prehistoric remains; but there is little consistency among the laws passed and many do not involve goods found on private property.[46] As Walter and Roger Echo-Hawk have written, "criminal statues in all fifty states very strictly prohibit grave desecration, grave robbing, and mutilation of the dead—yet they are not applied to protect Indian dead . . . [Native dead are still] 'federal property' to be used as chattels in the academic marketplace."[47]

In 1993, the Religious Freedom Restoration Act (RFRA) was passed and signed into law, thereby compelling the government not to "substantially burden religious exercise without compelling justification" and to "provide a claim or defense to persons whose religious exercise is substantially burdened by government." While this act may help to redress future infringement of Native American religious rights, it does not mention those rights specifically. This brings us fully into the present with the 1994 Native American Free Exercise of Religion Act (NAFERA). NAFERA is a bill amending the 1978 American Indian Religious Freedom Act (AIRFA) and includes, among other things, specific protections for the use of peyote by Native American Church members as well as protecting the religious rights of Native American prisoners who wish to practice traditional Native religions. The NAFERA bill was proposed as a means to put teeth into the policy statement of the 1978 act which has been largely perceived as ineffectual in court cases involving Native American religious freedom.[48] As of 1995, no government agency has developed actual regulations based on AIRFA; further, the U.S. Forest Service has been one of the most aggressive antagonists of AIRFA in the courts (particularly in *Lyng v. Northwest*). As Sharon O'Brien writes concerning AIRFA, "Testimony by American Indian witnesses and government officials clearly attest to the lack of federal administrative compliance with the law and congressional failure to rectify religious infringements through legislative reform."[49]

And where is AIM today? AIM is alive and well, continuing its long struggle for political and religious rights of Native peoples. In 1993, AIM reorganized into "an alliance of fully autonomous but reciprocally supporting chapters." AIM chapters are dedicated "to advance the cause of indigenous sovereignty and self-determination within its own context and regional conditions." Decisions of local and state chapters are made independently, emphasizing their local constituencies.[50] In April 1993, AIM held a Western Regional Conference of its many chapter organizations where AIM members were joined by John La Velle, the Santee Lakota founder of Center for the SPIRIT (Support and Protection of Indian Religions and Indigenous Traditions). San Francisco area-based SPIRIT is "a nonprofit organization of American Indian people dedicated to the preservation and revitalization of American Indian spiritual practices and religious traditions." La Velle announced a joint commitment with diverse tribal elders and the AIM chapters to continuing to work for the protection and maintenance of Native religious rights.

At the Lakota Summit V, in June 1993, an international gathering of United States and Canadian Lakota, Dakota, and Nakota nations, including five hundred representatives from as many as forty tribes, unanimously passed a "Declaration of War Against Exploiters of Lakota Spirituality." At the conference, Wilmer Mesteth, a traditional Lakota leader and instructor at Lakota Oglala College, spoke about the imitation and sale of Lakota ceremonies by non-Indian peoples. Mesteth, along with Darrell Standing Elk and Phillis Swift Hawk, drew up the declaration to warn non-Natives against the appropriation of Native spirituality.[51] AIM also has become more visible in a walk led by Dennis Banks and Mary Jane Wilson that began February 11, 1994, from Alcatraz island and which culminated in Washington DC, in July as a means to call attention to the continued imprisonment of Leonard Peltier—who many believe was falsely imprisoned and who is certainly the foremost symbol of Native American political and spiritual resistance.

The concerns of both AIM and SPIRIT are summarized in the Lakota Summit "declaration of war" against all "plastic Indians." This declaration expresses the frustration and anger that many Native peoples feel about the sale of Native

American religious objects as well as the marketing of Native ceremonies by unqualified and (usually) non-Native people (see appendix 1). Tourism that results in the sale of Native artifacts has been denounced as well as "New Age exhibitors [who] wrongfully [portray] themselves as Native Americans or [sell] ceremonies for profit."[52] AIM and SPIRIT sponsor political actions against institutions of higher education and confrontations with various institutions members of which are engaged in ceremonies that falsely claim to legitimate students as "pipe-carriers" or as representatives of Native religions. Confrontations have occurred with people claiming to lead or in other ways sponsor Native religious activities who are neither members of any tribe nor qualified by tribal standards to lead such events.

AIM and SPIRIT have adopted the terms "exploiters" and "exploitation" as part of a regional and national strategy to confront people, whether Indian or non-Indian, who profit from Native American religious traditions. Actions are presently underway by AIM to mandate tribal identification cards or tribal legal verification for anyone claiming to represent Indian people in any public forum, including powwow vendors and artisans. Anyone profiting from religious activities associated with a claimed tribal affiliation should be able to provide references from that tribe affirming the good standing of that person with tribal members. Finally, AIM delegates have resolved to work toward getting a bill to Congress making it illegal to falsely impersonate a medicine man or a medicine woman and to stop, where possible, the selling of ceremonies and sacred objects.

Other such Native groups have formed, including the League of Indigenous Sovereign Nations (LISN, May 1991, established on Piscatoway Native land in Port-Tobacco, Maryland); the Indigenous Peoples Caucus (IPC, Canada, 1993, Sulian Stone Eagle Herney, Mi'kmak); Native American Traditions, Ideals, Values Educational Society (NATIVE, 1993, founded by a Navajo mother of five, Betty Red Ant LaFontaine); and WARN (Women of All Red Nations) as one of the first Native American feminist movements. This feminist element has taken a more visible form in the recent Second and Third Continental Congress of Women of the Americas (1994, Washington DC; 1995 in Bejing) which included women from North, Central, and South America, Canada, and Russia, providing an opportunity for networking which may prove to be a formidable resource for Native political and religious actions.

In the summer of 1995, while attending a Sun Dance on Pine Ridge, I had several opportunities to discuss these issues with the full-blood traditional Lakota ceremonial leader who had invited me to that dance.[53] In our discussions, we touched on the history and background of oppression on the Pine Ridge reservation. His comments on Black Elk were particularly salient:

You know, Black Elk was part of a conspiracy, a cover up here among the Lakota. What he says there about the Indian religion being dead, over, was part of a plan to stop the oppression here at Pine Ridge. It worked too. After that book came out, things got better; we just said it was over, dead, a thing of the past. We had to still do it secretly, but things have gotten better. Now we can do it more openly and bring other people in. . . . I don't believe our religion is something that should be hidden or kept from other people who are not Lakota or Indian. But for a long time, we had to keep everything hidden, even from other Lakota.

These comments reflect more than a personal point of view. They express in many ways both the consequences of a long oppressive history and the resistance strategies that have led to the preservation of many traditional Native religious practices in the face of religious persecution. Caution still exists—this Sun Dance was by invitation only and closed to casual outsiders. Held back in the hills, there were no signs, no indications other than a single red cloth tied on a stop sign. On entering the dance grounds, a very large sign in red paint read, "No cameras or tape recorders allowed!" The entrance was watched day and night and roped off to anyone other than those approved or known to those posted at the entrance.

Perhaps one of the most fundamental of all strategies in the struggle for spiritual survival among Native Americans has been the constant theme of maintaining traditional religious integrity and not compromising religious beliefs or practices in the face of massive oppression and coercion. Accommodation has proven, in many ways, to lead to an erosion of traditional values in the face of a long and usually uncompromising, non-reciprocal assault on Native character and identity. Yet, political resistance in the late twentieth century has been moderated by a resurgence in Native religious practices, the leaders of which have constantly promoted non-violent tactics and an ethics of preservation, mutuality, and respect for tribal differences. All too often, these leaders have been labeled as "radicals" and "troublemakers" whose actions are seen as unjustly critical of majority rule. Such a response is a symptom of cultural blindness indicating a profound lack of awareness of the real history of Native American religious oppression.

The history of prophetic leadership has been one of cultural survival with a constant reaffirmation of the rights of Native peoples to formulate, and reformulate, their religious and communal identities through a validation of their own cultural pasts. Often this has required constant, bitter negotiation with non-Native peoples whose perspective is reinforced by alien cultural values. There is nothing "radical" about such resistance—it is a natural inclination to preserve valued cultural practices that are inseparable from a way of life and identity grounded in deep, abiding spiritual principles distinct from those imposed by aggressive missionization and assimilative government policies. In many ways, Native communities are actually proponents of the conservation of culture, of maintaining continuity with the past and of preserving long-held values. The prophetic foreground of visible resistance to cultural annihilation is more appropriately seen as a bulwark protecting a long and deeply held stability than as simply a reaction to aggressive settlement.

Another theme of this paper has been the way in which traditional spiritual movements act to facilitate intertribal cooperation without denying the diversity of religious practices or values of any particular community. This, it seems to me, is a lesson for all of us. There is a genuine need for all people involved in the study and practice of Native religious life to respect religious differences (which past generations of Euroamericans in particular have failed to do, including academics) in order to further the causes of religious pluralism as a basis for personal empowerment and religious identity. The character of religious resistance is grounded in the confrontation between various cultural monomyths and the struggle for any people to value the uniqueness of their own spiritual practices. Only when we fully affirm those practices as living resources for our mutual betterment can we move past the need for legislation and legal protections for what is, in fact, a right of all human beings—the free exercise of their religious beliefs.

APPENDIX 1:

DECLARATIONS AGAINST THE SALE OR APPROPRIATION OF
NATIVE CEREMONIES BY NON-NATIVES

There is a sequence of this type of proclamation reaching back to at least October 1980, where an early version was passed at Rosebud Creek, Montana, in the Northern Cheyenne Two Moons' camp. This document was signed by the following tribal spiritual elders: Tom Yellowtail; Larry Anderson; Izadore Thom; Thomas Banyacya; Phillip Deere; Walter Denny; Austin Two Moons; Tadadaho; Frank Fools Crow; Frank Cardinal; Peter O'Chiese. The text is as follows (circular in possession of author):

RESOLUTION:
FIFTH ANNUAL MEETING OF THE TRADITIONAL ELDER'S CIRCLE

It has been brought to the attention of the Elders and their representatives in Council that various individuals are moving about this Great Turtle Island and across the great waters to foreign soil, purporting to be spiritual leaders. They carry pipes and other objects sacred to the Red Nations, the indigenous people of the western hemisphere. These individuals are gathering non-Indian people as followers who believe they are receiving instructions of the original people. We, the Elders and our representatives sitting in Council, give warning to these non-Indian followers that it is in our understanding this is not a proper process, that the authority to carry these sacred objects is given by the people, and the purpose and procedure is specific to time and the needs of the people. The medicine people are chosen by the medicine and long instruction and discipline is necessary before ceremonies and healing can be done. These procedures are always in the Native tongue; there are no exceptions and profit is not the motivation. There are many Nations with many and varied procedures specifically for the welfare of their people. These processes and ceremonies are of the most Sacred Nature. The Council finds the open display of these ceremonies contrary to these Sacred instructions.

Therefore, be warned that these individuals are moving about playing upon the spiritual needs and ignorance of our non-Indian brothers and sisters. The value of these instructions and ceremonies are questionable, maybe meaningless, and hurtful to the individual carrying false messages. There are questions that should be asked of these individuals:

1. What Nation does the person represent?
2. What is their Clan and Society?
3. Who instructed them and where did they learn?
4. What is their home address?

If no information is forthcoming, you may inquire at the addresses listed [by those who signed], and we will try to find out about them for you. We concern ourselves only with those people who use spiritual ceremonies with non-Indian people for profit. There are many things to be shared with the Four Colors of humanity in our common destiny as one with our Mother the Earth. It is this sharing that must be considered with great care by the Elders and the medicine people who carry the Sacred Trusts, so that no harm may come to people through ignorance and misuse of these powerful forces.

Similar AIM resolutions were passed in 1982 and in the May 11, 1984, meeting at Window Rock, Arizona (circular in possession of author). These documents present concerns for the loss of Native ceremonies and religious practices to non-Native persons as a long-standing grievance with many Native people, as attested to by the 1993, Lakota Summit V.

1984 AIM RESOLUTION

WHEREAS the Spiritual wisdom which is shared by the Elders with the people has been passed to us through the Creation from time immemorial; and

WHEREAS the Spirituality of Indian Nations is inseparable from the people themselves; and

WHEREAS the attempted theft of Indian ceremonies is a direct attack and theft from Indian people themselves; and

WHEREAS there has been a dramatic increase in the incidence of selling of Sacred ceremonies, such as the sweat lodge and the vision quest, and of Sacred articles, such as religious pipes, feathers, and stone; and

WHEREAS these practices have been and continue to be conducted by Indians and non-Indians alike, constituting not only insult and disrespect for the wisdom of the ancients, but also exposing ignorant non-Indians to potential harm and even death through the misuse of these ceremonies; and

WHEREAS the traditional Elders and Spiritual leaders have repeatedly warned against and condemned the commercialization of our ceremonies; and

WHEREAS such commercialization has increased dramatically in recent years,

THEREFORE, be it resolved that the Southwest AIM Leadership Conference reiterates the position articulated by our Elders at the First American Indian Tribunal held at DQ University, September 1982, as follows:

Now to those who are doing these things, we send our third warning. Our Elders ask, "Are you prepared to take the consequences of your actions? You will be outcasts from your people if you continue these practices" . . . Now, this [warning] is another one. Our young people are getting restless. They are the ones who sought their Elders in the first place to teach them the Sacred ways. They have said they will take care of those who are abusing our Sacred ceremonies and Sacred objects in their own way. In this way they will take care of their Elders.

WE RESOLVE to protect our Elders and our traditions, and we condemn those who seek to profit from Indian Spirituality. We put them on notice that our patience grows thin and they continue their disrespect at their own risk.

NOTES

1. Prucha 1990:312–14; see Michaelson 1984 for an overview of this act.

2. Prucha 1990:160–61.

3. Prucha 1990:187–88.

4. Writing of the Commissioners of Indian Affairs are accessible in Prucha 1990; those writings that particularly express an intention to suppress Native religion and culture (1832–1901) are found on pp. 63, 73–74, 77–78, 124, 157, 160–61, 175, 177, 187–88, 200–201. With regard to the First Amendment, it is clear in the writings of both the secretary

of the interior and the commissioner of Indian affairs during this period that Native Americans were regarded as having no protection or guarantees under the Constitution and were in fact regarded as "alien nations" within the borders of the United States.

5. In 1818, Secretary of War John Calhoun wrote: "Our views of Indian interests, and not their own, ought to govern them. By a proper combination of force and persuasion, punishments and rewards, they ought to brought within the pales of law and civilization. Left to themselves they will never reach that desirable condition," Prucha 1990:32. The Indian Civilization Fund Act established a government fund "to employ capable [non-Indian] persons of good moral character to instruct Indians in the mode of agriculture suited to their situation; and for teaching their children reading, writing, and arithmetic," Prucha 1990:33.

6. Prucha 1990:3.

7. Loftin 1994:60.

8. Dowd 1992:xxii.

9. McLoughlin, 1994.

10. McLoughlin 1984:438.

11. Trafzer, 1986.

12. Dowd 1992:17.

13. Hirschfelder and Molin 1992:207; even earlier prophetic traditions are found among the Aztec and other Mesoamerican peoples; see Stephen Colston, " 'No Longer Will There Be a Mexico': Omens, Prophecies, and the Conquest of the Aztec Empire" in Trafzer 1986:1–20.

14. Hirschfelder and Molin 1992:66, 312; Champagne 1994:512–13.

15. Hirschfelder and Molin 1992:114–15; see also Champagne 1994:512–14.

16. Ruby and Brown 1989:6.

17. Hirschfelder and Molin 1992:295–96; Champagne 1993:520–21.

18. Hirschfelder and Molin 1992:94; see also Frank Owsley, "Prophecy of War: Josiah Francis and the Creek War" in Trazfer 1986:35–55.

19. Hirschfelder and Molin 1992:338.

20. See Joseph Herring, "Kenekuk, the Kickapoo Prophet: Acculturation without Assimilation" in Trazfer 1986:57–69; Hirschfelder and Molin 1992:145.

21. See Clifford Trafzer and Margery Ann Beach, "Smohalla, the Washani, and Religion as a Factor in Northwest Indian History" in Trafzer, 1986:71–86; and Ruby and Brown 1989:29–49.

22. See L. G. Moses, " 'The Father Tells Me So!' Wovoca: The Ghost Dance Prophet" in Trafzer 1986:97–113; Kehoe, 1989. Also of interest, see McLoughlin 1990.

23. For more on the Kiowa Ghost Dance, see Kratch 1992.

24. Prucha 1990:177; Commissioner Jones, in 1901, wrote of Indian education, "the Indian youth . . . [is] born a savage and raised in an atmosphere of superstition and ignorance, he lacks at the outset those advantages which are inherited by his white brother and enjoyed in the cradle. His moral character has yet to be formed. . . . In a

word, the primary object of a white school is to educate the mind; the primary essential of Indian education is to enlighten the soul" (Prucha 1990:200–201).

25. Hirschfelder and Molin 1992:38.

26. Prucha 1990:131–34, 135, 141–43. The 1872 distribution was listed by Commissioner Walker as follows:

Agencies		Indian Enrollment
Methodists	14	54,473
Baptists	5	40,800
Presbyterians	9	38,069
Episcopalians	8	26,929
Catholic*	7	17,856
Orthodox Friends	10	17,724
Congregationalist	3	14,476
Christian Church	2	8,287
Reformed Dutch	5	8,118
Hicksite Friends	6	6,598
Unitarian	2	3,800
Am. Board of Comm.	1	1,496
Lutheran	1	273
Total	73	238,899

*Catholic is much higher as Catholic Missions were long established before the creation of the BIC and there was a strong Catholic presence on many reservations not listed by the obviously pro-Protestant board.

27. Prucha 1990:200–201; See also Crow Dog and Erdoes 1990:28–41. In 1901, Indian Commissioner Jones wrote in his annual report: "These pupils are gathered from the cabin, the wickiup, and the tepee. Partly by cajolery and partly by threats; partly by bribery and partly by fraud; partly by persuasion and partly by force, they are induced to leave their homes and their kindred to enter these schools and take upon themselves the outward semblance of civilized life."

28. Josephy 1984:82.

29. Hendrix 1983:62–66.

30. See Al Logan Slagle, "Tolowa Indian Shakers and the Role of Prophecy at Smith River, California" in Trafzer 1986:115–36.

31. Stewart 1993:44–62; p. 60 gives a table of states which passed laws against peyote, of which only seven have been repealed.

32. Hirschfelder and Molin 1992:2.

33. Prucha 1990:222ff.; Stewart 1993:45.

34. Hirschfelder and Molin 1992:9–10; only after 1975 was the Bald and Golden Eagle Act modified to allow American Indians to "possess, carry, use, wear, give, loan, or exchange among other Indians without compensation, all federally protected birds, as well as their parts and feathers."

35. Prucha 1990:234, 264.

36. Prucha 1990:241.

37. Lewis 1990:65.

38. Josephy 1984:235–63; Crow Dog and Erdoes 1990:73–91.

39. Prucha 1990:264, 274–76.

40. Prucha 1990:293; Churchill and Morris 1992:17.

41. Prucha 1990:295; Hirschfelder and Molin 1992:6–7.

42. Moore 1993:86.

43. Hirschfelder and Molin 1992:193.

44. Hirschfelder and Molin 1992:238–39; for more on the Omaha Sacred Pole, see Ridington 1993.

45. This act is supported by the AAM (American Association of Museums) and the SAA (Society for American Archaeology) but limits the kind of objects legally subject to claims to avoid "raids on collections."

46. Hirschfelder and Molin 1992:32, 195, 305; for examples see 1976, Native American Historical, Cultural and Sacred Sites Act (California) and 1989, Unmarked Human Burial Sites and Skeletal Remains Protection Act (Nebraska).

47. Echo-Hawk 1993:68.

48. See Michaelson 1993; also Churchill and Morris 1992:20; see also Smith and Snake (1996) for a case study on peyote and its relationship to NAFERA.

49. O'Brien 1993:30–31 where she also calls the Lyng case "most restrictive interpretation" of AIRFA; 31–40 reviews the outstanding cases involved. See also Steve Moore's excellent review of AIRFA (Moore 1993) as well as Loftin 1994; also Deloria 1994.

50. The Edgewood Declaration of the International Confederation of Autonomous Chapters of the American Indian Movement (Edgewood, New Mexico, December 18, 1993); endorsed by 10 other AIM chapters at that time.

51. From "Lakota Declaration of War" by Valerie Taliman, published in *The Circle Newspaper*, July, 1993; three Native newspapers, *News From Indian Country, The Circle,* and *Native American Smoke Signals,* have all published articles on AIM and SPIRIT's present concerns.

52. A statement issued by SPIRIT and reprinted in Churchill 1994, says: "Therefore, we urge all supporters of American Indian people to join us in calling for an immediate end to the cynical, sacrilegious spectacle of non-Indian 'wannabes,' would-be gurus of the 'New Age,' and 'plastic medicine men' shamelessly exploiting and mocking our sacred traditions by performing bastardized imitations of our ceremonies. They are promoters of 'spiritual genocide' against Indian people; and while some of them may be guilty 'merely' of complicity in 'genocide with good intentions,' others have become aggressive in insisting on their 'right' to profiteer by exploiting and prostituting American Indian sacred traditions."

53. The leader of this particular Sun Dance, one of many on Pine Ridge, prefers to remain anonymous.

REFERENCES

Champagne, Duane. 1994. *Native America: Portrait of the Peoples.* Detroit: Visible Ink Press.

Churchill, Ward, and Glenn Morris. 1992. "Key Indian Laws and Cases." In *The State of Native America: Genocide, Colonization, and Resistance,* ed. M. Annette Jaimes. Boston: South End Press.

Churchill, Ward. 1994. *Indians Are Us? Culture and Genocide in Native North America.* Monroe ME: Common Courage Press.

Crow Dog, Mary, and Richard Erdoes. 1990. *Lakota Woman.* New York: Grove Weidfeld.

Deloria, Vine, Jr. 1994. "Sacred Lands and Religious Freedom." *American Indian Religions: An Interdisciplinary Journal* 1: 73–83.

Dowd, Gregory Evans. 1992. *A Spirited Resistance: The North American Indian Struggle for Unity, 1745–1815.* Baltimore: John Hopkins University Press.

Echo-Hawk, Walter R., and Roger Echo-Hawk. 1993. "Repatriation, Reburial, and Religious Rights." In Vecsey, *Handbook of American Indian Religious Freedom,* 63–80.

Hendrix, Janey B. 1983. *Redbird Smith and the Nighthawk Keetoowahs.* Welling OK: Cross-Cultural Education Center.

Hirschfelder, Arlene, and Paulette Molin. 1992. *The Encyclopedia of Native American Religions.* New York: Facts on File.

Josephy, Alvin M., Jr. 1984. *Now That the Buffalo's Gone: A Study of Today's American Indians.* Norman: University of Oklahoma Press.

Kehoe, Alice. 1989. *The Ghost Dance: Ethnohistory and Revitalization.* New York: Holt, Rinehart, and Winston.

Kracht, Benjamin R. 1992. "The Kiowa Ghost Dance, 1894–1916: An Unheralded Revitalization Movement." *Ethnohistory* 39: 452–77.

Lewis, Thomas H. 1990. *The Medicine Men: Oglala Sioux Ceremony and Healing.* Lincoln: University of Nebraska Press.

Loftin, John D. 1994. "Constitutional Law and American Indian Religious Freedom: A Tale of Two Worlds." *American Indian Religions: An Interdisciplinary Journal* 1: 37–72.

McLoughlin, William G. 1984. *The Cherokee Ghost Dance: Essays on the Southeastern Indians, 1789–1861.* Macon GA: Mercer University Press.

———. 1990. "Ghost Dance Movements: Some Thoughts on Definition Based on Cherokee History." *Ethnohistory* 37: 25–45.

———. 1994. *The Cherokees and Christianity, 1794–1870: Essays on Acculturation and Cultural Persistence.* Ed. Walter H. Conser Jr. Athens: University of Georgia Press.

Michaelson, Robert. 1984. "The Significance of the American Indian Religious Freedom Act." *Journal of the American Academy of Religion* 52: 93–115.

———. 1993. "Law and the Limits of Liberty." In Vecsey, *Handbook of American Indian Religious Freedom,* 116–33.

Moore, Steven C. 1993. "Sacred Sites and Public Lands." In Vecsey, *Handbook of American Indian Religious Freedom*, 81–99.

O'Brien, Sharon. 1993. "A Legal Analysis of the American Indian Religious Freedom Act." In Vecsey, *Handbook of American Indian Religious Freedom*, 27–43.

Prucha, Francis. 1990. *Documents of United States Indian Policy*. 2nd ed. Lincoln: University of Nebraska Press.

Ridington, Robin. 1993. "A Sacred Object As Text: Reclaiming the Sacred Pole of the Omaha Tribe." *American Indian Quarterly* 17: 83–99.

Ruby, Robert H., and John A. Brown. 1989. *Dreamer-Prophets of the Columbia Plateau: Smohalla and Skolaskin*. Norman: University of Oklahoma Press.

Smith, Huston, and Ruben Snake. 1996. *One Nation Under God: The Triumph of the Native American Church*. Santa Fe: Clear Light Publishers.

Stewart, Omer C. 1993. "Peyote and Law." In Vecsey, *Handbook of American Indian Religious Freedom*, 44–59.

Trazfer, Clifford E. 1986. *American Indian Prophets: Religious Leaders and Revitalization Movements*. Newcastle CA: Sierra Oaks Publishing Co.

Vecsey, Christopher (ed.). 1993. *Handbook of American Indian Religious Freedom*. New York: Crossroads Publishing Company.

Contributors

Thomas Buckley is associate professor of anthropology and American studies at the University of Massachusetts, Boston, where he is also academic director of the Native American Resource Center Project. He has done research and advocacy work in Native northwestern California since the 1970s and has published a variety of articles and essays on the Yurok Indians and on the history of anthropology in the region, including "The Pitiful History of Little Events: The Epistemological and Moral Contexts of Kroeber's California Ethnology," in *Volksgeist As Method and Ethic: Essays on Boasian Ethnography and the German Anthropological Tradition,* ed. George W. Stocking Jr. (University of Wisconsin Press, 1996).

Mary C. Churchill is an assistant professor of women's studies and religious studies at the University of Colorado at Boulder. Her essay is part of a larger manuscript project entitled "In the Spirit of Corn: Indigenous Theory and Cherokee Women's Literature." A mixed-blood Cherokee, she is involved in Native issues on the Boulder campus.

John A. Grim is a professor, and chair, in the Department of Religion at Bucknell University, Lewisburg, Pennsylvania. With his wife, Mary Evelyn Tucker, he has coedited *Worldviews and Ecology,* 7th ed. (Maryknoll NY: Orbis Press, 1999), which discusses the environmental crisis from the perspectives of world religions and contemporary philosophy. He co-organized a series of thirteen conferences on "Religions of the World and Ecology" held at Harvard University's Center for the Study of World Religions from spring 1996 to fall 1998. He is the author of *The Shaman: Patterns of Religious Healing among the Ojibway Indians* (Norman: University of Oklahoma Press, 1987); "An Awful Feeling of Loneliness: Native North American Mystical Traditions" in *Doors of Understanding: Conversations on Global Spirituality* (Steubenville OH: Franciscan Press, 1997); and "A Comparative Study in Native American Philanthropy" in *Philanthropy and Culture: A Comparative Perspective* (Bloomington: Indiana University Press, 1997).

Ronald L. Grimes is professor of religion and culture at Wilfrid Laurier University, Waterloo, Ontario, Canada. His book, *Deeply into the Bone: Re-Inventing Rites of Passage*, is forthcoming in Life Passages, a series published by the University of California Press. He is also author of *Marrying and Burying: Rites of Passage in a Man's Life* (Boulder: Westview Press, 1995) and *Readings in Ritual Studies* (Upper Saddle River NJ: Prentice-Hall, 1996).

Richard Haly is adjunct professor and research associate in the Department of Anthropology at the University of Colorado at Boulder. He is the author of two forthcoming books: "On Becoming a Mountain: Stories, Souls, and Order in an Aztec Landscape" and "Bones of the Night Sky: Ancestors, Information, and the Mesoamerican Cosmos." Currently, he is project ethnographer for the interdisciplinary "Proyecto La Malinche," funded by the National Geographic Society.

Inés Hernández-Ávila is associate professor of Native American studies at the University of California, Davis, where she served as chair of the department from 1996 to 98. Under her leadership the department launched several major initiatives, the most important of which was the completion and submission of a successful proposal to establish an M.A. and Ph.D. program in Native American studies. This graduate program, officially approved at the system-wide level in early November 1998, is the first of its kind in the country. She has recently finished a manuscript entitled "Dancing Earth Songs: Poems and Stories" and is working on a collection of essays entitled "Notes from the Homeland: Essays on Identity and Culture."

Lee Irwin is an associate professor at the College of Charleston, where he teaches in the religious studies program. He is the author of *The Dream Seekers: Native American Visionary Traditions of the Great Plains* (Norman: University of Oklahoma Press, 1994) and of various articles on Native religion, including "Native Voices in the Teaching of Native Religions," *Critical Review of Books in Religion* 11 (1998) and "Native American Spirituality: History, Theory, and Reformulation," in *The Blackwell Companion to Native American History* (Forthcoming, Cambridge MA: Blackwell Publishers, 2001).

Christopher Ronwanièn:te Jocks (Kahnawake Mohawk and Brooklyn Irish) is assistant professor of religion and Native American studies at Dartmouth College. He teaches and writes about contemporary Native American religious thought and practice, with particular interests in religious economics, language, and epistemology and in issues of religion and masculinity. His book on the religious dimension of contemporary Mohawk activism is nearing completion. He has published articles in several edited books, including *Endangered Languages: Current Issues and Future Prospects* (Cambridge: Cambridge University Press, 1998), *Redeeming Men: Religion and Masculinities* (Louisville KY: Westminster John Knox, 1996), and *Can Humanity Survive? The World Religions and the*

Environment (New Zealand: Awareness Book Co., 1996). He lives with his wife and son in the Upper Connecticut Valley of New Hampshire.

Clara Sue Kidwell is currently director of the Native American Studies Program and a professor of history at the University of Oklahoma. She is part Choctaw and is officially enrolled with the White Earth Chippewas. She has published "Systems of Knowledge" in *America in 1492* (New York: Alfred A. Knopf, 1991), *Choctaws and Missionaries in Mississippi, 1818–1918* (Norman: University of Oklahoma Press, 1995), "The Current State of Scholarship on American Indian Science and Technology," with Peter Nabokov, in *The Current State of Native American Scholarship* (Madison: University of Wisconsin Press, 1999), and "The Language of Christian Conversion among the Choctaws," *Journal of the Presbyterian History* (fall 1999).

Benjamin R. Kracht teaches American Indian studies and anthropology classes at Northeastern State University in Tahlequah, Oklahoma. He is the author of "The Kiowa Ghost Dance, 1894–1916: An Unheralded Revitalization Movement," *Ethnohistory* 39, no. 4: 452–77; "Kiowa," in *Encyclopedia of North American Indians* (Boston: Houghton Mifflin Company, 1996); "Kiowa Powwows: Continuity in Ritual Practice," *American Indian Quarterly* 18, no. 3: 321–48; and "Diabetes among the Kiowa: An Ethnohistorical Perspective," in *Diabetes as a Disease of Civilization: The Impact of Culture Change on Indigenous Peoples* (Hawthorne NY: Mouton de Gruyter, 1994). He lives in Broken Arrow, Oklahoma, with his wife, Kelly, daughter, Elena, and son, Robbie. His current research focuses on the differences between eastern and western Oklahoma Indians.

Melissa A. Pflüg teaches religion and anthropology at Wayne State University. She is the author of *Reclaiming a Sovereign Place: Ritual and Myth in Odawa Revitalization* (Norman: University of Oklahoma Press, 1998), "Breaking Bread: Ritual and Metaphor in Odawa Religious Practice," *Religion* 22 (1992); "Politics of Great Lakes Indian Religion," *Michigan Historical Review* (1992); and "Last Stand? Odawa Revitalizationists versus U.S. Law," in *Questioning the Secular State: The Worldwide Resurgence of Religion in Politics* (New York: St. Martin's Press, 1996).

Robin Ridington is professor emeritus at the University of British Columbia. He continues to write and do research from his home on Retreat Island, British Columbia. His publications include *Trail to Heaven: Knowledge and Narrative in a Northern Native Community* (Iowa City: University of Iowa Press, 1988); *Little Bit Know Something: Stories in a Language of Anthropology* (Iowa City: University of Iowa Press, 1990); and (with Dennis Hastings) *Blessing for a Long Time: The Sacred Pole of the Omaha Tribe* (Lincoln: University of Nebraska Press, 1997), which received honorable mention for the 1998 Victor Turner Prize for ethnographic writing. He and Jillian Ridington are currently working on "The Listener: A Narrative Fieldguide to Audio Ethnography," based on their fieldwork with the Dunne-za and the Omaha tribe.

Theresa S. Smith is a professor of religious studies at Indiana University of Pennsylvania. Since 1988 she has conducted field research in consultation with Anishnaabe people on Manitoulin Island and in Toronto, Ontario. She is author of *Island of the Anishnaabeg: Thunderers and Water Monsters in the Traditional Ojibwe Life-World* (Moscow: University of Idaho Press, 1995). Her most recent work in the area of Native American studies is "Yes, I'm Brave: Extraordinary Women in the Anishnaabe Tradition," *Feminist Studies in Religion* 15, no. 1 (winter/spring 1999).

James Treat teaches in the Honors College at the University of Oklahoma. His research focuses on contemporary Native religious issues, especially the relationship between tribal and Christian traditions in reservation and urban communities. He is the editor of *Native and Christian: Indigenous Voices on Religious Identity in the United States and Canada* (New York: Routledge, 1996) and *For This Land: Writings on Religion in America by Vine Deloria, Jr.* (New York: Routledge, 1999). Treat is an enrolled citizen of the Muscogee (Creek) Nation of Oklahoma.

Index

Armstrong, Raymond, 146, 153, 154, 155

Ashkisshe Sun Dance: authenticity approach
to, 52; as community event, 50; Crow Indian
Reservation performance (1941) of, 42, 53–54;
cultural identity implications of, 41–42;
diakaashe expressed during, 52–54; historical
loss and changes in, 56–57; old vs. new, 53–54;
ritualization of, 51–52. *See also* Sun Dance

Ashkisshe Sun Dance anniversary (1991):
brochure of, 55; described, 54; photo essay of,
51; understanding of, 55–56

authenticity approach: to *Ashkisshe* Sun Dance,
52; described, 38; embodied, 89; place and,
45–48; wilderness dualism of, 45–47

Aztec dance, 30

Aztec Thought and Culture (León-Portilla), 161

Baird, Spencer F., 108

Bakhtin, Mikhail, 97, 107, 118

Bald (and later Golden) Eagle Protection Act, 303

Ballew, Lauretta E., 241

Banks, Dennis, 303, 306

Banyacya, Thomas (Jenkins), 273, 274, 275, 276,
278, 282

Barnes, Joseph, 196

Bartram, William, 212, 214–15

"Bathing in the breath of Ki-je Manido" ritual,
134, 135

bear-walkers (*me'coubmoosa*), 132, 133

Beck, Peggy, 20

Beedahbun (Jesuit Anishnaabe Spiritual Center),
152

Bell, Kitty, 146, 152–53, 155

Bell, Leland, 148, 151

Bellecourt, Clyde, 303

Bellecourt, Vernon, 303

Beltran, Gonzalo Aguirre, 23

Benedict, Ernest, 278

Benedict, Ruth, 100–101

Bering Strait theory, 197–98

"Bible controversy" (Indian Shaker Church), 262,
264–65

Big Day, Heywood, 42, 55

Big Day, William, 54–55

Big Mountain relocation, 73

binary oppositions, 220, 221, 224–25. *See also*
purity vs. pollution paradigm

Black Bear, 122–23, 135

Black Elk, 307–8

Blackfeet ancestral reburial (1989), 305

Black Feminist Thought (Collins), 225

Black Hills land claims, 73

Blood Magic (Gottlieb), 223

Bly, Robert, 63

Board of Indian Commissioners, 241, 301

Boas, Franz, 99

Bommelyn, Loren, 264

"Border Crossing Celebration," 273

Borderlands (Anzaldúa), 162

Boston Peabody Museum, 305

Botone, 243

"The Boy and The Deer" (Zuni poetry), 108

Brightman, Robert, 104

Brown, Jennifer S. H., 104

Brown, Joseph Epes, 82, 224

Brown Otter, 123, 129, 134

Bruner, Edward, 266–67

Brush Dance, 262, 263, 264, 265

Bucknell University, 52

Buechel, Eugene, 117

buffalo doctors (Kiowa), 239

Buffalo Medicine Lodge, 239

Buffon, Géorges, 160

"Burden of Proof" policy (NMAI), 198–99

Bureau of American Ethnology, 205

Bureau of Indian Affairs, 283, 289

Bureau of Indian Affairs Circular 2970, 302

Bureau of Indian Affairs for the Indian Courts,
295

Butrick, Rev. Daniel Sabin, 215, 217, 218

cabildo (local government), 164

cajas de communidad ("community chests"), 165

Canadian Indian Act of 1884, 301

Canadian "White Paper," 286

cargo (religious office), 165

Carmody, Denise Lardner, 207

Carmody, John Tully, 207

Carson, David, 116

Castaneda, Carlos, 64, 74 n.2

Catholic Church: cross symbolism used by,
172–73; on inculturation of Stations of the
Cross, 152; Kiowa country missions by, 241;
Nahua adaptation of, 169–76; new evangelism
coming from, 146–47; peyote use condemned
by, 23; relations between Anishnaabeg and,
146–47; "serving the saints" practice of, 164–68.
See also Christianity; festivals

ceremonial ancestral lands, 18–19

ceremonial community, 61–62

ceremonies: *cofradías* (Brotherhoods) to sponsor,
165–66; exchange process in healing, 125–26;
Green Corn, 210, 213, 214–15, 216, 227 n.43;
Hopi clown role in, 195; Kiowa-Comanche
crescent moon peyote, 243–44, 249; knowledge
expressed through, 66; Nahua curing, 170;

conversation characterizing, 100; critiques on appropriation of, 63–65; cyberspace discussion on non-Native teaching of, 79–93; expressed through ceremonies, 66; historical study of, 71; inaccurate adaptations/interpretations of, 63–64; Iroquois Longhouse epistemological framework on, 65–66; of Nahua peoples, 176–79. *See also* Appropriation of Native American spirituality

Kodiak Island case, 199–200

LaBarre, Weston, 237, 242, 243
La Flesche, Franics, 109, 110
Lakota Summit V (1993), 306–7, 310
Lakota tradition: impact of Wounded Knee massacre on, 300; inadequacy of dualism to describe, 224–25; influence of, 29
Lakota Woman (Fire Lame Deer and Crow Dog), 116
Lame Deer, Seeker of Visions (Erdoes), 116
Landa, Bishop Diego de, 195
Lang, Julian, 17, 23, 263
language: culture/society as extension of, 220–21; missionary schools suppression of Native, 301; as system of signs, 220; weekly radio programs in Muscogee, 280
Lanman, Charles, 219
LaRocque, Emma, 104
Larsen Bay case, 199–200
Laughing Gull, 139, 140
La Velle, John, 306
Lawson, James, 212
Leach, Father, 153
League of Nations, Pan-American Indians, 277
League of North American Indians, 275, 276, 277
League of the Haudensaunee, 201
Le Jeune, Paul, 145
León-Portilla, Miguel, 161
Le Quier, Ojibwa Francis, 276
Lévi-Strauss, Claude, 220–21
Levy, Jerrold, 250
Lightningbolt (Storm), 117
LISN (League of Indigenous Sovereign Nations), 307
Little Big Horn College, 50
Little Bow, 243
Lockhart, James, 159, 163, 164, 165, 166
Lofaro, Michael A., 206
Logan, Beeman, 277, 278, 282, 283
Lone Wolf, 122, 127, 129, 131, 132, 135, 138–39, 140, 142
Lopez, Sam, 262, 263

Lyng v. Northwest Indian Cemetery Protection Association, 19, 45, 46–47, 306
Lyons, Oren, 268

Mabel McKay (Sarris), 114
Mails, Thomas, 65
Malinche role (Conchero sweat lodge tradition), 13–14
Malitzin (La Malinche), 13–14, 160
manidos (power-persons): contemporary rituals connecting to, 129–33; empowered identity through, 127, 128–29; forms taken during vision quest by, 131; gifting to establish relationship with, 124, 125; *pimadaziwin* (The Good Life) through, 129, 131, 137; powwows to establish relationship with, 137; sweat ritual to establish relationship with, 135
Manifest Destiny, 25
Manifest Manners (Vizenor), 41
Manitoulin Island. *See* Anishnaabeg of Manitoulin Island
Maria Sabina (Estrada), 20–21, 22
Maria Sabina and the Mazatec Mushroom Velada (recorded ceremony), 22
Martin, Calvin, 207
Massena Observer, 285
"matter out of place," 220
maxpe (sacred power), 42, 51, 52
mayordomía (sponsorship of festival), 166, 182, 183, 184
Maysayesva, Vernon, 200
McGaa, Ed ("Eagle Man"), 67
McKay, Mabel, 114, 118
McLoughlin, William G., 207, 217
McNickle, D'Arcy, 113
Means, Russell, 116, 303
Medicine and Magic (Aguirre Beltran), 23
medicine bag (*pinjigosaum*), 133
Medicine Bear, 132
medicine bundles (*xapaaliia*), 51
Medicine Crow, Joseph, 42
Medicine Fathers revelation, 54
Medicine Horse, Magdalene, 50
Medicine Lodge Treaty (1867), 240, 253 n.6
medicine-people, 129, 133, 142, 296
Medicine Woman (Andrews), 116
"Medicine Woman" (Sarris), 114
"Meeting of Indian Brothers": 1956, 274; combined meeting with Religious People (1963), 276
"Meeting of Religious People": 1956, 274; 1958, 275
Mennominee Termination Act (1954), 303

menstruation, 211, 213–14, 217, 223. *See also* women

Mescalero Apache, 242

Mesteth, Wilmer, 306

mestizos/mestizas/mestizaje: described, 29, 159, 161, 188 n.1; move into Cuetzalan by, 163; political impact of, 167–68

Methvin, Rev. John J., 241

Mexican nationalism: dynamics in Cuetzalan of, 163; hermeneutics of, 161–64; sources of, 160–61, 188 n.3; syncretism of indigenous religion and, 159

Mexican War of Independence (1810–21), 160

Mexico: conflict between culture of Nahua and, 158–59; domains of saints and ancestors in, 168–69; *mestizaje* of, 159; political order in, 186–88; "serving the saints" practice in, 164–67. *See also* festivals

Miccosukees, 275

midéwiwin (power to cure), 132

missionaries: to Anishnaabeg of Manitoulin Island, 145–46; Dawes Act (General Allotment Act) of 1887 and, 241; Grant Peace Policy control over, 301; to the Hoopa Valley, 258–59; Indian-white contact recorded by, 195–96; to Kiowa reservation, 241–42; Orthodox Friends (Quakers), 241; systemic failure of, 49. *See also* Christianity

"Missionaries" (song), 24–25

Missionary Conquest (Tinker), 41

missionary schools, 301

Mitchell, George, 303

Mohawk Cornwall Island blockade, 270–71, 272, 286

Momaday, N. Scott, 113, 236

monologism, 107

Mooney, James, 205, 212, 215, 216, 218, 219, 240, 243

Moore, Steven C., 18

Morelos, Fr. José María, 160, 161

Morgan, Thomas J., 296, 300

Morris, Elsie, 112

Morris, Wolf, 258

Morrison, Kenneth, 145

Mother Earth (Gill), 79

Mother Trinity, 172

Mount Graham observatory (University of Arizona), 73

Murray, Fr. Michael, 148, 149, 150, 154

Muscogee language, 280

museum collections, 196–99

Museum of Natural History (Smithsonian Institution), 196

mushrooms (peyote or *teonanúcatl*), 18, 21–22, 25, 33 n.35

"Myths of the Cherokee" (Mooney), 205, 215, 216, 218

NAFERA (Native American Free Exercise of Religion Act) of 1994, 305

NAGPRA (Native American Graves Protection and Repatriation Act) of 1990, 196, 198, 200, 201, 305

Nahua curing ceremony, 170

Nahua peoples: adaptation of Holy Trinity by, 171–73; adaptation of Our Father by, 169–71, 175; adaptation of Virgin Mary/Her-Skirt-Is-Jade by, 173–76; beliefs/knowledge of, 176–79; "cleansing the heart" practice by, 174; cultural conflict between Mexican and, 158–59; domain of saints and ancestors and, 169; parallel religious hierarchy of, 164; in San Miguel Tzinacapan, 168–69; Segura claims regarding culture of, 162; "serving the saints" practice and, 166–68; Spanish conquest and, 163–64. *See also* festivals

naming ceremony, 138–39

Nanabozho, 127

narratives. *See* stories

Natchat, 78, 94 n.2

National Forest Service, 19, 45

National Indian Youth Council, 276, 277, 281

nationalism. *See* Mexican nationalism

National Museum of the American Indian (Smithsonian), 198, 199

National Park Service policy statement of 1987, 304

Nations Remembered (Perdue), 207

NATIVE (Native American Traditions, Ideals, Values Educational Society), 307

Native American Church (NAC), 18, 98, 248, 250, 266, 302

Native American Movement, 276

Native American Religions (Carmody and Carmody), 207

Native American Religions (Collins), 206

Native American Religions, North America, 207

Native American Rights Fund, 18

Native Americans: accommodation strategy by, 297–98; belief system of, 34 n.56; census (1990) on, 195, 202 n.2; dehumanization of, 24–25; genocide of, 38; issues of self-representation by, 5–7; as misnomer, 35 n.60; need to recapture lost ways by, 16–17; new evangelism and, 146–47; representation of, 2; survival of, 257. *See also* indigenous peoples

Native American spirituality: circle of conversation characterizing, 100; commercialization of, 30–31; communication issues of, 2; defining spirituality in context of, 3; identity as core of, 98; problem of representation in study of, 4–7; requirements for the sharing of, 62; the sixties awakening of, 278–79; social complexity of concerns with, 7–8; successful representations of, 97–99; themes of, 1–2; various approaches to, 3–4; visionary transformation and, 100–101. *See also* spirituality

Native American Studies, 12

Native American tribes: cultural affiliation by, 197, 198; debates over origins of, 197–98; repatriation legislation and sovereignty of, 196, 197, 198, 200, 304–5

Native American Women's conference (Humboldt University), 32 n.6

Native-L, 78, 83, 94 n.2

Native Pentecostal Christians, 48–49

Native women. *See* women

nativistic strategy, 298

The Natural and Aboriginal History of Tennessee (Haywood), 218

Nature Power (Robinson), 105

Nazhikewizi Ma'iingan (Lone Wolf), 138

Nebraska repatriation law, 196, 197, 198

Nelson, George, 103–5

nemouhtil (Nahua soul-loss), 177

Neolin, 298

New Age: casual approach to spirituality by, 66; deceptive stories of, 116–17; Lakota Summit on commercialization by, 307, 310; Native American culture commercialized by, 30–31; Native American spirituality appropriated by, 25–28, 61–62

The New Indian (Steiner), 279

New Spain, 160, 161. *See also* Mexico

A New Voyage to Carolina (Lawson), 212

New World discovery, 23–25

New York Times, 273

Nez Perce stories, 16–17

Night-Hawk Society, 302

Nimipu people, 22

NMAIA (National Museum of the American Indian Act) of 1989, 196, 198, 200, 304–5

Nokomis (Moon), 134

non-Native instruction/perspective: arguments favoring teaching by, 88–90; cyberspace discussion on teaching using, 79–93; integrity and intent of, 43, 45, 47; of New Age, 25–28, 30–31, 61–62, 66; objections to, 86–87; requirements for desirable, 90–93; stories by anthropologists as, 266–67; substantive arguments regarding, 88–90; unspoken implications of objections to, 87–88; value of disinterested knowledge and, 89–90. *See also* academia

Norris, Ella, 263

North American Indian Unity Caravan, 278

Northwest Indian Cemetery Protection Association, Lyng v., 19, 45, 46–47, 306

Oakes, Richard, 287

O'Brien, Sharon, 306

"Observations" (Bartram), 215, 216

Ocean Bay Tradition site (Larsen Bay), 199

Odawa traditionalists: on contemporary collective rituals, 133–42; on contemporary personal rituals, 129–33; on empowered identity/rituals of community, 127–29; focus of, 121; on identity interdependence with the dead, 140; on identity through ethical relationships, 123–27, 137, 142; on *pimadaziwin* (The Good Life), 121–22, 123, 128, 129, 142, 143; on prayer, dreams, and visions, 130–32, 142–43

Ojek, Rose, 286

Oklahoma Cherokee Ketoowa, 301–2

Old Koniag site (Larsen Bay), 199

Olsen, Loran, 17, 23

Omaha people, 111–12

The Omaha Tribe (Fletcher and La Flesche), 109–11

ondedw (Kiowa upperclass), 237

O'odham cultural affiliation claims, 200

oral tradition, Native American, 103. *See also* stories

Original Cherokee Community Organization, 281, 282

Orthodox Friends (Quakers), 241

Otis, George, 196

Our Father, 169–71, 175

Owens, Louis, 113

Palmer, Alice, 236

Palmer, Gus, 249

pan-Indianism movement, 98, 266, 267

panoliz (an expense), 165

Papounhan, 298

Payne, John Howard, 215, 216

Payne Papers, 215, 216, 229 n.90

Peltier, Leonard, 306

Perdue, Theda, 207

personal rituals (contemporary), 129–33

Peynetsa, Andrew, 108

The Peyote Cult (LaBarre), 237

peyote (*teonanúcatl*), 18, 21–22, 25, 33 n.35, 242–43, 249, 305
Peyote Way, 51
pimadaziwin (The Good Life): contributing to collective, 130–31, 140–41; described, 121–22; empowerment/healing sources of, 129, 131; ethical relationships and, 123, 128, 137, 142
pinjigosaum (medicine bag), 133
pipe-carriers, 130, 132, 133, 142
pipe ceremony, 133–34, 143 n.3
Pipe-Tomahawk Clan, 283
place: authenticity and, 45–48; saints equated with, 168
Plan de Iguala (1821), 161
Pole ceremonies, 111–12
politics of recognition: academic study use of, 39–40; community survival approach to, 48–50; Native American identity and, 42–45; Native American studies and, 37
Poncet, Fr. Joseph, 145
Pongonyuma, James, 273
Pontiac, 298
pooling resources, 126
Porter, Tom, 283, 285, 286, 287
"A Portion of Indian History, Part I" (booklet), 282
"positive structure," 220
postcolonial theory, Native American, 37
Pouce-Coupe, Mary, 102–3, 105
powwows: described, 135–36, 144 n.4; intertribal dances of, 136–37; spiritual benefits of, 143
PPS (Partido Politico Socialista) [Mexico], 187
Pratt, Mary Louise, 11, 12, 13
prayer: during Kiowa-Comanche crescent moon peyote ceremony, 243–44; Kiowa religious practice of, 237, 250; limited literature on Indian, 236–37; Odawa traditionalists on, 130–32
Presbyterianism, 258, 266
PRI (Mexico), 187
Problems of Dostoevsky's Poetics (Bakhtin), 97
Prophet Dance tradition, 300
prophetic leadership, 298–300, 308–9
"Propitiation or Cementation Festival" ceremony, 217
Pulekukwerek (Yurok myth), 259
purgation tradition, 212
Purity and Danger (Douglas), 220, 223
purity vs. pollution paradigm (Cherokee belief system), 214–16; Bartram's discussion on, 214–15; dualism/binary opposition issues of, 220, 221, 224–25; Hudson's description of, 208, 221, 224–25; Hudson's description of, 208–12; literary mentions of, 207; Mooney's

discussion of, 215–16; Payne papers on, 216–18; sources for Hudson's interpretation of, 212–14, 218–21; weaknesses of, 225–26. *See also* Cherokee religious traditions

Rabasa, José, 23
Rainbow Coalition, 195
"Rainbow Tribe" (Eco-Tribe) encampments, 27
"The Real Omaha," 111–12
reciprocity, 126
Red Buffalo, 243
Red Power movement: Alcatraz occupation by, 287, 303; birth of, 276; growing concerns with, 283. *See also* activism, Native; intertribal traditionalism
reducciónes (relocated indigenous communities), 164
Reformed Presbyterian Church of North America, 241
Religion (listserv), 83, 94 n.2
religions, Native American: AIRFA and, 17–18; approaches to study of, 41–42; Apsaalooke/Crow case study on, 50–57; belief system of, 34 n.56; Christianity and, 24–25; Circular 2970 protecting, 302; conflicts marking the study of, 82; cyberspace discussion on non-Native teaching of, 79–93; demonization of, 23; dialogic approaches to, 39; ethnic criteria argument and study of, 39–41; historic oppression of, 295–97; inculturation of Christianity and, 146–58; integrity and intent in study of, 43, 45, 47; Native American Church/Navajo Tribal Council decision and, 303; oppression of, 300–303; survival approach in study of, 49–50; volume on Pueblo, 92
religions, South American, 40–41
religious freedom: additional legislation on, 305–6; AIRFA and, 17–18, 45, 295, 304, 305, 306; ceremonial ancestral lands and, 18–19; *Employment Division vs. Smith* on, 18
remohpoh (Yurok Kick or Doctor Dance), 261, 262
repatriation of objects: cultural affiliation claims and, 197, 198–99, 200–202; legislation on, 196, 197, 198, 200, 304–5; resistance of academic community, 200–202
representation characteristics, 97–99
Resolution: Fifth Annual Meeting of the Traditional Elder's Circle, 309–10
"Retrospective Essay" (Wasson), 21
revivalist/resistance movements: AIM as, 303–4, 306, 310; Four Mothers Society as, 301–2; Native values/beliefs emphasized by, 297–98; prophetic

leadership of, 298–300, 308–9. *See also* activism, Native

RFRA (Religious Freedom Restoration) of 1993, 305

Rice, Julian, 116, 117

Rickard, Clinton, 272, 273, 275, 276–77

Rickard, Karen, 276

Rickard, William, 275, 276

Ritual Criticism (Grimes), 80

rituals: Apsaalooke/Crow, 50–51; "Bathing in the breath of Ki-je Manido," 134, 135; contemporary collective, 133–42; contemporary personal, 129–33; empowered identity and community, 127–29; Ghost Dance, 98, 245–48, 300; *Gi-be Wiikonge* (Ghost Supper), 139–40; gift exchange, 124–26; giveaways as community, 138; "going to the water," 210, 213, 216, 228 n.69; Green Corn, 210, 213, 214–15, 216, 227 n.43; identity approach to, 51–52; identity of friend vs. foe, 126–27; identity through ethical relationship, 123–27; myth and *Ashkisshe,* 55; peyote, 18, 21–22, 25, 33 n.35, 242–43; powwows as, 137–38; types of sweat, 134–35. *See also* ceremonies

Roberts, Helen Heffron, 23

Robinson, Harry, 105–7, 118

Roman Catholic Church. *See* Catholic Church

Rose, Wendy, 40, 41, 43, 44, 45, 63, 65

Rothenberg, Jerome, 22

Rothrock, Mary U., 218

"Rules for Indian Courts" (1892), 296, 300

runners, 16, 32 n.15

Run Toward the Nightland (Kilpatrick and Kilpatrick), 205

Sabina, Maria, 20–23

The Sacred (Beck, Walters, Francisco), 20

"Sacred Formulas of the Cherokees" (Mooney), 205, 215, 218

sacred objects, 111–16

Sacred Pole ceremonies, 111–12

Saddle Mountain Baptist Church, 247

Saddle Mountain Kiowa community, 241

Sahlins, Marshal, 125

Saint Lawrence Seaway project, 275

saints' festivals (San Miguel Tzinacapan), 179–85

Sanchez, Walter, 108

Sankadote, 243

San Miguel Tzinacapan (Mexico): Nahua culture of, 168–79; "serving the saints" culture in, 167–68. *See also* festivals

Sapir, Edward, 99

Sarris, Greg, 113, 114–15

Saussure, Ferdinand de, 220

Schineller, Peter, 147

Scholem, Gershom, 90

Scollon, Ronald, 99

Scollon, Suzanne B. K., 99

Scott, Joan W., 225

Second Annual Report of the Bureau of [American] Ethnology (Cushing), 107

Second Continental Congress of Women of the Americas, 307

Secret Native American Pathways (Mails), 65

Segura, Andrés, 162

"Self-Evidence" (Douglas), 223

Sequoya, Jana, 11, 12, 13, 31

The Serpent Symbol, and the Worship of the Reciprocal Principles of Nature in America (Bartram), 216

"serving the saints" practice, 164–68

Setzepetoi (Afraid-of-Bears), 246

"Seven Drum Religion" songs, 22

"shadow-visions," 43–44, 52

Shaughnessy, Florence, 261

Shenandoah, Leon, 270, 271, 282, 284

Sherzer, Joel, 99

Shilling, Glenna, 285

Shining Shirt, 299

Shoshoni/Crow Sun Dance. See *Ashkisshe* Sun Dance

Sidney, Angela, 98

Sierra Norte de Puebla (Mexico), 16, 164

Silko, Leslie Marmon, 28, 113, 114, 115, 118

Sioux. *See* Lakota tradition

"Sisterhood of the Shields," 63

Slocum, John, 259–60, 302

Slocum, Mary, 260

Smith, Employment Division vs., 18

Smith, Marian, 266

Smith, Redbird, 301

Smithsonian Institution, 196–97, 305

Smohalla, 299, 300

smudging, 133

Soaring Eagle, 134

songs: during Kiowa-Comanche crescent moon peyote ceremony, 244; "Missionaries," 24–25; Native American spirituality in, 98; "Seven Drum Religion," 22; "Teteo Innan, Temazcalteci," 14; White Roots of Peace programs using, 287

South American religions, 40–41

Southeastern Ceremonial complex, 98

Southeastern Indians: historical/ethnographic sources on, 212–21; literature on belief systems of, 205–12; synchronical vs. diachronical